BISON
BOOKS

General Alpheus S. Williams

the
Civil War
letters
of
General
Alpheus S. Williams

FROM
THE
CANNON'S
MOUTH

edited
with an
introduction
by
Milo M. Quaife

Introduction to the Bison Books Edition
by Gary W. Gallagher

University of Nebraska Press
Lincoln and London

Introduction to the Bison Books Edition © 1995 by the University of
Nebraska Press
Manufactured in the United States of America

⊖ The paper in this book meets the minimum requirements of American
National Standard for Information Sciences—Permanence of Paper for
Printed Library Materials, ANSI Z39.48-1984.

First Bison Books printing: 1995
Most recent printing indicated by the last digit below:
10   9   8   7   6   5   4   3   2   1

Library of Congress Cataloging-in-Publication Data
Williams, Alpheus S. (Alpheus Starkey), 1810–1878.
From the cannon's mouth: the Civil War letters of General Alpheus S.
Williams / edited with an introduction by Milo M. Quaife; introduction to
the Bison Books edition by Gary W. Gallagher.
p.   cm.
Originally published: Detroit: Wayne State University Press and Detroit
Historical Society, 1959.
Includes bibliographical references (p.   ) and index.
ISBN 0-8032-9777-7
1. Williams, Alpheus S. (Alpheus Starkey), 1810–1878—Correspondence.
2. Generals—United States—Correspondence.   3. United States. Army—
Biography.   4. United States—History—Civil War, 1861–1865—Personal
narratives.   5. United States—History—Civil War, 1861–1865—
Campaigns.   I. Quaife, Milo Milton, 1880–1959.   II. Title.
E467.1.W72A4   1996
973.7'82—dc20
95-21199   CIP

Reprinted from the original 1959 edition by Wayne State University Press,
Detroit, and the Detroit Historical Society.

Grateful acknowledgement is made to the Mary E. Murphy Fund of the Detroit Historical Society for financial assistance toward the editing and publication of these letters.

Introduction to the Bison Books Edition

Gary W. Gallagher

From the Cannon's Mouth ranks among the best published collections of letters by any Civil War officer. Brigadier General Alpheus S. Williams served throughout the conflict, taking part in major campaigns in the eastern and western theaters and forging an admirable record as a brigade, division, and corps commander. His letters include descriptions of battles and places, unvarnished assessments of various Union generals, and revealing material about important political and social issues. Whether interested in details of military operations, daily life in the Army of the Potomac, morale among Union officers, or the war's impact on the southern home front, readers will learn much from this testimony. They also will discover that Williams, who was incapable of dull writing, invariably holds their attention.

One strength of the book is in its excellent accounts of battles and campaigns: First Winchester, Cedar Mountain, Antietam, Chancellorsville, Gettysburg (though part of the text is lost), Atlanta, and the March to the Sea. Williams's anticipation of fighting at Antietam during the night of 16 September 1862 is typically memorable: "I shall not . . . soon forget that night; so dark, so obscure, so mysterious, so uncertain; with the occasional rapid volleys of pickets and outposts, the low, solemn sound of the command as troops came into position, and withal so sleepy that there was a half-dreamy sensation about it all; but with a certain impression that the morrow was to be great with the future fate of our country." He concluded, "So much responsibility, so much intense, future anxiety! and yet I slept as soundly as though nothing was before me." Riding over the field two days after the battle, Williams came upon Confederate dead in the Sunken Road. "In one place for nearly a mile," he observed, "they lay as thick as autumn leaves along a narrow lane cut below the natural surface, into which they seemed to have tumbled. Eighty had been buried in one pit, and yet no impression had apparently been made on the unburied host."

Although unquestionably a hard fighter, Williams often seemed satisfied merely to avoid decisive defeats and habitually urged caution in pressing the Army of Northern Virginia.[1] In the aftermath of

Union failure at First Winchester, he suggested that a "successful retreat is often more meritorious than a decided victory." He denounced
an "impatient public" that urged pursuit of the retreating Confederates after Antietam: "[T]hese anxious souls know nothing of our preparations, nothing of the force or resources of the enemy," wrote Williams a month after the battle. "It would seem as if they thirsted for
blood; for stirring accounts of great battles." Similarly, after the Army
of the Potomac withdrew to the north bank of the Rappahannock
River after suffering defeat at Chancellorsville, he believed that neither "the most extravagant self-conceit nor the wildest lunacy could
bring anyone to the belief that with our reduced army we can, with
the least prospect of success, cross the Rappahannock just now. . . .
offensive operations are out of the question." After Gettysburg, Williams insisted that the Confederates outnumbered the Army of the
Potomac. The Federals must exercise caution in this circumstance:
"[T]he Rebel army under Lee. . . . is constantly falling back on reinforcements and his base of supplies. We are moving away from both
and daily decreasing in numbers." "Besides," he added, "as an invading army, we must almost of necessity attack, and the odds are always
greatly against the attacking party in two armies like those now opposed."

Transfer to the Western Theater in the fall of 1863—away from the
specter of R. E. Lee and his famous army—changed Williams's attitude. During the Federal advance from Chattanooga to Atlanta in
May–June 1864, his letters betray little of the excessive caution common in those written in Virginia during 1862 and 1863. Battles at
Resaca, New Hope Church, Kennesaw Mountain, and elsewhere left
Williams chastened but not discouraged. "I am not so confident as
some, as our real base of supply is far away and the line we depend
upon a very long and uncertain one, subject to accidents and destruction by the feeblest party," he commented as William Tecumseh
Sherman's Federals approached the Chattahoochee River in early
July 1864. "And yet with the fair chances of war on our side, I think
we will get Atlanta." Overall, Williams's letters offer excellent comparative evidence regarding factors that influenced northern expectations of success in Virginia and the Western Theater.[2]

Williams minced no words in assessing fellow officers. Calling J.K.F.
Mansfield "an officer of acknowledged gallantry," he also noted that
at Antietam Mansfield was "greatly excited," exhibited "a very nervous temperament and a very impatient manner," and brought his
corps onto the field in a formation that invited significant casualties.
"Feeling that our heavy masses of raw troops were sadly exposed,"

wrote Williams, "I begged him to let me deploy them in line of battle, in which the men present but *two* ranks of rows instead of *twenty*, as we were marching, but I could not move him." Biting criticism and a touch of humor enliven the evaluation of John Pope. "Suffice it to say . . . that more insolence, superciliousness, ignorance, and pretentious-ness were never combined in one man," Williams observed following the Union defeat at Second Bull Run. Four days later he added, "I had a great disgust for him for his pomposity and swagger, though I was glad that we had one head to the army—even a cabbage head!" Elsewhere, Williams wrote that Nathaniel P. Banks seemed "to get sick when there is most to do," accused Samuel W. Crawford of skulking and perhaps intentionally wounding himself at Antietam, and characterized Ambrose E. Burnside as "a most agreeable, companionable gentleman and a good officer" who was not "regarded by officers who know him best as equal to McClellan in any respect." As for George B. McClellan, perhaps he had "too much of the Fabian policy, but in judging of this one must not forget that he has been placed in circumstances where to lose the game would have been to lose all."

Williams clearly shared McClellan's aversion to making hard war on the rebels early in the conflict (his intense dislike for Pope likely stemmed in part from the latter's pronouncements about hanging Rebels and destroying their property). He deplored depredations against civilians, taking pride in the fact that noncombatants looked to him as a Yankee general who would protect them. "My reputation for kindness and leniency preceded me," he wrote from Winchester, Virginia, in March 1862, "and scores of people have come to me and said, 'We hear you are disposed to treat us with kindness, and we beg you to do this and that to aid us.' " Williams considered it a "matter of congratulation to know that my soft words have made more Union friends than hundreds of harsh generals could accomplish. Indeed, I feel that all that is needed is kindness and gentleness to make all these people return to Union love." Sixteen months later he surveyed the countryside around Snickersville, Virginia, with palpable sadness. "The fields which we left last winter all forlorn and desolate-looking, are now planted all over with corn and grain," he began, "but are for the fifth time terribly cut up again, as two or three corps encamped on them and whole acres of wagon trains. I pity the poor people who live where armies encamp."[3]

Another year of bitter warfare transformed Williams on this score. He defended Sherman's expulsion of civilians from Atlanta on the grounds that "the people could not stay there and subsist. . . . It became a matter of necessity and mercy, therefore, to send them away. . . ." Near the end of the war, he cheerfully recounted the harsh treatment of South Carolinians during Sherman's march across their state. "South Carolina will not soon forget us," he claimed. "A blackened swath seventy miles wide marks the path over which we traveled. . . . The first gun on Sumter was well avenged." The departing Union army left South Carolina's houses "comfortless and shabby, and its people at home rusty, ignorant, and forlorn." In language foreign to his letters of two or three year earlier, Williams concluded of South Carolinians that "the tornado of war may do them good in the end."[4]

Williams initially shared with McClellan and other conservative Democrats a wish to restore the Union without ending slavery; however, he became a somewhat reluctant convert to the idea that emancipation would be necessary to defeat the Confederacy. Disavowing a newspaper report in September 1862 that quoted him as supporting Lincoln's preliminary proclamation, he nonetheless conceded a willingness "to sustain any measure I thought would help put an end to this cursed rebellion." He accepted the proclamation partly because it seemed to him a political gesture that would free slaves no faster than would have been the case as Federal armies advanced into the Confederacy. In any circumstances, he hoped to avoid "the promiscuous slaughter that would follow an immediate emancipation of slaves in the South"—though he left unclear whether he foresaw a slaughter of enslaved black people, their white owners, or both.

Williams supported the Republican administration in the election of 1864 because "its great aim, in the emergency which absolves small things, is right. It goes for fighting this rebellion until the Rebels cry, 'Enough!'" Preservation of the Union represented the "great aim" of which Williams approved, and a continuing lukewarm attitude toward emancipation may be inferred from the statement that he had "no particularly strong personal reasons for loving the existing Administration, nor do I, in everything, admire its policy or measures."

None of Williams's letters credits black people with efforts to achieve their own emancipation. During the spring of 1862, he commented that few slaves left their masters to seek freedom—"although they all understand that the rear is open to them." Apparently pleased to see the Federals arrive, they "probably think some great benefit is to accrue to them, but they show very little desire to quit their present homes. . . . If the abolitionists could see things as they really are here they would have less confidence in the aid the Negro is in concluding this war." More than two and a half years later, as Sherman's army rested in Savannah after the March to the Sea, Williams described a conversation with an elderly black man who maintained that he and his wife prayed every night for Union victory. "I have no doubt there are hundreds of thousands of honest old pious Negroes all over the South who are nightly putting up the same heart yearnings and petitions for our success," stated Williams. "I have been astonished to find how widespread amongst field hands, as well as house servants, the idea is that the Yankees are coming to set the captive free, and how long his feeling has existed."[5]

In addition to the passages about black people in the South, Williams's letters address other facets of life behind the lines in the Confederacy. On several occasions he identified strong unionist sentiment, as when he mentioned "hundreds of Union-loving people" in Winchester who welcomed the Federal army in March 1862 and "told me their sufferings and their grievances and how they have waited for our coming. . . ."[6] He also repeatedly stressed the run-down appearance of southern towns and villages and dismissed poor whites as utterly inferior to northerners. A letter written after his troops transferred to Tennessee in 1863 touched on both of these themes. "All the towns along this railroad excepting Murfreesboro are the veriest pretenses, most of them sounding names and nothing else," sniffed Williams, "and the people—the 'poor white trash'—are disgusting: the mere scum of humanity, poor, half starved, ignorant, stupid, and treacherous." The absence of draft-age white men in the countryside and towns spoke of the extent of southern white mobilization. From near Fayetteville, North Carolina, in March 1865, Williams noticed "no young men, save the deformed, the sick or wounded, and deserters (pretty numerous). Everybody else had been forced into the service, even to decrepit old men of sixty and upwards, lots of whom came to us to be paroled or to be sent home." In these and other ways, the letters underscore the overwhelming impact of war on southern society.

Tension between West Pointers and nonprofessional soldiers serves as a final important theme in Williams's letters. Although innocent of formal military training, Williams had seen duty with a Michigan regiment during the war with Mexico and considered that experience more valuable than much of the coursework completed by cadets at the U.S. Military Academy. Like John A. Logan and other nonprofessionals who demonstrated aptitude for command during the Civil War, he railed against what he saw as a closed system that blatantly favored West Pointers. "[T]he whole West Point influence is against any man who did not happen to spend four years of his life in that institution," he wrote bitterly in December 1861, "and any man who has been there, even for a few months, no matter what his natural stupidity or his indolent, inefficient habits, his ignorance acquired or habitual, is fit for all responsibility and all power." He had witnessed enough of such unqualified men to develop "a most ineffable disgust with the whole thing" and suspected that West Point's principal legacy to its graduates was "superciliousness, arrogance, and insolence." The fact that Williams spent virtually the entire war at the grade of brigadier general suggests that his notions about West Point favoritism may have been well founded.[7]

The critical reception accorded *From the Cannon's Mouth* was largely positive. One reviewer likened the book to a "literary gold mine" of wartime testimony. Another affirmed that "Civil War scholars are always grateful for a volume of letters written by a high-ranking officer who held important commands in pivotal engagements." The standard bibliography on the Civil War lauded this "long run of letters [that] presents an undiluted picture of war" and pronounced it "especially valuable for Sherman's campaigns."[8] Historians have cited *From the Cannon's Mouth* innumerable times over the past thirty-six years, confirming the high estimate of most of the reviewers. Because the original edition has been long out of print and relatively difficult to find, many students of the war have known Williams's letters only through excerpts quoted in other works. This Bison Books edition makes a classic title readily accessible to the large audience it deserves.

NOTES

1. For a provocative discussion of why many soldiers in the Army of the Potomac may have been cowed by R. E. Lee and the Army of Northern Virginia, see Michael C. C. Adams, *Our Masters the Rebels: A Speculation on Union Military Failure in the East, 1861–1865* (Cambridge: Harvard University Press, 1978 [reprinted in 1992 by the University of Nebraska Press as *Fighting for Defeat*]).

2. John White Geary also served as a Union general in the East and the West. His letters, which may be read with profit in conjunction with those of Williams, are collected in John White Geary, *A Politician Goes to War: The Civil War Letters of John White Geary*, ed. William Alan Blair (University Park: Pennsylvania State University Press, 1995).

3. For another description of the ravaged Virginia landscape at about this time, see Arthur J. L. Fremantle, *Three Months in the Southern States: April–June 1863* (1864; reprint, Lincoln: University of Nebraska Press, 1991), 223. "The country is really magnificent," Fremantle wrote from near Sperryville, Virginia, on 21 June, "but as it has supported two large armies for two years,

it is now completely cleaned out. It is almost uncultivated, and no animals are grazing where there used to be hundreds. All fences have been destroyed, and numberless farms burnt, the chimneys alone left standing. It is difficult to depict and impossible to exaggerate the sufferings which this part of Virginia has undergone."

4. Charles Royster's *The Destructive War: William Tecumseh Sherman, Stonewall Jackson, and the Americans* (New York: Alfred A. Knopf, 1990) and Mark Grimsley's *The Hard Hand of War: Union Military Policy toward Southern Civilians, 1861–1865* (New York: Cambridge University Press, 1995) offer perceptive discussions of the shift toward harsher war.

5. For different opinions about the question of self-emancipation, see Ira Berlin and others, *Slaves No More: Three Essays on Emancipation and the Civil War* (New York: Cambridge University Press, 1992), and Mark E. Neely Jr., "Lincoln and the Theory of Self-Emancipation," in John Y. Simon and Barbara Hughett, eds., *The Continuing Civil War: Essays in Honor of the Civil War Round Table of Chicago* (Dayton, Ohio: Morningside, 1992): 45–60.

6. On the plight of unionists living behind Confederate lines, see Stephen Ash, *When the Yankees Came* (Chapel Hill: University of North Carolina Press, 1995).

7. John C. Waugh, *The Class of 1846: From West Point to Appomattox, Stonewall Jackson, George McClellan and their Brothers* (New York: Warner Books, 1994), explores the ways in which West Point bound cadets together, and Thomas W. Cutrer, *Ben McCulloch and the Frontier Military Tradition* (Chapel Hill: University of North Carolina Press, 1993), examines tensions between West Pointers and officers who did not attend the Academy.

8. *Civil War History* 6 (March 1960): 111 [unsigned book note]; *The American Historical Review* 65 (April 1960): 692 [review by Warren W. Hassler Jr.]; Allan Nevins and others, eds., *Civil War Books: A Critical Bibliography*, 2 vols. (Baton Rouge: Louisiana State University Press, 1967, 1969), 1:176 [annotation by James I. Robertson Jr.].

foreword

HENRY D. BROWN · DIRECTOR
DETROIT HISTORICAL MUSEUM

The publication of selections from the General Alpheus S. Williams Papers on the Civil War marks an important new undertaking for the Detroit Historical Society and Wayne State University Press, both of which have enjoyed a long and fruitful association. This is their first sponsorship of the reproduction and editing of original source materials, a type of publication that makes original sources more readily available to those who in turn write about our heritage for the general reader. The book will be a contribution for writers and students of the history of the American Civil War. The Press and the Society consider publication of this type of basic source material a logical part of their contribution to a deeper understanding of our local and national heritage.

It is singularly appropriate that this initial project of scholarly editing of original sources should be concerned with the period of the Civil War, for the coming centennial of that conflict has directed national attention to the need for additional published source materials. While the major contribution of the volume will be to make more readily available important original materials on the Civil War, the letters themselves contain some of the finest depictions of warfare as it actually is which can be found anywhere in literature.

The publication of the Alpheus S. Williams Papers was made possible through the bequest of the late Mrs. Fred T. Murphy to the Detroit Historical Society. For fifteen years prior to her death in November 1956, Mrs. Murphy had been most active in local history projects as a member of the Museum Building Fund Committee, a member of the Board of Trustees of the Detroit Historical Society, and a member of the Detroit Historical Commission, 1946–1956.

As a daughter-in-law of General Russell A. Alger, the wife of Frederick M. Alger from 1901 until his death in 1933, Mrs. Murphy was deeply concerned over the proper means of emphasizing the important contributions of Union participants in the Civil War. General Alger, a contemporary of General Williams, was not only a distinguished participant in that conflict but later served as commander of the Grand Army of the Republic, Michigan Governor and Senator, and Secretary of War. It may be recalled that it was through Mrs. Murphy that the late Mrs. Charles B. Pike, daughter of General Alger, became interested in the proposed building for the Detroit Historical Museum, and that her generous gift initiated the building fund drive, which culminated in the present Museum structure.

The Detroit Public Library generously granted permission for the Society to publish the Alpheus Williams Papers in the Burton Historical Collection and cooperated wholeheartedly in the details incident to preparing them for publication. While the bulk of the papers had been copied some years ago, much copying and recopying of material still had to be done. Members of the Museum's administrative staff, particularly Miss Patricia Butkowski, Secretary to the Director, contributed substantially to the completion of this phase of the work.

Dr. Milo M. Quaife, from 1924 to 1947 Secretary-Editor of the Burton Historical Collection of the Detroit Public Library and a distinguished historian and editor, called our attention to the significance of the Alpheus S. Williams Papers. The Society and the Press were fortunate in enlisting Dr. Quaife's services as editor. His long and important contributions in the field of editing original source materials is well known to many of the individuals who will make use of this volume. Members of the Society will recall that Dr. Quaife delivered the Lewis Cass Lecture in 1954 and that in 1956 he was presented a citation by the American Association for State and Local History for distinguished contributions to the field of American national and local history.

preface

My procedure in preparing the letters for publication should be explained to the reader. Since they are chiefly family letters, written by a devoted parent to his young daughters, the originals contain a great deal of domestic and private material which possesses no interest for the present-day reader. Partly for this reason, in part to avoid useless expense, all of this material has been deleted from the present version. Like all other authors, General Williams occasionally committed errors of grammar or of orthography. To reproduce these in print would serve no useful purpose, and such corrections as the individual circumstances required have been made; also as a matter of course, such details as capitalization and punctuation have been standardized. It is perhaps unnecessary to add that none of the deletions and changes have been animated by the motive of suppressing or altering Williams' expressions of opinion.

I am under obligation to numerous individuals and institutions for assigning the editorial task to me and making the publication of General Williams' letters possible. I am grateful to Mrs. Margaret Barbour, the general's granddaughter, for her sympathetic interest and support. Mr. Henry D. Brown, Director of the Detroit Historical Museum, and Dr. Harold A. Basilius, Director of Wayne State University Press, whose respective institutions have jointly sponsored and financed the book, have given me their constant support, along with much technical assistance. Professor Alexander Brede, Editor of the Wayne State University Press, has competently performed the copy reader's task of whipping the manuscript into final shape for printing. From Mrs. Elleine Stones, former Chief, and Mr. James Babcock, present Chief, of the Burton Historical Collection of the Detroit Public Library, within whose pleasant domain the editorial work has been chiefly performed, I have received unfailing service and cooperation in facilitating the task. Nor should acknowledgement be omitted of the helpful interest of Dr. Alfred

H. Whittaker or the many services rendered by Miss Dorothy Martin, Archivist of the Burton Collection, along with the usual courteous services of the remaining members of the staff, which contribute so much to render the Collection a peaceful haven of historical research. For the reproduction of the old illustrations I am indebted to the excellent photography of Mr. Joseph Klima, Jr. The index is the work of Mr. Simon Greenfield. Last but not least may be noted the help accorded by Letitia, my permanent secretary and wife.

M.M.Q.

contents

illustrations

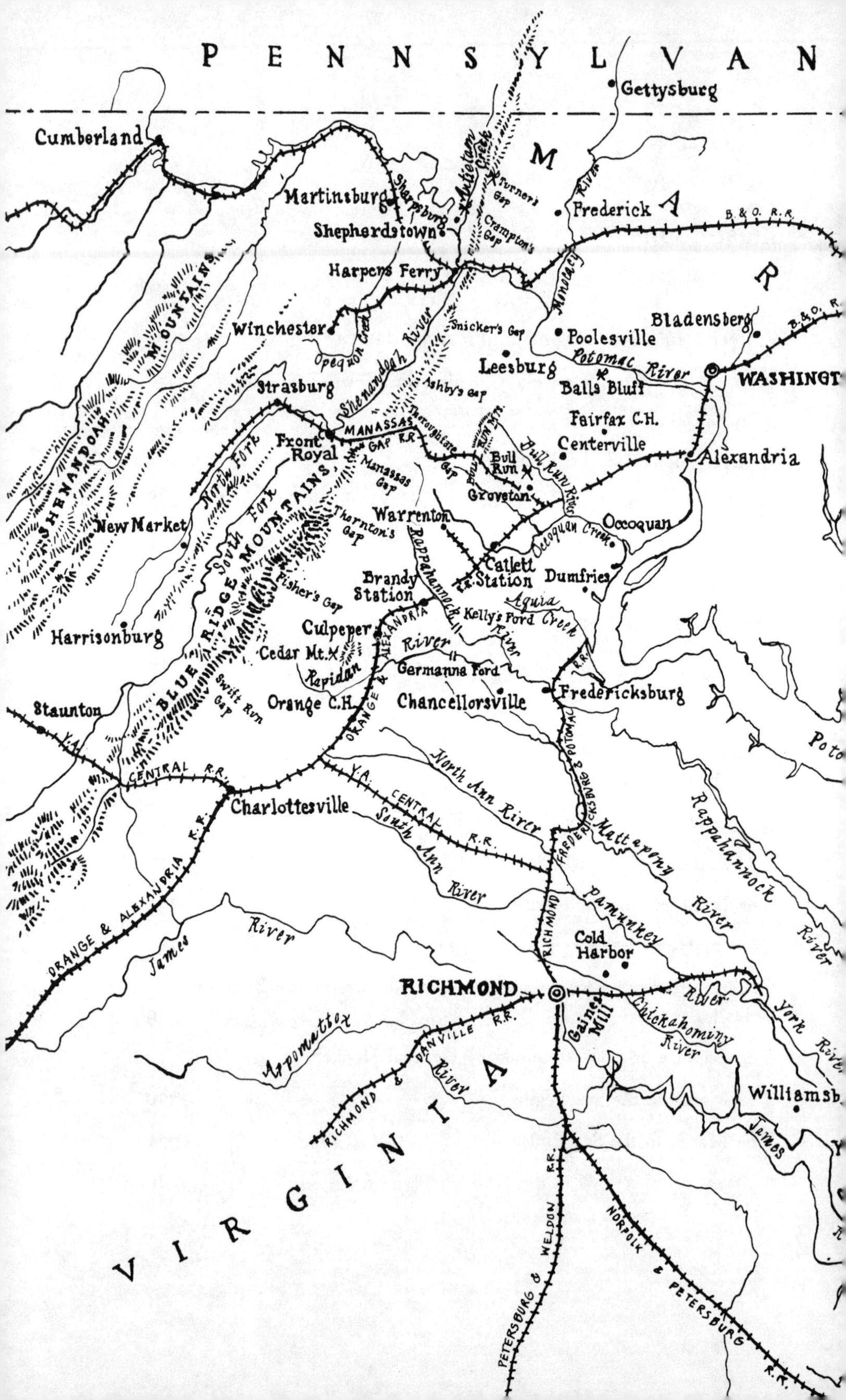

PENNSYLVAN
Gettysburg
Cumberland
M
A
R
Martinsburg
Sharpsburg
Antietam Creek
Turner's Gap
Crampton's Gap
Frederick
B. & O. R.R.
Shepherdstown
Harpers Ferry
Monocacy River
MOUNTAINS
Winchester
Opequon Creek
Shenandoah River
Snicker's Gap
Poolesville
Bladensberg
Leesburg
Potomac River
Balls Bluff
WASHINGT
Strasburg
Ashby's Gap
Fairfax C.H.
Centerville
Alexandria
SHENANDOAH
Front Royal
MANASSAS GAP R.R.
Manassas Gap
Thoroughfare Gap
Bull Run
Bull Run Mts.
Bull Run River
Groveton
North Fork
New Market
South Fork
Warrenton
Thornton's Gap
Occoquan
Occoquan Creek
Catlett Station
Dumfries
Brandy Station
Rappahannock River
Fisher's Gap
Aquia Creek
Kelly's Ford
Harrisonburg
BLUE RIDGE MOUNTAINS
Culpeper
Cedar Mt.
Rapidan River
Germanna Ford
Fredericksburg
Chancellorsville
Orange C.H.
ORANGE & ALEXANDRIA
Swift Run Gap
Staunton
Y.A.
CENTRAL R.R.
Charlottesville
North Ann River
FREDERICKSBURG & POTOMAC
Y.A. CENTRAL R.R.
South Ann River
Mattapony River
Rappahannock River
Pamunkey
Poto
ORANGE & ALEXANDRIA R.R.
James River
Cold Harbor
RICHMOND
Gaines Mill
Chickahominy River
York River
Appomattox River
RICHMOND & DANVILLE R.R.
Williamsb
James
VIRGINIA
PETERSBURG & WELDON R.R.
NORFOLK & PETERSBURG R.R.

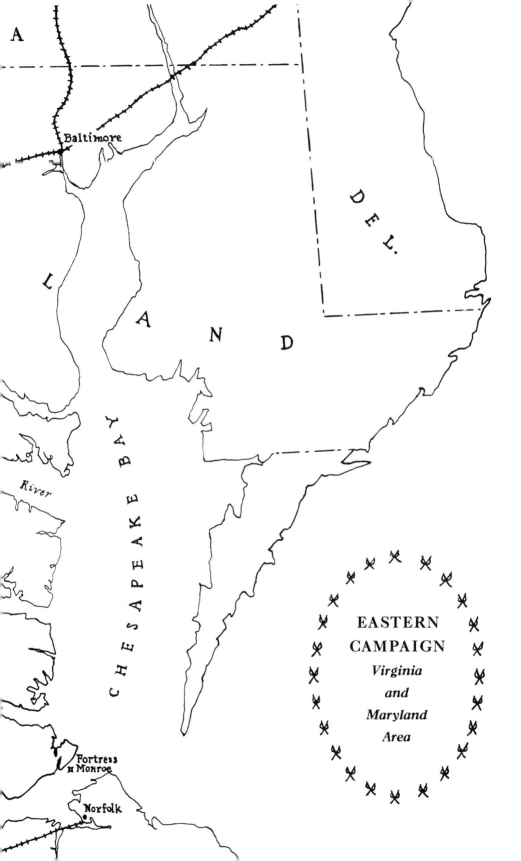

**EASTERN
CAMPAIGN**
*Virginia
and
Maryland
Area*

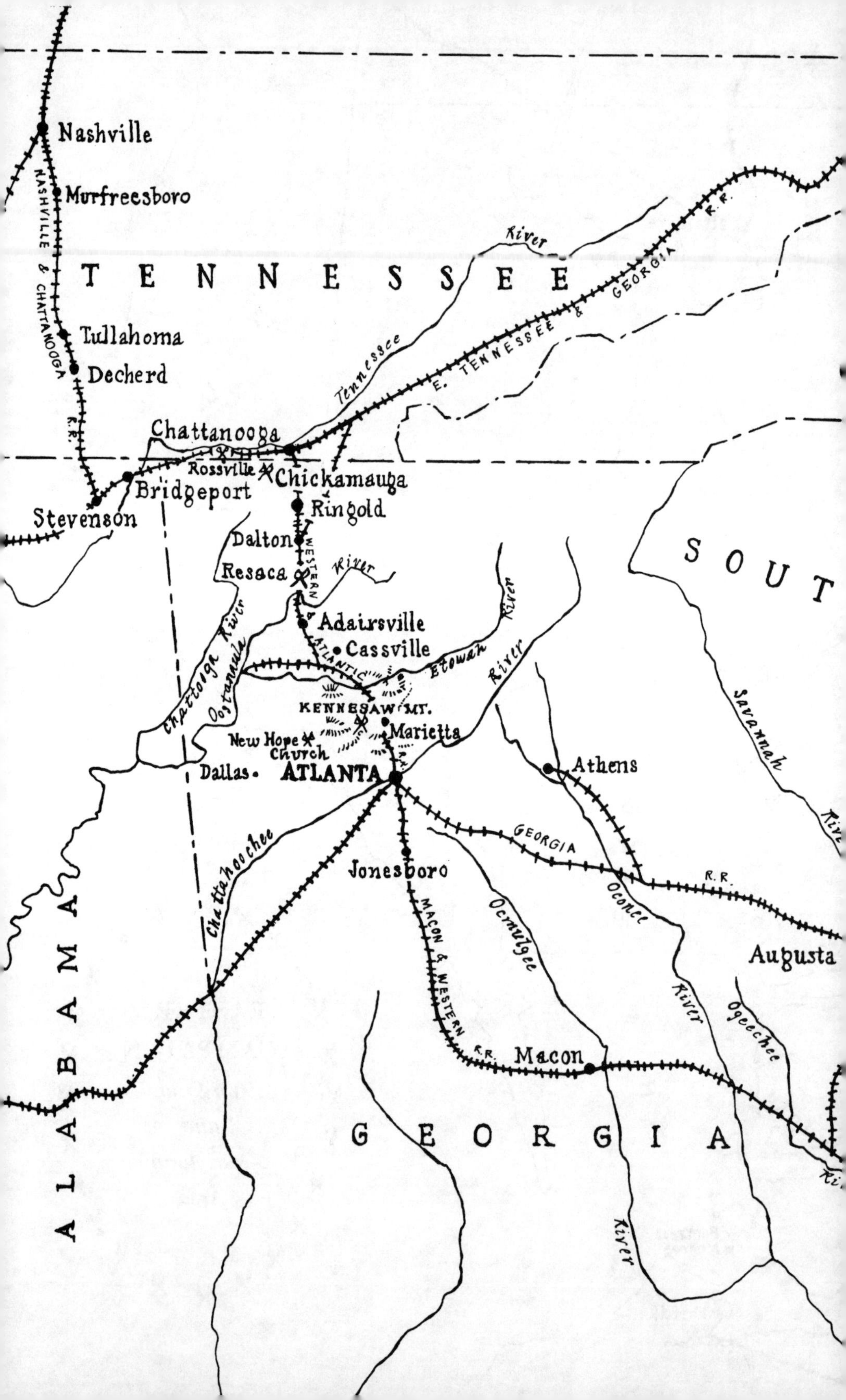

Nashville
Murfreesboro
NASHVILLE & CHATTANOOGA R.R.
TENNESSEE
Tullahoma
Decherd
Chattanooga
Rossville
Chickamauga
Bridgeport
Stevenson
Ringold
Dalton
Resaca
Adairsville
Cassville
WESTERN & ATLANTIC R.R.
KENNESAW MT.
Marietta
New Hope Church
Dallas
ATLANTA
Jonesboro
Athens
Augusta
Macon
GEORGIA R.R.
MACON & WESTERN R.R.
E. TENNESSEE & GEORGIA R.R.
Tennessee River
Chattooga River
Oostanaula
Etowah River
Chattahoochee
Ocmulgee River
Oconee River
Ogeechee
Savannah River
SOUT
ALABAMA
GEORGIA

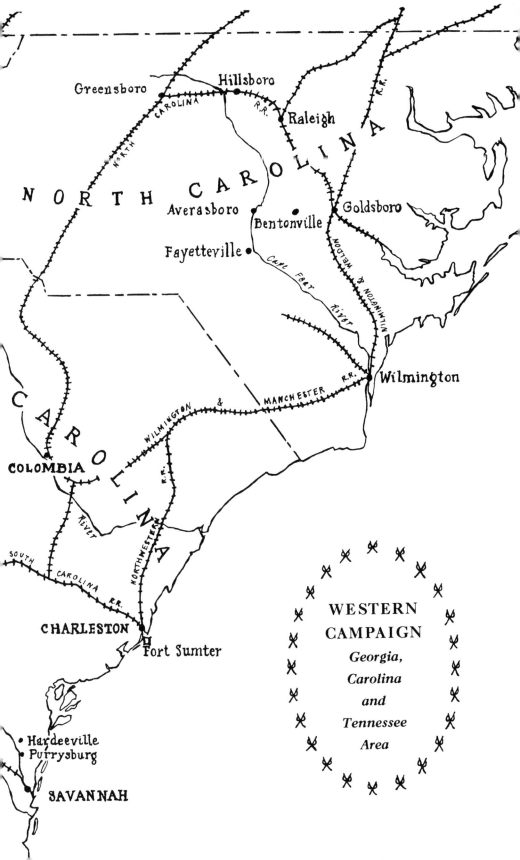

Greensboro Hillsboro

NORTH CAROLINA R.R.

Raleigh

NORTH CAROLINA

Averasboro Bentonville Goldsboro

Fayetteville

Cape Fear River

WILMINGTON & WELDON

CAROLINA

WILMINGTON & MANCHESTER R.R.

COLOMBIA

River

N.R.

NORTHWESTERN

Wilmington

SOUTH CAROLINA R.R.

CHARLESTON

Fort Sumter

Hardeeville
Purrysburg

SAVANNAH

WESTERN
CAMPAIGN

Georgia,

Carolina

and

Tennessee

Area

Historical
Introduction

historical introduction

Over the main cross roads of Detroit's Belle Isle Park looms the equestrian statue of "a weary man on a tired horse." [1] It was erected in 1921 as a memorial to General Alpheus S. Williams, Detroit and Michigan's best-loved soldier. Around it flows a stream of automobile traffic which long since provoked the proposal that the statue should be removed to a more suitable location. Yet still the General reins his steed, serenely unperturbed by the noise around him, and the prediction may be hazarded that any serious effort to banish him to a more secluded scene will be met with a storm of public disapproval.

Surface indications to the contrary, polyglot Detroit sincerely cherishes the memory of her historic past. Statues, bronze markers, and other memorials abound throughout the city's older area, directing the attention of the passing throng to the actors and actions of former times. For almost a century the venerable City Hall has displayed on its exterior walls the statues of four notable figures of the remote past. Statesmen and politicians, poets and other dreamers—Christopher Columbus and Franz Schubert (who did not live in Detroit), railroad stations, both "Underground" and actual, churches and trees and hospitals and toll gates—these and many others populate the city's pantheon. Belatedly, therefore, the city bestirred itself, now half a century ago, to erect a permanent memorial to its foremost soldier, General Alpheus S. Williams.

Williams was born in the village of Deep River, Connecticut, on September 20, 1810.[2] His father died when Williams was but eight years old, and his mother during his seventeenth year, leaving his future training to the care of family relatives. Left to him, also, was a reputed patrimony of $75,000, a very considerable fortune a century and a half ago.[3] Following his graduation from Yale in 1831, for several years he devoted his time to an intermittent study of law and a series of extensive travels, both in America and Europe. According to his biographers the

3

legal study was pursued at Yale, yet his journal preserved in the Burton Historical Collection of the Detroit Public Library discloses that in the early winter of 1831–32 he was studying in New York under the tutelage of a Mr. Hall. It further discloses that he did not take his legal studies too seriously. In early January 1832, he responded to an invitation from "Miss H" to visit Philadelphia and from there went to Washington. About this time he decided to accompany his brother on a voyage to Brazos Santiago at the southern tip of Texas, which was then a Mexican possession. On April 22, 1832, he began the voyage, bidding goodby to the law with this light-hearted valedictory: "farewell to law, Alph's occupation is gone."

Whether he resumed it upon his return to New York remains unrecorded, but in the spring of 1833 he embarked upon another southern tour, extending to Charleston and thence up the Savannah River and through the Cherokee country to New Orleans. The following spring he undertook another extensive tour, extending this time to Ohio and St. Louis. He was back in New Haven by the end of July, and in October 1834, he embarked upon a prolonged tour of Europe. The intervals between these several excursions afforded his only opportunity to master the intricacies of the legal profession, whose practice he presently entered upon.

In short, it seems apparent that for several years following his graduation from Yale he was chiefly intent upon dissipating his patrimony. He was abetted in this pleasant task by Henry Wikoff, a young Philadelphian, who for several years was his classmate at Yale. To escape expulsion by the college authorities, Wikoff had hastily departed from New Haven to spend his senior year at Union College, from which he was duly graduated in 1831. Possessed of an ample inheritance and a no-less ample stock of self-assurance, he now set out to see the world. Whether he persuaded Williams to join him in his travels, or vice versa, remains unrecorded. At any rate, for several years the two young men toured America and Europe as companions.[4]

They sailed from New York in mid-October 1834 on a tour which was to last a year and a half. From Le Havre the fellow-travelers proceeded to Paris in one of the ponderous French diligences, drawn by five stout Norman horses. Awaiting them in Paris was the actor Edwin Forrest, an old-time friend of Wikoff's guardian. Already widely famous

4

in America, Forrest had embarked upon a prolonged European excursion, with Wikoff and Williams as his traveling companions. The trio of tourists had excellent introductions, along with plenty of money, and they found little or no difficulty in establishing contact with many of the leading characters of the time.

After experiencing the delights of Paris for two or three months they departed upon a tour of Italy. Upon its conclusion they returned to Paris in the spring of 1835, intent upon paying a visit to England and Scotland. During its progress Wikoff conceived the project of a journey to Russia, and thence southward to Constantinople and Jerusalem. Williams, however, whose funds were running low, stoutly declined to embark upon such a journey; Wikoff and Forrest departed for the Baltic and Saint Petersburg, and Williams returned alone to Paris, where he passed the ensuing winter. On March 6, 1836 he bade farewell to Paris and France, arriving in New York after an "agreeable" voyage of thirty-eight days.

Before him lay the sober task of earning a living and mastering his profession. Why he fixed upon Detroit as the scene of his future activities has nowhere been recorded. However, in 1836 the city was enjoying its first great boom. Western immigration and speculation in wild land were running at flood tide, and as the natural gateway to Michigan and the farther West Detroit offered promising inducements to an aspiring professional man. Hither, therefore, Williams came, and from the day of his arrival on August 12, 1836, until his death forty-two years later Detroit remained his home.

One of Detroit's leading citizens from the close of the War of 1812 was Charles Larned, soldier, lawyer, and civic leader. A native of Pittsfield, Massachusetts, he had gone to Kentucky prior to the outbreak of the war to "read" law in the office of Henry Clay. When the news of Detroit's downfall arrived, the young law student enlisted in a Kentucky regiment which was hastily raised and with it marched northward to join the army of General Winchester. There he shared in that leader's disastrous campaign, which was highlighted by the River Raisin defeat and massacre of January 22, 1813.

Along with Lewis Cass and many another soldier who had served in the war, upon its conclusion Larned made Detroit his home, and until his death in 1834 he combined the practice of law with the holding of various public offices. Meanwhile, in 1816 he married his boyhood sweetheart, Sylvia Colt of Pittsfield, and began the rearing of a numerous family. Julia, the eldest daughter, married Lewis Allen, and Catherine married John G. Atterbury, with whom Williams some months after coming to Detroit established a legal partnership. Jane Hereford, sister of Catherine and Julia, quite early in life married Benjamin Pierson. The union was soon terminated by his death and on January 16, 1839 the young widow became the bride of Alpheus Williams. Four months later he recorded in his journal that his married life was "flowing on like the peaceful current of a gentle river, happy as the day is long." Mrs. Williams died a decade later at the early age of thirty. Five children had been born of her union with Williams, two of whom died young. The others, Irene, Charles Larned, and Mary, will claim our subsequent notice.

In 1840 Williams was elected Probate Judge of Wayne County. Atterbury, meanwhile, developed a desire to exchange his legal calling for that of the ministry, and about the year 1843 Lewis Allen succeeded to the interests of the legal partnership. Williams' term of Probate Judge expired in 1844, but he had begun the assumption of other duties which continued to distract his attention from the law. In 1842 he became president of the Bank of St. Clair (removed about this time to Detroit). On November 10, 1843, he purchased the Detroit *Advertiser*, a daily paper, which he continued to own until January 1, 1848. In April 1849, he began a four-year term of service as postmaster of Detroit. The postoffice occupied the first floor of the Old Mariner's Church, which stood, until its recent removal, at the northwest corner of Woodbridge Street and Woodward Avenue. During Williams' incumbency of the office he had a staff of five assistants. Among other civic offices which he held at various times were colonel of the volunteer night watch (in 1849), recorder (1845–48), and member of the Board of Education (1856–57).

It was perhaps inevitable that a young man of Williams' temperament and energy should manifest an interest in military activities. Joseph Greusel, one admiring biographer, even affirms that he was born with a predilection for military life and that his travels in America and Europe during his early manhood were undertaken for the express purpose of studying the scenes of former battles and the reasons for the successes and defeats associated with them. Of this remarkable "pre-dilection," we have found no evidence prior to his removal to Detroit in 1836. It is not improbable, however, that, like other young men, he was interested in the military companies which constituted one of the very few forms of organized athletic activity in the era prior to the Civil War. At any rate, on November 26, 1836, he was admitted to membership in the Brady Guards, a company then recently organized, and from this time forward he assumed an increasingly prominent role in the military activities of the city. In 1838 the company was called into active service, performing patrol duty for several months during the continuance of Canada's Patriot War. In 1839 Williams was elected first lieutenant of the company, and in 1843 and 1846 its captain. The Mexican War was now at hand and Williams was appointed lieutenant colonel of the Michigan regiment which late in 1847 departed for the scene of conflict. It arrived in Mexico too late to participate in any battles, but during the winter and spring of 1848 it performed garrison and outpost duties. In the early summer the regiment returned to Detroit, where it was mustered out on July 23.

Although it had won no particular glory in the war, the opportunity had been afforded to Williams to master the routine of military life and to experience at first hand the many problems in which such service abounds. His reputation, too, as an active leader of military affairs in Michigan had been materially enhanced. Upon the death of General Brady in 1851 the Brady Guards became moribund. Its place in the life of the city was assumed by the newer company of Grayson Guards, which had been organized in 1850. In November 1855 this organization gave place in turn to the Detroit Light Guard, with Williams as its captain and leader. In 1859 the company evolved into a battalion of two companies, with Williams as its major. With this step, his pre-Civil War military education was completed.

Two years later came the firing on Fort Sumter and in its wake the holocaust of America's bloodiest war. In Michigan, public opinion overwhelmingly supported President Lincoln and the preservation of the Union. "Secession is revolution," said Governor Blair in his inaugural address in January 1861, "and revolution is the overt act of treason and must be treated as such. . . . It is a question of war the seceding states have to face."

This forthright declaration was followed by appropriate measures looking to belated preparation for waging war. General Williams was appointed brigadier general of state troops and from June until August he conducted a school of military instruction at Fort Wayne. Meanwhile new regiments were being organized in rapid succession, and before the war ended the state had sent over 90,000 men into the Union service, from which practically one in six was never to return.

In August 1861, Williams was appointed by the President a brigadier general of United States volunteers, to take effect as of May 17. Ordered to Washington at the beginning of October, he was assigned to General Banks' command which constituted the right wing of the newly-created Army of the Potomac, then stationed in the general vicinity of Harpers Ferry. From this time until the close of the war he was in constant service save for a single month's leave of absence in the winter of 1863–64. Repeatedly during the war he was given command of a division or of an army corps, winning the unvarying commendation of his superiors and the warm devotion of his soldiers. Yet, save for the relatively meaningless award of a brevet major generalship in January 1865, he ended his service as he had begun it, with the rank of brigadier general.

Why the promotion so clearly merited was withheld from him is difficult to understand. That he despised the arts of self-glorification and refused to woo the favor of the correspondents who followed the armies affords a partial explanation. Whatever the further reasons may have been, the fact remains clear that in the matter of official preferment he was the forgotten man of the Union Army. "In my judgment," wrote an officer of his staff in later years, "General Williams was one of the finest military commanders in the eastern army, and had he been fairly treated would have found his proper place at the head of it. He had all the attributes of manhood, was brave as a lion, was thoroughly versed in all the arts of war, and had a genius that inspired him where other men failed in a pressing emergency." [5]

Admittedly this is the statement of a friend and admirer, but it finds ample support in the commendations of such military authorities as General Sherman, General Hooker, General Slocum, and General Thomas. In sum, although General Williams failed to obtain official promotion he enjoyed the confidence of his military superiors, the affection of the members of his military staff, who gave expression to it by the gift of a magnificent sword, and the love and admiration of his soldiers, who awarded him the title of "Pap" Williams.

Both the quality and the volume of General Williams' wartime correspondence is amazing. Throughout the war he recorded his activities in a personal journal, most of which has unfortunately been lost. He maintained a constant correspondence with his daughters, frequently writing separate and more or less identical letters to each of them. Commonly he wrote them amid the crude surroundings of active campaigning; frequently, when subject to a constant flow of interruptions from members of his staff and others; at times, when beset by weariness or with the booming of cannon and the staccato reports of rifle fire assailing his ears. Yet into them he poured the scent of flowers, the singing of birds, the shocking sights of a military hospital, the hardships endured and the valor displayed by the common soldiers, the grandeur of mountain scenery, and the uproar of armies locked in desperate battle. With their aid the reader still may view the windrows of Confederate dead at Antietam, the headlong stampede of Union troops at Chancellorsville, the struggles of drowning mules trapped in the mud of a Virginia winter, the amazing spectacle presented by Sherman's tatterdemalian army emerging from its march through the Carolinas; or hear once more the voice of a woman in the darkness welcoming the conquering Union army as it entered doomed Atlanta.

General Williams' family in 1861 consisted of his son, Charles Larned, who was born in 1841, and his daughters, Irene and Mary, born respectively in 1843 and 1846. Upon Williams' entering the army, the family was broken up, never to be restored. Larned (as he was commonly called) accompanied his father to the army, although he refrained from enlisting. After about a year of employment, chiefly in connection with the quartermaster's department, he obtained work in Philadelphia, where he remained for several years, and where he married in February 1869. For many years he was attached to the office of Major Farquahar of the Engineer Department of the United States Army. In 1883 he entered upon an eighteen-year clerkship in the United States Engineer's office at Detroit. Transferred in 1901 to the Lake Survey, he served as chief clerk until his death in 1919.

Irene Williams (the Rene of the letters) passed the war years with her family relatives in Detroit and Connecticut or in the study of music at Philadelphia and possibly elsewhere. On January 18, 1866 she married William J. Chittenden, a member of the noted Chittenden hotel family. For several decades he served as manager and proprietor of the well-known Russell House at the corner of Woodward Avenue and Cadillac Square, subsequently the site in turn of the Pontchartrain Hotel and the National Bank of Detroit. Throughout her married life Mrs. Chittenden was active in social and patriotic society activities. She died at Chicago on April 7, 1907, while en route from the Pacific Coast to her home in Detroit. Of her several children, only Margaret, who married William T. Barbour, is still living. To her we are indebted for the preservation of General Williams' letters and for their gift in recent years to the Burton Historical Collection of the Detroit Public Library.

Mary (Minnie in the letters) was entrusted to the care of the family relatives in Connecticut, and two years passed before she saw her father again. She married Major Francis Farquahar, a West Point graduate in the class of 1861, who was attached to the Engineer Department of the army. For many years, until his death in July 1883, he was engaged in engineering activities on the Upper Mississippi and around the Great Lakes. His widow outlived him more than half a century, dying on February 7, 1935. In 1921, then the only living member of her father's family, she witnessed the unveiling of his monument on Belle Isle.

The close of the war left Williams without an occupation and with but limited financial means. He presently accepted the offer of an appointment as military administrator of the Ouachita District, comprising much of southern Arkansas, then a crude frontier region whose residents were much addicted to the late Confederacy and to acts of violence. Early in 1866 he resigned his commission, and upon his return to Detroit was appointed minister resident to the Central American republic of San Salvador, where he remained for three years. Returning once more to Michigan, he waged an unsuccessful campaign for governor in 1870 and two successful ones for election to Congress in 1874 and 1876.

His career was terminated by his death at his post of duty on December 21, 1878. As chairman of the House Committee on the District of

Columbia he had won deserved credit for the probity of his conduct in an era when graft and dishonesty in the conduct of public office was commonplace. In 1875, with his children long since married and scattered, he established a new home by marrying Mrs. Martha Tillman, the widow of a well-known Detroit merchant, who survived him. He was accorded a funeral marked by expressions of public esteem and grief such as falls to the lot of but few men. His material monument is the imposing statue erected to his memory on Belle Isle. His wartime letters to his daughters, now first published after the lapse of almost a century, may well become an even more enduring monument.

1. Thus characterized by John C. Lodge at the unveiling of the monument in October 1921. Whether it was the sculptor's intention to produce this effect may be doubted. Instead, he seems to have sought to depict the general checking his steed while he pored over a road map.

2. Without exception, apparently, his biographers erroneously affirm that he was born at Saybrook. Saybrook village, at the mouth of the Connecticut River, is in the New England town of Old Saybrook. Deep River, which lies some miles to the northward, is in the town of Saybrook. Apparently the confusion of the biographers derives from this multiplicity of names.

3. For this and some other biographical details we are dependent upon "Winder's Memories," first published in the Detroit *Sunday News* (subsequently the *News Tribune*) in 1893–94. John Winder, the author, was a pioneer Detroit lawyer and official, whose host of interesting memories were subsequently republished, with additions, by Robert B. Ross, under the title of *The Early Bench and Bar of Detroit from 1805 to the End of 1850* (Detroit, 1907). Both the book and the newspaper file are now exceedingly rare items.

4. Wikoff was a puzzling, as well as a fascinating, character. Although he authored several books, one of them a 600-page volume devoted to his personal history, the year of his birth and even the name of his father remain unknown. Possessed of fortune and an engaging personality and a brilliant intellect, throughout his life he moved in the best circles of society. Yet he made the pursuit of pleasure his chief occupation, and his uncompleted autobiography bears the significant title, *Reminiscences of an Idler* (New York, 1880). For a sketch of his life see the *Dictionary of American Biography*. (Hereafter cited as *Dict. Am. Biog.*)

5. The statement of Captain B. W. Morgan at the time of General Williams' death.—Undated newspaper clipping in the Chittenden scrapbook, in the Burton Historical Collection.

I

Organizing
an
Army

Until the firing upon Fort Sumter in April 1861, despite increasing debate between North and South, practically no preparation for waging a war had been made. That event signalized the close of the era of peaceful discussion and the resort to trial by battle. The profusion of volunteers for the army, in North and South alike, was only equalled by the almost complete absence of arms and other material essential to the existence of an army. Along with this went a similar lack of experience in the organization and conduct of armies. Only in the costly school of trial and error could capable leaders be found and disciplined armies created. Thus in the opening months of the war an impatient public opinion hopefully anticipated a prompt invasion of the South and an early end of the war, while the military authorities held back, arguing the need of better preparation for their task.

The situation in Michigan illustrates fairly closely the conditions elsewhere throughout the North. Prior to 1861, the state had twenty-eight volunteer militia companies with an aggregate strength of but 1241 officers and men. In response to Governor Blair's appeal, ten of these companies rushed to Fort Wayne in Detroit, where on May 1, 1861 they were mustered into the United States service as the First Michigan Infantry Regiment. On May 13 the regiment departed for Washington, to participate soon afterward in the battle of Bull Run, the opening combat of the war.

ON THE EVE OF BULL RUN

Washington,
Saturday, July 13th, 1861.

My Dear Minnie:

I have just found your dear and affectionate letter on my return from the other side. I have but a moment to thank you and to say that I am well, and I can find no paper at hand but this envelope.[1]

I am sure, however, that you will be glad to get even a line from me. I have been visiting all the camps on this and the Virginia side. There are over 80,000 men in camp within ten miles of Washington. Each camp is isolated and therefore the show is not great, but as you ride from one to the other for a whole day you become impressed with the immensity of the gathering.

I have seen our friends Lew Forsyth and wife and Cousin Marion but have not seen Cousin Maria yet. I expected to have been home to-day, but am waiting the passage of a law authorizing the appointment of generals. I have the promise of an appointment, but after all it depends much on the kind of law passed by Congress. I was very cordially received by the Secretary of War and by the President, and have made the acquaintance of a host of [illegible], generals, etc. etc., besides meeting scores I have known before. . . .

Your Affectionate Father,
A.S.W.

❖

Detroit, [Sept.] 28th, 1861.

My Dear Daughter:

I have just time to say that I shall (D.V.) leave . . . for Washington Monday evening and expect now to stop a few hours in Philadelphia on Wednesday next. The 8th Regiment went last night and Brodheads' cavalry go tonight. . . . Larned went last night with my staff, horses, and baggage. So we break up. Minnie will write you the news. Love to all.[2]

Your Affectionate Father,
A.S.W.

IN SEARCH OF A COMMAND

Washington, Oct. 4th, 1861.

My Dear Daughter Irene: [3]

I reached here all safe but hugely annoyed by crowded cars and drunken soldiers. Found my staff and Larned anxious for my arrival. Horses and baggage all arrived safe, and through the courtesy of Col. Rucker are safely deposited and stabled in his private quarters.[4]

Yesterday I occupied a hot day in the War Department and military offices, reporting myself and seeking directions for my brigade. I had an audience of Gen. Scott and was received very graciously and kindly. I have not yet seen Gen. McClellan. Indeed, he is not easily seen, being almost constantly in the saddle on the other side. I, of course, saw his Assistant Adjutant General and the Chief of his Staff, Gen. Marcy.[5] I expect an order today, but don't yet know my destination.

Yesterday I was much encouraged that I should have a full brigade of Michigan troops. Today it is intimated to me that I shall be sent to Banks' division.[6] He has no brigadier general and is posted, as you probably know, on the upper Potomac in the vicinity of Harpers Ferry. I only regret this because I fear I shall have no Michigan troops, and have command of strange regiments. However, we must make the best of a bad case, if it is a bad case. The matter, however, is not definitely settled. I have had a second interview with Gen. Marcy today on the subject. . . . I saw Mrs. Smith a moment yesterday. Kirby, who is now here, has the colonelcy of an Ohio regiment and is going to Columbus, Ohio.[7] Mrs. Smith will probably go with him and spend the winter in Cincinnati, where Kirby's residence will be ordered. . . .

Ever Your Affectionate Father.

◈

CAMP LIFE BEGINS

Camp near Darnestown, Md.,
Saturday night, Oct. 12th, 1861.

My Dear Daughter:

Here I am away up amongst the hills of Maryland about two miles from the Potomac and about twenty miles above Washington. Imagine a pretty high hill (mountains in our state), on top a thick wood, at the bottom a small rapid stream, a valley spreading out for a quarter of a mile or so and bounded on the opposite side by higher hills formed into projecting knobs by lateral ravines. On one of the largest of these is the encampment of Gen. Banks, staff and escort, foot and horse. On our hillside are my eight or ten tents, sheltered by the woods in the rear. Just within the woods are our servants' tents and farther in, the picket for our horses, sheltered as well as may be by a hedge of bushes and covered by one of our tent flies.

Nearby is William Dollarson's cooking apparatus.[8] Around about on the hills (all in sight save one) are the regiments of my brigade as follows: 2nd Massachusetts, Col. Gordon; 5th Connecticut, Col. Ferry; 28th New York, Col. Donnelly; 46th Pennsylvania, Col. Knipe; 19th New York, Maj. Ledlie; Co. A, Rhode Island Battery, Capt. Tompkins; in all, nearly 5,000 men.

The country round about is beautiful, varied into high hills and fertile valleys with numerous small, rapid, clear streams. Altogether it is a delightful spot, especially towards sundown when the bands of the regiments strike up for the evening parades and the hillsides in front are covered with moving bodies of troops and the bugle calls from the neighboring brigades float up the valleys and are echoed along the hillside.

It seems queer, though, and almost magical to be transported in such a brief time from a quiet home to this bustle and stir of battalions of armed men, where civil life is really hardly observable and military pomp and preparation cover everything, the cultivated and uncultivated land and man and beast, with the trappings of war. But you will ask, How did you get there? Well! To go back to my last letter to you from Washington, when I was in daily expectation of a brigade of Michigan troops. On Saturday last I received an order to report forthwith to Gen. Banks, with an intimation (to soften my disappointment) that Gen. Banks was in need of a brigadier, and that I would find a responsible command. So on Monday, as soon as we could gather together our tents and other necessaries, we mounted horse and with three wagons drawn by double mule teams set forward to our unknown destination. . . .

We had a slow and pleasant ride till towards evening when we were overtaken by a tremendous shower, and we took shelter for the night at a small village inn at Rockville. I never saw it rain harder, and the wind blew a tempest. It was a hard night for the poor soldiers, many of whom are out on picket guard all night without shelter. The next morning we started forward in a drizzle and reached Gen. Banks' headquarters about noon. On my way I rode off the line a few rods to visit Gen. Meade, who commands a brigade eight or ten miles below.[9]

We dined with Gen. Banks, who gave me orders for my brigade, and I started out to select a camping-ground, which I found without difficulty in the position I have attempted to describe.

We were strangers, and none of the regiments near offered me the least assistance. Gen. Banks promised to send me a detail of men but none came. So we all set to work, myself, Capt. Wilkins, Lt. Pittman, Larned, and the three servants, none of whom but Capt. Wilkins and myself had ever seen a tent pitched. However, we were all pretty snugly located before dark and William had opened our mess chest and prepared a very comfortable meal of broiled ham and soda biscuits, and upon this diet we were obliged to feed for a couple of days before we could find fresh meat or bread. The country people bring in nothing, being pretty much all Secessionists, and those disposed to sell have been fairly eaten out by our large army. Man and beast find small pickings. Our horses had a little poor hay for a day or so and then a little corn, but at length we have ferreted out the resources of the land and have meat for ourselves and oats and hay for the horses.

My Yorkshire proves a splendid animal, afraid of nothing and full of life and spirit. We are kept very busy in posting ourselves up with the brigade. I am in the saddle a good deal, visiting the several regiments. Capt. Wilkins is kept employed with a clerk and one or two other assistants and a mounted orderly in answering applications, making the daily details for guard, pickets, duty officers, recording orders, and generally providing for our large military family of 5,000 men, to say nothing of the hundreds of teams and horses. For the latter, especially, we have much trouble in providing day by day, forage being very scarce and very dear.

Our daily routine is: up at reveille (sunrise); William gives us a cup of strong coffee soon after and breakfast in an hour. By eight o'clock the reports begin to arrive from the several regiments, and then sergeant-majors [begin] to copy orders and the general applications for leave, furloughs, for quartermaster's or commissary's stores, for all kinds of wants. Orders from division headquarters follow, all to be copied, repeated in a new order, and distributed to the several regiments.

We have improvised a few desks out of packing boxes and on these we do most of our writing. Breakfast over, I mount (as soon as the consolidated report of all the regiments is made up and signed) to visit the regiments in turn. I do not get back much before dinner time. After dinner I am again in the saddle with some duty to do. In this way the days seem short, and by eight or nine o'clock we are all in bed.

We know little of what is passing beyond our immediate vicinity. The two other brigades of this division are commanded by Gens. Abercrombie and Hamilton.[10] They lie near at hand but neither have as large and, I think, not as good regiments as I have. You will see that I have troops from five different states, among them the famous Rhode Island Battery with James' rifled cannon. This company was at Bull Run battle and gained a good reputation. The 2nd Massachusetts is a splendid regiment; the colonel and lieut-colonel are both graduates of West Point. The 5th Connecticut is commanded by Col. Ferry, a member of Congress from that state, a man of great energy and industry but I think not much of a soldier.[11] The other regiments are tolerably well officered, and all but one have been in service since May.

Now Minnie dear, I have told you pretty much all I can think of about myself and my matters. Larned makes himself useful, but not exactly in the way I wish. I shall put him in the adjutant general's office. He prefers outdoors. He received your letter yesterday in which you mention an eight-page letter to me, which I grieve to say has not come to hand. I have not received a single letter from you nor from Irene since I left her, but my companions are in the same plight. Neither Capt. Wilkins nor Lt. Pittman have heard from their wives. It is strange how irregularly letters come to us here at home. It was better in Mexico. However, keep writing, I suppose they will turn up.

I commenced this letter last evening and am finishing it on a box upon which my early cup of coffee has made some blots. You must hardly expect a neat letter from camp. I fear this is scarcely legible. We have orders to hold ourselves in readiness to march within twenty-four hours and hence all writing places are occupied now as early as reveille. I think it more than probable we shall not move at all, but the preparation of two-days' cooked rations, all the fuss and bustle, is as necessary as though the march were certain. . . . We talk of you often in our Detroit mess. You are a great favorite with my staff officers, and Father, you know, never wearies hearing your praises.

Your Affectionate Father,
A.S.W.

◈

ROUTINE OF CAMP LIFE

Camp near Darnestown, Md.,
Oct. 16th, 1861.

My Dear Daughter: . . .

Your first letter was only received today by the hands of Larned, who after much perseverance got it out of the Washington Post Office. He went down last Monday with a train to get us some necessaries, but on arriving in Washington found that his memorandum was lost, so back he posted, arriving at camp about noon, and was off again mounted on horse-back at one o'clock. I was very much pleased with his perseverance and energy in the matter. I gave him your messages. He promises to write you on his return. I see by the New York papers that they have a report that Gen. Banks' Division has been attacked and badly cut up, all of which is without foundation. We have not been even threatened, unless an occasional shot across the river at our pickets can be called threatening, so you see you must not be alarmed at any rumors.

I have no idea that we shall be attacked until we cross the Potomac. We, none of us, can guess what our movements are to be. I have a fine brigade. One of the regiments, 2nd Massachusetts, is the best volunteer regiment I ever saw and drills like regulars. The 2nd Connecticut is under the command of Col. Ferry. The Rhode Island Battery has James' rifled cannon and is the same battery which gained distinction at Bull Run. The New York and the Pennsylvania regiments are well commanded and are making efforts to improve. On the whole, I am well-satisfied, though I should have preferred one or two regiments from Michigan.

We have had very fine weather for some days, with splendid moonlight nights. Within the hearing of my camp are probably eight or ten regiments, all with excellent bands, besides several camps of artillery, cavalry, and independent zouave companies with bugles and trumpets. In consequence, we have a profusion of music at all hours, but especially during the moonlight evenings. The hillsides and projecting knobs which lie around our circular-formed valley are covered with tents, and at night when the lights are lit and the camp fires blazing and the bands playing the scene is very striking and beautiful. I should like to transplant you here for an evening if I could safely send you back to Aunt Kate's for a lodging. I am sure you would enjoy the sight and the music, to say nothing of my society.

The country around us is much broken with hills and valleys. Some of the rides along the narrow bridle paths by the side of considerable streams are very romantic. I am a great deal in the saddle from necessity, and like it amazingly. Day before yesterday I rode over twenty-five miles and yesterday about fifteen to visit one of my regiments on detached service. In one of my rides I visited the camp of the 7th Michigan, Col. Grosvenor. It is about two miles towards the river from Poolesville. I was received with great eclat. You will remember this is one of the regiments in my camp at Fort Wayne. It is a very fine regiment.[12] The sergeants, and corporals, even, rushed out to greet and shake hands with me.

According to the custom of the army I am obliged to live and travel in considerable state, though you know I have not much fondness for the ceremonies of military life that have not immediate influence upon its efficiency and discipline. I have a guard detailed for me every day at my own camp by the several regiments, in turn. They turn out and present arms every time I leave or return. Behind me rides a mounted orderly, whenever I leave camp, and as soon as I approach the encampment of a regiment, the sentinels begin to pass the word, "Turn out the guard," "The Brigadier General." Out rolls the guard of a hundred men or so and I am obliged to ride along the front, cap in hand, to acknowledge the salutation, while the drummers beat a furious tattoo upon their drums and the guard presents arms. I go through this process at least once a day with all my regiments, and then leave instructions to "never mind the guard," which means do not turn out on my approach again today.

The details I have to attend to are very considerable, so much so that I have a clerk detailed besides my staff. All the issues from the quartermasters and commissaries I have to approve, all charges for courts martial, all applications for furloughs and leaves, and all reports. In short, everything for 5,000 men has to pass under my supervision, besides the daily detail of guards, officers of the day, etc. Still we have greatly simplified much of this circumlocution system and saved half of our labor. I find time after morning business to visit most of the regiments, to examine the condition of the camps, hospitals, kitchens, etc. Each morning my field officer of the day, whose duty it is to visit and supervise each camp night and day, makes me a long written report, and all his complaints and suggestions I generally attend to in person as the most effectual way of correcting error and improving matters generally. To do all this I am up at sunrise or thereabouts and to bed about nine o'clock, and during these moonlight nights about ten o'clock. . . .

Your Most Affectionate Father,
A.S.W.

◈

BEFORE THE BATTLE

Camp at Edwards Ferry,
Oct. 23rd, 1861.

My Dear Rene:

I am on the point of moving over with my brigade. Have been in the mud and rain forty-eight hours, mostly without sleep and marching by night. I have only time to enclose the money you asked for, and to say that if I fall or am taken prisoner you must help Larned to support yourself and Minnie. You are able and willing and full of energy and confidence. Larned is pretty well used up and nervous. He will write soon.

You will hear by telegraph if anything occurs, long before this reaches you. God bless you my daughter and have you always in his holy keeping.

Most Affectionately, Your Father,
A.S.W.

◆

DISASTER AT BALL'S BLUFF

Camp near Muddy Brook, Md.,
November 5, 1861.

My Dear Lew: [13] . . .

Now as to war matters. We are having the devil's own weather and have had since we were so suddenly woke up from our quiet camp near Darnestown. I made a forced march with my brigade, got orders while inspecting a regiment, left all standing, tents, hospitals, etc., with a camp guard, and commencing after dark I was at Edwards Ferry before daylight, having performed nearly twenty-five miles, part of the way in a cold rain and deep clay mud. Gen. Banks had no knowledge of the intended movement till 5 o'clock P.M. nor did any of us know of the disaster to poor Baker till we reached Poolesville, five miles from Edwards Ferry. Here I was taken to the telegraph office and shown Baker's full dress hat and uniform, two ball holes through the hat and several through the coat. His corpse lay in a house nearby. [14]

From this point to the Ferry the road was full of stragglers and ambulances with wounded. Not a man carried his arms. All professed to have thrown them into the river and swam for life. They told enormous stories, and very pitiable if true. Every man was the last of his company. Arriving at the ferry, we had a doleful position on the muddy banks, crowded with arriving troops, cold rain, and high winds. I posted my men in the woods, found Gens. Banks and Stone looking dolefully around a camp fire and waited till daylight to pass over my brigade.

When daylight came, I found the means of transit were two small boats and one canal boat, capable of carrying perhaps one hundred

men and occupying an hour or so in being poled over by awkward boat-
men. The river was much swollen and very rapid, about one-quarter
mile broad or more, and in the misty, dull morning light it didn't look
at all pleasant. Gen. Abercrombie's brigade was ahead of me, having
come by the shortest route. I waited and waited in the rain till nearly
2 o'clock, when orders came to bivouac and but a few hours after came
the sudden rattle of small arms and the booming of big guns from
over the river. We had a stirring sight for a half hour or so, in full
view from the high banks on our side. All at once the fight stopped, the
guns ceased fire, and there was a painful silence over the other side,
especially as the smoke settling down over the field, we could see
nothing of the position of our troops. In a short time we learned that
the enemy had fled, and subsequently we had positive intelligence that
they lost sixty men killed in this short conflict.[15]

My brigade was ordered under arms again and soon we went on a
double-quick to the ferry, the men cheering all the way, and considering the weather, the march, the means of transportation, and all things
else, were in excellent spirits, better, I confess, than I was, though I
assumed an especial alacrity and good cheer at the prospect of passing
over. We didn't get over, however, for the cavalry had possession of
the boats and it was dark before even they could move. After some
delay we were ordered back for the night.

The day following was a furious gale, so strong that only one or
two boats crossed. Our poor fellows already over lay in the mud day
and night without shelter and badly provisioned. We were hourly
expecting an attack upon them and we had no means to reinforce them.
I contrived to get over one company of sharpshooters to scout on the
south side of Goose Creek, where we had not one man and from which
direction our flank was exposed. There was a furious popping of skirmishers all day and we could see bodies of their troops in position on
the hills behind. My brigade was taken down to the ferry, my artillery
embarked on the boats, and after dark I was ordered back again to
remain in readiness to embark during the night. I tumbled myself onto
my bed full-armed, expecting to be called at any moment. I did not
awake till morning, when I found my scouting officer at hand to report
that all our troops had recrossed and left the "sacred soil" to its own
people.

Gen. McClellan had been in camp the day before all day. No general officer, unless Gen. Banks, knew his decision till it was carried out during the night by the withdrawal. During the gale of Wednesday I had put all my regiments in tents behind the first roll of the high bank, my wagon train having followed me up as I ordered and the same day my supply train arrived, so that my whole brigade was well provided. It was mighty cold, however, and I regret to say that few fences within a mile of Edwards Ferry had even a foundation rail left. We remained in camp within full reach of their guns and shells till Saturday, but as my brigade was in advance I took the precaution to send my whole wagon train (which with its hundreds of mules and heavy wagons is no joke in a stampede) five miles to the rear.

On Saturday (26th) we broke up and marched by the river road to this point, reaching this [place] after dark and encamping pell mell, weather raining, in an open space surrounded by woods of evergreens. I have since got all my regiments into the evergreens, well protected from the high winds, which blow furiously more than half the time. We are about a mile in direct line from the river, which my brigade has been picketing for nearly five miles on the banks of the canal, but which I have had narrowed down to two and a half miles. All the roads are also picketed, which besides the camp guards takes nearly one man in four of my command on duty every night.

Since coming to this camp, we have had two furious northeasters and last night ice formed very thick. All the troops of my brigade have overcoats, but the single blanket and such worn-out tents are poor protection. The men are suffering badly, though strange to say in this brigade we have less sickness than before marching to Edwards Ferry. The other brigades, which are encamped west of me in open and elevated plains, are suffering much more, and sickness has greatly increased and is increasing. As division officer of the day yesterday I had to visit every regiment of the three brigades and was in the saddle from 9 o'clock till sundown. I found one Indiana regiment without overcoats, and yet doing duty on the river as pickets. This is too bad and any country ought to be damned that suffers it.

We have not been molested from the other side. Their scouts and pickets show themselves, but scarcely a musket is fired. I go along the tow-path with as much feeling of safety as I should on the Erie Canal.

Yesterday, I went two or three miles down, part of the way with an escort of dragoons (my officer-of-the-day hangers-on) but received no recognition from our saluting friends opposite. Indeed, picket shooting is getting to be voted barbarous. Up at Edwards Ferry they exchange visits now, crossing over and having contabs. . . .

No one here (not [even] Gen. Banks) can guess what is to come next. We talk of winter quarters at Frederick, at Poolesville, at Rockville, at Washington, and now and then it is guessed that we are to follow the southern expedition. In the meantime, we watch the opposite shore, but I fear don't *pray* much, but rather swear. I shall not comment on the sad repulse at Conrad's Ferry near Edwards Ferry. I have my opinion of the whole movement—the originator, the motive, and the expectation. McCall was at Darnesville (nearly opposite our present camp) reconnoitering. Stone was at Poolesville. Baker was burning for a fight. A few horsemen crossed, rode towards Leesburg, and came back reporting no enemy at Leesburg or on the road. There seemed a golden chance to get ahead of McCall and take Leesburg by a simple march. One rickety boat transported over two or three small regiments and a few men [were] held ready to be passed over in an equally singular way at Edwards Ferry. It is plain that nobody expected to be driven back or come back in a hurry, for it was simply impossible to do so with the transit means at hand. Gen. Banks, fifteen to twenty miles distant, was not notified of the movement. Gen. McCall at Darnesville moving toward Leesburg was not notified, for on the same day he made a retrograde movement of twelve miles, thus leaving the enemy at liberty to go to Leesburg. Gen. McClellan was not notified till Baker was defeated. It was therefore plainly an unpremeditated and unprepared effort, and failed, as nine out of ten such hasty affairs will.

Who was to blame, I know not—but I do know that there is a mighty amount of stupidity in those papers who lay the affair to Gen. Banks. Gen. Stone's division is not under Gen. Banks' command. It is (like Gen. Banks') one division of Gen. McClellan's Army of the Potomac. On the very morning that Baker crossed, Gen. Banks was at my tent talking over the probabilities of crossing and expressed his opinion that no advance on the upper Potomac could be made till further movements were had before Washington. At 10 o'clock the same day, hearing that some movement was on foot above, he telegraphed and got answer that there was no intention of crossing, or something to that effect! This was received after Baker's column had actually in part crossed the river!

It was not till Baker was driven back that Gen. Banks was telegraphed to send one brigade to Conrad's Ferry and Hamilton's brigade (being nearest in position) was put in motion. At the same time the other two brigades were ordered to move to Seneca Ford, and I had actually marched nearly four miles toward the mouth of the Seneca before a second telegraph directed us all toward Poolesville and Edwards Ferry. My night march was increased nearly eight miles by this operation. Our editors seem to speak as if Gen. Banks commanded the whole line of the upper Potomac. It is not so. McCall commands one division below—partly over the river. Banks comes next and Stone one above, each three brigades, but there was no 25,000 men at Edwards Ferry, nor half of that number. There is a great overestimating of troops on this line. The regiments are greatly reduced in number and some never had over 750 men. If the estimates made of troops around Washington are equally erroneous then indeed there is good cause to remain stationary. Besides, our troops are miserably armed. Our fine 7th Regiment, Col. Grosvenor, which was across the river at Edwards Ferry, is armed with the Belgian rifle, not one in ten of which can be discharged. I have one regiment with guns of three different calibers and I found a regiment yesterday with guns of four different calibers. What are we to think of such indifference to the effectiveness of troops? This whole matter is weekly reported by me, and I doubt not sent up. But in truth we have no good guns, and to all uses of war, we should be just as strong with half the men we have well-armed as we are now. But enough. I am sending you an intolerable letter. Give much love to Jule and Syl and Cousin Maria and Mary, and to little Jule one of my provoking kisses. I shall hope to hear from you often—give us the little news. Our letters are provokingly slow, but they do come. . . .

Yours Affectionately,
Alph.

P.S. Don't mention what I have said about Banks' telegraphs or our forces.

Can't stop to read over. A. S. Williams.

ALL QUIET ALONG THE POTOMAC

Camp near Muddy Brook, Md.,
Nov. 9th, 1861.

My Dear Daughter:

I wrote you a pretty long letter a few days since in which I promised photographs of my headquarters' log cabin. The weather has been so stormy since that I have not been able to get them printed. We have had two violent easterly gales with rain followed by high northeasterly winds, very cold and disagreeable.

Yesterday we had a fine day, quite Indian summer like. The day before was clear but cool with high winds. As division officer of the day I rode all day from 9 A.M. till sundown, visiting all the regiments of the three brigades, the several picket guards on the road, the cavalry and artillery camps, and finishing up by following the river pickets for miles (along the tow-path of the canal, which runs on the margin of the Potomac) partly on horseback and partly on foot. My brigade has been picketing the river bank for nearly five miles, from Great Falls to the mouth of the Muddy Branch. About 200 men are put on each afternoon carrying 24 hours' rations and returning the following evening after being relieved.

It is a hard duty, as the poor fellows are not allowed fires and the weather has been very inclement. Still they go on with wonderful cheerfulness. There is a strange excitement in the prospect of shooting at one another across the river. We have had, however, very little picket firing and do not encourage it. The Rebels appear on the opposite bank, but so long as they remain quiet we do not trouble them. The river has been unusually high, overflowing the banks of the canal and wholly submerging the island. Since I wrote you last (I think) Gov. Blair and suite paid me a visit and dined with us.[16] . . .

Dr. Antisell joined us as brigade-surgeon a few days ago. He is a very agreeable and intelligent addition to our mess.[17] Capt. Whittlesey has received his appointment as brigade quarter-master and been ordered to report to me, so you see I am getting my staff filled up pretty much as I wished.[18] The young officer who is acting-assistant-commissary of subsistence is from my native village of Deep River and is a most excellent and efficient officer. He has the strong recommendations of the regular commissary and will probably get his appointment and be permanently put on duty with me. This, with the appointment of one more aide (which I can make from lieutenants) completes my staff. I expect Capt. Whittlesey some time next week.

All my regiments are now encamped in evergreen woods, except the 19th New York, which is two or three miles distant guarding the division supply train. They are very comfortably located and much less exposed than the regiments of other brigades, encamped on high table lands open to all the high winds of the season. Two of my regiments have cut out the small scrub pines and grubbed up the roots making a square completely hedged in, in which they pitch their tents, and on the edge of the square piled up the bushes so as to completely cut off the cold winds. Almost every tent has its fire, which is built in the mouth of a trench in the front. The trench is carried through the tent covered over with flat stones and earth and terminating behind in a turf chimney surmounted by a barrel to increase the draft. In this way the fire is carried under the tent; the stones, once heated, keep up the warmth a long time, and a tent is made very comfortable. Others dig deep cellars and build regular fire-places, carrying the chimney through the ground under the wall of the tent to some distance away and use the barrel for a chimney.

In one regiment (28th), which is encamped among trees of larger growth, the men are building log huts along the line of streets. If we are left in position long this whole regiment will be hutted. I have a busy brigade and am much pleased with it. I fancy it is far the best in the division in all respects, in drill, policing, good order, and cheerful discharge of any duty. In marching, I believe (since my forced march to Edwards Ferry through the rain and mud) that I can beat any troops in the Army of the Potomac. . . .

I should like to visit you at Christmas and perhaps we may be so placed in winter quarters that I can get away. While, however, operations are liable to be active and we are still in the field I do not like to be absent one day. All the other generals of this division have been away and both, I believe, are in Washington now. I intend to stick close to the camp till the prospect of any movement this season is closed. There is some talk about winter quarters. Gen. Banks has intimated that we shall move soon, but I think he is not much better advised than the rest.

It has been thrown out that we may follow the southern expedition as a reinforcement. I think all movements are in suspense awaiting information from that source.

In the meantime we hear, day after day, the booming of cannon above and below us and our minds are kept conjecturing "what is up." Yesterday, all day, we heard reports of heavy guns, and a few days before we were sure that Gen. McCall was engaged below Danesville. Dr. Antisell, who came up, says the rumor below was that all our division was fighting the enemy and that the cannon reports came from our direction. In the meantime, around the whole front of our encampment the rolling drill ground, covering a space of several hundred acres, is on every pleasant day a scene of the most lively and pleasant kind. Several regiments are engaged in all kinds of drill, some by battalion, some by companies, some skirmishing, some forming squares, some charging in line of battle; in short, employed in all manner of maneuvers. While the regiments are marching out and in, the bands play, and occasionally, when the companies are at rest. This scene begins at 8 o'clock A.M. when all regiments "mount guard" and all bands play in succession. Then comes the drill by companies till near 11 o'clock, then for two or three hours the space is cleared, excepting [for] straggling details and mounted orderlies. In the afternoon the regiments appear again by battalion, all the bands playing and the sounds very discordant sometimes, from the quantity of instruments from different directions. In a few moments, the whole space will be covered by the changing and moving masses and detachments of men, and the sound of many voices giving hoarse and loud orders takes the place of musical instruments.

Towards sundown the drills stop and the music begins again, till the regiments form for evening parades skirting along the circular line of the evergreen woods, and all in full view of our log-cabin home. The scene is then most animating and cheerful. I often wish you were here to enjoy it, knowing your fondness for this military display and for the music of bands. In the evening, before tattoo, the bands generally play again, in turn, and now and then one comes round to serenade the General.

Tattoo comes and then taps, all lights are extinguished, all noise hushed, except the outrageous braying of mules or the more agreeable neighing of horses or perhaps the call of some far-off sentinel, who calls loudly the number of his post, with a yell for "Corporal of the Guard." Then may be heard in the stillness of the night the tramp of horses, some officer, with his escort, going the "grand rounds"; or perhaps a single horseman can be heard dashing furiously over the hills in the direction of division headquarters, coming as if he bore a message of vast importance, which, though often delivered at midnight, turns out to be nothing more than a leave of absence or a detail for next day, or some other insignificant matter which might as well have been delivered next day.

When the days are fair, I ride with some of my staff over the country to get familiar with the many byroads and bridle paths. It is a country full of commanding views and pleasant prospects. Almost every hill one ascends gives him a far-off view of hill and dale and river. From some we get long peeps into Virginia. We have on these highest points regular signal stations, with a corps of officers in permanent charge. Communications are made at fixed hours with Washington below and as high up as Point of Rocks and Harpers Ferry—in the daytime, by a series of flags, and by night by varied-colored lamps, after the system invented by Major Ayers, who is in command of the corps.

The highest point for signals is Sugar Loaf Mountain, which rises some few miles above Edwards Ferry in the shape of a loaf of sugar, several hundred feet above any surrounding hill. It is a prominent and conspicuous point from the whole line of the river. From the station at its top one can plainly see Leesburg on one side and Frederick, Maryland, on the other. The next station below is a hilltop near our camp. To gain a higher elevation, an old dry tree on the hill is used and ascended by ladders. Away up in its branches they have fixed a sort of nest where through the strong telescopes used one can see away down to Chain Bridge and away up to Edwards Ferry, the camps of Gen. Stone's division being plainly visible.

It is, indeed, a grand prospect, and along the whole distance long patches of the Potomac gleam out towards a pleasant sunset, seeming like silver lakes. Everything, of a quiet afternoon, such as we have had several times, looks so peaceful and home-like, the cattle grazing on the hillsides, the smoke curling from the many farmhouses, that one can hardly realize that thousands are armed for battle on either side of that pleasant river and amid those quiet valleys. But so it is, and one's heart feels heavy in the thought that it is so.

You will be glad to hear that my horse is doing finely, notwithstanding his outdoor exposure to rain and wind, and his occasional deprivation of hay or oats. The whole division is much troubled to procure forage. I am obliged to send the wagons of my brigade 25 miles for hay and oats. The roads are now so heavy that the mules consume much of the load before they return, or on the return. When you reflect that we have in the division about a thousand four-mule-wagons, besides the horses of officers, artillery, cavalry, and various staff departments, you will comprehend somewhat the difficulty we have to feed them. The country immediately about us is not very productive, and the farmers have been pretty closely skinned and complain bitterly that they are often obliged to sell at prices fixed by the government. I fear their complaints are well founded, but "necessity knows no law." Still, I think the government should make liberal prices.

There is a great rush to me at each new encampment for guards for houses. I have invariably tried to protect the people, and always send out small pickets to houses near our camps; and yet, in spite of all endeavors and all efforts of commanders of regiments, there is a good deal of rascality done; mainly, however, I think, by the hordes of unenlisted teamsters, drovers, and hangers-on, who are a necessary appendage to an army. I am greatly annoyed by daily complaints and try hard to correct the evil and do justice where damage is done. I fear, however, we are suffering the usual consequences of an armed occupation, making more enemies than friends. Indeed, I fear there is not much real loyalty in this part of Maryland, and that the people would greatly rejoice to see us driven out. They *talk* very patriotic. . . .

Ever Your Affectionate Father,
A.S.W.

◈

ARMY DRILLS AND NEEDS

Camp near Muddy Branch, Md.,
Nov. 24th, 1861,

My Dear Daughter:

Your last letters have reached me with much better regularity and all have come to hand. The last, with the enclosure of your school report, was very gratifying. . . . I was much pleased with Aunt Kate's letter. I shall answer it soon, but at present my time is much occupied. I have, in consequence, somewhat delayed writing you or Irene longer than usual, and I shall be obliged now to make a short letter. I could write you in the evening, but that our small log cabin, 12 by 15, is full of the desks of staff officers and their assistants, who keep up a constant talk about forage, rations, abstracts, requisitions, claims, prices, supplies, and the like with the regimental quartermaster and others who seek the night to make arrangements for the succeeding day. Add to this a very smoky chimney and all the [illegible] of a crowded cabin, with all writing tables occupied, and you can imagine I have a poor chance for letter writing.

The past has been a tolerably pleasant week and I have improved it by a review of my brigade and brigade drills, in which all my regiments are maneuvered together. We make a great show in these "evolutions de luxe," especially as they are mainly done in double-quick, and the regiments being very well drilled the movements are made with wonderful precision and accuracy. Would you not like to see four or five regiments closing up into mass, then deploying into line of battle, then moving rapidly to the front in "echelons" forming squares all in one grand oblong parallelogram, then separating into squares of single regiments, oblique and direct; in short, taking all manner of offensive and defensive positions and all moved without confusion or disorder and controlled as by a single thought to the same end?

Mine is the only brigade in this division which has these drills, and consequently we have a large crowd of spectators from the three brigades and from the host of civilian employees of the army. It was quite an imposing affair, *we* all think. I found a large field of many hundred acres where I could form all my regiments in one line. After marching in quick time, each regiment marched past in double-quick to the music of its own band. It was very handsomely done, for all my regiments but one have been nearly five months in service and move on the double-quick with the regularity of veterans. They trot off with knapsack packed, canteen and haversack and cartridge box, with forty rounds of ball cartridges, as if nothing was on their backs. On the whole, you see, I am well pleased with my brigade, and what is perhaps more important, I think the brigade is well pleased with me, but this may be fancy.

We have all been expecting to move from our present position to Rockville or Frederick for winter quarters. It is rumored today, however, that we shall not go into winter quarters at present, but must hold on here to await events. We are in a sorry position. The roads, even the best ones, are almost impassable, and the new ones cut for military purposes and to get into our camps are for all practicable value quite so. In riding in yesterday from the camp of one of my regiments I found lots of mule wagons stalled in the mud, some with broken tongues and others badly disabled in other ways. If this is so while the weather is comparatively good, what may we not expect as soon as the winter days begin in reality?

So far the season has been, for a week at a time say, one day heavy rain, the next a cold, strong north wind, gradually lessening into a tolerably mild Indian summer day. This would end in another heavy north-east rain. Thus we seemed to be just in that point where a constant strife is going on between the north and south winds. Tonight we have a regular snow storm with a northerly wind. My heart bleeds for the poor fellows picketted along the river with little shelter, many without blankets, and some without overcoats. I have been unremitting in my efforts since I joined the brigade to get all this necessary clothing supplied and have sent all my colonels to Washington and some to their states to get overcoats and blankets. They have been promised over and over again. Many have been supplied, but not all.

There seems [to be] a great want of foresight somewhere, a great negligence in preparing for the future. I don't pretend to say where, but I know that our volunteers could be clothed and ought to be. Their exposure in this weather all through these stormy nights is bad enough with the best clothing, but without overcoats and blankets it is barbarous and will cost the government in pensions and hospitals ten times the

35

value of good warm clothing. If mittens are not provided before the winter cold comes, thousands will be disabled by frozen fingers and hands.

My regiments have very bad tents, but they are making all sorts of huts and warm shelters for winter and when inside their tents will get along pretty well, I think. Most of them have got fireplaces inside, so have regular log houses, others have mounted tents on log basements. It is quite a curiosity to go through the camps and see the various devices to keep warm. With new tents we could keep warm all winter, I think.

I fear you were too much alarmed at the Edwards Ferry affair. The exposure to me is not very great, and what I most feared in that river crossing was that we should have hard work to get back if Beauregard had sent, as he could, a large force to attack us. But he did not, and we, fortunately, did not stay to give him a chance. Leesburg is about as near Centerville (the Rebels' large army) as Washington. Of course we could hardly expect to stay long at Leesburg without a big battle.

I have not yet sent the photographs; I am waiting to get one of myself and some others. If I don't get them this week I will send those I have by express. Love to all. I have forgotten to tell you how useful we have found your "housewife." [19] Capt. Wilkins and Mr. Pittman [20] talk of you often and wish to be remembered. Capt. Whittlesey has not yet arrived; we expect him soon. I should like to send my things to Annie to be overhauled. I think she would find some things out of sort. Larned has no "housewife." Can't you make him one? I will write you again in a few days and talk about Christmas.

Your Affectionate Father,
A.S.W.

◈

REMOVAL TO WINTER QUARTERS

Headquarters, 3rd Brigade,
Camp near Frederick, Dec. 7th, 1861.

My Dear Daughter:

A letter from Aunt Patty received just before I left Camp at Muddy Branch says that you had not heard from me for four weeks,

If this is so, my letters must have miscarried, for the longest interval has not been over two weeks. I must have written you at least five letters from Camp Muddy Branch while we were there but about four weeks. You must not think it strange nor that you are forgotten if my letters are very irregular, for I have not only constant occupations but subjects of incessant thought. It is an easy matter for you, who have literally nothing that *demands* daily attention, to write to your friends. If you had the care and supervision of a town of 4,000 people you would find the time for writing not easily got at.

As I wrote you in my last, we have changed camps and I am now perched up in the hills which form part of the chain of the Blue Ridge. We are westward of the city of Frederick about three and one-half miles. Back of us lies a high range of wooded hills, and as we have the southern slope on a gravelly soil, with several small mountain streams running close to us, with plenty of wood, we can say that our camp for cold weather is most eligibly located. My headquarters are in a farmer's house, nicely situated, with a two-storied corridor or stoop running the whole length of the house. We have one large room for office and eating-room, one bedroom (small) for myself and Larned, and one large one for my staff. For the first time in two months I have slept in a room and on a bed! So rapidly do we acquire new habits of life that it seems strange, and as the weather is very fine I almost regret my tent and field bed!

The country about us is exceedingly beautiful and picturesque. We are just in the first hills of the mountain range and my regiments are encamped up a narrow ravine or valley which runs east and west into the ridge, called Catoctin Mountains. East of us, perhaps fifteen or twenty miles, is another range of mountains or high hills called Parr's Ridge. Between these two ranges lies a most beautiful and fertile valley, rolling in great undulations and cultivated to the highest perfection. In the center of this valley is the ancient and rather fine-looking city of Frederick, a place of several thousand inhabitants, renowned for the wealth of its citizens and for its Secession proclivities. At a distance, its lofty spires and its long range of cement[?] buildings and other public edifices give it a very picturesque appearance. From our headquarters we can overlook a greater part of this valley, and the city, though distant over three miles, seems (especially, through the present hazy atmosphere) to be almost within a stone's throw.

So much for my location: We broke up camp on the morning of the

4th inst. (Wednesday) moving with all my regimental and brigade supply-trains of over a hundred four-horse wagons. The other brigades had moved each a day before the other. The roads had been terrifically bad, so deep in mud that we found it difficult to get forage for our numerous cattle. But fortunately the weather became freezing cold and the road hard, but as rough as the popular song makes the road over Jordan. However, I made fifteen miles the first day, bringing up wagons and everything promptly and encamping long before sundown on a superb ground on the banks of the Little Seneca, on the "Mudpike" from Rockville to Frederick.

The next morning we were on the march a little after sunrise. The day was beautiful, a veritable Indian summer day, and I anticipated a pleasant march. Before reaching the village of Clarksburg, however, we began to be annoyed by the stragglers of other regiments which had preceded us one day. Presently we overtook the wagon train of an entire regiment, which had stalled or been neglected on the way. You will think that passing a few wagons is no great matter, but if you had had a little experience in getting heavily-laden vehicles stretching out three miles or more over roads running over abrupt and rocky hills and through deep, narrow gullies and ravines you would have some appreciation of the labor and delay.

We succeeded, however, in passing the train, but as we proceeded we began to meet long lines of returning wagons. The stragglers of one regiment (the 1st Maryland) unattached to any brigade, fairly lined the road, drunken and furious with liquor and committing all sorts of depredations and outrages. In the villages especially, the rum-shops had all been taken possession of, and the most violent conduct was being exhibited. I had no empty wagons and could not encumber my command with drunken prisoners, so all I could do was to clear out and shut up the groggeries and drive the rascals out of the villages into the country.

I was necessarily annoyed all day, and as savage and angry as a tiger, especially as those drunken stragglers were most intent upon giving their rum canteens to my men and occasionally manifested their high regard by a grand discharge of loaded muskets, fired without especial regard to range or aim. On one occasion a wagon-load fired a volley at some of their comrades lying drunk by the roadside. Fortunately the balls took effect on the rails instead of the persons of their friends. I expected to hear of wounds and loss of life, but I believe nothing was killed but hogs, dogs, and cattle.

In spite of all these annoyances and delays I reached the Monocacy Junction (three miles from Frederick) with my whole command about 3 o'clock P.M. The wagons of the regiments, with all the tents, forage, etc., did not get up at all, and these regiments were obliged to bivouac in a pretty frosty night without shelter of any kind. We found quarters in a nice house and I (for the first time in two months) had a room and a great, broad bed! All by myself! Our host and hostess were very kind and agreeable, the latter a remarkably pretty woman, and as I had not seen a passable face for a long time I enjoyed the sight as a novel entertainment.

Our trains got up in the night and we were off again soon after sunrise. I halted outside Frederick, closed up my ranks, and marched through the city in grand style, colors flying and music playing. They complimented us by saying that we made a fine show, much better than the other brigades. I rode at the head of the brigade with my staff of six. The whole population was out, and the flag of our Union was displayed very generally.

Today I have been into Frederick for a short time on business and to report to Gen. Banks, who has his headquarters there. I found the place very ancient in appearance, but with a good many elegant private residences. I hear the people are very hospitable, and that if we seek it or assent to it we shall be very generously entertained here. As for myself, I think I shall desire to keep very quiet. I have lost pretty much all desire for the gay *monde*.

I made the acquaintance yesterday of a Gen. Klemmer, who lives some ten miles east and is one of the active and prominent Union men of the state. I was introduced to a good many other gentlemen, but I was deeply impressed with the idea that while they regret the disseverance of the Union and are willing to treat us kindly, they have, after all, no very strong feeling for our side, believing, probably, that all hope of a restoration of the Union as it was is gone. However, I shall probably be here some weeks and shall see and know more. Nobody seems to know our future destination. Of course, there are all kind of rumors; for going south and going west; for breaking up the division and sending us all ways. I think nothing definite has as yet been decided, but that toward spring we shall be reinforced and sent down the valley of the Shenandoah, or toward western Virginia.

But this is all guess. I don't think Gen. Banks knows his future movements. He is not very communicative, even to those near him in command, and although always pleasant and courteous, he cannot be said to be a companionable person. I think he is oppressed somewhat with a position novel and untried, and full of responsibilities of a character so different from those he has had heretofore that he feels ill at ease. He is an officer of excellent judgment and good sense, but not familiar with military routine or etiquette, and he has for an adjutant general an officer who knows less of military [life] and [is] of less experience than he. I regard the whole state of things as unfortunate for Gen. Banks and, perhaps, *en consequence,* unfortunate for us who have the honor to command his brigades.

I think the army, and perhaps the political influence at Washington, is against him. You know that old army officers think that no man can be qualified to command who is not a graduate of West Point and has not spent at least fifteen years as a *clerk* in an army bureau or on duty at a frontier post as a lieutenant to a command of a dozen men, where there are no books, no drill, no military duty, nothing but a vast amount of whisky drinking, card playing, and terrific, profane swearing; and where, as a consequence, men forget in a year or so all they could learn in four years, and acquire habits of the most indolent and unambitious and dissolute kind. And yet, with honorable exceptions, such are the men who, in the eyes of one another at least, and I fear, too, of a good share of the public, are fit to command our armies or have any responsible positions in this war.

At least, the whole West Point influence is against any man who did not happen to spend four years of his life in that institution, and any man who has been there, even for a few months, no matter what his natural stupidity or his indolent, inefficient habits, his ignorance acquired or habitual, is fit for all responsibility and all power. I have seen much of these men and I confess to a most ineffable disgust with the whole thing. I begin to think that all the prominent acquisition obtained there is superciliousness, arrogance, and insolence. Of course, there are noble exceptions, men of military taste and ambition, to whom that institution has been the alphabet of knowledge they have gained afterwards and who would have been under any circumstances good military men. But to set it down as certain that a graduate of West Point is *ipso facto* a good officer would be like pronouncing every graduate of Harvard or Yale a man of learning—or classical knowledge—or a learned lawyer, or doctor. As these graduates forget their Latin and Greek, so these West Pointers forget their tactics, their strategy, their logistics, or exchange what little they knew for skill in whist, euchre, monte, and billiards. But I have unintentionally run into a disquisition.

The other brigades of Gen. Banks' division are east of Frederick about the same distance that mine is west, so we are quite six miles apart. . . .

Your Affectionate Father,
A.S.W.

◆

WINTER QUARTERS AT FREDERICK

Camp near Frederick, Md.,
Dec. 18th, 1861.

My Dear Daughter:

We received an order last night, or rather early this morning, to be ready for a rapid march toward Williamsport. As we were all un-packed and housed, in fact, quite settled down in our farm-house head-quarters, it created a good deal of bustle and confusion. However, we were all ready bright and early, when a countermand was received with orders to be on the alert. Our domestic arrangements, however, are left in great disorder while we await the next movement. As I may be on the road in a short time I embrace the leisure of suspended orders to write you. You will know by telegraph long before this reaches you whether we have left Frederick or not. So you can direct your letters as heretofore— "Headquarters, 3rd Brigade, Gen. Banks' Divn. near Frederick."

We have had two weeks of very charming weather which our major general has improved by a series of reviews of all his brigade and in-dependent regiments and detachments. My brigade was reviewed last

Friday, that is four regiments, the artillery having been detached to be consolidated into one battalion.

I see that the Baltimore papers give us a very favorable notice. I send you a slip from the *Sun*. After the review I drilled the whole brigade together in some very showy movements, such as forming squares by regiments in echelon on the double-quick; forming oblique squares of battalions; marching to the front on double-quick of battalions in mass, and divers such things which none of the other brigades had attempted. I also passed the general on the second time at double-quick, each battalion closed in mass and taking the double-quick step from its own music. On the whole, we of the 3rd Brigade think we rather excelled in the maneuvers, though the 1st had better ground and had just secured their new uniforms.

I accompanied Gen. Banks as a part of his cortege in all the reviews. His retinue, made up of the brigadier generals, his own large staff, and the brigade staff, with a large escort of cavalry, made a very showy cavalcade. Most of the officers were in full dress, epaulettes and chapeaus. I went each time in my simple shoulder straps and un-dress cap. At my own review, I came out in full feather, with my full regulation dress: chapeau, yellow sash, epaulettes, red second[?] belt, and all. As everybody seemed bent on "fuss and feathers" I thought I would show them that we were provided with the article! It was quite an accident that I had them, as I have no great fancy for the pomp of full dress, but, on the whole, I am rather glad I was prepared.

Since I wrote you, Col. Brodhead, 1st Michigan Cavalry, has joined our division. He is encamped on the other side of Frederick, about six miles from us. I have been to see him once. His regiment is finely mounted and he seems to have a fine lot of men. I fear they know, as yet, very little of cavalry drill. Indeed, I doubt if any of the large drafts of cavalry will be of much service, except as outposts, escorts, patrols, and the like. However, I suppose the government knows where to place its 60,000 cavalry.[21]

I have been so busy I have not seen much of Frederick or its people. I probably shall not, as I am from three to four miles away. I have, however, mounted on a bright sunny day the apex of a mountain knob, one of the highest of the Catoctin Range, and had a most extensive prospect of the two broad valleys on each side of that range of mountains. The one east (in which Frederick lies) as seen from this elevation of from 1,500 to 2,000 feet was exceedingly vast and impressive. The Eastern Range, which down in the valley seems high and broken, looks from my mountain peak like a gentle and gradual swelling up of the surface into a smooth ascent. Down south towards the Potomac is the Sugar Loaf, which seems to terminate that range. All between, for miles and miles up and down, are the square lots of the cultivated farms (green now with winter wheat) and the white farmhouses, looking in the distance and in the bright sunlight very neat and attractive.

On the other side of the Catoctin we had the smaller but equally beautiful valley which lies between it and the South Range. In its center is the neat and considerable village of Middletown, and far off in the southwest the mountain gap through which flows the Potomac at Harpers Ferry. The famous Maryland Heights, which has been the scene of various conflicts, looms up just beyond the river-gap. So much for scenery.

I am sorry I shall not be able to be with you for Christmas. . . .

Love to all. Larned promised, and I thought did write you all about our Thanksgiving under canvas. It was no grand affair, but we had turkeys and chickens, and William made a big effort. . . .

Your Very Affectionate Father,

·A.S.W.

◈

A MILITARY EXECUTION

Headquarters, 3rd Brigade,
Near Frederick, Md., Dec. 23, 1861.

My Dear Daughter:

I wrote you a few days ago, I think, while under orders and expecting to be off at once for Williamsport, Md. Since then the order has been countermanded, but we are held subject to a movement at once when ordered. The weather, in the meantime, which has been spring-like since we arrived, has changed to the very most tempestuous, snowing, sleeting, raining, freezing, and altogether of the most un-

FROM THE CANNON'S MOUTH

pleasant character. My poor fellows are badly prepared for it, as we have been expecting daily to move and but little "hutting" has been done in some of the regiments, in expectation of going away soon. Besides this, our hundreds of public horses are in the open air, exposed to sleet and cold rain, freezing as it falls. One such day will cost the government more than lumber to cover the whole army would. There will be hundreds of horses and mules dead tomorrow morning. The very high wind and low temperature will make sad havoc. . . .

To multiply the depth of a "blue Monday," we had an execution by hanging a private of my brigade on the parade ground today at 2 P.M. The culprit was named Dennis Lanaghan. While on a march just three months ago, he deliberately loaded a musket and shot the major of his regiment, the 46th Pennsylvania, simply because the major had compelled him to follow a wagon, and on his refusing had tied a rope to him for a short time. He was partly intoxicated at the time, but when sober was a very bad man. He has been in the hands of the provost guard of the division ever since, and after one or two trials set aside for irregularity in the order organizing the court, he was finally condemned a few weeks since.

I received an intimation for the first time yesterday that he was to be executed today, and this morning a party from Frederick began putting up the scaffold on a knoll in the center of the field we use for drills. At 12 o'clock I received the notification of the execution. The unpleasant office was performed by the provost marshall, and my brigade was present only as spectators. The day, as I have mentioned, was half-sleety, half-snowy, and with a high, cold wind. The ceremonies were very short. The rope was adjusted, a Catholic priest whispered something to the prisoner, a black fellow pulled the cord and let fall the drop. The man fell about two feet and literally died without a struggle. There was but an almost imperceptible drawing up of his legs and not a movement besides. The troops marched off leaving a small guard, and the affair was all over in ten or fifteen minutes.[22] . . .

On Wednesday is Christmas. I have been thinking that we have never before been absent from one another at Christmas. Rene and Larned have been away, but I think we have always been together. The day to me is full of associations. Happily for you, while you can remember the happy scenes of the past, you can look joyfully to the future. I have reached that age when "Merry Christmas" has no cheerful sound, but is rather full of sad remembrances of the many, many dear ones who used to enjoy the festive days with me but are here no more. In short, my dear Minnie, I have got so old that I begin to live in the past and hardly take into account the future on earth. But it gives me pleasure to see you merry and cheerful, and I most cordially wish you a Merry Christmas and a Happy New Year. . . .

Believe me as ever, Your Affectionate Father,

A——

1. The letter was written on both sides of a split-open envelope. Here, as elsewhere throughout the letters, as far as practicable, private and personal details have been deleted.
2. Although this letter was dated August 28, accompanying information discloses that it was actually written a month later. The official *Record of Service of Michigan Volunteers in the Civil War, 1861–1865* (hereafter cited as *Record of Service of Michigan Volunteers*) discloses that Colonel Brodhead's First Michigan Cavalry left Detroit for Washington on September 29, 1861 and that the Eighth Infantry Regiment, mustered at Detroit on September 23, departed for Washington on the 27th of this month. General Williams' succeeding letter of October 4, announcing his then recent arrival in Washington, harmonizes with the supposition that he left Detroit on Monday, September 30. The following Wednesday, when he planned to be in Philadelphia for a few hours, fell on October 2, and the letter of October 4 states that he had spent the preceding day at the War Department.
3. From long-hand copy; original manuscript missing.
4. Daniel Henry Rucker (1819–1910) of the Grosse Ile Rucker-Macomb family. He entered the army in 1837, served in the Mexican War, and in the Civil War attained the rank of major general. The daughter of his second wife, Irene Curtis Rucker, became the wife of General Philip H. Sheridan.
5. For General Randolph B. Marcy (1812–87) see the *Dict. Am. Biog.* He was General McClellan's father-in-law.
6. Nathaniel P. Banks of Massachusetts, politician and Civil War soldier, under whom General Williams was about to serve. For a sketch of his career see *Dict. Am. Biog.*
7. A letter of General Williams to his daughter, Irene, written July 24, 1855, states that Mrs. Smith, widow of Captain E. Kirby Smith who was killed at Molino del Rey in 1847 is momentarily expected on a visit, and that "young" Kirby, evidently her son, now at West

45

Point, will accompany her. The son, Joseph Lee Kirby Smith graduated from the Academy in the class of 1857. He was appointed colonel of the Forty-third Ohio Regiment on September 28, 1861 and died at the age of twenty-six on October 12, 1862 from wounds received at Corinth, October 3–4. According to the *Dict. Am. Biog.*, Confederate Lieutenant General Edmund Kirby-Smith was a younger brother of Captain E. Kirby Smith and thus was an uncle of our present subject. Various allusions in the letters of General Williams disclose that Mrs. Smith was an old-time family friend.

8. The 1861 *Detroit Directory* lists George W. Dollarson, colored, as a baker, and Mrs. Dollarson of the same address as an embroiderer. One may surmise that William was their son.

9. George Gordon Meade, subsequently commander of the Army of the Potomac and victor of Gettysburg.

10. General John J. Abercrombie, a graduate of West Point in the class of 1822, a veteran of the Mexican War and of long years of frontier service, and Charles S. Hamilton, a West Point graduate of the class of 1843. For their military careers see George W. Cullum, *Biographical Register of Officers and Graduates of the U.S. Military Academy at West Point.* . . .

11. Colonel Orris S. Ferry was a lawyer who had been a Republican member of Congress from 1859 to 1861. Following the war he was a member of the Senate until his death, November 21, 1875.

12. The Seventh Michigan Infantry, chiefly composed of militia companies from various towns, was mustered into service at Monroe on August 22, 1861 and left the state for the seat of war on September 5. Of its total number of enlistments throughout the war (1375) slightly more than one-half (691) were casualties from wounds, diseases, etc. Over 13 percent (183) were killed in action or died as the result of wounds received.

13. Lewis Allen of Detroit. His wife (Julia Larned Allen) and General Williams' deceased wife were sisters.

14. Edward D. Baker, prominent as an orator and politician, and a personal friend of President Lincoln. The battle of Ball's Bluff, October 21, in which he was killed, was a very minor military operation. Coming soon after Bull Run, however, and like that battle a Union defeat, it had important consequences. General Stone, who dispatched his troops across the Potomac without orders from General McClellan, was arrested, imprisoned, and officially disgraced. The popular demand for a scapegoat induced Congress to create the Committee on the Conduct of the War, which until the end of the war maintained a vigilant oversight of the Administration and its armies. As yet the nation was unaccustomed to scenes of bloodshed, and the armies were

chiefly composed of amateur soldiers, a condition which is illustrated in the present letter.

15. This description deals with the minor engagement near Edwards Ferry on the afternoon of October 22, 1861. A relatively small force of Confederates attacked the Union force under General Abercrombie on the south side of the Potomac, abandoning the assault when it found itself outnumbered by the Northern soldiers. General Abercrombie reported a loss of one man killed by the enemy and another killed "by mistake." In addition, General Lander, who was present for some unexplained reason, suffered a flesh wound in the leg. See *War of the Rebellion: A Compilation of the Official Records of the Union and Confederate Armies* (Washington, 1902), Series 1, V, 336–38 and 354–55, for conflicting official reports of the action. (Hereafter cited as *Official Records.*)

16. Austin Blair, one of the active founders of the Republican party, was governor of Michigan from 1861 to 1865. Although he had been one of the floor leaders for Senator Seward at the Chicago Republican Convention of 1860 which nominated Lincoln for the Presidency, in his role as governor, Blair was a vigorous advocate of Lincoln's measures and he became not the least distinguished member of the notable group of Northern "war governors." In his inaugural address (January 3, 1861) he proclaimed the power of the Federal government to defend itself and his certainty that it would do so, warning the seceding states that it was a question of war which faced them. Under his leadership the First Michigan (three-months) Regiment was the first regiment of western troops to reach Washington, and a precursor of the vigor with which the Michigan state government supported the President throughout the war.

17. Dr. Thomas Antisell, subsequently medical director of the Twelfth Corps.

18. Franklin W. Whittlesey of Ypsilanti, who entered the service as a captain in the First Michigan Infantry, April 20, 1861. He attained the rank of colonel of the regiment and was honorably discharged for disability, March 18, 1863.—*Record of Service of Michigan Volunteers.*

19. A container for keeping needles, thread, scissors, etc.

20. Captain William D. Wilkins, assistant adjutant general, and Lieutenant Samuel E. Pittman of the First Michigan Infantry were members of General Williams' staff.

21. General Williams' distrust of the cavalry branch of the Union army was well-founded. "Who ever saw a dead cavalryman" became a commonplace gibe throughout the army in the early years of the war. In its latter half, under the leadership of such men as Pleasonton, Kilpatrick,

Sheridan, and Custer, the Union cavalry became a fair match for its Confederate counterpart. As for the First Michigan Cavalry, after more or less arduous service in the Shenandoah Valley and around Washington, in the course of which Colonel Brodhead was mortally wounded, and in the second battle of Bull Run, August 30, 1862, it was assigned, early in 1863, to General Custer's Michigan Cavalry Brigade comprising the First, Fifth, Sixth, and Seventh regiments. Under his leadership the brigade acquired a reputation fairly comparable to that of the famous foot-slogging Wisconsin-Indiana-Michigan Iron Brigade.

22. An interesting comment concerning this execution was supplied following General Williams' death in 1878 by the provost marshal who conducted it. Early on the appointed day of execution he went with a corps of workmen to erect the gallows. The severe storm of sleet and rain threatened to demolish the structure unless additional ropes to anchor it could be secured. The site was near General Williams' headquarters tent and the provost marshal applied to him for an order on his wagonmaster for the needed supplies. General Williams, however, declined, saying: "Spare me the necessity of issuing an order. You can, no doubt, find what you want." The tremulous voice and moistened eye of the general commanded the provost marshal's respect. Years later, upon meeting him, the incident was alluded to, when General Williams said he would have given his right arm if by so doing he could have spared the culprit's life.—Unidentified newspaper clipping dated about January, 1879, in Burton Historical Collection, Williams' file.

II

Up and
Down the
Shenandoah

UP AND DOWN THE SHENANDOAH

Whatever other faults General McClellan displayed, he was a fine organizer and drill-master. Throughout the winter of 1861–62 he was busy with plans for the capture of Richmond. Meanwhile, General Banks' command would invade Virginia by way of the Shenandoah Valley. Banks was a good politician but only a mediocre military leader. Against him was pitted Stonewall Jackson, the outstanding military genius of the Confederacy. Although badly outnumbered by the several Union armies opposed to him, Jackson triumphed over all of them. He fell short, however, of his objective of destroying Banks' army, which escaped intact across the Potomac. In the letters which follow General Williams narrates the triumphant advance and subsequent retreat of General Banks' army in this first invasion of the Shenandoah Valley.

HORRORS OF BORDER WARFARE

Hancock, Md., Jan. 31, 1862.

My Dear Daughter:

I have not heard from you for nearly a month, except through Irene, that your eyes were troubling you again. I suppose this is the reason you have not written.

I have been able to write you but once since I reached this place. My hard march up found little relief here. I found the village full of new and undisciplined troops, infantry, cavalry, and artillery, without order or decency. I got my first intimation that I was to be put in command on my way up and had no instructions what to do. The weather was intensely cold and the ground so frozen that a tent-pin could not be driven. There was not a vacant foot in town, so I bestowed the regiments of my brigade in barns and in all manner of places outside, and went to work from the moment of my arrival, telegraphing right and left, and I have kept it up pretty busily ever since.

When I reached here the Rebels were in large force within ten or twelve miles, extending from the hills opposite to Unger, fifteen miles below. They have been moving about cautiously ever since, but have made no great demonstrations towards me. My patrols are sent over almost every day and go nearly up to Bath,[1] where the Rebels have a garrison. But I operate very cautiously, as I am under orders to hold this post and await further instructions.

But I am here where I see the horrors of this war in its worst forms. All the Union people on the other side (mostly in moderate circumstances) have been stripped of everything that could be eaten or used. Their husbands have generally fled to this side, leaving wives and children at their little homes, hoping to save their furniture or some small property to bring away hereafter. These wives fill my office daily and fill my heart with pain at the recital of their sufferings and deprivations. Many of them are living on corn meal alone and have been for weeks. I tried to help a few, but the number is altogether too great for one poor private purse and I have given up in despair. Every day male refugees arrive who have spent nights in the woods to avoid Rebel pickets. They all bring sorrowful tales of misery all through the adjoining counties. Prices of everything are exceedingly high, and want very general amongst the poorer classes. What these poor people will do to sustain life all winter is more than I can imagine. I have sent over several armed parties to bring families away, but in most cases the parties are too far away to bring their effects to the river.

This town, since the new regiments were sent to Cumberland, is very orderly and my troops behave well. I am sorry to say that the troops who were obliged to flee from Bath behaved very badly. All the houses were deserted when the Rebels fired upon the town and had not been occupied. The retiring troops, having forded the river to their arms in extremely cold weather, seized upon the houses and destroyed a great deal of property wantonly, besides eating up all the provisions of every house. The complaints of housekeepers are very numerous, and well-founded, I fear. It annoys and frets me exceedingly.

I have now five regiments of infantry, six pieces of artillery, and two companies of cavalry, besides some unattached companies. The weather has been snowing and raining till the mud is impassable. I have over 800 horses and mules to feed, to say nothing of the several thousand men. What with the bad roads, I find it no easy job, especially as the mules are pretty much used up by exposure to cold and wet and hard work. However, we hold on and hope for better weather. . . .

Your Loving Father.

❖

DIFFICULTIES OF WINTER WARFARE

Headquarters, 3rd Brigade,
Hancock, Feb. 3, 1862.

My Dear Lew:

Your letter by Capt. Wilkins came to hand some time ago, but I was in the midst of cares and duties of the most insistent and irritating nature. I had gone to Washington on Sunday [2] to meet Irene and had a very pleasant time with her and Cousin Marion on Sunday afternoon. On Monday morning, I received telegraphs and orders in hot haste to join my brigade forthwith. I started in the first train with Dr. Antisell and had a most disagreeable time from Frederick in chase of my brigade which preceded me twenty-four hours. The march of so many men and wagons had beat the road to the condition of ice and our mules being uncalked worked all sorts of antics over the high hills which lie at right angles to the road from Frederick to this place. By dint of perseverance, we made forty miles and overtook the brigade the same night [January 6] at Clear Spring. In the meantime, I had received a telegraphic order to precede the command and relieve General Lander at this place. I made great haste to do so, and faced the anti-summer temperature of below zero in crossing the high mountain west of Clear Spring and after much tribulation was safely set down at Hancock on Wednesday 8th inst.[3]

I found here five regiments of infantry of the newest and most mobbish species. During the shelling of the town on Sunday previous [January 5], the people had left their houses, food, furniture and all, which our troops (some fording the river arms deep and others sent up from below) had occupied and literally appropriated to themselves. Food, furniture, forage, fuel and all had been used and destroyed without thought or decency. Three of the regiments were new and had been armed with Belgian [rifles] the day of the attack. They knew nothing of camp, garrison, or other military duty, and were literally a mob firing their loaded muskets right and left and playing the very devil generally.

I did not wait to get my overcoat off before I began a reform. I appointed a provost marshal and gave him a guard as soon as my own brigade came up of reliable men [and] ordered a report of the strength of regiments, established a grand guard and outposts four miles up and down the river, shut up the groggeries, and filled up several respectable sized rooms with arrested rowdies. Two of these regiments had lost all their camp and garrison equipage and the weather was cold to zero. Every particle of space in the whole town was crowded. Retiring citizens from the country rushed upon me with violent complaints of robbery, plunder, destruction of all their edibles, and with all the ten thousand complaints of a people scared out of their homes at a moment's notice, which a hungry and irresponsible soldiery had taken possession of.

To add to [my] tribulations up came my four regiments, three of them without winter tents and the ground so frozen that tents could not be pitched at any rate. I hardly know now how I disposed of them—

some in barns outside, some in canal boats, and some in bivouac. But the thing was done, and I went to my blankets a tired and anxious man. I had at least 6,000 men crowded into a little village, not 500 yards from the opposite bank [of the river] held by the enemy in force not less than 15,000 with twenty pieces of artillery. It seemed but a stone's throw to the high hills opposite, which looked down upon this town, which is at the foot of the hills on our side. I had eight pieces of artillery—four of smooth bore six-pounders and four Parrotts. Reports brought to me were that Jackson and Loring held Bath in great force and extended in a continuous camp up to the high hills opposite, and that they intended to renew the shelling of Hancock as soon as the weather moderated.

I was full of concern that they might begin that night. If so, we should have had a scene of confusion that I am not anxious to witness. The town, as I have said, is at the foot of high hills right on the river bank and is completely commanded by the opposite shore. So is the road approaching from below for at least eight miles. It runs along the hillsides for all this distance, hemmed in by precipitous ridges and slopes and overlooked by the hills on the Virginia shore at not more than half-musket distance in many places, and in no place out of range. It was a pleasant predicament to be in if those twenty-odd guns had opened upon us and had enfiladed, as they could, our only retreat and the route of all our supplies. I found one road to the rear leading towards Pennsylvania, a very hard road, but I ordered my wagon train to park two miles out upon it, and made arrangements to take all the regiments as promptly as possible behind the hills and then hammer away with artillery.

There we stood for two days, while I had my scouts, civil and military, across the river and up and down to get information. I myself mounted a high ridge five miles above called Round Top from which I could see far and wide over Dixie from an elevation of 2,000 feet. But I could see nothing but camp fires extending for miles away down the valleys but behind intervening hills.

On the 3rd day I learned that the Rebels were moving away—leaving an inferior force behind—but a large camp a few miles below. Lander above had got the same news and descending from Romney he fell back towards Cumberland.[4] Gen. Kelley, who was still there, telegraphed me to send reinforcements.[5] I was but too glad to get rid of my green ones and forthwith started all the infantry but my own brigade on the road to Cumberland. In the meantime, the telegraph line, which I had reconnected through the enemy's country for ten miles, was cut again and I was isolated from Kelley. By the aid of mounted men every five miles I established a communication by the road (forty miles). I was under orders to hold this post but to go to Lander's aid if he was attacked; so I was obliged to keep my command under marching orders with cooked rations for days, Lander being in a constant stew—at times full of fight and asking me to join him in a five-days' march, bivouacking in the open air and depending upon our haversacks for provisions. Expecting to be ordered to this service, I sent back to Hagerstown all my baggage, but the powers above (military) I think put an end to Lander's quixotic expedition, which would probably have resulted in frozen feet to hundreds, if nothing more disastrous. I confess I had no stomach for such an expedition, especially [since] with all my care many of my men were already frostbitten.

My Dear Lew: Sitting in your parlor or resting quietly snug in your warm bed it may seem very easy to talk of winter campaigns and to call out "Onward" in mid-winter. But if you will come down to these snow-clad hills and take one midnight's round to my outposts, see poor devils in rotten tents not fit for summer, talk to the sentinel on his two-hours' round without fire, see the damnable roads, figure up how much provisions it takes to feed a few thousand daily, hear the *cries* not of men only but of half-frozen animals (mules and horses) of which I have upwards of 800—half frozen and half killed by work—witness the effort it takes to get in forage, which I buy from twenty to thirty miles away, to transport subsistence stores thirty miles away, you will be satisfied that in winter months a stationary force has about all it can do to subsist itself, especially in the rain, snow, and mud we have had for the last twenty days. For while it freezes hard at night, it thaws in the valleys by day, or it snows on the hills and rains in the valleys. Altogether I have never seen such cursed weather and such devilish roads.

I should like to photograph you one day's work here. I have five regiments of infantry, six pieces of artillery, and two companies of horse. In the morning begin the reports, and with them the requisitions for things wanted. I have been four months trying to get things absolutely necessary for comfort. I have had requisitions for thousands of shoes and have received but 500 for two months. I have hundreds of men nearly shoeless. But for supplies from the states [they] would have been absolutely barefooted. I had men who could not march from Frederick for want of shoes! I have written and telegraphed, cursed and swore, and pleaded and begged, and in return have had promises that they should be sent forthwith. But they came not. Just fancy in this age soldiers left without shoes in this war for the Union and that in midwinter and in a campaign!

Again, but two of my regiments have Sibley tents, the only ones you can live in in winter, because [they are] the only ones in which you can use a stove.[6] One of the other regiments has common wedge tents used all through the three months' campaign and literally in shreds. One other has almost equally bad—wholly unfit for this season. These regiments have hutted themselves up to our march here. Now it cannot be done. I have for months had the promise of Sibley tents but they come not! I made requisition for bugles for skirmishing drill four months ago. They are needed for the efficiency of my command. I have had the promise of them fifty times, but do not get them.

Same of axes and intrenching tools—same of everything. It takes months to have a requisition filled, yet I see the papers every now and then boast of how excellently our troops are provided. It is all sham, except in rations. We have never wanted for an abundance to eat. It is the only department that is provided, or if provided makes its regular issues. In all other things the troops are woefully neglected. But for provisions made by states and for articles the men buy for themselves they would suffer extremely. Half of my men are in boots bought for themselves. I can say nothing about troops near Washington, but speak only of those at a distance. It may all be the fault of our own division departments. I know I don't fare worse than the other brigades of Gen. Banks' division. On the contrary, [I] fancy I am somewhat ahead of them in getting supplies. If I were Gen. Banks, with his political influence, I should understand in a few days where the fault lies. He seems to take it easy and make abundant promises.

I have run rather unintentionally into complaints. As it is against regulations, you will please not read [this] to others, but keep [it] to yourself. It is one of the curses of our service that no complaint can be uttered but to the proper authorities, and they regard them not. I could tell a tale that would smash up the whole department of sleepy old-fogy quartermasters and I am sorely tempted to do so. I doubt not that there are in our depots an abundance of everything I require to make my men comfortable, but they cannot be got out under three months' time. In spite of all this my command is unusually healthy for the fatigue and exposure they have had, nor do they complain. Their eagerness to get into Dixie is amusing. I send out daily small parties as patrols. There is a great effort from all the regiments to get on this duty which though full of fatigue is full of excitement and hairbreadth escapes.

But if we have suffered some, Jackson's command has suffered more. We have reliable information that he sent back over 1,200 frozen and sick men during the few days he lay opposite. People who came over yesterday say that his sick and disabled fill every house from Bath to Winchester and that many amputations have taken place from frostbites. His whole command was exposed to a heavy snow-storm, followed by intense cold. I see the Dixie papers confirm the reports of his disasters. He lost a good many men, too, from our Parrott guns, which were admirably served, every shot landing plump into his batteries, upsetting his guns, killing his horses, and throwing his men into confusion. A loyal man who was on that side told me that men were killed by some of the last shots thrown purposely high, at least two miles from the river bank. On their side, the firing was miserable. They literally did no damage to the town, though some shots passed through roofs of houses and some shells exploded in the streets. Not a person was wounded. Most of their shot fell short or passed high over the town into the hills beyond.

The country around this [place] is most splendidly picturesque. After the day's work, I take a horseback [ride] for a couple of hours each day to make myself familiar with the roads and the country. The day after I took command here my scouts discovered the frame of a bridge about two miles up [river] which had been all prepared for laying across the river. I supposed, therefore, that they intended to cross at that point and I was greatly in hopes they would attempt it. I could have demolished their whole 15,000 [men] in thirty minutes by close calculation. I did not disturb their bridge till the main force had left. I then sent a party over and threw it into the river.[7] The river here was

58

favorable when I arrived, but has been very high most of the time since. I found only a single flatboat, carrying perhaps sixty men. There are some canal boats, but they are too cumbersome to be served in the rapid current. I have applied for authority to build boats and could have enough in a week to carry half my command, but I have no response. So of Bath, the famous Berkeley Springs, I got reliable information that the force left there did not exceed 500 men, with one Brig. Gen. (Carson) and two or three field officers, considerable baggage and all that. I had discovered a mountain pass to their rear cutting off their retreat perfectly. I applied for permission to try it. It was an easy and sure thing, but I got no response. That cursed Ball's Bluff haunts the souls of our chiefs, and perhaps it is well it does. We are too much divided and are operating on the periphery while they stand in the center. I could plan a campaign to seize upon Winchester and relieve all the country north and northwest and open the Balt. and Ohio Railroad beyond molestation. If you will look at the map you will see how completely it is the key to the whole of the country now occupied by Jackson and Loring. It is in the most fertile valley of Virginia which leads down to Staunton, cutting their most important railroad and completely turning the entrenchments at Manassas, but I have no room, or time for more. . . . Love to all.

Affectionately,

A.S.W.

◆

BOASTING OF GENERAL LANDER

Hancock, Feb. 19, 1862.

My Dear Daughter:

It is so long since I have written to you that I forget when and where I left off, but it matters little, as I have been here in Hancock watching the course of events, somewhat anxious on account of the erratic movements of my next military neighbor, Gen. Lander. I see now, to my great surprise, by newspapers and his own reports that he has been doing great things, though I have been for four weeks in constant com-

59

munication with him at Patterson Creek, from which place he has not moved till the last week, without suspecting his glories. He talks in his report to Gen. McClellan of having opened the railroad from Cumberland to Hancock, while in fact I have had possession of all this road from Hancock half way to Cumberland for nearly four weeks, and have twice established the telegraph line over the whole route.

I see, too, he reports of the daring and successful reconnoissance of some one of his colonels as far as Unger twenty-two miles south, when in fact my patrols had been there several days before and I myself with other officers and an escort of only four mounted men had ridden nearly to the same place but two or three days before, crossing the Potomac seven miles above and returning to a point opposite this place, after a circuit of several miles. In truth, until last Sunday Gen. Lander knew nothing of the railroad or the other side of the Potomac for twenty miles above. The whole of that region has been held by my pickets, who have had possession of the railroad bridge over the Big Cacapon and below for five to ten miles. I confess my astonishment, therefore, to see in the Baltimore papers today a long account of Gen. Lander clearing the line of the railroad and opening the route for Gen. Williams' brigade to cross, and a complimentary order of the Secretary of War to Gen. Lander for his valuable services.

I belong to Gen. Banks' division of the Army of the Potomac and Gen. Lander commands a division of the Army of Western Virginia. Our boundary line is the Potomac and the western slope of the Alleghanies. I am, therefore, on the extreme right of the Army of the Potomac and cannot go beyond that line without especial orders, though I have sent my pickets far over my line. In this way I have held the railroad (Baltimore and Ohio) on the other side of the Potomac for miles, because Gen. Lander, retiring from Romney, had taken post fifty-odd miles distant at Patterson Creek. The only damage done to the road was partial injury at the Big Cacapon before I came up, which was repaired in a day and the cars can now run from Wheeling to this place, though they have been down but once.

Wednesday, February 26, 1862.

I wrote this some time ago and have been to Frederick since and just returned. . . . We shall march again tomorrow, I suppose for Williamsport and then for "Dixie." You will hear all about us by telegram, but don't be alarmed. I think the enemy will not wait for us, even at Winchester. We shall go in strong force if Gen. Banks is not mistaken.[8] I will write you a line or so when I get a chance. . . .

Your Affectionate Father,
A.S.W.

❖

THE ADVANCE TOWARD WINCHESTER

Bunker Hill, Va., Mar. 8, 1862.

My Dear Daughter:

This is a little hamlet twelve miles north of Winchester on the pike from Williamsport. My headquarters are in a small room of a small house. I have a bedroom adjoining, which just holds my bed. The others, servants and all, occupy our office-room rolled in blankets at night. We are glad of any shelter, for the weather has been very rough, worse than our Detroit March. Indeed, I don't know when I have [not] been exposed to bad weather, but my health is good and my spirits never better.

We left Hancock on March 1st and marched to Williamsport the same day, twenty-three miles. At this point I commenced crossing the river on a single scow ferry-boat. It took me twenty-four hours to get across two regiments and their trains. Consequently, I was nearly three days in passing over my six regiments of infantry, a company of artillery and two companies of cavalry. My advance regiments took possession of Martinsburg without opposition, the Union people welcoming us and the non-Union, for the most part, running away. It was at this point that the Rebels last summer destroyed over fifty locomotives of the Ohio & Baltimore Railroad, the melancholy ruins of which still stand on the track. On Wednesday last I left Martinsburg with my brigade expecting to meet the enemy in force at this place, but he had evacuated and we found nothing but a small picket of cavalry and a few infantry. My cavalry advance dashed into the town, a few rounds of musketry were fired from the houses, we captured five or six of them, and then our anticipated battle was all over without loss to us.

61

I happened to be in advance with some officers and got considerable of the fever of the rush and thus was one of the early ones in.

Yesterday I sent out a reconnoitering party towards Winchester which was attacked by a considerable force in the woods. My troops drove them easily but we had three men wounded and Capt. Wilkins' fine horse (Prince), which you will recollect, was struck in the shoulder and badly hurt. We killed six of the enemy and wounded seven. They were all cavalry. These fellows are very daring. After we drove them off yesterday they came back at night and fired on my pickets. They are driving all round outside of my lines picking up soldiers on furlough and stealing horses and other property of Union men. I hope to trap some of them soon.

I have the advanced position now and on the extreme right of the Army of the Potomac. My brigade has now six regiments of infantry, six pieces of rifled cannon and two companies of cavalry, the largest command I have had, at least 5,000 men. On my left is Gen. Hamilton and beyond him toward the Shenandoah the other brigades of Gen. Banks' division. Behind late Gen. Lander's, now Gen. Shields' division is coming up, a part having arrived at Martinsburg. I don't know what is ahead, but I think we shall drive them forward without much trouble. . . .

I write you hurriedly. My little office is crowded with all sorts of men for all sorts of business. I am now really "monarch of all I survey," and all the people about, as well as my own troops, think I should supply everything and do everything. Love to all. . . .

Ever Your Affectionate Father,
A.S.W.

◈

OCCUPATION OF WINCHESTER

Winchester, Mar. 13th, 1862.

My Dear Daughter:

I have merely time to say that we are in Winchester. I left Bunker Hill day before yesterday, my brigade in advance. I skirmished all the day with my light troops and occasionally shelling the woods with six pieces of artillery, which I held in advance. I have since learned that we killed several of the Rebels. I had but one man wounded. We encamped at night within five miles of this place, the Rebels with their artillery in full view of us. Several earthworks were observable, and we looked forward for a great battle in the morning. My whole brigade was under arms at 4 o'clock yesterday and at daylight we moved forward, four regiments in advance with nearly 800 skirmishers leading, covering the hills in a line for nearly three miles. The morning was beautifully spring-like and the sky as clear as crystal. We moved with great caution, as all the hills showed entrenchments. It was an exciting sight as our long line of skirmishers moved forward and mounted in a long row of single men towards the batteries, looking in the distance like a swarm of ants crawling up the hillsides.

We watched with our glasses as they reached the works, and observed several persons advance from them in front as they approached. Presently we saw them all going to the rear and our front line of videttes pouring over the line of entrenchments without opposition. Soon the large fort came in sight and the left line of skirmishers approached and halted and sent back word that the fort was in front and apparently occupied. They were ordered to "feel" them cautiously, and forward went the whole line, and soon we saw them tumbling over the parapets and the bayonets brightly glaring in the morning sun.

We knew then that the town was ours, and gathering up the whole command, ten regiments, two batteries (ten guns), and four companies of cavalry, we advanced on the town en masse, myself and Gen. Hamilton, who just ranks me, riding in advance.[9] As we reached the outskirts the mayor and council met us and surrendered the city of Winchester, asking protection to private property. We then marched most of the regiments through the town. Many of the people hailed our entrance by waving handkerchiefs and some by showing the Star-Spangled Banner. It is nearly a year since it has been shown in Winchester. . . .

I lost, in advancing from Bunker Hill, five men wounded. It is the only brigade in Gen. Banks' division which has had a man wounded. Indeed, I have led the whole advance, and yet you probably will not see my brigade mentioned. I was joined at Bunker Hill by Gen. Hamilton, who ranks me on the list of generals, though appointed the same day. He sent me in advance the first day and in command the second day, and yet as he ranks me I have no doubt his name alone will get the credit. However, I court nobody—reporters nor commanders—but try to do my whole duty and trust it will all come out right. But I can't help seeing how much personal ambition is mixed up with all these operations, small fame at the expense of the great purpose we have in hand.

It took me all day yesterday to get my regiments in position, and at night I went to my camp-bed the tiredest man you can think of. I have a great many incidents I should like to tell you, but I have no time. Since we arrived, scores of generals have come up. Gen. Shields, Gens. Gorman, Abercrombie, Sedgwick, and I know not how many more. I have had amusing scenes with wives of Rebel officers and others for protection of property, and in one instance with the wife of Col. McDonald, a colonel in the Rebel army, to whom I applied for quarters.

My reputation for kindness and leniency preceded me and scores of people have come to me and said, "We hear you are disposed to treat us with kindness, and we beg you to do this and that to aid us." Indeed, I think I am looked upon as the only soft-hearted man in command, but it is a matter of congratulation to know that my soft words have made more Union friends than hundreds of harsh generals could accomplish. Indeed, I feel that all that is needed is kindness and gentleness to make all these people return to Union love. They think we are coming to destroy, and seem to be astonished when we don't ransack their houess and destroy their property. If I had time I should love to tell you of the hundreds of Union-loving people who have told me their sufferings and their grievances and how they have waited for our coming, and how their neighbors have deceived them with the idea that the "Yankees" (all of us are Yankees) were going to destroy them. . . .

Love to all,

Yours Affectionately,
A.S.W.

P.S. Don't be anxious. I think we shall drive all before us without trouble.

A.S.W.

FIRST BATTLE OF WINCHESTER

Strasburg, 20 miles south of Winchester, Va.,
March 30th, 1862.

My Dear Daughter:

I wrote you last from Winchester, after I had been put in command of a division (three brigades) of troops and was on the point of marching eastward across the Shenandoah. One of my brigades left on Friday, the 21st, and the other two and myself on Saturday, the 22nd. We reached the Shenandoah with our long trains Saturday night, and the head of the column, including one brigade and train and part of another brigade, had passed, when the pontoon bridge gave way. It took nearly all day to repair it. In the meantime I had received information that the enemy had returned in considerable force to Winchester and were threatening an attack. Gen. Shields was there with his division. I halted my brigade, which was still on this side, and sent it back to Berryville to be ready to reinforce Gen. Shields.

In the meantime, the river was rising and the bridge bid fair to go away altogether, leaving my command on two sides. I stood by the bridge to watch its safety, expecting to cross the other brigade the next day. At daylight in the morning, however, a messenger brought the word that there had been a fight before Winchester, that Gen. Banks had left for Washington the same day, and that Gen. Shields had been wounded in a skirmish the day before. I was much wanted. I mounted my horse and with a small escort of cavalry set out in hot haste for Winchester. My 1st Brigade was already on the march for the same place. On reaching Winchester I found that Gen. Banks had returned and assumed command and was then following up the retreating enemy. I stayed long enough to order my brigade to follow, and to feed myself and horse, and started for the front.

I overtook Gen. Banks seven or eight miles out. The enemy was in sight, with a strong rear guard of infantry, cavalry, and artillery, but retiring from one strong position to another. We followed them all day till near sundown. At their last stand a battery from my brigade was brought up and they were driven helter-skelter from their position, leaving behind several killed and wounded, with tents, etc. The troops of Gen. Shields' division had been engaged in battle the day before [10] and had marched fifteen to twenty miles after a night-watch on the battlefield. My brigade (the old third that I commanded for so many months, now commanded by Col. Donnelly, senior colonel) had marched thirty-six miles since the preceding evening and with but two hours' rest.[11]

We could follow no farther, so the whole command bivouacked on the field, many a poor fellow supperless. My wagons were thirty miles away with no order to follow, for I did not expect to follow so far, but I found comfortable lodgement in a farmhouse and sufficient to eat. I do not give you any description of the battle or the battlefield, where at least four to five hundred lay dead, nor of the wounded which filled the houses of Winchester and all the little villages on our march this side.[12] You will see pictures enough, often greatly exaggerated, in the newspapers. We came and occupied this place and five miles in advance on Tuesday last and are waiting certain events for future operations. Two of my brigades are now here. The third is over the Shenandoah. Which way we go next is not decided, but I think you'd better direct to me, "Comdg. 1st Division 5th Army Corps (Banks), Winchester."

This place is most beautifully situated in a narrow valley, where the spurs of the Blue Ridge terminate in bold, precipitous bluffs on one side, and a regular unbroken ridge bounds the other. My fatigues the last week have been immense and my responsibilities and anxieties beyond description. If I had been one day later in marching from Winchester I should have had command in the battle and I think could have done a good deal more than was done. Indeed, the wound of Gen. Shields and the absence of Gen. Banks left the whole thing in charge of a colonel, and those who ought to know say the matter managed itself pretty much and the victory was gained by simple hard fighting under great disadvantages of position and movements. Whether true or not, it is quite certain that men do better when those who have been their chief commanders are present. In this view of the case, with only my old brigade to assist, I think I could have captured all Jackson's guns and been a major general! The last thought is rather selfish, but it seems to be a very prominent (too much so I fear) motive in all hearts hereabouts. . . .

Your Affectionate Father,
A.S.W.

FRATERNIZING WITH THE ENEMY

Camp near Edinburg, Va., April 9, 1862.

My Darling Daughter:

I have been reading over your letter of latest date (received March 14) and wondering what has become of the many you have written since, for I know full well that you write me weekly. I wrote you last from Strasburg a week or so ago. On the 1st we moved to this place, banging all the way at the rear guard of the Rebels. There was not much loss, I fancy, on either side as the artillery had the whole work at long range. We lost one killed and some wounded by bursting shells. Long before reaching this place we saw the heavy columns of smoke from the burning bridges over the considerable stream that flows just in advance of the town, one a road and the other a high railroad bridge. They burned all the bridges on the railroad; one just back of this, a monstrous piece of trestle work over a hundred feet high across a chasm of many hundred feet.

The day was beautifully spring-like, the finest we have had, and what with the banging of big guns, the long lines of troops and baggage wagons, it was quite a day of excitement. Many of the shells of the Rebels burst hundreds of feet in the air, giving the semblance of pyrotechnics got up for our entertainment. When, however, a piece from one of them struck a poor fellow sitting quietly on some railroad ties, splitting his skull and dashing his brains in all directions, the poetry of the shelling was changed to a sad realization of these dangers.

We found the stream (Stony Creek) too deep for fording and the whole command encamped on this side. Our advance occupies the town of Edinburg and for several miles along the ridges which lie this side of the stream, while the Rebel advance is for the most part in plain sight on the opposite ridges and in the woods beyond. Every now and then the big guns on both sides open on one another with tremendous noise. After awhile the Rebels withdraw and all is quiet except an occasional popping of the advanced pickets. We have had several skirmishing parties across the stream to protect our bridge builders and we generally drive them back, but they appear again as insolent as ever as soon as our troops retire. We have lost one man only in all this banging and shooting, though several of their shells have fallen in unpleasant vicinity to our quarters in Edinburg. My headquarters are a mile back from the town and we are in comparative quiet, except the noise of the guns.

We are still following up the valley of the Shenandoah. On the left of the road is one of the ridges of the Blue Ridge, running in an almost uniform altitude of fifteen hundred feet. Occasionally a "gap" opens through the ridge, which is always evidence of a cross-road leading toward Warrenton, Culpeper Court House, or some other considerable town east of the Blue Ridge. On our right is a more unequal ridge of the North Mountain, broken into peaks and sending off spurs into the valley, contracting sometimes to a narrow space. We passed one but a few miles back called the "Narrow Passage," where there is only a kind of natural bridge, just wide enough for a road over a very deep ravine. It is the same place where the high railroad bridge was burned. The pike and the bridge are close together. It is a very strong military position, and we expected great opposition to its surrender. At a house close by, elegantly furnished, owned by a young lady, Gen. Jackson had his headquarters for some time. The place was abandoned very soon after our artillery opened on it from a distant hill. The young lady with a sister remain at home, though the house is in part occupied by one of my brigade commanders as headquarters. The place is called Willow Glen Cottage. It has a very picturesque location with two mountain streams coming from the west and the Shenandoah flowing far down in a deep valley on the east and winding away to the base of the Blue Ridge. The night after we arrived I went to call upon the brigade commander and met the band of one of his regiments coming to serenade me. I took them back to Willow Glen and gave the young ladies the benefit of the music. They were very pleasant and chatty but rank Secessionists, having brothers and other friends in the Rebel army. The scene from the house was exceedingly beautiful. The troops had marched without tents and one brigade had bivouacked from the road far up the hillsides and built a very large number (countless as seen from the piazza) of camp fires. There was just enough of the new moon to make "darkness visible" and to give a magical effect to the whole scene. I don't know as I have ever seen a sight more striking and impressive, especially as the music of the band—the murmur of the thousand voices from the bivouac and the occasional cheer from the men as some patriotic air struck their fancy, taken up and carried on away to the far off ridges—gave additional effect to the eye picture. This, however, is the occasional poetry of war.

Our marches for the past month, and, indeed, before, have been generally in sleet, snow, and cold rain, after bivouacking in storms,— almost always, on the march without tents. Today and for three days past the weather has been fit for the middle of winter. Snow, rain, sleet and freezing, till every tree is covered with ice and the ground white with snow. After several warm days it comes with especial severity. The men are for the most part in tents, excepting always the large force which in front of the enemy are obliged to keep on picket and other guards. The poor animals are fairly shriveled up with the ice and sleet. Forage is very scarce, in fact, all stripped off from this section, and what is worse, our long marches over wet roads have destroyed fearfully the poor shoes issued by the government. I have at least 4,000 men in my division who are shoeless completely, or so nearly so that they cannot march. Shoes issued to my men in Winchester are already entirely worn out! Such is the fraud that contractors are permitted to put upon poor soldiers! I can hardly conceive of a crime more fitly punished by death. We should be far in advance but for these constant draw-backs, which fairly unfit an army for march[ing]. . . .

Your Affectionate Father,
A.S.W.

◈

A MILITARY PAGEANT

Camp near Sparta, 4 miles south of New Market, Va.,
April 20, 1862.

My Dear Rene:

We have made another forward movement. The command left our camp near Woodstock Thursday morning at daylight and reached New Market about dark. The day was unusually warm and we had the customary amount of banging of big guns and an occasional pop of small arms. At Mt. Jackson we halted for several hours to give time for a flank movement of two brigades. Across a stream in front of the town is the strongest position we have met, and at this point we supposed the Rebels would give battle. We had contrived, by a dash of cavalry, to save the covered bridge over the North Fork. After shelling the ridge occupied by the enemy we drew up our entire force on the broad river bottom on both sides of the road, covering the columns by a cloud of skirmishers extending several miles. Cavalry and artillery were intermingled in masses amongst the infantry. The field from the high riverbank on the north could be overlooked for miles, and every corps could be distinctly seen. It was a splendid spectacle, the finest military show I have seen in America. Indeed, I have never before seen a single plain upon which so many troops could be displayed, this side of our western prairies.

I watched the advance for some time from a high bluff, as the troops were obliged to march slowly over the soft wheat-fields. Before they reached the foot of the hills in front, I mounted and rode forward on the road, but the enemy had vanished. They fired only two guns and limbered up and sped. We saw nothing more of them till we reached New Market. Ashby, who commands the Rebel cavalry, early had his horse killed and came near losing his own life, as the ball passed through his saddle.[13] My brigades had the advance all day. They passed through New Market after dark and encamped on the south side, or rather bivouacked on the ground. The next morning we moved forward four miles to a small stream on which we are now in bivouac.

The rascals fought us all the way out and we had some beautiful practice with rifled guns. We chased them some three miles in advance of this. They burned every bridge, even to the little culverts, and made a tremendous bonfire of their camp some miles ahead of us. But as they know the country and have fine roads they are too fast for our infantry. As for the cavalry, it is good for kicking up a dust, doing foraging, capturing horses and stealing them, and for not much else. The material is good enough, but they are poorly drilled and poorly mounted. The horses have not been over half-fed during the winter and of late have been severely handled. The Rebel cavalry seems much better drilled and have better horses. At any rate, they scale the fences most beautifully and show themselves very fearless till our rifled guns open, when they put out rapidly.

We contrived to capture two lieutenants and a few privates. The night before we left Edinburg four companies of infantry from my division captured fifty-odd—a whole company—of Ashby's cavalry, officers and all. They were conducted by a Union man and they were fairly surrounded before they knew of our approach. As I write, eight prisoners are brought to me. Deserters are very common. But this is a great country and a beautiful one. I have never seen so beautiful and apparently so fertile a valley. It improves greatly as we advance. There were points on our march on Thursday that one never tired looking at. We have still the same mountain ranges on either hand, perhaps six miles apart, and the same rolling valley between, but the ridges are more broken into peaks and gaps and the valley is occasionally traversed by spurs and dotted by solitary peaks, which rise like sugar loaves from an even surface.

Some of the wives and daughters of officers have followed us as far as Edinburg, amongst them, Mrs. and Miss Copeland, Lt. Col. of the 1st Michigan Cavalry. I think, however, that they are out of place and must be a source of great anxiety and annoyance. For example, an order to march usually comes at midnight and the troops are expected to be under arms before daylight. Everything must be packed and placed in wagons. As we carry all our cooking utensils and mess furniture, to say nothing of the office desks, table, etc., etc., we find enough to do without looking out for the effects of wives or daughters. However, *chacun à son gout*. It may all be very fine, "but I don't see it." I prefer to think of you as safe in Philadelphia.

We are under orders to move forward again. Our men's shoes are following somewhere in rear of us, but we seem to keep in advance and many men are fairly shoeless. I hope they will catch us soon. . . .

Your Affectionate Father,
A.S.W.

◈

THE ADVANCE TO HARRISONBURG

Harrisonburg, Va., April 29, 1862.

My Dear Daughter:

I wrote you from camp near Sparta last week. This camp was about four miles below New Market. My 1st Brigade moved down to within four miles of this place a week ago and the second came down on

Thursday last, and both advanced and took position in front of the town on the road running eastwardly toward Gordonsville, upon which Jackson's forces had retreated. I was obliged to ride about ten miles a day through pelting rain, sleet, and snow before we left our last camp to attend a board for examination of officers. In consequence I caught a terrific cold all over and have had my first ill day since I have been in the service. We have had the most infernal weather, such as I never saw in Michigan in the month of April. The hills were, till yesterday, quite white with snow in spots, and while at our last camp we had two heavy snow-storms and rain enough to make a young deluge, I was out of sorts only a day, but I was obliged to ride over twenty miles on a pretty hard-going horse with sore limbs and aching head. However, I kept my feet all the while and am now quite well again. There is nothing like my universal remedy-diet.

This valley thus far continues to be beautiful—even more so than farther "down," as they call toward the north, more diversified and picturesque. We have reached the end of the ridge that has hemmed us in on the east, and now the valley spreads out in that direction to the Blue Ridge, while the loftier and irregular tops of the Alleghanies are plainly visible on the west, stretching far away toward the south. The intervening valley is broken into many conical-shaped knobs, which give a most singular appearance to the view as seen in the late afternoon from a high hill east of town. The town is beautifully situated in the bottom of the valley and has around it many elegant country seats. It is altogether the most attractive-looking town I have seen in the valley.

Our cavalry were sent forward toward Staunton a few days since but found the bridges burned over the streams below, which were not fordable just now. Jackson's army is east of this from fifteen to twenty miles on the slopes of the Blue Ridge. He has a very large bridge between us and him. It is said that he has it ready for burning. We fear he has been largely reinforced and intends to turn upon us here or wait for us in his present strong position. We have had several pretty strong skirmishes with him and taken several prisoners; lost one ourselves, and several killed and wounded.

The road toward his present camp is in a wretched condition. I think we shall be obliged to remain here some days. I hardly know what will be the next movement. We are now pretty well advanced into the interior and are a long way from the base of our supplies. As we have neither railroad nor water transportation we find it no small task to keep our force supplied in rations, forage, and clothing. I contrived to get shoes for most of my division at the last camp, but our wants are still many. The troops have had to bivouac much of the time in rain and snow with such shelter as they could put up out of rails, boughs, etc., but it is wonderful how inventive and ingenious they become in providing for themselves. I am sorry to say, however, they do not always respect private property, though persons are seldom molested.

The Negro population increases as we go south, and although they all understand that the rear is open to them, very few leave their masters. Indeed, many of them are afraid of us at first, probably from big stories of our cruelties that are told them. They seem glad at our coming and probably think some great benefit is to accrue to them, but they show very little desire to quit their present homes. In truth, they are much attached to localities, and but for the fear of being sold south I don't think a dozen could be coaxed away. As it is, probably fifty have come in and are employed by our quartermasters. If the abolitionists could see things as they really are here they would have less confidence in the aid the Negro is in concluding this war. Their masters say that they become more insolent and lazy on our advance, and that is the only good we are likely to do them. . . .

Your Affectionate Father,
W.

◈

RETREAT TO STRASBURG

Strasburg, Va., May 17, 1862.

My Dear Daughter:

You will see that we have made a retrograde movement. I cannot explain the reason, because I really don't think there *is* any. If there be one, it is unknown to us here and is confided to the authorities at Washington. We regard it as a most unfortunate policy and altogether inexplicable, especially as we had the game all in our hands, and if the

moves had been made with the least skill we could easily have check-
mated Jackson, Ewell, and Johnston, instead of leaving them to attack
and drive back Milroy, as we hear they have done.[14]

I cannot explain to you, and I am not permitted to complain, but if
the amount of swearing that has been done in this department is recorded against us in Heaven I fear we have an account that can never
be settled. But here we are with a greatly reduced force, either used as
a decoy for the Rebel forces or for some unaccountable purpose known
only to the War Department. Imagine our chagrin in marching back,
like a retreating force, over the same ground that we had driven the
Rebels before us, and having the galling reminders of our defeat, and
that without a gun being fired or a man killed. But all this is private
and not to be repeated outside of your home. The worst part is that we
have put ourselves in a most critical position and exposed the whole
of this important valley to be retaken and its immense property of railroads and stores to be destroyed.

I have had a wearisome march of several days through heat and dust
most intolerable. All our vast trains of stores, etc., had to precede us,
and we followed in the fine powder that these miles of wagon wheels
pounded up for us. We have finally come to a stand here; that is, my
decimated division is here and a few other troops, while others have
been detached on some wild-goose chase after the enemy. I am getting
terribly disgusted and feel greatly like resigning. How a few civilians
at a distance can hope to manage this war is inconceivable. I sometimes
fear we are to meet with terrible reverses because of the fantastic tricks
of some vain men dressed in a little brief authority. If we do not, it is
because the Almighty interposes in our behalf. . . .

I wrote to Aunt Patty some time ago, I fear a very blue letter, for I
have been hugely out of sorts for some time. With all our victories, I
do not feel we are gaining much. There is so much jealousy and detrac-
tion, in and out of Congress, so much selfishness, such a struggling
after self-aggrandizement, so little pure and disinterested and in-
genuous patriotism, that I shudder for the future. If we have a reverse,
God help us! You do not see it as I do, and perhaps I am morbidly
alive to it. But I am so surrounded by its presence, I see it so palpably
in Congress, in the heart-burnings and bitterness of our commanding
generals, in the divisions and sub-divisions of our forces to give com-

mand to favorites, in the sacrifice of power which lies under our hand, just to checkmate some rival or to destroy some dreaded popularity, that I tremble at some great disaster. Was the whole government, civil and military, united and actuated by one great and engrossing and ﬁne purpose, this rebellion would be destroyed in two months. As it is, I fear it may yet destroy us.

But enough of this. I am disheartened just now by events transpiring about me and probably look on the dark side of everything. But when I see three military departments lying side by side divided and power-less, which if united might combine an irresistable force which could march to Richmond, I feel disgusted and heart-sick. Such are the departments commanded by McDowell, Banks, and Fremont. The latter has literally done nothing, and is in a position to do nothing. Banks could do but little because his force has been taken away for the others. McDowell is drawing away other troops to make a great show and bluster. If these forces were all in one column they could drive all before them out of Virginia. But this is a grumbling letter, written late at night. Perhaps I'll write in better humor tomorrow.

How long we shall be here and where go next, I can't say.

Goodbye, Love to all,

Your Affectionate Father,

A.S.W.

◈

PERPLEXITY OVER THE RETREAT

Strasburg, Va., May 21, 1862.

My Dear Daughter:

I received yours of the 16th this morning. I have already explained to you in a previous letter why we are here. The whole of this is un-explainable, especially as we occupied a position from which we could in one movement have interposed between the commands of Jackson and Ewell and thus have saved Milroy and Schenck from being driven back with loss. But the whole movement comes from the highest command and we are neither authorized to criticise nor complain. I

75

could say much more, but it is not advisable. I trust we shall be safely extricated from a dilemma, that, to speak mildly, was unnecessarily brought about. I have no idea how long we shall be here or where [we will] go next. I probably know as much as General Banks. . . .

I am glad you are doing something for the comfort of the sick and wounded soldiers. You can hardly imagine how these little matters comfort the sick and the dispirited; how they are remembered in after years. The smallest attentions—a simple kind word falls often with wonderful influence upon their hearts and will be repeated to you years hence, if you should chance to meet them. . . .

My headquarters are at a large brick house just outside of Strasburg, a very old and very stately mansion of an old Virginia family. The lady is a widow with a pretty large family of girls, children and stepchildren. She has a governess from Massachusetts, a very pleasant young lady who has been here during the whole Rebel war and is, in fact, quite a Secessionist. So the officers say. I have had very little to say to any of them. The young men have very pleasant concerts with the family every evening. . . .

Your Affectionate Father,
A.S.W.

◈

SECOND BATTLE OF WINCHESTER AND FAILURE OF THE CAMPAIGN

Williamsport, May 27, 1862.
My Dear Daughter:

I can fancy your anxiety after the recent telegraphic tidings from Banks' column. I therefore telegraphed you yesterday that I was safe here. We have had a very unpleasant time through anxious and laborious days and sleepless nights, such as I fancy would make old age come prematurely.

On Friday evening last [15] we got conflicting rumors of an attack upon our guard at Front Royal, a small village about twelve miles east of Strasburg where a considerable valley, parallel with the valley in which Strasburg is, crosses the Shenandoah. Through this valley is a stone pike, and there are several mountain gaps through which good roads at this season connect with the stone pike from Strasburg to Staunton. As there is a good road from Front Royal to Winchester, the Rebels with sufficient force at Front Royal could easily intercept our line of march and cut us off from our supplies, especially as the occupation of Front Royal destroyed the railroad line that connected us with Washington.

I think I have several times written you that I regarded our position as very critical. It was in reference to this very matter, all which has taken place, almost exactly as I feared. Ewell's division, estimated at from 10,000 to 15,000 troops, had been joined in the valley below Front Royal by Jackson's brigade of 8,000 to 12,000, and they moved with great rapidity and secretly upon and actually took by surprise, the regiment (1st Maryland) doing guard duty there. I do not think fifty men escaped, and the few who did passed the night in the woods on their route to Winchester. It was near midnight, therefore, before we knew the extent of our disaster.

By some strange fatality a large quantity of clothing and other public stores for the use of the department had been placed in depot there, and it is rumored a considerable number of excellent arms. All this was grabbed by the hungry Rebels. By a singular coincidence the 1st Maryland of the Rebels was the leading infantry regiment in the attack on the 1st Maryland of our service. The Rebel cavalry, in which arm they are very strong, did the business, however, and, I fear, committed fearful and outrageous slaughter. The stories told by the escaped and the runaways on these occasions are not always to be believed. If they were, one would be obliged to think men turned to brutish beasts, such instances of bloody and monstrous butchery of wounded and unresisting men are narrated. Amongst the killed was Col. Kenly of Baltimore, who commanded the regiment. He was a marked character, a most perfect gentleman and as brave a soldier as ever wore a sword. Amongst the many friends in the service who have fallen within the past few days, I know of none whose death has so deeply touched me. His regiment was attached to my old brigade while I was at Hancock, and at his own earnest request. I have, of course, seen much of him almost daily since. I shall not soon forget his cheerful face and courteous bearing.[16]

But to my narration of events. When the fact was patent that a very large force had possession of the railroad and was crossing the river towards Winchester, orders were immediately issued to start our immense trains of wagons, commissary, quartermaster, ordnance for division brigades and regiments—several hundreds—toward Winchester, and the command to hold itself ready to follow. As you have never seen, you cannot appreciate the difficulties of moving these long mule-trains or the impediments they make to a rapid march, especially in retreat, when hurry and confusion, frightened teamsters and disordered teams, break-downs and collisions and ten thousand nameless things conspire to make up the turmoil and increase the disorder. The great wonder is that they ever get off, but they do move, and under all the circumstances with wonderful expedition.

Our trains on this occasion (as we were moving all our supplies) reached for miles, indeed, almost a continuous line of wagons from Strasburg to Winchester, twenty-two miles. The troops marched about 10 o'clock A.M. Guards had been sent with the wagons, but anticipating an attack in force, we were obliged to hold our forces together as much as possible to meet it. The rumors of large forces of Rebels gathered as we marched, till it became almost a certainty that Winchester was in possession of the Rebels in force, at least 20,000 men. These rumors were corroborated by the frequent attacks upon our trains by cavalry at different points, creating much disorder and no little loss of mules and vehicles. Wagoners are proverbially scary and on the first alarm they cut traces, mount horses, and decamp. This is often done when not an enemy is within miles, and it is a singular fact that our losses on this march were at a long distance from the actual points of attack. Still, under all the difficulties, we succeeded in bringing through our long line of wagons with wonderful success, but the labor to the men was very great and our rear guard was engaged with the Rebel skirmishers till long after midnight.

As we approached Winchester we were agreeably surprised to find that the enemy was not before us, and that the flag of our Union was still flying from the public buildings. The regiments encamped on the elevations just outside of town so as to cover the two roads leading towards Front Royal and Strasburg. I had been up all the night before, and what with the excitement and responsibilities I was weary enough, but the rumors of approaching forces were too reliable and the probabilities of an unequal contest the next day, as well as the hurrying and necessary preparations for the events that were sure to open at daylight occupied my mind and time until midnight.

In the meantime the booming of artillery and crack of the outpost muskets kept up as if the Rebels knew we were sleepy and were determined to keep us from rest. I had been in bed, it seemed to me, not half an hour before a terrible rapping at my door roused me from the deepest sleep. In rushed a bevy of staff officers with Gen. Crawford, who has just joined us, just from Gen. Banks, with positive information that the Rebels were before us (probably around us) in tremendous force of not less than 20,000 infantry, cavalry, and artillery. The General must see me at once to arrange the program for the morning. Of course I was obliged to lose my second night's sleep. The General had information that we should be attacked in the morning by a superior force, and the question of our best position to defend our trains and stores, as well as to keep ourselves from annihilation, had to be discussed.

It was decided to make a fight as we were, in front of the town. I had but 3,500 infantry and ten pairs of Parrott guns with six useless brass pieces to resist a force estimated by nobody at less than 15,000 and by most (prisoners and citizens) at 25,000 troops.[17] The prospect was gloomy enough. That we should all be prisoners of war I had little doubt, but we could not get away without a show of resistance, both to know the enemy's position and to give our trains a chance to get to the rear. I hurried up my own wagons and sent them off to get the advance, if possible, and after sundry preparations and a hurried cup of coffee found the daylight coming on.

The Rebel guns opened fire at the earliest dawn and the banging to and fro became incessant. Larned came up for instructions as the heavy gun-firing began and I, of course, ordered him to put out with Capt. Whittlesey's wagons without delay. He seemed very cool for him, and probably did not realize the difficulties that surrounded us. He says now that the Parrott shells make a terrible noise and he does not like them at all. He seems to think he has been in imminent danger, though I think no shell came within half a mile of him.

I shall not undertake a minute description of our fight. By direction of Gen. Banks I joined him at his headquarters and we rode to the front. The sun was just rising, but the heavy smoke from the guns so obscured a cloudless sky that it smelt sulphurous and looked dismal. I rode to the center of the brigade on the right, which occupied a series of knobs, on the highest of which one of our batteries was playing away manfully. The whiz of the Parrott shells going and coming kept the air quite vocal and, strange to say, had an exciting effect upon my unstrung nerves. I felt rather exhilarated than depressed. There is a singular fascination and excitement about the banging of guns and rattling of musketry with the pomp and circumstance of war.

After riding along this brigade and examining the front through my field glass for a while, I rode to the left where three regiments of my old brigade were posted. They had already been warmly engaged with the infantry and had gallantly repulsed them, almost annihilating a North Carolina regiment. Their dead and wounded lay thickly scattered along the front of one of our regiments. Some of our officers went out and talked with them. They all expressed regret that they had been fighting against the Union. I was rejoiced to find my old brigade doing so well. Every man semed as cool and cheerful as if preparing for a review. They lay in order of battle behind the crests of hills ready for another attack. Away off the hills were seen the moving masses of the enemy, evidently preparing to out-flank us and get to the rear while their batteries were opening in new directions and fresh troops were constantly coming up. The colonel in command of the brigade had already counted *nine regimental colors* that were moving up to crush out this small brigade of only three regiments, numbering not over 1,500 men.

The case certainly looked hopeless enough, but officers and men seemed composed and defiant. Fearing that we were about being turned on this flank, I started for the right wing to get reinforcements. I stopped a few moments to confer with Gen. Banks, and pushing on had hardly reached the valley which intervened between the two wings when a furious fusillade began on the right. Their cannons opened with tremendous vigor and apparently from a dozen new batteries. As I was obliged to ride across the line of fire of most of them, it seemed to me that I had become a target for the whole Rebel artillery. Several shells passed in most unpleasant proximity to my head with a peculiar whizzing sound that made one involuntarily bob his head.

I dashed on as fast as my horse could carry me, but before I could reach the front I saw our artillery were limbering up and that a regiment on the right (the 27th Indiana) was getting into confusion and many men running back. I dashed at them with such of my staff as were with me and made all sorts of appeals to rally them. The men would stop for a while, but before I could get them in line a new batch of fugitives would break all my efforts. Presently the whole regiment came pouring back in a confused mass. I saw the case was hopeless with them, and directing an officer to rally them behind a stone wall in the rear, I pushed to the right, where were posted four companies of the 1st Michigan Cavalry. I saw near the head of the column Maj. Town, who came forward to meet me with zeal and spirit. I ordered him to dash up the hill and if a chance opened to charge and hold in check the enemy who were rapidly rushing up to the position deserted by our Indianians. Town took his men to the crest of the hill gallantly and I went forward with them to get a look at the position of the enemy.

As we reached the brow of the hill a most terrific fire of infantry was opened upon us from a long line which extended beyond my extreme right. The air seemed literally to be full of whizzing bullets, which stirred up currents of wind as if the atmosphere had suddenly been filled with some invisible cooling process. The cavalry could do nothing before such an overwhelming force and it went down with great rapidity. I stopped just long enough to know that I could see nothing of value through the smoke in front, and looking to the left I saw the whole line of the brigade retiring in order and yet rapidly to the rear. I put spurs to my horse, descended partly down the hill and was beginning to think I should spend a time in Richmond if I did not hurry, especially as I was penned in by a heavy stone wall. I dashed my horse at a point where two or three stones appeared to have been knocked off the top and although he is a pretty heavy beast (not my favorite gift horse) I think he appreciated the occasion for he cleared the wall most gallantly and carried me safely over into a narrow lane. At this moment all my staff officers were away on duty except Capt. Beman, who also took the wall.

As this lane was well under cover I thought it my duty to make a second effort to get a look at the enemy and consequently turned up the hill again but had not got far before the colors of the Rebels, infantry and cavalry, appearing on the top warned me I had no time to lose to withdraw the two brigades. I therefore sent word to Col. Donnelly, commanding the 1st Brigade, to retire by the east of the town and Col. Gordon, 5th Brigade, to pass his regiments through the town to the pike to Martinsburg. It was hurrying times, as you can well imagine, with the very large force that was pressing us on all sides. I rode through one of the side streets and was saluted by a shot from a window which came near finishing Capt. Beman. It was necessary to make great efforts to stop a stampede, especially as the early fugitives had been joined by several unarmed sick from Shields' division, who were scattering alarm with great vigor. These, with a great number of wagons of sutlers and citizens and some army conveyances were whipping and hallooing and creating great alarm.

I overtook, after a while, one of our batteries, which I got into position. I then seized upon every straggling officer and began to reassure the men by forming them in squads, but the difficulties of calming men in such condition is enormous. You can have no idea of the confusion. All of the regiments but one were fortunately passing to the rear in pretty good order, some of them admirably; but still the fugitives continued to increase and the danger of a rout was imminent. There is a strange sympathy in courage and in fear, and masses seem to partake of one or the other feeling from the slightest causes. For instance, on reaching the first woods, with several other mounted officers, I succeeded in getting quite a line of fugitives established and ready to make a stand. Just at this time, down came a company of Michigan cavalry, running their horses at full bent. My line of brave fellows broke at once and went off in double-quick. On the other hand, but a few moments afterward two companies of other cavalry came from toward Martinsburg riding toward the enemy and shouting with drawn sabers. Our fugitives received them with cheers and seemed at once to recover from their alarm.

From this onward to Martinsburg even the leading rabble marched coolly and in quiet. The artillery was placed in position at all good points and the main force of the cavalry, kept in the rear by Gen. Hatch, with the infantry columns on either flank, protected us from much injury, though the assaults by cavalry and battery were frequent. One column of two regiments of Donnelly's brigade followed a parallel road on the right flank and did not join us, but crossed the River Potomac some seven miles below. One other mixed column of cavalry

and infantry with twenty-odd wagons, having been cut off on Saturday
night, took the road towards Hancock and crossed the Potomac at
Cherry Run, all sound. The rest of the command halted an hour or
more at Martinsburg and then resumed the march toward Williamsport,
where it was supposed the river was fordable for men.

Our whole train (nearly 500 wagons) had preceded us to the river
and I began to congratulate myself that we were well out of a bad
scrape and that I should get a sound sleep in Williamsport that night.
Judge of my disgust, then, when within three or four miles of the
river I came upon the rear of our train and was told that the river was
not fordable except for horse-teams and horsemen, that it was between
four and five feet deep and of great rapidity. With a heavy heart and
weary limbs I began to work my way to the ferry through the jam of
teams and wagons and guns and caissons and forges, intermingled with
straggling cavalry and mounted men. It was already dark and the road,
which winds through gullies and descends a series of steep hills to the
river for miles, it seemed to me, was not easily followed with my poor
eyesight, but after hard labor and a great deal of swearing, I fear, I
reached the plateau by the river.

Here it seemed as if all the wagons of the army were in "corral,"
that is, drawn up in close lines and packed together almost in mass,
covering acres of ground. I worked my way to the ferry and found the
single scow-boat (by means of which with my brigade alone I was
three nights and days in crossing over in March) busy at work taking
over the sick and wounded. I was cheered, however, by hearing that my
personal baggage had arrived early and was across the river. Hoping
to get some relief by the prospect at the ford, I worked through the
crowd of mules and vehicles down to the point where the river is
entered. Big fires had been built upon both sides to guide the crossing,
and horsemen and horse-teams were struggling in the river to get across.
The river here is over 300 feet wide and the current exceedingly rapid,
especially where the water is the deepest.

The descent into the river from the bank is very muddy and each
wagon, as it went in, stalled on the start and then the poor animals
would struggle and flounder in the rapid stream, which reached nearly
to their backs, till many a horse and scores of mules were drowned. I
saw it was a desperate chance for getting our teams over, and as for

FROM THE CANNON'S MOUTH

the men, who were busily building large fires along the hillsides and cooking their suppers, I felt most sadly for them, for not one could possibly pass through that fierce current of a broad and gloomy river.

The poor devils had been without anything to eat, as the fight began in the morning before they had cooked breakfast, and they had marched thirty-five miles without an ounce to eat in their haversacks. I thought of the desperate confusion of horses and wagons and men should we be strongly attacked after it was known that at least five to one were after us; of the demoralized condition of our troops, consequent upon a march of sixty miles (with but one meal) in two days and an almost constant succession of combats and one heavy battle; of the probabilities that we should be followed to the river and attacked, at least by daylight, before a tithe of our men could be crossed and while all our immense train was parked ready to deepen the awful confusion that must follow.

I saw I had another sleepless night before me, and as I had been fasting all day my appetite, as well as my philosophy, prompted me to seek sustenance without delay. So I made for a small house, which I found full of sick and wounded, and the surgeons were actually dressing a horrible arm mutilated by a shell, while others were waiting to be cared for. But the horrible and the careless are strangely mingled in war. A private soldier recognized me as I entered and said he had just made some coffee which he would cheerfully share with me. We sat down to the same table. I found bread and sugar, while he drew from his kit butter and his sugar rations, remarking that he always took care of the subsistence; that while he had enough to eat he could march forever.

The small room filled with hungry officers and men, and it became almost a fight for our small pot of coffee. It shows how discipline works, for my friend, the private, was quite sure to announce my name and rank to save his coffee pot, and it is to the credit of tired and famished men that they always gave way on the announcement. But as I had given up my horse to a wounded soldier during the afternoon, the matter, after all, was only reciprocal. Ah! Rene, the experience of that long, sixty-mile march and the deaths and wounds which a few hours brought under my notice seems now as a great and horrible nightmare dream. My great responsibilities and anxieties I could not then realize, and I felt as cool and collected as on a common march. But they come back to me now, and I just begin to realize under what a tremendous pressure of feeling and rapid thought I was all the while acting. I had no time to think of myself, because I was so filled with the great danger that surrounded the thousands who looked to me for direction.

All Sunday night I walked from the ferry to the ford and then to Gen. Banks' quarters—in wagons by the way—to see what could be done to hasten the safe transportation of our men. Fortunately we had dragged back two pontoon boats which were launched, and a scow was found, and we began about 2 o'clock the morning of Monday to get our men rapidly over. The wagons, too, were getting slowly over the ford, but some wagons stalled and mules drowned and the white-covered boxes stood in the river, some times three and four together, as monuments of danger to those who followed.

The men all dropped to sleep as if dead. The campfires, which blazed briskly on our first arrival, died out. Nothing was heard but the braying of mules and the rolling of wagons moving toward the ford and the occasional obstreperous cursing of some wagon-master at the unruly conduct of his team. We had pushed forward towards the rear a section of artillery and some infantry and cavalry to watch the approach of the Rebels, but so convinced were our men of the vastly superior force of the enemy that they were poorly prepared to resist an attack. I waited impatiently, and yet mostly anxiously, for daylight. The regiments not on duty were brought down to the front and stood quietly waiting their turns to cross. We sat there for hours around the campfires of Gen. Banks, talking of the past and discussing the probabilities of the morrow; the major general and four brigadier generals, Banks, Williams, Hatch, Crawford, and Greene. The last-named two had joined us just before the retreat to command brigades, then commanded by colonels.

I had my horse unbridled and fed from oats picked up from the thrown-away forage, and I unbuckled the martingale and fixed my sword and pistol and other weighty traps so that I could be ready to swim the stream after I was satisfied that further efforts were useless. I was determined to trust to my horse, and as I knew the ford would be over-crowded I decided to take the deep current and trust to the swimming qualities of my horse. So I tied him near the bank with Lt. Pittman's [horse]. Capt. Wilkins and Beman had got separated from us, and Whittlesey was with his train and St. Augustine, ordnance officer, was with his wagons, ready to destroy the ammunition in case of necessity.

My escort of cavalry was reduced to half a dozen who had followed me vigorously all day, and especially one black-eyed boy, who seemed to be, through the fight and even afterwards, like my shadow. He never quit my side, but with a quiet, determined manner was always ready to answer when I called. His name is Lemcke, and he is from Michigan. I have not yet had time to look him up and reward him for his devotion.[18]

At length daylight came. The river had fallen half a foot but the mule-trains were constantly balking and the mules drowning, till there were dozens of wagons and two pieces of artillery in the stream, blocking up the way and increasing the difficulties. So we went to work with ropes to draw them out and succeeded so as to open the way again. Then down came the cavalry to try the ford. With all my fatigue, I could not but laugh at the scene. The strong current would take some away down stream. Others would ride fearlessly over and with little trouble. Several got so confused that they lost the ford and swam away down the river in the middle of the stream. Each horse seemed to have some peculiarity. Now and then a rider would be thrown and would disappear, floundering in the water. Some would run against the stalled wagons, and altogether the scene was most confused, and in spite of its real seriousness and danger was in fact laughable.

But the enemy came not, and after a while, what with fixing the ford entrance and what with improvised facilities of transportation, matters began to be more hopeful and cheerful. At 9 o'clock or so, being satisfied all was safe, I crossed on the ferry. Most of the men were then over, and the wagons were getting along rapidly. I hoped to get some rest, but on this side I found so many things to attend to that it was hours before I could throw myself on a bed. After three days and nights of incessant fatigue and without sleep, you may be assured I slept soundly, and yet awoke unrefreshed. But I am now pretty well again, and yet not over the soreness of muscle and general debility consequent on such long efforts.

I cannot tell you now what our loss has been; probably 800 in killed, wounded, and missing. My infantry force was not far from

3,500 men. The cavalry is made up of so many incongruous organizations that I can say nothing of it, except that it did nothing for us, except as a part of the rear-guard under Gen. Hatch. With him they were useful and efficient, but there were so many straggling and running here and there to the great confusion of order and discipline that I regretted they were not all away.

To sum up, Rene, we have marched sixty-odd miles in two days, with nearly 500 wagons and have brought them all in with the exception of perhaps 50; have fought numerous combats and one severe fight, in the face, and in spite of the best efforts of from 15,000 to 20,000 Rebels. A successful retreat is often more meritorious than a decided victory. We were certainly very successful in our defeat, for which I think "good luck" should have the main praise. We have got off in pretty good order, but if you were a politician I could tell you how easily all this could have been avoided and how, instead of being a defeated and dispirited army, we ought now to be in Staunton or beyond, with Jackson and Ewell defeated fugitives and the whole Rebel crew driven back far beyond the line of Richmond. A singular blunder, a division of our forces and a neglect to send to us troops which were there in this valley has led to all this disaster and unhappy loss of life, property, and territory.

I write this under constant interruptions and have no time to revise. As I am only half recovered to my usual condition you must make it out the best way you can. . . .[19]

As ever,

Your Affectionate Father,

A.S.W.

◈

REASONS FOR THE DISASTER

Williamsport, June 2nd, 1862.

My Dear Daughter:

I wrote a long account of our "skedaddle" (new but very expressive phrase in the army) to Rene and told her to send it to you. I hope you have received it before this. We had a most disagreeable retreat, marching nearly seventy miles—some of the troops more—in two days, fighting two-thirds of the way with one severe battle in front of Winchester, and passing three nights without sleep. We brought off nearly 500 wagons containing all the supplies of the department. We were attacked by at least 20,000 men. We had to oppose them only two [illegible] brigades of my division of about 3,600 infantry, 10 Parrott guns, and 6 smooth-bore guns, and perhaps 1,500 scattered, discordant, and unorganized and very poor cavalry that literally did nothing but make an occasional show of a portion of themselves. Five hundred of them separated from us and took a different direction and several hundred more fled and spread enormous reports of our destruction. As we were separated from our provision wagons, our men had but one meal in two days, except what they picked up on the way. Our loss in killed, wounded and missing is pretty large, being at least one-fifth of the command. Considering the force attacking us, it is less than might have been expected.

I believe I have several times told you that I thought we were in a critical position. If I have not, it was because I did not wish to alarm you. But the War Department seemed determined to strip Gen. Banks of his whole command to make new departments and new armies at points where there was no enemy. For instance, Gen. Fremont lay directly in our rear and without a possibility of meeting an enemy unless we were driven back. Yet the War Office gave him an army of 30,000 men [and] Gen. McDowell an army of 40,000 or more, while Gen. Banks' command was reduced to the number above stated, in face of two columns of the enemy not less than 10,000 each and but one or two days' march from us.

In order to get us somewhat out of the way (I suppose), we were ordered to return to Strasburg, a three days' march, and here we were obliged to hold the debouches of two valleys (at both points large public stores were in deposit) twelve miles apart. The two columns of Ewell and Jackson were one in each of said valleys and good stone pikes led directly to our valuable deposits. How anybody of common sense could have expected any other result than what followed, I cannot imagine. But the wise "powers that be" at Washington, whose policy seems to be to divide our forces into the weakest and smallest commands, and in this way give time and chance for the Rebels to combine and overwhelm us, did not seem to think we were in danger. On the contrary, they were every day spreading us out over a long railroad line, making us thinnest where we were most exposed and where by a sudden attack our railroad communication could be broken and the rest of our command isolated and surrounded. . . .

The War Department has undertaken the management of the whole war from its bureau in Washington and it has a chronic trepidation that Washington City is in danger of being attacked. If we are not wholly destroyed by its policy, it is because Providence interposes to save us. We have under Banks, McDowell, and Fremont at least 80,000 troops which could be united in one week and overwhelm everything by a movement up this valley to Staunton and to Lynchburg, and from that point move directly on the flank of the Rebel army at Richmond. Not a Rebel enemy would dare to remain behind us either in western or northern Virginia. This movement could and should have been made two months ago, while we were at Harrisonburg, before we were ordered to retrograde. Two brigades of my division and Gen. Shields' division numbered probably 14,000 men; Blenker's division and other troops within a few days' march (at Winchester), numbered 12,000. A part of my division, at least 5,000 men, were east of Strasburg, two days' march. At least 30,000 men could have been concentrated within five days.

We had then before us Ewell's division, 12,000 strong or less, at the crossing of the forks and of the Shenandoah south-east of us, twenty miles off. Jackson's division [was] marching to Staunton with 12,000 more and 4,000 of Johnston's, and massing to attack and defeat, as he did, on Gens. Milroy and Schenck in the mountains. A march of twenty miles would have placed us at Staunton between Ewell and Jackson's divisions, pinning up Jackson in the mountain passes, from which he could not possibly escape, and forcing Ewell to run away if he could, which I doubt from the then condition of the roads. Just at this very moment Shields' division was sent to McDowell and we were ordered back to Strasburg, and Blenker was sent from Winchester away up to Romney and then round to Franklin to join Gen. Fremont!! Marching hundreds of miles out of the way and away from the enemy to get to a place not forty miles from Harrisonburg where we were!

In truth, the War Department seems to have occupied itself wholly with great efforts to give commands to favorites, dividing the army in Virginia into little independent departments and creating independent commanders jealous of one another, and working solely for their own glorification and importance. If we had had but *one general* for all these troops there would not now be a Rebel soldier this side of the railroad from Lynchburg to Richmond. But enough of this. Tell Uncle John that the regulations do not permit me to grumble nor criticise, and he must not compromise me with this information.

Love to all,

Your Affectionate Father,

A.S.W.

1. Bath, better known as Berkeley Springs, is in Morgan County, West Virginia, some five or six miles southwest of Hancock.
2. Actually on Saturday, January 4.
3. That is, on January 8.
4. General Frederick W. Lander, killed on March 2, 1862.
5. General Benjamin Franklin Kelley.
6. The Sibley tent was conical in shape, like the tepee of the Plains Indian tribes, and large enough to house several soldiers in relative comfort. A ventilation device at the top permitted the use of a stove or other fire at the center of the tent.
7. This bridge had been constructed by General Jackson on January 5, for the purpose of crossing the Potomac to capture Hancock. Upon learning of the arrival of Union reinforcements there, he abandoned the project, preferring to direct his force to the recapture of Romney. See his report in *Official Records*, Series 1, V, 392.
8. General Banks was about to launch the first invasion of the Shenandoah Valley. General Jackson was in possession of Winchester at this time.
9. Charles Smith Hamilton, a West Point graduate in the class of 1843. At the opening of the Civil War he was appointed colonel of the Third Wisconsin Infantry Regiment, and on May 17, 1861 was commissioned a brigadier general, on the same day as General Williams.
10. The battle of Kernstown, March 23, 1862, in which General Jackson was defeated. For a comprehensive account of the battle and the succeeding operations by General Nathan Kimball, who in the absence of General Shields commanded the Union army, see *Battles and Leaders of the Civil War* (reprint edition, New York, 1956) II, 302–13.

11. Historians still comment with admiration on the feats of Jackson's infantry who marched "thirty miles in twenty-four hours." The letters of General Williams disclose that when properly led, Union soldiers were quite capable of meeting the best efforts of Jackson's famed "foot-cavalry."

12. "I did not stop, in my haste to get to the front, to visit the battlefield in front of Winchester, but from some of my officers I hear it presented a horrid sight. The dead (several hundred) lay pretty much all in a small space where the fight had been thickest. They were un-buried on the second day, at least the Rebels were. The wounded were taken in early. They filled all of the public and many of the private buildings in Winchester, and all along our route they were in villages and houses. Some wounds made by our shells were ghastly enough.

"The ladies of Winchester for the first time made their appearance in the streets, carrying comforts to their own wounded, [but] *not to ours*. I am much disgusted with the samples I have had of female Secesh. It has been my endeavor to treat them all courteously and kindly, but their manners, even under the gentlest language and [illegible] are anything but maidenly or ladylike. I say this after making all allowance for wounded pride and bitter feelings."— Letter to daughters, March 27, 1862.

13. Turner Ashby was a native of Fauquier County, Virginia, and a some-what notable leader of Confederate cavalry in the early months of the war. He operated chiefly in the lower Shenandoah area in 1861–1862 until he was killed near Harrisonburg on June 6 of the latter year.—*Dict. Am. Biog.*

14. General Jackson had defeated Milroy at McDowell on May 8, 1862, compelling the latter to retreat northward toward Franklin, West Virginia. This letter indicates that as late as May 17 General Williams had but little, if any, knowledge of the defeat.

15. General Jackson captured Front Royal on Friday, May 23, 1862. The letter discloses that General Williams learned of the affair late on the same day.

16. The report of his death was unfounded. Although wounded, Colonel Kenly survived to serve throughout the war and to die peacefully on December 20, 1891.

17. As commonly in warfare, the strength of the Confederate army is ex-aggerated. Yet Jackson had twice as large a force as General Banks' army, which was, in effect, General Williams' division, and the success-ful withdrawal of the Union army across the Potomac marked an important failure for General Jackson. According to one admiring biographer the failure was caused by the ability of the vanquished Unionists to retreat faster than the victorious "foot-cavalry" could follow them—an apparent reflection upon the marching capacity of

the latter.—Allen Tate, *Stonewall Jackson: The Good Soldier* (New York, 1928), pp. 150–51.

18. August Lemcke from Marquette, who enlisted in Company B, First Michigan Cavalry on August 23, 1861. He was discharged for disability, January 9, 1863.—*Record of Service of Michigan Volunteers*, Vol. XXXI.

19. Not the least remarkable thing about the battle and the retreat of the Union army was the writing by General Williams of this 5,000-word account of it on the day following his escape.

III

Cedar Mountain
and
Second Bull Run

CEDAR MOUNTAIN AND SECOND BULL RUN

Despite the fact that in the Seven Days' Battle before Richmond McClellan had inflicted much heavier losses upon the Confederates than his own army had sustained, his inaction following their conclusion made clear to the world that the campaign had ended in failure. Still seeking a general who would lead the Army of the Potomac to victory, President Lincoln offered its command to General Burnside, who promptly declined the responsibility. In his desperation the President now called General Pope from the West, to whom was entrusted the direction of the newly-formed Army of Virginia. Boastful, vainglorious, and incompetent, Pope promptly led his army to humiliating defeat and a retreat behind the defenses of Washington. Once more General Williams' command, badly outnumbered, stood face to face with Stonewall Jackson's grim soldiers. At Cedar Mountain on August 9 he fought desperately, despite the blundering of the higher command, sustaining one of the heaviest losses, for the numbers engaged, of any battle of the war. The letters which follow fairly disclose the practically unanimous condemnation of the leadership and character of General Pope.

TRAPPING STONEWALL JACKSON

Williamsport, June 3rd, 1862.

My Dear Daughter:

I shall go over the river as far as Martinsburg tomorrow probably. Our men have not been supplied with lost blankets, knapsacks, etc., but Gen. Banks is very impatient to get into Virginia again. . . . Our troops, one of my brigades, are in Martinsburg again and it is rumored that McDowell or Fremont is in Winchester. I suppose we are to do over the old story and go a third time through the valley. When we get well up we shall again be left alone to be driven back. The government seems determined to play the game of fast and loose. . . .

Some of our officers taken at Winchester have returned on parole. The Rebels had left the town and paroled all the officers. Col. Kenly, 1st Maryland, is alive but wounded, not dangerously. Col. Murphy is a prisoner, not wounded. Our prisoners are well treated since the fight. They contrived to pick up a good many stragglers and sick men, but took very few able-bodied men who stayed by their colors.

Where we shall go next is very uncertain. I shall be better able to tell you at Martinsburg. The B. and O. Railroad was not much damaged. Indeed, the Rebels seem to have been on a rapid foray for stores, unless they have gone back to try fortunes with McDowell and Fremont. If these officers have made a junction, Jackson can never get out of the valley. If they have kept separate, as I fear, he will be apt to beat them *seriatim*. Our commanding generals are fishing so much for personal popularity that I think they care but little for the general cause, when it conflicts with private interest.

I am quite well and over my fatigue. Indeed, I see nobody quite as tough as I am. . . .

Love to all,

Your Affectionate Father,
A.S.W.

❖

FAILURE TO TRAP STONEWALL

Winchester, June 16, 1862.[1]

My Dear Daughter:

Your letter of the 10th reached me yesterday. I came up from Williamsport to Martinsburg on Thursday last, spent a pleasant evening with the family of Commodore Bornman, U.S.N., consisting of several daughters and other female relatives, all very agreeable and strongly for the Union. The next day I came on here and now have quarters in a fine old house built on the site of old Fort Loudon of the French and Indian War times. The family is thoroughly Secesh but very civil to me, probably for the reason, given by one of the ladies, that she had heard that I treated all with great kindness and politeness. I wonder if they will remember this if I am taken prisoner.

My troops are scattered from this place to Front Royal. I was glad to meet on my arrival several officers of my 2nd Brigade, which has been absent since our attempted march to Centerville. They had come up as a committee to see Gen. Banks and get an order restoring them to my command again. They have been under Gen. McDowell and are terribly disgusted with him. I felt much pleased at the preference shown for my command. Gen. Banks telegraphed to Washington, but the War Department under some unaccountable influence of Gen. McDowell refuses to order them back to my division.

The pretense is that Gen. McDowell is about to do some great operation. I hope he will. He made a great failure in pursuing Jackson. Officers of his command report that he marched to within four miles of Strasburg and heard the guns of the first fight between Fremont and Jackson, when he ordered a halt and subsequently counter-marched to Front Royal and started, himself, forthwith for Washington. If he had followed closely he could have destroyed Jackon. Instead of that, Jackson seems to have cut up pretty badly Shields' division (a part of McDowell's) sent to intercept him at Port Republic bridge. Matters were very unskillfully managed, or Jackson's army would now be among the things that were.

Indeed, I am heart-sick at the want of common sense in all the management of affairs outside of McClellan's army in Virginia. In this valley it would seem that we are to be the sport of changing policy. I would I were well out of it, even in the hardest place of the army. I can stand anything except the gross stupidity that someone is guilty of. You must not be surprised to hear we are all travelling over the Potomac again, though we have troops enough in West Virginia, if properly combined, to drive away everybody this side of Richmond. We have too many district commands and too many independent commanders.

I am greatly pressed for time. All my regiments are yet unsupplied with things lost on the retreat, knapsacks, blankets, haversacks, canteens, and the like. Three weeks have gone, and we ought to have had everything in three days. I feel sick when I think of the suffering and sickness which these insincere and wicked plays [?] do and will cause among our men. . . . I am wearied, annoyed, tired, and distressed to death, and yet my tough constitution stands it all as if made of iron. Alas, this fearful responsibility which others direct and you cannot control where you are most responsible. . . .

Your Affectionate Father,
A.S.W.

◈

A PROPHETIC FORECAST

Near Front Royal, Va., June 22, 1862.
My Dear Daughter:
I wrote you last from Winchester. We came down here on Thursday last and met a warm reception from our old companions. The men of my old brigade turned out en masse and cheered me vociferously. Some of them remarked that I was a re-inforcement equal to a brigade. This is very flattering, for perhaps I prefer the love of the men to the favor of the government. We are now on the spot where the 1st Maryland Regiment was attacked before our retreat, and the camps are nearly at the place where the last stand was made. I trust we are not to go through the same disaster, though I confess to you I have my apprehensions, so badly are we overlooked and neglected and so confident am I that the Rebels intend to make a desperate effort for this valley. If the government is wise it will direct its fears this way

and not toward the fortified front of the capital. If Maryland is ever invaded, it will be through this valley—mark my prediction.[2]

We have received a great acquisition of prominent officers, and have here and hereabouts generals enough to command an army four times our number. Shields and four or five brigadiers have just gone off, but Fremont, Banks, and Sigel, major-generals, and Craword, Greene, Cooper, Slough, and several others besides myself still flourish in this little army. One would suppose the government was determined to scare the Rebels by a show of general officers. . . .

I have not had a line from you since you left Philadelphia, but our mails are very irregular. We are now literally in the field. There are few dwellings hereabouts; the few are very large, but have a run-down air—very a la Virginia. It is not easy to account for, but this whole beautiful valley with its productive soil presents very few indications of prosperity. Houses and appurtenances have an air of neglect and dilapidation. I think they are all in debt and spend yearly more than they raise. . . .

Your Affectionate Father,
A.S.W.

◈

BATTLE OF CEDAR MOUNTAIN

Culpeper, Aug. 17, 1862.

My Darling Daughter:

I have not found time to write you a line since our battle on the 9th, and it was with much difficulty that I could get a telegraph through.[3] Gen. Pope for some reason shut down on everything and thousands of anxious people were kept anxious for days waiting a single line.

We came up here from Washington Court House in a two days' march, dusty and hot in the extreme. Being in the rear, I did not reach this place till after midnight on the night of the 8th (day before the battle) and as I was obliged to see my divisions in camp, it was after 2 o'clock before I got to sleep in a small room of a small toll-house outside of town. There were a dozen or so of us jammed into one room.

At 10 o'clock the next morning news came that the enemy was

99

advancing in force upon one of my brigades which had moved the night before six miles or so to the front. We left everything standing and moved off to their support. We found the brigade just beyond a little stream called Cedar Run and within a mile of a mountain whose northern side slopes gradually up into a considerable elevation. The country was much wooded, with intervening strips of cultivated land. The position was a bad one and I immediately wrote back to Gen. Banks to that effect. He came up, however, soon afterwards, about the time my second brigade (Goodwin's), which I had gone ahead of, arrived. The enemy had opened with his cannon the moment I arrived, but was soon silenced by ours. From this to 3 o'clock, there was no firing. After my brigades were put in position, our cook got us up a good lunch of coffee, ham, etc., and I invited many field officers of my old brigade to join me. After lunching, we all lay down under a shade [tree] and talked over the events of the ten months we had been together, and everybody seemed as unconcerned and careless as if he was on the lawn of a watering place instead of the front of a vastly superior enemy. Col. Donnelly of the 28th New York, a great joker and full of humor, was in excellent spirits and cracked his jokes as joyously as ever.

Sorrow and misfortune seemed far away and yet of all the field officers of these three regiments (mine) not one, five hours afterwards, was unhurt. Everyone was either killed or wounded. Col. Donnelly, 28th New York, mortally wounded; [4] Col. Knipe, 46th Pennsylvania, twice wounded and nearly insane from a wound in the head; Col. Chapman, 5th Connecticut, wounded and a prisoner; Lt. Col. Brown, 28th, New York, lost his arm; Maj. Cook killed, and Lt. Col. Stone, 5th Connecticut, killed; Maj. Blake, a young man graduated at Yale last year, badly wounded and a prisoner. Two of the adjutants were killed and one wounded. Nearly all the sergeants killed. In the 28th New York every officer in action was killed or wounded. In the 46th Pennsylvania five lieutenants only escaped, in the 5th Connecticut six lieutenants escaped.

The 10th Maine, a new regiment in this brigade, was almost as badly cut up. In Goodwin's brigade the loss was not so great, but in the 2nd Massachusetts, a regiment whose officers are of the Boston elite, four captains were killed outright, all of them young men of great fortunes and of the highest standing. The major was also wounded. Lt. Col. Crane of the 3rd Wisconsin was killed. He was a most excellent man and very popular. Out of the 3,400 infantry of my division at least 1000 were killed, wounded, or missing, but few missing.[5] This does not include the slightly wounded who returned to duty.

The battle was opened by artillery about 3 o'clock. At 5, I had placed my brigade in the woods and orders were sent to push through and if possible take a battery which was doing great mischief to our left (Augur's division). It was in this effort to pass the open ground, which was successfully accomplished, and in the woods beyond where they had concealed their reserves, that we suffered so severely. For two hours the volleys of infantry were incessant and the roar of artillery seemed hushed in the din of small arms. By the aid of the 2nd (Gordon's) Brigade we held on till dark, though it was every moment apparent that we were greatly outnumbered and exposed to flank movements. We then slowly withdrew to our old position, wondering what had become of the 12 or 15,000 of our troops (Rickett's and part of Sigel's corps) which we had passed in the morning on our way out, not over four miles from the battlefield. If they had arrived an hour before sundown we should have thrashed Jackson badly and taken a host of his artillery. As it was, they came up some time after dark and took up a position that greatly relieved us.

We had, however, several instances of tremendous cannonading and the Rebels tried once seriously to force our lines. I came very near being caught in it. I was riding towards a road in front of which I had been directed to mass my division, or what was left of it. When but a few rods off, a spirited fire of infantry was opened upon us. Just in front of me was Gen. Gordon and an escort of cavalry. Fortunately we were in a small hollow and the balls passed over us. There was, however, a general stampede of officers and dragoons. Just behind us Gens. Pope and Banks were sitting dismounted with a good many staff officers and escorts. This was a hurrying time with them and altogether the skedaddle became laughable in spite of its danger. In front of the woods not over 500 yards off was an infantry regiment just come up, which opened fire with very little regard to friend or foe, and I fear killed some of our horses if nothing else.

I contrived to get beyond the line of fire pretty soon. The Rebels almost immediately opened with a heavy fire of artillery to which two of our batteries (twelve pieces) on the flank promptly responded. It was a grand sight, especially as our batteries were well served and knocked the Rebels to pieces rapidly. Finding the Rebel shells passed far over me, I stood on a little knoll and enjoyed the sight vastly. It was a flaming pyrotechnic display. In the morning, I counted over twenty dead Rebel horses, and they left one lieutenant and several men killed on the position of their battery. They didn't stay long after our guns got the range and quiet reigned the rest of the night.

It was a glorious moonlight, too, but what with fatigue and excitement and extreme thirst I can't say I was in the best frame [of mind] to enjoy it. I had sent my escort away in the afternoon to search the woods on the right, and after dark, all my staff officers to search for stragglers. So after riding with Gen. Banks to the river after water, I picked up a bundle of wheat or rye straw, took my horse to a fence near the front, unbridled him, tied the halter about my arm, and went to sleep while he munched straw.

After an hour or so I woke up and rode to the rear again to find water and see if my stray companions could be found, but I discovered nothing but two bareheaded[?] staff officers of General Banks and so I came back to my old stand and dozed till daylight. As the first streaks of light appeared, I discovered two haystacks, and hoping for a few for my horse went over to them. Here I found a strange medley of general and staff officers and privates all mixed up in the straw. Amongst others, Gen. McDowell appeared to me as I had taken a roost for a small nap before the fight was renewed, as I was assured by Gen. Pope it would be by sunrise. I wish he had kept his promise, for I feel confident we should have punished them badly. I found, too, that my troops had gone to the rear and that all the other troops had been massed in columns of brigades. I had heard the rumbling of vehicles, which I dreamed or imagined to be ambulances with wounded, but which was the moving of artillery. Everything was solemnly still except this rumbling and an occasional suppressed tone of command.

I found my troops and all my staff (except Captain Wilkins) a mile or so to the rear. They had been looking for me almost all night, but not so far to the front. Poor Wilkins was missing. He was seen safe after the fight coming from the right where I sent him. He probably was run upon by the Rebel pickets when alone and captured. We heard the next day he was a prisoner and several have since come in who saw him. He is not wounded. I miss him greatly now, for Gen. Banks was run against by a horse in the skedaddle and on the following day turned over the command to me and went into town. I have since been incessantly at work till after midnight. I contrived to finish a hurried letter to Rene yesterday and now I am writing you at midnight. The applications I receive from all sources for everything, for telegraph, transportation, protection, etc., and the thousand reports and returns, the looking after the broken troops of two divisions, the numberless papers to be endorsed and forwarded, the hundreds of matters to be examined and approved, you cannot imagine.

We have a new general, too, who has new rules, with a new staff just from the bureau that make all the trouble and vexation possible. I pray for Gen. Banks to get well. To add to all, the adjutant general of the corps was wounded (Maj. Pelouse). My adjutant general and the adjutant general of the 2nd Division were both taken prisoners. I have nobody on my staff to help me but Lt. Pittman, who is adjutant general and aide. The quartermaster and commissary have their duties outside. . . .

I was ordered with the remnants of our corps into town on Wednesday last, and have command of all the troops here and about. How long we shall stay here I can't guess. A good many troops are in advance, but not as many, I fear, as the Rebels can bring up from Richmond. I hope to see the day we shall meet them with at least equal numbers, and on fair grounds. But our generals seem more ambitious of personal glory [than] of their country's gain, at least some of them. . . .

> As ever, Your Affectionate Father,
> A.S.W.

❖

THE SECOND BULL RUN CAMPAIGN

August 26, 1862.[6]

My Dear Daughter:

I am now near Fayetteville, about seven miles from Warrenton. For ten days I have not been able to change clothes and only now and then to wash my face—sleeping under trees or on the unsheltered earth—and generally vagabonding up and down the Rappahannock. I have not been able to write you for two good reasons. 1, I have had nothing to write on. 2, A general order has stopped all letters going out. I might add a third—that day and night we have been literally under arms, liable at any moment to be called into action or into a fatiguing march. If I ever get settled, I will give you a detailed history of the last week. I have had hard service and hard traveling, but I think the past week's experience puts all other labor and privations to the shame. All our baggage has been forty miles from us and we have been at times, officers and men, literally with[out] bread or meat. Every minute came a new order—now to march east and now to march west, night and day.

Such a vagrant-looking set of officers from the major general down was never seen. We have been on the march today, having left Waterloo Bridge yesterday. I find here an officer who is going to Washington, and I use him to smuggle through a note.

I don't know if we shall get mails up or not but I suppose we shall, as I received a letter yesterday, but none from you for ten days. Where all this will end, I cannot guess. We are getting some reinforcements but nothing to what we should have. A few of us—my division reduced in the late battle to half its muster and almost without officers—are compelled to do an immense duty, enough to kill iron men. We have been under fire of shells almost continuously and at times most incessant and tremendous. After hard labor and great losses of life we are back where we were when Gen. Pope published his famous order that we must look to no lines of retreat and that in his western campaigns he never saw the backs of his enemies. In short he boasted greatly, at which we all laughed and thought he would do better to stay where we then were till he got men enough to do half what he threatened. But I have room for no more. Say to Minnie that I will write her by my first private chance.

Your Affectionate Father,
A.S.W.

◆

Camp near Rockville, September 8, 1862.
My Dear Daughter:
With the exception of my short pencil note, I have not been able
to write you since the fight at Cedar Mountain but once I believe. . . .
For two weeks, we were without knowledge of the outer world. To
look back upon those two weeks of anxiety, sleepless nights, long marches,
and almost incessant battling, it seems like a long nightmare when one
wakes up feverish and exhausted, and but indistinctly can recall what
has happened to him.

A few days after our Cedar Mountain battle, the command of the
army corps was turned over to me by Gen. Banks, and I was ordered
to move the corps to Culpeper and take command of all the troops
there. We were there several days but most incessantly and vexatiously
occupied. I was almost always up till after midnight. The loss of so
many general and field officers threw matters into confusion.

I had got the books and papers of the corps together and was getting
matters straightened when orders came for us to pack up for a sudden
march on Rappahannock Crossing. We had our tents pitched in [the]
large front yard of a Dr. Herndon and I was most comfortably located. But on the 17th ult. at 2 p.m. we were obliged to pack up and
start our trains, but the corps was to remain as a rear guard to all of
McDowell's wagons. Mine were got out of town early, but McDowell's
and Sigel's came lurching by all night while myself and staff were
watching and waiting. It was 10 o'clock the next morning before I
could put my column in motion.

While I was waiting, sleepy and impatient, soon after sunrise a
cavalry officer brought up and delivered over to me Maj. Fitzhugh, a
general of Gen. Stuart's Rebel cavalry. He was well dressed and a very
gentlemanly young man. I invited him to take coffee with me, as it
was just ready, and afterwards I took his parole not to attempt to escape.
He was mounted on an elegant horse, a present of his wife, parting
with which seemed to be his great grief. He rode with me all day. I
gave him a dinner on the road. I crossed the Rappahannock before
sundown at the railroad crossing and took up a line of battle on the
south side of the railroad along the river and bivouacked. My wagons
had all gone back on some quartermaster's orders and our best shelter
was the woods, to which we took with our prisoner. I kept him till

the afternoon of the next day, took his parole to report to Gen. Halleck in Washington, and then shipped him on the railroad. He almost shed tears when I took him aside and offered him such funds as he might need for present uses. He acknowledged most warmly my kindness, which he had not expected, and seemed sincerely affected. So strangely are the extremes of friend and foes brought near. So strangely does war mix our passions and our better feelings.

The enemy opened his big guns upon us the next day, Wednesday, but harmed only the forces (McDowell's) on our right. Thursday night we moved down towards Berry's Ferry to support [Gen.] Reno. Slept within woods in a big rain storm, ordered back next morning, stayed in woods.

Friday, 22d, ordered up river to support Sigel. Encamped near Beverly Ford, terrific shelling all day. Moved troops to woods in rear of Sigel, who attacked the enemy with infantry. Gen. Bohlen was killed.[7] Sigel lost badly, though I see the newspapers give him the false reputation of having taken 2,000 of the Rebels! In the morning (Saturday) the woods we were in were shelled and several fell close to us. A 12-pound round shot passed directly over our impromptu breakfast table just as we left it, whereupon we mounted our horses and moved out of range.

Saturday, 23d, followed Sigel's corps towards Warrenton Springs along the Rappahannock. It was a day of very slow marching over very bad roads. Sigel had a long train with him and we were obliged to lie in the road for hours for his command to go by. . . . Reno's corps followed us. Just before night a tremendous cannonade began in front followed by heavy volleys of musketry. It was dark before we halted for the night. Sigel was in advance up[on] a narrow, bad road. Reno some miles in the rear. The enemy was reported in force across a narrow creek. We were crowded into a small open space surrounded by heavily wooded hills. I went forward to see Sigel. Found him in a farmhouse full of Dutch staff officers and several general officers: Gen. Carl Schurz, Milroy, and Schenck were there. All anticipated a big battle next day.

I got home through a horrid road by the light of a lamp carried by a mounted orderly about 2 o'clock in the morning. The next day we reconnoitered early towards Warrenton Springs—got the column on the road following Sigel about noon. As soon as we reached the hills overlooking the Springs, the Rebels opened firing[?] with their guns. Ours were soon in position and for hours we had the fiercest artillery duel that has happened in this war. While it was going on, I was obliged to march my division along a wooded hill directly in the rear of our batteries and under the direct range of the Rebel guns. The shells whizzed and burst over us and the cannon shot cut the trees and branches like rattling hail, and yet strange to say not a man of the 1st Brigade that I was leading was injured. In the midst of the wood we found a lady (the wife of one of Sigel's staff) and two officers closely hugging the side of a big tree. As we came up one officer (an old German of most military aspect), alarmed apparently by a shell bursting near, threw himself flat upon his saddle and spinning his horse by ferocious kicks high on his rump, he skedaddled in about as laughable a way as can be conceived. None of us could help a grin quite audible even though all probably would have been glad to emulate his speed.

We passed safely through these woods and obtaining an open space in a deep hollow, we halted for an hour or so while the duel of big guns kept up. Finally, a corps of pioneers reached the bridge over the Rappahannock and set fire to it. We marched off up the Warrenton Pike till we reached a cross road towards Waterloo Bridge which crosses the river between Warrenton and Springville, our old route when we first began the campaign under Pope. We encamped on the road about two miles from the bridge. Sigel in front of us still and his eternal trains all night as they had all day stopping our march. The next morning, we marched towards the bridge, but soon fell into Sigel's confused ranks. I was leading the corps, and as we were ascending a hill Sigel appeared in his long cloak and broad-brimmed hat, looking as if he might be a descendant of Peter the Hermit. He was terribly enraged that Gen. Banks should order his corps to march through his ranks. He lifted his arms up and spread out his cloak as if he was about to give a benediction. It was a tremendous cursing in mixed German and broken English. Altogether the scene was very laughable, and we all laughed heartily as soon as we could get our faces away from the enraged general. I calmed his resentment in a short time by assuring him that Gen. Banks had intended no disrespect, and that I would take the responsibility of moving the corps back and uncovering his troops, which I did in five minutes. I saw the enraged general soon afterwards expending his surplus wrath on a very black Negro, whom he was having soundly thrashed, probably for neglecting his breakfast.

Same day, Monday, the 25th, we received orders to march in all haste towards Bealeton Station, about three miles from the Rappahannock. It was rumored that the Rebels were moving towards Thoroughfare Gap to cut our communications. We marched some miles, passing McDowell's corps, or part of it, on the way. We were halted for the night in a fine camping ground. At last I halted the corps there as Gen. Banks was absent in Warrenton. The next morning we moved forward, but were halted in the woods after a few miles and stayed all night. Wednesday (27th) we again moved forward to Bealeton and followed up the railroad towards Warrenton Junction. We encamped at night with[in] a mile of Warrenton Junction. Fitz John Porter's command were ahead of us and thousands of his stragglers covered the route.

The next morning (28th) we marched to Kettle Run near Catlett's Station. There we halted over night and had time to look at the battleground of Gen. Hooker's division, which took place the day before.[8] Gen. John C. Robinson (Capt. Robinson of Detroit) was one of his brigadiers. As I came up with the rear of Porter's corps in marching out in the morning, I came across the 16th (Stockton's) Michigan Regiment. Capt. Tom Barry, formerly a clerk at Tillmans, was commanding the regiment.[9] I found several officers I knew, among them Robert Elliott. We left Kettle Run and marched to Bristow Station and Manassas Junction. All day before we had heard the sound of heavy firing northwest and north of us, but no order came to move nor did we hear a word from Pope. Today we could see from the fortifications of Manassas the fight going on—the smoke of cannon and of infantry firing.[10] About 3 p.m., just as the cloud of smoke seemed thickest in the center, and when, too, it seemed that our troops were receding (as afterwards proved true), we were ordered to march back four miles to Bristow Station. All night we were without information save what came from rumor with its thousand tongues. We were away off on one flank with a little decimated corps of not 6,000 fighting men. If our troops were driven our chances of getting away were small. I had taken the corps back by order. It was nearly dark when we reached our camping ground. I could not find Gen. Banks and so made my dispositions for the night as best I could. I slept soundly in spite of uncertainty and doubt and anxiety.

Early the next morning Gen. Banks sent for me and showed me an order to burn all public property and march via Brentsville. The rail road bridge had been burned by the Rebels, leaving on the south side hundreds of our wounded and sick, besides miles of cars full of army stores and provisions. The wounded and sick we had taken off to Centerville by wagon, but the goods were there and the torch was soon applied and a tremendous bonfire, whose smoke went up high into the heavens, broke out for miles along the railroad. At the same time our ammunition wagons were set on fire and many of our ambulances. Explosions followed like salvos of artillery. I had for my headquarters carriage an ambulance and one wagon, which we had contrived to secure to carry our forage and food. These I determined to keep. I got them off safely and have them yet. Gen. Banks burnt up his private baggage almost wholly. We saved a good many ambulances. The day was rainy and the road we took to Brentsville muddy and heavy.

At Brentsville we turned off to the left and after [marching] up hill and down we came out on the plains near Manassas and crossing Bull Run we encamped on the hills near Blackburn Ford. This is the point where your Gen. Tyler and our Gen. Richardson began the attack on Thursday before the unfortunate battle of Bull Run. The affair was considered a failure, and I believe (justly or unjustly I can [not] say) both Tyler and Richardson were considered censurable. We remained here guarding the bridge over the ford that night and part of next day. It was here that we began to get some definite intelligence of the disasters of the fights on Saturday. We heard, too, the death of poor Fletcher Webster, who had spent a day and night with me at Culpeper on his return from leave at Marshfield. He was in great spirits there and was anxious that the battling might begin. Here, too, we heard that Col. Brodhead was wounded and a prisoner. He has since died and his body sent home.[11] Col. Roberts, too, of the 1st Michigan [Infantry] was reported killed.[12] Fifty of my personal acquaintances and friends were reported killed or wounded. Such is war. Our troops had fallen back and lay as thick as leaves in Vallombrosa in rear of the bare hills of Centerville.

In the afternoon, we were ordered towards Fairfax Station by a road running parallel to the pike from Centerville to Alexandria. We had nearly reached a cross road to Fairfax Court House when a heavy fire of infantry opened on our left, apparently not half a mile distant. We had just been ordered by a staff officer to halt and there we lay on the road while the musketry rattling and cannon now and then boomed out above the rattling din. Amidst it all began the most furious storm of thunder, lightning, and rain I have ever been exposed to. The firing slackened somewhat, but in each lull of the storm it would begin again furiously. Then the thunder would begin again and such lightning, apparently striking the trees in our very midst. All this kept up until dark, when guns and thunder all stopped and the silence was oppressive. I crawled into my ambulance and slept soundly from fatigue. In the morning, we learned that Gens. Kearny and I. S. Stevens had been killed in the fight near us and that we had lost several hundred killed and wounded. The enemy were forced back, but it cost us valuable lives, two of the best officers in the service.[13]

After waiting half a day in the road, we were finally moved forward with orders to proceed to the forts near Alexandria. This was Tuesday (2nd inst.). It was midnight before we got into bivouac on the hills behind the forts near Washington. We groped about for hours before we could find a place to stop, trying to find Franklin's corps.[14] We fetched up in the grove of a gentleman's country seat. I fear as the night was cold that our long [illegible] in the Rebel land did not prepare our troops to abstain as they should from burning the man's fences. It was very cold, strangely so, and our men for over two weeks had been days without rations, marching without shelter, bivouacking in storms and wearied and fretting beyond endurance. Indeed, Rene, I should not be willing to try a description of what our men were exposed to in this terrible seventeen days. Our trains had all been sent away and we were always finding forage and subsistence burnt up just as we were getting near it.

All this is the sequence of Gen. Pope's high sounding manifestoes. His pompous orders issued in Washington and published in the daily telegraphs all over the country with great commendation of the press and apparently of the people greatly disgusted his army from the first. When a general boasts that he will look only on the backs of his enemies, that he takes no care for lines of retreat or bases of supplies; when, in short, from a snug hotel in Washington he issues after-dinner orders to gratify public taste and his own self-esteem, anyone may confidently look for results such as have followed the bungling management of his last campaign. A splendid army almost demoralized, millions of public property given up or destroyed, thousands of lives of our best men sacrificed for no purpose. I dare not trust myself to speak of this commander as I feel and believe. Suffice it to say (for your eye alone) that more insolence, superciliousness, ignorance, and pretentiousness were never combined in one man. It can with truth be said of him that he had not a friend in his command from the smallest drummer boy to the highest general officer. All *hated* him. McDowell was his only companion and McDowell is disliked almost as much, and by his immediate command he is entirely distrusted.

But enough of this. We were allowed a day's rest near Fort Albany and then ordered to the front and have led the advance up to this point. We are now within a few miles of where I began my service with the old brigade a year ago. What a contrast. The three regiments of that brigade (one has been transferred) are here yet in name, but instead of 3,000 men they number altogether less than 400 men present! Not a field officer nor adjutant is here! All killed or wounded! Of the 102 officers not over 20 are left to be present! Instead of hopeful and confident feelings we are all depressed with losses and disasters. Instead of an offensive position the enemy is now actually in Maryland and we are on the defensive. What a change! After such vast preparations and such vast sacrifices. This has been called a "brainless war." I can't tell you of the future. We are accumulating troops this way and shall doubtless have some severe conflicts. If we fail now the North has no hope, no safety that I can see. We have thrown away our power and prestige. We may become the supplicant instead of the avenger. . . .

The trains left us at Culpeper, and we did not see them again till we crossed the river. They luckily escaped the raids at Catletts and Fairfax. . . .

I am again in command of the army corps and worked to death. Gen. Banks seems to get sick when there is most to do. I see that the 24th Michigan, Col. Morrow's [regiment], is ordered to this corps.

Four other regiments are ordered to us, but they are so green in officers and men that little can be expected.

Love to Auntie and children. I will write as often as I can.

Your Affectionate Father,

A.S.W.

1. Reproduced from a typewritten copy. The original letter is missing.
2. General Lee's two invasions of the North, ending respectively at Antietam and Gettysburg, were by way of the Shenandoah Valley.
3. The battle of Cedar Mountain, August 9, 1862, the first encounter in the Second Bull Run campaign. In it, General Banks' command, 8,000 strong, fought desperately General Stonewall Jackson's 20,000 men, being driven in retreat toward nightfall, as General Williams relates.
4. Colonel Dudley Donnelly, wounded on August 9, died at Culpeper, August 15, 1862.
5. General Williams' Second Corps bore the brunt of the battle and sustained all but a minor fraction of the Union losses (2,216 men in a total for all units engaged of 2,381). Of the total loss reported, 585 are ascribed as "captured or missing." General Williams, however, states that the missing were but few, leaving the implication that almost all of the 585 were either captured or killed. General Jackson's report of the battle acknowledges a loss of 1,314 killed, wounded, and missing, and adds that this was "probably" about one-half the Union loss. Since the latter were outnumbered two to one, the proportionate Union loss was correspondingly greater. Jackson was so gratified over the victory that he ordered a divine service to be held in the army on August 14, to give thanks for past victories and to implore the continued divine favor for the future. See *Official Records*, Series 1, XII, Part 2, 136–39 and 181–85.
6. A penciled note written on scrap paper. The Second Bull Run campaign was now approaching its climax in the defeat of General Pope's army and its withdrawal within the defenses of Washington on August 29–30, 1862. A second letter of similar tone was written on the same day by General Williams to his other daughter.
7. General Henry Bohlen, a native of Germany, was appointed colonel of the Sixty-fifth Pennsylvania Infantry on September 30, 1861. He was commissioned a brigadier general, April 28, 1862, and was killed in the battle of Freeman's Ford on August 22, following.
8. The battle of Kettle Run on August 28, 1862 was another Union defeat. For General John C. Robinson's report of it see *Official Records*, Series 1, XII, Part 2, 421–22.
9. Thomas B. W. Stockton of Flint, a West Point graduate of the class of 1827, served as colonel of the First Michigan Regiment in the Mexican

War 1847–48. In 1861, at the age of fifty-nine, he became colonel of the Sixteenth Michigan Infantry. He was captured at Gaines' Mill in the Peninsular campaign, June 27, 1862, and was exchanged on August 12, following. Thomas J. Barry of Detroit was commissioned captain of Company A, Sixteenth Regiment, on August 1, 1861. He was wounded in the battle of Manassas on August 30, 1862.—*Record of Service of Michigan Volunteers*, Vol. XVI.

10. The first day's battle of Second Bull Run, Friday and Saturday, August 29–30, in which General Pope unsuccessfully attacked Jackson's force.

11. Colonel Brodhead was wounded in the action of August 30 and died on September 2.

12. Horace S. Roberts of Detroit entered the military service (three months) as a captain in the First Michigan Infantry Regiment on April 20, 1861. On August 10, 1861 he was commissioned lieutenant-colonel of the reorganized (three-year) First Michigan Regiment, of which he became colonel on April 28, 1862. He was wounded at Gaines' Mill, on June 27 and was killed on the second day of Second Bull Run, August 30, 1862.—*Record of Service of Michigan Volunteers*, Vol. I.

13. This was the battle of Chantilly, September 1, 1862, in which General Jackson unsuccessfully sought to gain the road by which General Pope's defeated army was withdrawing toward Fairfax Court House. For the careers of General Isaac I. Stevens of Washington Territory and General Philip Kearny, see *Dict. Am. Biog.*

14. General William B. Franklin, whose military career proved stormy. The conduct of his corps at the Second Bull Run battle provoked a testy exchange of letters between General Halleck and General McClellan, the former accusing someone (presumably McClellan) of disobedience to orders and the latter replying with a tart request for definite instructions, since he resented being accused of disobedience when he had "simply exercised the discretion you imposed in me."—*Official Records*, Series 1, XII, Part 3, 723. For General Franklin's career see *Dict. Am. Biog.*

IV

Northward
to the Potomac
and Antietam

NORTHWARD TO THE POTOMAC AND ANTIETAM

The Confederate victory at Second Bull Run on August 29 and 30 presented to General Lee two alternative courses of future action. Lacking the resources required for a successful investment of Washington, he could concentrate his army at a suitable base between that city and Richmond, there to await a renewed Union invasion; or he could improve upon the current demoralization of the Union forces to launch his own invasion of the North in the hope of rallying the people of Maryland to the Confederate cause and of obtaining its recognition by the governments of western Europe.

The decision was made quickly and on September 3 Lee's army began the northward march which was to culminate two weeks later at Antietam. But the people of Maryland did not rally to the Confederate banner. In need of supplies from Virginia, Lee divided his army, sending General Jackson to capture Harpers Ferry, which commanded the northerly end of the Shenandoah route. Meanwhile General McClellan, who had been restored to the command of the Army of the Potomac, followed the Confederate invaders, interposing between Lee's army and the cities of Washington and Baltimore. At this juncture blind chance dealt General Lee a stunning blow. He gave to three of his generals identical copies of an order detailing his plans for the movement of his army. One of the copies became lost and was picked up by a Union soldier. Conveyed to General McClellan, it disclosed to him the division of the Confederate army and gave him the opportunity to crush Lee before Jackson could rejoin him. In turn, a Confederate sympathizer who learned of McClellan's possession of the order, reported this information to Lee, who took position behind Antietam Creek, where he awaited McClellan's attack. The ensuing battle of

Antietam, fought on September 17, was probably the bloodiest single day's fighting of the entire war. Although the Union forces were again badly mismanaged, Lee's army was so severely punished that all thought of continuing the invasion of the North was abandoned, and the army was glad to escape to the friendly shelter of Virginia, whither the Army of the Potomac slowly followed it. One will seek long for a more stirring description of a great battle than the one which General Williams penned to his daughters from his camp near Harpers Ferry on September 22, but five days after the battle.

EN ROUTE TO ANTIETAM

Camp near Damascus, Md., Sept. 12, 1862.

My Dear Daughter:

I have not written you (excepting a scrawl in pencil) since we were in camp near Cedar Mountain. I have not been able to, for we were over two weeks without pen, ink or paper—almost without food—sleeping every night in our clothes—often without taking off my spurs! —and without one opportunity to change our underclothes.

What with marching through woods and bushes my only coat is exceedingly ragged, and I have doubtless, in the eyes of the new regiments, added to our old corps much the aspect of a jail bird or loafer. Indeed, we old veterans are much amused at the fresh and gaudy show of our new volunteers. I have no doubt they are equally disgusted with our forlorn appearance. I have now about 3,000[?] of these jolly fellows, who have marched up from Washington without tents and with no shelter but blankets and some overcoats. They think they are suffering amazingly, and I fancy, as it is raining tonight, that they are not as comfortably placed as they were a few weeks ago under their paternal roofs, as they have not the knack of old soldiers of extemporizing shelters out of rails and blankets and pieces of boards. I doubt if they won't by tomorrow begin to look to the ragged regiments for comfort.

I have not time to write you of my experiences since we left Culpeper. I have sent Rene a long account, and if you wish to read it ask her to send it to you. Suffice it to say that for over three weeks we have been scarcely a day without marching—for at least seven days without rations, except what a poor country afforded to a very large and hungry crowd. Our horses fed on the grass of the country. At length we reached the fortifications opposite Washington, about the last of the army of Pope, which never took thought of lines of retreat or bases of supplies.

I think I prognosticated to Uncle John through a letter to you that Pope would prove, as he did, a vain, weak, and arrogant man. From the first, I had a great disgust for him for his pomposity and swagger, though I was glad that we had one head to the army—even a cabbage head! We rested but one day in camp near Alexandria and have since had the advance. Gen. Banks has been in command of the corps but a few days since the battle of Cedar Mountain, and since we reached the fortifications, relinquished it altogether. I have had the advance toward Frederick till today. This morning I came up from five miles below, and pitching my headquarters tent on the cross road have been entertaining my friends of Burnside's command, which has been filing by all day. He has over 30,000 men. Just think of the procession! Gen. Willcox commands a division in Burnside's command (2nd Corps) and dined with me as he came by.[1] He is looking remarkably well, never better I think, certainly fatter than formerly. Gen. Burnside passed almost all the afternoon in my tent with Gen. Parke,[2] Cox[3] and others.

The 17th Michigan belongs to the command and many of the officers stopped to see me.[4] A few days ago my camp was within a few rods of the 7th Michigan and many of the officers who were in the School of Instruction at Fort Wayne called upon me. Indeed, I have repeatedly met Michigan officers of late, and they all greet me with great cordiality.

I have been coöperating with Gen. Sumner's corps. In it is Gen. Dick Richardson, commanding a division.[5] I find he has been made a major general, but there seems to be great contempt for him among his brother officers of rank. I did not see him, but Captain Norvell, his assistant adjutant general, came to see me.[6]

I have been intensely occupied. The loss of the principal officers of the corps has greatly perplexed me, and the [labor entailed by the] re-organization of commands which have lost field and staff and company officers, as well as all their books and papers, is immense. We march all day or are under arms all day, and then pitch our main tent and write half the night. While I write, my office tent looks like a bureau office in Washington. Five clerks, two staff officers, and some outsiders are all at work at a long table through the center. Orderlies are coming and going with dispatches. Reports are coming in from brigades and divisions and the establishment looks as if we had sat down for a season's work, and yet in an hour everything may be packed in wagons as it was an hour ago and we off for some other locality.

Tell Uncle Lew we are approaching the Rebels in large force. Burnside on the right, myself next, Sumner next, Franklin next. There will be a great battle or a great skedaddle on the part of the Rebels. I have great confidence that we shall smash them terribly if they stand, more confidence than I have ever had in any movement of the war. We move slowly but each corps understands the others, and when we do strike I think it will be a heavy blow. Tell Uncle Lew to pay those notes as his judgment dictates. I will write him if I am not on the march at daylight. . . . Don't be frightened about me, but believe me,

As ever, Your Affectionate Father,

A.S.W.

❖

EN ROUTE TO ANTIETAM

Camp near Frederick, September 13, 1862.

My Dear Lew: . . .

I have been so long without a clean shirt that I am rejoiced to be so near a town that I may reasonably hope to find a haberdasher to-morrow. It is just a month that I have been without rest or sleep of a reasonable kind. Tonight I have straw under a blanket! Think of that luxury!

The enemy have gone towards Hagerstown. We shall find them that way, I think, though they evidently begin to fear we are too many. I reached this (near Frederick) this noon, having forded the Monocacy with my corps. Gens. Hooker, Burnside, Sumner, and Franklin are near at hand.

The big guns have been banging all day, but little injury done about here. We have chased them across the South or Cotoctin mountains. What a pretty circuit I have made. My march for Dixie began here, and here I am after a year, with a crippled nation's *defenders*.[7]

I can't write more, for at every halt I have an infinitude of matters to examine and decide and write about.

Love to all. I wrote Minnie a day or so ago.

Yours Affectionately,

A.S.W.

❖

SOUTH MOUNTAIN AND ANTIETAM

Camp near Sandy Hook,
Near Harpers Ferry, Sept. 22, 1862.

My Dear Daughters:

I wrote you last from Damascus, I think, on the 11th inst. On the 12th we moved to the neighborhood of Urbana, after a circuitous and tedious march. On the 13th we marched to Frederick expecting an attack all the way. We forded the Monocacy and encamped about a mile east of the city. It was a year ago nearly that we marched through Frederick with flying banners. Alas! of those gallant troops (the old 3rd Brigade) how few remain. On Sunday the 14th we were ordered forward from Frederick crossing the Catoctin Mountain by a very rough road, east of the pike upon which we were encamped a year ago. The road took us very near our old campground at a small hamlet called Shookstown. I found all the people knew me, and I was fairly deluged with peaches, apples, etc. Ascending the mountain, we heard the reports of distant artillery and once on the summit could see that a fierce engagement was going on across the valley and in the gorges of the opposite range of mountains.[8]

We were hurried down and marched over rough roads and finally about sundown I got an order to bivouac the corps. Before, however, the regiments had filed into the fields a new order came to follow Gen. Sumner's corps over the ploughed fields toward the musketry firing heard in front. I had ordered a supper (after a meal-less day) at a farmhouse and went back to get it and to look after my artillery which had got astray in our field and erratic marches. We had a good meal and I mounted to follow the command when I heard that Capt. Abert, U.S. Topographical Engineers, of my staff had been seriously injured by the fall of his horse. Having directed his removal to the house where Dr. Antisell was, I rode back but met a staff officer on the way with a report that the corps was ordered to Middletown to report to Gen. McClellan. Thither I started in the darkest of nights, but at Middletown could hear nothing of my corps. So I rode from there toward the mountain gap where the fighting had been and got as far as our advanced pickets but could not find my corps.

Back I went to Middletown again, but could get no knowledge of my command. But here I heard with sad heart that Gen. Reno, one of the best officers and bravest fellows, had been killed in the engagement.[9] But one day before he had spent at Damascus half a day with me, full of spirits, full of confidence, and full of good feeling. Of all the major generals he was my *beau ideal* of a soldier. You will remember that he commanded a corps which followed ours along the Rappahannock. I had been thrown much with him. His frankness, absence of pomp and parade, his cheerfulness under all circumstances—that indescribable something in manner, had made me love him at first sight. I could have cried when I heard of his death, but for the thousand cares that oppressed me and for the heavy duties which close up the tender impulses of the heart.

Hearing nothing of my command I again rode to the front and on the pike found a portion of our regiment sleeping calmly with no knowledge of the rest. Soon afterward I found a mounted orderly, who directed me to a by-road leading up through the mountain defiles, and following this I at length at 2 o'clock in the morning found the rear division of my command bivouacking near the column of Hooker, which had been engaged with the enemy. I lodged under the best tree I could find, and at daylight got my whole command under arms and went forward to see what was to be done. On the top of the pass I met almost the first [man] I knew, Gen. Willcox, who commands a division. The dead lay thick in front, but I could see nothing beyond as the mist hung heavily on the mountain. Our troops, however, were already in motion and skirmishers were firing right and left as they pushed the Rebels forward.

Going back to my command, I met Gen. Mansfield, who had just arrived from Washington to take command of the corps. He is a most veteran-looking officer, with head as white as snow. You may have seen him in Washington. His home is at Middletown, Conn. and he has been inspector general of the army for a long time.[10] With this new commander came an order to march. I went back to my division, rather pleased that I had got rid of an onerous responsibility. We crossed the fields to the Hagerstown pike. Our new commander was very fussy. He had been an engineer officer and never before had commanded large bodies of troops.

Onward we went after being delayed for other columns to pass.

Crossing the South Mountain we descended rapidly to Boonsboro where the people, as at Frederick, received us with great rejoicing. I did not tell you that in marching my corps through Frederick we were greatly cheered and ladies brought bouquets to me as commander. The same enthusiasm followed us everywhere. Citizens met us on horseback and the whole population seemed rejoiced that we were chasing the Rebels from the state. At Boonsboro we passed south towards Sharpsburg, taking across lots and in all sorts of out of the ways. We encamped at a crossroads and for the first time for weeks I slept in a house, the home of a Mr. Nicodemus. As I was getting my division into camp I saw other troops arriving and an officer darting up to me put out his hand eagerly to greet me. It was the topographical engineer captain with whom Alph. and Ez. went to New Mexico, now Col. Scammon of an Ohio regiment.[11] I did not feel very kindly, I fear, and yet he looked so changed and so glad to see me that I greeted him in return. He went away and I have not seen him since.

The next morning we were ordered hurriedly to the front, Gen. Mansfield, in an excited and fussy way, announcing that we should be in a general engagement in half an hour. Over we went across lots till we struck a road and after a three-mile march we were *massed* in close column in a small space where the shells of the enemy's guns fell close to us. A high ridge in front did not seem much protection. We lay here all day, and at night fancied we were going to rest. I sought a tent with one of my colonels, who gave me the best bed I had seen for weeks.

During the afternoon, amongst the troops marching up I had seen Col. Stockton and other old friends. It was evident that the Rebels were standing for a fight. Their lines were plainly visible from the elevation in front and one battery had been playing all day with ours. I had got fairly asleep when along came a message to get under arms at once. Oh, how sleepy I was, but there is no help at such times. Up I got and in a few moments the head of my division was moving along an unknown road. We passed a stone bridge over the Antietam and then branched off into the fields. Gen. Mansfield and his escort led the way, but it was so dark and the forests and woods so deep that I could not follow and was obliged to send ahead to stop our leaders repeatedly.

After a weary march we halted in some ploughed ground and I was told to put my division in column in mass. It took a long time as I had five new regiments who knew absolutely nothing of maneuvering. At length about two o'clock in the morning I got under the corner of a rail fence, but the pickets in front of us kept firing and as often as I got asleep Gen. Mansfield would come along and wake me with some new directions. At length I got fairly asleep and for two hours was dead to all sounds or sensations. I shall not, however, soon forget that night; so dark, so obscure, so mysterious, so uncertain; with the occasional rapid volleys of pickets and outposts, the low, solemn sound of the command as troops came into position, and withal so sleepy that there was a half-dreamy sensation about it all; but with a certain impression that the morrow was to be great with the future fate of our country. So much responsibility, so much intense, future anxiety! and yet I slept as soundly as though nothing was before me.

At the first dawn of day the cannon began work. Gen. Hooker's command was about a mile in front of us and it was his corps upon which the attack began. By a common impulse our men stood to arms. They had slept in ranks and the matter of toilet was not tedious, nor did we have time to linger over the breakfast table. My division being in advance, I was ordered to move up in close column of companies —that is a company front to each regiment and the other companies closed up to within six paces. When so formed a regiment looks like a solid mass. We had not moved a dozen rods before the shells and round shot came thick over us and around us. If these had struck our massed regiments dozens of men would have been killed by a single shot.

I had five new regiments without drill or discipline. Gen. Mansfield was greatly excited. Though an officer of acknowledged gallantry, he had a very nervous temperament and a very impatient manner. Feeling that our heavy masses of raw troops were sadly exposed, I begged him to let me deploy them in line of battle, in which the men present but *two* ranks or rows instead of *twenty,* as we were marching, but I could not move him. He was positive that all the new regiments would run away. So on we went over ploughed ground, through cornfields and woods, till the line of infantry fight began to appear.

It was evident that Hooker's troops were giving way. His general officers were hurrying toward us begging for support in every direction. First one would come from the right; then over from the center, and then one urging support for a battery on the left. I had ridden somewhat in advance to get some idea of the field and was standing in the center of a ploughed field, taking directions from Gen. Hooker and amidst a very unpleasant shower of bullets, when up rode a general officer begging for immediate assistance to protect a battery. He was very earnest and absorbed in the subject, as you may well suppose, and began to plead energetically, when he suddenly stopped, extended his hand, and very calmly said, "How are you?" It was Gen. Meade. He darted away, and I saw him no more that day. Hooker's troops were soon withdrawn and I think were not again brought into the field. Was it not a strange encounter?

I had parted with Gen. Mansfield but a moment before this and in five minutes afterward his staff officer reported to me that he was mortally wounded and the command of the corps devolved on me. I began at once to deploy the new regiments. The old ones had already gotten themselves into line. Taking hold of one, I directed Gens. Crawford and Gordon to direct the others. I got mine in line pretty well by having a fence to align it on and having got it in this way I ordered the colonel to go forward and open fire the moment he saw the Rebels. Poor fellow! He was killed within ten minutes. His regiment, advancing in line, was split in two by coming in contact with a barn. One part did very well in the woods but the trouble with this regiment and the others was that in attempting to move them forward or back or to make any maneuver they fell into inextricable confusion and fell to the rear, where they were easily rallied. The men were of an excellent stamp, ready and willing, but neither officers nor men knew anything, and there was an absence of the mutual confidence which drill begets. Standing still, they fought bravely.

When we engaged the enemy he was in a strip of woods, long but narrow. We drove him from this, across a ploughed field and through a cornfield into another woods, which was full of ravines. There the enemy held us in check till 9½ o'clock, when there was a general cessation of musketry. All over the ground we had advanced on, the Rebel dead and wounded lay thick, much more numerous than ours, but ours were painfully mingled in. Our wounded were rapidly carried off and some of the Rebels'. Those we were obliged to leave begged so piteously to be carried away. Hundreds appealed to me and I confess that the rage of battle had not hardened my heart so that I did not feel a pity for them. Our men gave them water and as far as I saw always treated them kindly.

The necessities of the case were so great that I was obliged to put my whole corps into action at once. The roar of the infantry was beyond anything conceivable to the uninitiated. Imagine from 8,000 to 10,000 men on one side, with probably a larger number on the other, all at once discharging their muskets. If all the stone and brick houses of Broadway should tumble at once the roar and rattle could hardly be greater, and amidst this, hundreds of pieces of artillery, right and left, were thundering as a sort of bass to the infernal music.

At 9½ o'clock Gen. Sumner was announced as near at hand with his corps.[12] As soon as his columns began to arrive I withdrew mine by degrees to the shelter of the woods for the purpose of rest, to collect stragglers, and to renew the ammunition. Several of the old regiments had fired nearly forty rounds each man. They had stood up splendidly and had forced back the enemy nearly a mile. The new regiments were badly broken up, but I collected about one-half of them and placed them in support of batteries. The regiments had up to this time suffered comparatively little. The 3rd Wisconsin and [the] 27th Indiana had lost a good many men, but few officers. I began to hope that we should get off, when Sumner attacked, with but little loss. I rode along where our advanced lines had been. Not an enemy appeared. The woods in front were as quiet as any sylvan shade could be. Presently a single report came and a ball whizzed close to my horse. Two or three others followed all in disagreeable closeness to my person. I did not like to hurry, but I lost as little time as possible in getting out of the range of sharpshooters.

I should have mentioned that soon after I met Gen. Hooker he rode toward the left. In a few minutes I heard he was wounded. While we were talking the dust of the ploughed ground was knocked up in little spurts all around us, marking the spot where musket balls struck. I had to ride repeatedly over this field and every time it seemed that my horse could not possibly escape. It was in the center of the line of fire, slightly elevated, but along which *my* troops were extended. The peculiar singing sound of the bullet becomes a regular whistle and it seems strange that everybody is not hit.

While the battle was raging fiercest with that division the 2nd Division came up and I was requested to support our right with one brigade. I started one over to report to Gen. Doubleday and soon followed to see what became of them.[13] As I entered the narrow lane running to the right and front a battery opened a cross-fire and Pittman and myself had the excitement of riding a mile or so out and back under its severest salutations. We found Gen. Doubleday sheltered in a ravine and apparently in bland ignorance of what was doing on his front or what need he had of my troops, except to relieve his own, but I left the brigade and came back. Finding a battery, I put it in position to meet the flank fire of the Rebel battery and some one else had the good sense to establish another farther in the rear. The two soon silenced this disagreeable customer.

It was soon after my return to the center that Sumner's columns began to arrive. They were received with cheers and went fiercely toward the wood with too much haste, I thought, and too little reconnoitering of the ground and positions held by us. They had not reached the road before a furious fire was opened on them and we had the infernal din over again. The Rebels had been strongly reinforced, and Sumner's troops, being formed in three lines in close proximity, after his favorite idea, we lost a good deal of our fire without any corresponding benefit or advantage. For instance, the second line, within forty paces of the front, suffered almost as much as the front line and yet could not fire without hitting our own men. The colonel of a regiment in the second line told me he lost sixty men and came off without firing a gun.

Sumner's force in the center was soon used up, and I was called upon to bring up my wearied and hungry men. They advanced to the front and opened fire, but the force opposed was enormously superior. Still they held on, under heavy losses, till one o'clock. Some of the old regiments were fairly broken up in this fight and what was left were consolidated and mixed up afterward with the new regiments. The 46th Pennsylvania, Col. Knipe, and the 28th New York, Capt. Mapes, commanding, were especially broken. Col. Knipe has just returned to duty from his wounds. He had but one captain (Brooks) in his regiment present and he was killed early. The 2nd Massachusetts, which had done excellent service in the first engagement, was badly cut up and its lieut. col. (Dwight), mortally wounded. At 1½ o'clock I ordered them back, as reinforcements were at hand.

While this last attack was going on, Gen. Greene, 2nd Division, took possession and held for an hour or more the easterly end of the wood— struggled for so fiercely—where it abuts on the road to Sharpsburg. A small brick school house stands by the road, which I noticed the next day was riddled by our shot and shell. Greene held on till Sumner's men gave way towards the left, when he was drawn out by a rush and his men came scampering to the rear in great confusion. The Rebels followed with a yell but three or four of our batteries being in position they were received with a tornado of canister which made them vanish before the smoke cloud cleared away. I was near one of our brass twelve-pound Napoleon gun batteries and seeing the Rebel colors appearing over the rolling ground I directed the two left pieces charged with canister to be turned on the point. In the moment the Rebel line appeared and both guns were discharged at short range. Each canister contains several hundred balls. They fell in the very front of the line and all along it apparently, stirring up a dust like a thick cloud. When the dust blew away no regiment and not a living man was to be seen.

Just then Gen. Smith (Baldy Smith) who was at Detroit on the light-house duty, came up with a division.[14] They fairly rushed toward the left and front. I hastily called his attention to the woods full of Rebels on his right as he was advancing. He dispatched that way one regiment and the rest advanced to an elevation which overlooked the valley on our left, where the left wing had been fighting for several hours. The regiment sent toward the woods got a tremendous volley and saved itself by rushing over the hillside for shelter. The rest of the brigade got an enfilading fire on a Rebel line and it broke and ran to the rear. One regiment only charged the front, as if on parade, but a second battery sent it scampering.

On this ground the contest was kept up for a long time. The multitude of dead Rebels (I saw them) was proof enough how hotly they contested the ground. It was getting toward night. The artillery took up the fight. We had driven them at all points, save the one woods. It was thought advisable not to attack further. We held the main battlefield and all our wounded, except a few in the woods. My troops slept on their arms well to the front. All the other corps of the center seemed to have vanished, but I found Sumner's the next morning and moved up to it and set to work gathering up our stragglers. The day was passed in comparative quietness on both sides. Our burial parties would exchange the dead and wounded with the Rebels in the woods.

It was understood that we were to attack again at daylight on the 19th, but as our troops moved up it was found the Rebels had departed. Some of the troops followed, but we lay under arms all day, waiting orders. I took the delay to ride over the field of battle. The Rebel dead, even in the woods last occupied by them, was very great. In one place, in front of the position of my corps, apparently a whole regiment had been cut down in line. They lay in two ranks, as straightly aligned as on a dress parade. There must have been a brigade, as part of the line on the left had been buried. I counted what appeared to be a single regiment and found 149 dead in the line and about 70 in front and rear, making over 200 dead in one Rebel regiment. In riding over the field I think I must have seen at least 3,000. In one place for nearly a mile they lay as thick as autumn leaves along a narrow lane cut below the natural surface, into which they seemed to have tumbled. Eighty had been buried in one pit, and yet no impression had apparently been made on the unburied host. The cornfield beyond was dotted all over with those killed in retreat.

The wounded Rebels had been carried away in great numbers and yet every farmyard and haystack seemed a large hospital. The number of dead horses was high. They lay, like the men, in all attitudes. One beautiful milk-white animal had died in so graceful a position that I wished for its photograph. Its legs were doubled under and its arched neck gracefully turned to one side, as if looking back to the ball-hole in its side. Until you got to it, it was hard to believe the horse was dead. Another feature of the field was the mass of army accouterments, clothing, etc. scattered everywhere or lying in heaps where the contest had been severest. I lost but two field officers killed, Col. Croasdale, 128th Pennsylvania and Col. Dwight, 2nd Massachusetts, several men wounded. Gen. Crawford of the 1st Brigade was wounded, not severely. I marvel, not only at my own escape, as I was particularly exposed, on account of raw troops to be handled, but at the escape of any mounted officer.

The newspapers will give you further particulars, but as far as I have seen them, nothing reliable. . . . The "big staff generals" get the first ear and nobody is heard of and no corps mentioned till their voracious maws are filled with puffing. I see it stated that Sumner's corps relieved Hooker's. So far is this from true that my corps was engaged from sunrise till 9½ o'clock before Sumner came up, though he was to be on the ground at daylight. Other statements picked up by reporters from the principal headquarters are equally false and absurd. To me they are laughably *canard*.

On the afternoon of the 18th I received orders to occupy Maryland Heights with my corps. They are opposite Harpers Ferry, and had just been surrendered by Col. Miles.[15] I marched till 2 o'clock in the morning, reaching Brownsville. Halted till daylight, men sleeping in the road. I slept on hay in a barn. Started by sunrise up the Heights and marched along a rocky path on the ridge to the Heights overlooking Harpers Ferry. I left my artillery and train at Brownsville. Occupied the Heights without opposition. Found there was no water there; left a strong guard and took the command down the mountain on the east side. Sent a brigade over the river and a regiment to Sandy Hook. This morning (Gen. Sumner's corps having come up) I have sent one division over the river to Loudon Heights and one part way up Maryland Heights in front. The Rebels are in sight in and about and this side Charleston and to the west toward Shepardstown. What is to be done next I know not. It will be my fate, I fear, to go a third time up the valley. Heaven forbid! The valley has been an unfortunate land for me. My friends think I shall get a major generalship. I should if I was of the regular army; but not being such nor a graduated fool I suppose I shall remain a brigadier. Gen. Banks never moves for any of his command, unless solicited personally. Nobody in his corps has received promotion, though he seems to have gathered some newspaper laurels. . . .

It is now nearly six weeks that I have hardly halted a whole day, and when I have it was under orders to be ready to move at a moment. I am so tired and uneasy of this kind of sleepless life. On the march up my command was one day eighteen hours under arms and marching most of the time. But I am well and bear it better than anyone.

Affectionately, my Daughters,

Your Father,

A.S.W.

◈

RETURN TO THE POTOMAC

Camp near Maryland Heights, Opposite Harpers Ferry,
Sept. 23, 1862.

My Darling Daughter:

I have written a long joint letter to you and Rene but have sent it for her first perusal. You will get it almost as early as this. I write just a line or so as I know you are anxious to hear that I am well. I have had no time for writing and indeed no pen, ink and very little paper. It is now nearly two months that we have been daily on the march, or under arms ready to march at a moment's notice. We have had neither tents nor baggage. I have done a deal of my excellent sleeping under fences and trees and occasionally in a hay mow. I am undergoing an excellent tuition for a loafer's life: ragged clothes and sleeping in the open air.

We came down here two days ago under orders to occupy the Maryland Heights, which Col. Miles had so ignobly given up. I marched my corps till 2 o'clock in the morning, let them sleep two hours in the road at the foot of the mountain range, ascended at daylight to the crest of the ridge, and then marched over the stoniest ground to the high bluff which overlooks the Potomac at Harpers Ferry. We had six miles' march over rough, jagged, and loose stones. Just before reaching the Heights we passed the recent battlefield between a portion of Miles' infantry and the Rebels. The country people were there picking up arms, and the stench proved abundantly what was said by them, that many bodies were still unburied. The position was a very strong one, amongst large rocks and crags on the top of a narrow ridge. Two thousand men ought to have kept 20,000 at bay. . . .

I sigh for a leave that I might see you and Rene for a few days. It seems to me that I have done a lifetime of labor and exposure in the past two months. But to all appearances, we have just begun a new campaign. If it goes on with the same bloody issues as the past two weeks have seen, there will be nothing left from privates to generals. It will be a Kilkenny cat affair—both sides used up. In the last battle we had, I think, some ten or eleven general officers killed or wounded. My only wonder is that anyone escaped. I was myself under fire from sunrise to nearly 2 o'clock P.M. We went in without breakfast and came out without dinner. The major generals with big staffs will gobble up all the glory, judging from newspaper reports. But there is an unwritten history of these battles that somebody will be obliged to set right some day. Generals are amazingly puffed who are not ten minutes on the field. Corps are praised for services done by others. Commands that were hours behind the line, when the battle raged fiercest, are carrying off the reputation (in newspapers) of saving other corps from defeat. These reports are got from staff officers of the absent corps. The reporters are often members of the staff. . . .

Poor Gen. Mansfield, who took command of our corps two days before the battle, was an excellent gentleman, but a most fussy, obstinate officer. He was killed just as the head of our column reached the battlefield and I, of course, had command of the corps for the rest of the day. I had not parted from him five minutes when he was reported to me mortally wounded. Gen. Crawford, who commands a brigade of my division, was also wounded but not very seriously. But my long letter—written very hastily—will give you all the details I can find time to write. We have been so long without a halt and so much disorganized by battle and marching that I have an infinite deal of work to get reports of present condition. . . .

There are so many major generals anxious to command corps that I shall probably have a new commander soon. It is only wonderful that I have held the command so long.

Your Affectionate Father,
A.S.W.

❖

REASONS FOR FAILURE AT ANTIETAM

Camp near Harpers Ferry,
September 24, 1862.

My Dear Lew:

For the first time for weeks, I have found time to look over old letters which have become marvellously dirty in my pockets. I find yours of 5 August, I will answer the business part. . . .

Your famous 24th Regiment was assigned by general orders to my division just as we reached Rockville on our way up, but it never reported, nor have I had any explanations.[16] If it had come along Col. Morrow would have had a chance to take that battery he promised your good people in his last speech. At any rate, he would have got a terrible baptism of fire and blood. I had five new regiments. Some of them were badly peppered, and it took hard work to keep them anywhere, when once broken. They went in very valorously, but as neither officers nor men knew the first thing of movements they could not change positions without breaking and being rerallied. They were of superb material, and if they had had the drill of my old brigade, would have done fearful execution.

What has become of the rest of the 300,000? We can't have over 20,000 of new troops with us, if as many. The 17th Michigan did nobly in the mountain fight on Sunday.[17] It was a free fight in the woods and hills. I met Gen. Willcox in the pass, who praised them greatly. They are in his division. The old Michigan 7th suffered severely at Antietam. They are in Sumner's corps and in a different part of the field from us, though our corps is a part of Sumner's command, two corps being put under one commander. We were detached the night before to support Hooker's attack. I enclose a copy of my report of the battle of August 9th at Cedar Mountain.[18] It comes rather late, but we have really been separated from everything for weeks. I wore one shirt about three weeks. We have marched every day but four, and on those days we were under orders for immediate movement.

We punished the Rebels severely in the last battle.[19] The number of dead they left on the field was enormous. In some places whole regiments seem to have fallen in their tracks. If McClellan's plan had been carried out with more coolness by some of our commanding generals, we should have grabbed half their army. But we threw away our power by impulsive and hasty attacks on wrong points. Hundreds of lives were foolishly sacrificed by generals I see most praised, generals who would come up with their commands and pitch in at the first point without consultation with those who knew the ground or without reconnoitering or looking for the effective points of attacks. Our men fought gloriously and we taught the rascals a lesson, which they much needed after Pope's disaster. They out-numbered us without doubt, and expected to thrash us soundly and drive us all pell mell back towards Washington. As it was, they sneaked out of "my Maryland" at night leaving their dead and wounded on the field. Even dead generals were left within their lines unburied. Their invasion of Maryland has been a sad business for them. If you can find any Detroit editor who desires to publish my report, you can give it to him *sub rosa*. I suppose I have no right to publish myself without authority. Still, I see others get into the papers, and I suppose this can be got in without coming from me. . . .

Yours Truly,
A.S.W.

◆

REORGANIZATION OF THE ARMY

Sandy Hook, Oct. 5, 1862.

My Dear Daughter:

I have had time to write you but once since I came here and I really cannot recall what I wrote you in that. We have had most beautiful weather: warm days and cool nights; some days as warm as summer. Although I have had hard work, the quiet and absence of constant marches has been delightful. I have *thirteen* new regiments sent to this corps, all, or nearly all, with green officers and most of them just out from the States. One from Connecticut (29); eight from New York (117, 123, 127, 137, 138, 140, 145, 149); one from New Jersey (13); and three from Pennsylvania (124, 125, 128). You can well fancy that these green regiments give an infinite increase of work to get them into shape. Besides this, the old regiments, from loss of records and officers—especially the field and staff—had got into a disorganized state, which required inspections, examinations, enforcement of discipline and orders. An immense number of reports about everything and everybody. I have not got through yet, for as fast as one thing is disposed of and daylight begins to appear, a new batch of labor is laid out by a new order. Gen. McClellan is an indefatigable officer in organization. Nothing seems to escape his attention or his anticipation. Every endeavor is made, and constantly kept up, to enforce drill and discipline and to create an *esprit de corps* and confidence. I have met no officer at all his equal in this respect. But he keeps everybody hard at work.

I have sent in my report of the battle of Antietam.[20] I was obliged to make it out on short notice and before the subordinate reports were all received. We had 1,744 killed and wounded, quite one-fourth of our whole number in action. Gen. Sumner came to see me yesterday and was quite complimentary, stating that he had mentioned my name and had recommended me for promotion. He commanded the center, or properly right, in the action. Gen. Hooker, whose corps we relieved in the morning of the battle, sent his aide for a copy of my report, with a message that he was greatly pleased with my disposition of the troops and hoped he should be so fortunate as to have my assistance if he ever had another battle. Gen. Banks has also written me that he has strongly urged my promotion and congratulates me upon the splendid conduct of the corps. All the general and field officers of the corps have petitioned for my promotion. So I think I may well hope, at length, to be a major general. I think I am more pleased, however, with the commendations I have received from our best generals than with the prospect of getting rank, though I don't despise the latter. I still have command of the corps, the only brigadier who has so important a position. I can hardly expect to hold it long with so many ranking officers seeking the place. The President was here a few days since. I had quite a long talk with him, sitting on a pile of logs. He is really the most unaffected, simple-minded, honest, and frank man I have ever met. I wish he had a little more firmness, though I suppose the main difficulty with him is to make up his mind as to the best policy amongst the multitude of advisers and advice. . . .

I have just heard from Rene. She has not received my long letter after the battle of Antietam. I fear it has miscarried, which I should much regret, as I cannot write another. I will send you the next long letter, but I hope we shall not have a second Antietam immediately, unless the salvation of the Union depends upon it. I think we are fighting and have fought battles enough to have saved this Union, if they had been properly directed. This corps alone (the smallest) has lost between 4,000 and 5,000 men in battle within two months. The sacrifice would be less to be regretted if one did not feel that half of it has been fruitless and useless. All of Pope's losses were worse than waste of human life or limb. It was an absolute encouragement to the Rebels and resulted in the sacrifice of thousands more. . . .

I have a new brigadier general, just reported. Brig. Gen. Kane, brother of Kane the navigator. He is a small man and very precise.[21] Here he comes on business and I must stop.

Your Affectionate Father,
A. S. Williams

◆

PREPARATIONS FOR A NEW CAMPAIGN

Camp at Sandy Hook, Md.,
Oct. 17, 1862.

My Dear Daughter: . . .

We are still, you see, at the same place. There are daily rumors of a forward movement and we have daily reconnoissances with the usual accompaniment of big guns and a great deal of noise; not much wool. With all our efforts it seems almost impossible to get the troops into good condition for the field. Old regiments are much reduced and disordered, if not demoralized by loss of officers, by battle and disease. Majors are commanding brigades and lieutenants, regiments. While this lasts an efficient force cannot be made, and if we advance we shall soon retrograde. Yet I see by the newspapers that an uneasy and impatient public are demanding an immediate advance. We have the same old story—"demand." Yet these anxious souls know nothing of our preparations, nothing of the force or resources of the enemy. It would seem as if they thirsted for blood; for stirring accounts of great battles. No sooner is one story of bloody fights grown cold than the outcry is for another. Men and women who groan and sigh over a railroad accident which kills two and wounds six, seem to delight in the glowing description of a battle which leaves upon a single field 20,000 killed and four times as many wounded. Strangely inconsistent is poor human nature! . . .

We have a good many Michigan regiments in the corps not many miles off, but it will seem strange to you to be told that old friends may be within a mile or two of one another and never know it, except by chance. But it is so; nobody knows anybody not of their immediate command. The white shelter tents cover now an immense area in this vicinity. As seen from Maryland Heights, which terminates in an abrupt bluff on the very edge of the Potomac, the view is really magnificent and grand. On the west side the whole valley of the Shenandoah spreads out between the two rivers and mountain ranges away up to the bluff near Strasburg and Front Royal, sixty miles away. For several miles along the interior slope of Bolivar Heights, which run across the triangle between the Potomac and the Shenandoah, the *tents d'bris* of Sumner's corps shine in the purest white. Away south on Loudon Heights, higher than Bolivar, are seen the tents of the 2nd Division of my corps. On the east, along up Pleasant Valley for four or five miles, are thickly dotted the camps of my corps and Burnside's. Half way down the Maryland Heights on a considerable plateau, where are the big-ship Dahlgren guns of one hundred-pound caliber and the thirty-pound Parrotts, are thickly posted two brigades of the 1st Division of my corps. On the very pinnacle of the Heights is an observatory, where are stationed the flagmen of the signal corps. From this prominence you can overlook all this, to say nothing of the many villages and towns that peep out from the grove patches through the Shenandoah Valley, nor of the narrow gap below where the Potomac seems to have burst through the Blue Ridge.

Oct. 22nd.

I wrote this far some days ago, since which I have been very busy turning over the command to Maj. Gen. Slocum, who has been assigned to it. He is a New Yorker, a graduate of West Point. Was on the Peninsula, of course. Nobody gets permanent command or promotion, I believe, unless he was on the Peninsula. However, while there are so many major generals commanding divisions, I could hardly hope to be left long as a brigadier in command of a corps. Our people complain some and there is a general regret amongst the officers that I could not retain command.

This morning while [I was] at breakfast Mr. Reuben Rice, Mr. Hammond of Chicago, and others out west peeped into the mess-tent. I was greatly surprised. They stayed but a few moments, on their way to Antietam battlefield. Mrs. Hammond was with them. In riding around yesterday I fell upon "John Brown's School House," so called, a small log building in a ravine of the mountain where John Brown hid his army when he seized Harpers Ferry. The people [here] about speak of him as a quiet, inoffensive man in his bearing and some say he was a very kind-hearted creature.

I enclose you a button I cut from a dead Rebel officer's coat on the battlefield of Antietam. I also send you a very puffy paragraph which somebody sent me anonymously. A letter from Rene says it was in the Philadelphia *Press*. I have no idea who the writer is, as I have seen no reporters and don't recognize the initials. I send you also a letter from Gen. Banks for safe keeping. I have only a carpet bag for all my effects. We are reduced to the smallest scale. . . .

I suppose we shall move soon. Such seems to be the impression, and the public pressure is terrible.

The public knows nothing of our actual strength or preparation. If we fail, that same dear public will howl our condemnation. . . . The paymaster has not yet come and I have nearly three months due me.

Your Affectionate Father,

A.S.W.

P.S. The paymaster has just arrived and says, "Take off that mark that I am not here."

◆

CLAMOR FOR A NEW CAMPAIGN

Sandy Hook, Md.,
Oct. 26, 1862.

My Dear Daughter: . . .

Our mails have never been more irregular than for the past ten days or so. Everything now goes to headquarters and is scattered to everybody's corps except the right one.

Yours of the 18th only came day before yesterday. I have been under orders for instant march ever since and have been constantly employed to get all the readiness possible. By some fatality, or by the general crowding, we are lacking much. There seems to be an unaccountable delay in forwarding supplies. We want shoes and blankets and overcoats—indeed, almost everything. I have sent requisition upon requisition; officers to Washington; made reports and complaints, and yet we are not half supplied. I see the papers speak of our splendid preparations. Crazy fools! I wish they were obliged to sleep, as my poor devils do tonight, in a cold, shivering rain, without overcoat or blanket and under one of those miss-named "shelter tents"; a mere sieve, which filters the water over one in a nasty mist and gives no warmth. I wish these crazy fools were compelled to march over these stony roads barefooted, as hundreds of my men must if we go tomorrow. When will civilians who know nothing of our preparation or the force and strength of the enemy learn to leave war matters to war men, who have means of knowing their duties, their capabilities, and their chances? We are driven "forward" by the popular outcry. I can only hope we shall not be driven back disgraced and the country fatally put in jeopardy.

This grumbling is for your eye alone. Here I say nothing and it won't do for a general officer to complain, even in private letters. But let me tell *you* that we cannot successfully invade Virginia from this point. We must have water transportation or large railroad carriage to subsist our troops the moment we leave our depots. There are but few passable roads in Virginia. We cannot now live on green corn. We are under orders and I shall do my best and hope for the best. . . .

Your Affectionate Father,
A.S.W.

EMANCIPATION OF SLAVES

Camp at Sandy Hook, Md.,
Oct. 28, 1862.

My Darling Daughter:

I have written to Larned and Uncle Lew so recently that I can give you little news of myself except that I am still here, part of our corps moving over the river and a great number of troops marching up and down. I am kept very busy with these changes, especially as there has been a reorganization of our corps. The 2nd Division had become, from a multitude of commanders and other causes, pretty much demoralized, and so our new commander has infused new life into them by transferring a part of my division and two of my best colonels to command brigades there. These changes have delayed us a few days, but I suppose we shall move in a day or so. . . .

The weather is getting very cool and our accommodations are not good. We have not made our usual fire places, as we have been anticipating a movement. The poor fellows in shelter tents, which are really no shelter, as they are made of thin cotton cloth, are suffering much and the new regiments are full of sickness.

I like our new corps commander very much so far, though he does not strike me as of wonderful capacity.[22] In my division I believe I have told you I have a new brigadier general, Kane. He is a brother of Kane, the Arctic navigator and the same man whom Uncle Lew will remember was sent *via* the Pacific by our government to settle the Mormon troubles, while our troops were marching toward Utah. He is a little man of rather *petit-maitre* manners, but full of pluck and will. He was badly wounded at Cross Keys and taken prisoner.

The rest of my brigades remain the same. I have tried hard to get some of the colonels made brigadier generals, but have not succeeded. Indeed, Gen. Banks' corps has never yet had a promotion except in the regiments made by states. We begin to think the general has either very little influence or very little courage to use it. The latter, I think. He is very fearful of losing power by an over-exercise of it. As he seems to have got considerable glory, we naturally think that his subordinates should have a little. At least, it is hard to see how a commanding general can gobble up all the credit of success. . . .

I see somebody has printed a pretended extract from one of my private letters approving of the President's proclamation.[23] I don't remember to have written any such sentence, though I have repeatedly said that I was prepared to sustain any measure I thought would help put an end to this cursed rebellion. I should dislike to see or hear of the promiscuous slaughter that would follow an immediate emancipation of slaves in the South. There is no fear, however, that slaves will be freed any faster than our troops get possession of Rebel territory, and this was the case before the proclamation. I don't think matters are much changed by that document. . . .

      Love to all,

Your Affectionate Father,

A.S.W.

1. Orlando B. Willcox of Detroit, a member of the West Point class of 1847. He served in the regular army from his graduation until 1857, when he resigned his commission to begin the practice of law at Detroit. In 1861 he became colonel of the First Michigan Infantry (three-months) Regiment. At the battle of Bull Run, where he commanded a brigade, he was wounded and captured, remaining a prisoner until August 19, 1862, when he was exchanged. He was immediately promoted to the rank of brigadier general and assigned to Burnside's corps, with which he served at Antietam and subsequently throughout the war. Like General Williams, he frequently held higher commands than his rank called for. Unlike Williams, he was rewarded with promotion to brevet major general of volunteers, and in 1867 to the rank of major general in the regular service. Save for a short period in 1866, he served in the army until his retirement in 1887.—*Dict. Am. Biog.*

2. John G. Parke, a West Point graduate in the class of 1849, served in the engineer corps of the army until 1861 when he was commissioned a brigadier general of volunteers. He was closely associated with General Burnside, for whom he served as chief of staff at Antietam and Fredericksburg. He remained in the regular army until he was retired at his own request on July 2, 1889, after forty years of service.—*Dict. Am. Biog.*

3. Jacob D. Cox of Ohio, lawyer, politician, Union general, governor of Ohio, and Secretary of the Interior under President Grant. He achieved distinction both in military and in civil life.—*Dict. Am. Biog.*

4. The Seventeenth Michigan was one of the "new" regiments of the army, although it was not assigned to Williams' command. It was mustered at Detroit on August 21, 1862 and departed for Washington five days

later. As yet (September 12) it had seen no fighting. Its bloody baptism in the art came at South Mountain on September 14, and three days later it participated in the battle of Antietam, sustaining heavy losses in both battles.—*Record of Service of Michigan Volunteers*, Vol. XVII.

5. Israel B. Richardson, a West Point graduate in the class of 1841 and a veteran of the Mexican War. Following that war he served at various western posts until his resignation with the rank of captain, September 30, 1855. Thereafter until 1861 he was a farmer at Pontiac, Michigan. In May 1861 he became colonel of the Second Michigan Infantry. On July 4, 1862 he became a major general of volunteers. Mortally wounded in the battle of Antietam on September 17, he died at Sharpsburg, November 3, 1862. His military career was notable and nothing has been found in the published records to support the statements of General Williams concerning him.—*Dict. Am. Biog.*

6. John Mason Norvell of Detroit entered the service on April 22, 1861, as second lieutenant of Company I, Second Michigan Infantry Regiment. On August 30, 1861, he was appointed captain and aide-de-camp on General Richardson's staff, and on August 22, 1862, major and assistant adjutant general. He resigned his commission on June 21, 1865. He subsequently entered the regular army, serving as lieutenant and as captain until his retirement, December 27, 1890. He died on December 18, 1893.—*Record of Service of Michigan Volunteers*, Vol. II.

7. Here, also, he was destined to be a year later, still with "a crippled nation's defenders," enroute this time to Pennsylvania and Gettysburg.

8. This was the battle of South Mountain, September 14, 1862. On September 9, at Frederick, General Lee issued his famous "lost order," outlining his plan of operations. While his main army marched westward from Frederick through South Mountain, Stonewall Jackson was to detour southward, capture Harpers Ferry, and then hurry northward to rejoin Lee, when the combined army would advance by way of Hagerstown into Pennsylvania. Unfortunately for Lee's plans, a copy of the order fell into the hands of a Union soldier and was brought to General Williams' headquarters. Armed with its information, General McClellan pushed his pursuit of Lee, capturing the mountain gaps in the hard-fought battle of September 14, and compelling Lee to retire toward Sharpsburg, where the battle of Antietam was fought on little Antietam Creek on September 17. Although the immediate battle ended in a stalemate, it proved to be a Union victory, for Lee was compelled to abandon the invasion of the North and retire to Virginia. The uncertainty attending the movements of the army on the day of South Mountain is shown in General Williams' account of his efforts to reach the field of battle. Concerning the lost order see General D. H. Hill's defense and General Lee's estimate in the *Virginia Magazine of History and Biography*, LXVI (April 1958), 161–66.

9. Major General Jesse L. Reno, for whom see *Dict. Am. Biog.* Fort Reno, Wyoming, Fort Reno, Oklahoma, and the city of Reno, Nevada, were subsequently named in his honor.

10. Joseph K. L. Mansfield was a West Point graduate in the class of 1822. Assigned to the engineer corps of the army, he performed distinguished service in the Mexican War. In 1853, through the influence of Secretary of War Jefferson Davis, who also had served in the Mexican War, he was promoted to the rank of colonel and appointed inspector-general of the army. In July 1862 he became a major general, and upon McClellan's reorganization of the Army of the Potomac was given command of the Twelfth (Gen. Williams') Corps. He joined the army two days before the battle of Antietam, September 17, 1862 in which he was mortally wounded.—*Dict. Am. Biog.*

11. Colonel E. Parker Scammon, a graduate of West Point in the class of 1837. He served in the Mexican War and on various surveys and other engineering works until June 4, 1856 when he was dismissed from the army for disobedience to orders and other alleged misconduct. The New Mexico survey alluded to by General Williams occurred in 1855–56. He was appointed colonel of the Twenty-third Ohio Regiment on June 14, 1861, attaining the rank of brigadier general October 15, 1862.—Cullum, *Biog. Register of Officers and Graduates of the U.S. Military Academy.*

12. Edwin V. Sumner, born in 1797, entered the army in 1819 and served continuously until after the battle of Fredericksburg, December 13, 1862, in which he commanded the right grand division of the army. Relieved from duty with the Army of the Potomac at his own request, he died the following year (March 21, 1863). He was a favorite of General Scott in the Mexican War, and, apparently, of General McClellan in the Civil War. It has remained for General Williams' pen to record his mishandling and the consequent needless slaughter of his troops at Antietam. See *Dict. Am. Biog.*

13. General Abner Doubleday of New York, reputed "father" of the game of baseball. He was a West Point graduate in the class of 1842 and a veteran of the Mexican War. In April 1861 he fired the first shot at Fort Sumter in reply to the Confederate bombardment. Appointed brigadier general in February 1862, he succeeded to the command of a division at South Mountain when its commanding officer was wounded. He served with distinction in the battle of Gettysburg, where, upon the death of General Reynolds on the first day of the battle (July 1) he succeeded to the command during the remainder of the day. While stationed at San Francisco, 1869–71, he obtained the charter for that city's first cable street railway. See *Dict. Am. Biog.*

14. William Farrar Smith, a West Point graduate in the class of 1845, for many years served as a topographical engineer. At the opening of the

Civil War he was appointed colonel of the Third Vermont Regiment, and in August 1861 commanded a division of the Army of the Potomac. In July 1862 he became a major general and commanded a division in the battle of Antietam. Undoubtedly a brilliant engineer, his military career was marred by indulgence in indiscreet criticism of his superiors.—*Dict. Am. Biog.*

15. On September 15, immediately before the battle of Antietam.
16. The Twenty-fourth Michigan was a new regiment which was mustered into service at Detroit on August 15, 1862. It left for Washington on August 29, where for some reason not learned it was diverted from General Williams' command and had no part in the Antietam campaign.
17. The battle of South Mountain, September 14, 1862.
18. The report is printed in *Official Records*, Series 1, XII, Part 2, 145–49.
19. The battle of Antietam, September 17, 1862.
20. Printed in *Official Records*, Series 1, XIX, Part 1, 474–78.
21. Thomas Leiper Kane of Philadelphia, an ardent Abolitionist. At the outbreak of the Civil War he organized a regiment of hunters and backwoodsmen, an undertaking repeated by Theodore Roosevelt in the Spanish-American War of 1898. He was appointed a brigadier general on September 7, 1862. Illness compelled his retirement from the army on November 7, 1863. His brother, Elisha Kent Kane, was a West Point graduate in the class of 1841. Addicted to a life of adventure, he achieved great renown by his determined search (1850–55) for survivors of the Sir John Franklin Arctic Expedition. His book, *Arctic Explorations* "lay for a decade with the Bible on almost literally every parlor table in America."—*Dict. Am. Biog.*
22. General Henry W. Slocum. Upon further close association Williams became a warm admirer of his superior.
23. The preliminary Emancipation Proclamation, issued September 22, 1862.

V

Virginia Mud
and Winter Quarters,
1862-63

VIRGINIA MUD AND WINTER QUARTERS, 1862–63

Safely back in Virginia from his futile invasion of the North, General Lee prepared as best he might to repel another advance of the Army of the Potomac. But McClellan procrastinated, despite the proddings of President Lincoln, while the autumn weeks during which a campaign might be waged slipped away. At length, near the close of October he ventured to cross the Potomac with a newly-refurbished army, moving so deliberately that on November 7, the President relieved him of the command, which was given to General Burnside. The action marked the sunset of McClellan's military career, yet the appointment of Burnside brought no improvement in the situation. He was quite unfit to command the Army of the Potomac, which he accepted only in obedience to a military order. The sorry tragedy of Fredericksburg in December followed in due course, by which time the bottomless mud of Virginia's roads brought a halt to further operations. Meanwhile, the command of General Williams, marching to join Burnside, arrived too late to participate in the battle of Fredericksburg, and after a desperate struggle with the Virginia mud went into winter quarters at Stafford Court House, close to the lower Potomac and but a few miles north of Fredericksburg. Here it remained until April 1863, when under a new commander the Army of the Potomac once more resumed the road to Richmond.

PROSPECTS FOR A NEW CAMPAIGN

Near Sandy Hook, Md.,
November 16, 1862.

My Dear Lew:

Larned arrived last Monday bringing your letter, which was gladly received. He also brought Rene with him from Philadelphia, and I have had her on horseback for the whole week, visiting all points of interest in this romantic part of our country. Rene will probably give Minnie a full description of her visit to the battlefield and her numerous rides over the mountains and to the camps in this vicinity. So I will not bore you nor myself with them. I have deposited her in a farmhouse nearby, but about all she does there is to sleep and eat breakfast. The rest of each day she is in my camp or on excursions.

My division is now spread out from Point of Rocks to Opequan Creek, one brigade being in Loudon Valley on the south side of the Potomac. How long we shall remain in this diluted condition, I can't guess. Rumors are rife that Jackson and A. P. Hill are about to make a descent upon the line of the Potomac. We are too thin to make any considerable resistance except at Harpers Ferry or its vicinity. I hardly think the attack, if any, will be made here. But for the fact that Jackson is the most reckless and often foolhardy of men, I should hardly expect any Rebel movement in the direction of the Potomac.

Yet he has twice made these movements and escaped punishment right under the noses of our superior forces. He may do so again. Last winter, you will remember, he marched 15,000 men to Hancock and Romney and lost about half his command by cold and consequent illness. Last spring he chased us out of the valley and threatened this point while Fremont and McDowell lay on either flank with over 60,000 troops. The rascal escaped when all his own officers gave up all hope.

Our corps is left here but for how long no one can guess. I supposed we should move on Martinsburg as soon as our other corps had reached the Rappahannock, and I think this was McClellan's design. What will be done now I cannot imagine. I have no faith in a campaign in Virginia from this or any other overland route. The topographical features of the country, the miserable state of the country roads, the necessity of heavily guarding such a long and exposed line of communication must render success with a politic and shrewd enemy almost impossible. They have done and are still doing what I anticipated, falling back on their supplies and reserves, and thus extending our lines and weakening our force as we move towards the interior. Somewhere on the railroad where important communications are threatened they will fight, if attacked. Their policy has always been this, except that unfortunate (to them) invasion of Maryland. In doing this they were laboring under the same or similar difficulties that oppose our invasion. Their numbers were reduced, and they were sadly straitened for subsistence. The history of war proves that an united people can in the end overwhelm any superior invading force, if acting purely on the defensive. These Rebels had at Antietam at least 20,000 more men than we had. If they had been on the Rapidan instead of the Potomac their position would have been successfully defended and our army would have retired.

Burnside is a most agreeable, companionable gentleman and a good officer, but he is not regarded by officers who know him best as equal to McClellan in any respect.[1] I coincide in this belief, though I am personally far better acquainted with Burnside than McClellan. Perhaps McClellan has too much of the Fabian policy, but in judging of this one must not forget that he has been placed in circumstances where to lose the game would have been to lose all. My idea is that the cursed policy of this war has its origin at Washington. Old fogyism has ruled in every department. Trepidation for the safety of the Capital seems to have paralyzed all faculties of preparation and promptness.

Yours Affectionately,
A.S.W.

Rene is in my tent and sends love. She will write soon. I will write you again soon, but in these quiet times I have nothing of interest to say. You quite surprise me about the Antietam letter, as it was written in great haste amidst a multitude of duties.

◈

EN ROUTE TO THE RAPPAHANNOCK

Fairfax Station,
Sunday night, Dec. 14, 1862.

My Dear Daughter:

I am so far on my march, very fatigued and full of a thousand duties. After you left me at Harpers Ferry I soon mounted to go to the front. I spent all the day in Loudon Valley in sight of Mr. Longbridge's barn and of my old camping ground. With all my looking through field glasses I could get no signs of any of you. About 4 o'clock, with a heavy heart—the heaviest I have had in this sorrowful war—I took up the line of march with the 3rd Brigade. As its wagons were not up I ordered it into camp about two miles west of Hillsborough shortly after dark. With a small escort of cavalry I proceeded on and overtook Knipe's brigade at Wheatland, about nine miles from Harpers Ferry. Knipe had a nice house for his headquarters and I slept comfortably with him under his blankets. On Friday I marched the first two brigades to Goose Creek, passing through Leesburg. The 3rd Brigade was left to wait its wagons. We found a good camping ground and my headquarters in a farmhouse.

At daylight we were on the march. Some rascally fellows set fire to three stacks of hay belonging to my farmer. I was intensely angry, as well as grieved for the distress of the family, as this was their only subsistence. It was the first of this kind of wanton destruction I have seen, and was occasioned by Knipe's refusing to let the men use the stacks for bedding. On Saturday we marched to the deserted mansion (Chantilly) of the Stuart family, connections by marriage of Washington's family. In his attic our men and officers found autograph letters of Washington, Mrs. Washington, and others of the family connections. The place, which was once magnificent, has been occupied by cavalry and its fine grounds utterly ruined. You can hardly conceive such a picture of destruction and desolation. It is one of the pictures of civil war.

This morning we left Chantilly at 9 o'clock, halting two or three hours at Fairfax Court House. Reached this point about dark. The roads this side of Fairfax Court House are abominable, and worse, they say, ahead. My 3rd Brigade has caught up. The weather has been fine, but it has thawed the snow and frost and left the roads almost impassable. Many trains passing over them have cut up deeply what never was very good. I am tonight trying to reduce the miles of wagons and reducing weight so as to pass through the sloughs ahead. You cannot imagine the difficulties of marches at this season, on short rations, short forage, bad roads, bad preparations, and the like. Think of moving a force of 10,000 men with all its supplies in wagons over a stripped country in the month of December. The thing looks impossible, and yet we have done it so far and I have no doubt I shall get through with a fagged command.

I am without intelligence from the active world for four days. We have rumors of great fighting at Fredericksburg and severe losses.[2] I suppose we are bound for the same place, as we go now to Stafford Court House. I shall be there within four days. Write me via Washington, 1st Division, 12th Corps. I am very anxious to hear from you. Tell Minnie that I will write her as soon as I get to a camp where I can stay one day. God knows when that will be. . . .

Your Affectionate Father,
A.S.W.

❖

DISCOURAGEMENT OVER FREDERICKSBURG

Camp near Fairfax,
Dec. 19, 1862.

My Dear Daughter:

After floundering four days in such roads as were never seen in the earliest days of the Northwest I am again back in camp with my division at this place. My leading brigade reached the Neabasco River four miles from Dumfries.

I wrote you Sunday P.M. a short note from this place. We left on Monday morning, having taken the precaution to reduce my trains as much as possible. I sent Augustine with the surplus ammunition and shells with all the extra baggage to Aquia Creek via Alexandria. With the rest of our baggage and my division I began the march early Monday morning and after a hard day's work reached Wolf Run Ford over the Occoquan and passed over it with all my division long before dark. I encamped myself about two miles beyond the Occoquan at a cross roads where stands the remnant of an old Baptist church known for years hereabouts as the "Beacon Corner Church." My brigades were all well up and we should have gone farther but for the rear of Geary's division, which I overtook here and which had delayed us the day before.

Before daylight the next morning my troops were in motion, Knipe's brigade leading. About 12 o'clock I received orders to halt until further orders. Knipe had reached the Neabasco at a point near the Potomac. Kane was about two miles behind, and Gordon's brigade (Murphy commanding) was two miles or so behind him. Toward evening I was notified that we were to countermarch the next morning. It had rained the night before and during the morning and the roads—red clay—were indescribable. Our long trains cut them up fearfully and it really seemed impossible to return. I ordered the troops to march before daylight and difficult as was the route the 2nd and 3rd brigades succeeded in reaching this place before night. Knipe's brigade and all our trains crossed the Occoquan and I spent the night in a house on the banks of that creek. The night before I was in a house on the Neabasco. The other nights I passed in tents.

Altogether I have never had so disagreeable and difficult a march. How my trains got over such roads I cannot now guess, but they have all returned safe, though shattered, with the loss of but one mule. I reached this place about 11 o'clock yesterday. Geary's division is returning today. Where we are going to it is difficult to say. I suppose we shall remain hereabouts as a reserve until the movements of the Rebels are known. The disaster at Fredericksburg affects us all deeply. From our standpoint it seems a most unaccountable sacrifice of life with no results. I am glad I was not there. I am as discouraged and blue as one well can be, as I see in these operations much that astonishes and confounds me and much that must discourage our troops and the people. Who is at fault I know not, as I am not in a position to judge. . . .

Your Affectionate Father,
A.S.W.

SKIRMISHING WITH GENERAL STUART

Camp near Fairfax Station, Va.,
Dec. 31, 1862

[My Dear Daughter:]

Christmas has come and gone so gently and with so little of the circumstance of holidays that I was not made aware of its presence. A day or two afterward I was just sitting down to send you a remembrance, which would aid you in remembering others, when I was ordered to march my division towards Wolf Run Shoals as Dumfries had been attacked. So with three days' rations in our haversacks we started to find Stuart, leaving this depot (by orders) almost without a guard at all. At Wolf Run Ford I drew up my three brigades on the hill slopes in a most picturesque spot and occupied with my artillery the fortifications and rifle pits made by the Rebels last year and waited orders from Gen. Slocum, who had gone toward Dumfries with Geary's division to relieve Col. Canby, who was there with three regiments and had been assaulted all the day before by Stuart.

We could hear nothing of Canby's condition as the Rebel cavalry occupied the roads between us in force. Every now and then we could hear Geary's guns shelling the woods in his advance, a favorite mode he has of skirmishing with artillery. About 3 P.M. (Sunday) a runaway cavalryman brought us word that all our cavalry pickets on the Occoquan below to the village had been driven off and that Stuart had crossed with 4,000 men and two guns, making toward Fairfax Station.

Here was a pleasant fix. We had left all our personal luggage, to say nothing of the stores, at the junction unguarded. I at once dispatched a brigade back with four guns and before sundown occupied our camp here and the whole road from this to Wolf Run Ford. I dispatched messengers to Fairfax Court House to have the line of railroad between this place and Alexandria guarded. If this had been done we should have caught Stuart in a trap, as we held the Occoquan River and the whole west line. His only escape was by Burke's Station on the railroad between this and Alexandria.

Stuart came up as far as Mt. Carmel Church within two and one-half miles of my line and then struck off towards Burke's Station, where he cut the telegraph wire and damaged the railroad somewhat and then passed on around Fairfax Court House. I had no cavalry and could not find out his movements till too late. His men were all mounted. The authorities in Washington, where probably are 5,000 cavalry, were asked to send out on the railroad but I cannot hear that the least movement was made. On the contrary, it is reported here that they ordered our troops to defend Alexandria, as it was threatened by a cavalry raid!

I kept my whole division under arms or on the move for nearly forty-eight hours. Thus we let a few thousand cavalry ride through our lines while our cavalry is cut up into small parties of fifty or a hundred scouring around the country to little or no purpose. Although Stuart began to cross the Occoquan over a bad ford at 11 A.M. in the face of a hundred or more of our cavalry, no information was brought me, and then by chance, until nearly 3 P.M. The reason was that our cavalry pickets ran away, each man for himself, and took the most convenient route to a safe place. They did not even resist the crossing at a ford where but two men could pass at the same time. I marched my division back to its old camp day before yesterday, everybody much disgusted at the result. . . .

It is more than fifteen months since we parted at the Central Railroad with a heavy heart, both of us, and with that vast uncertain future overshadowing our souls. How I have longed to see you, my darling daughter, no one but an anxious parent can guess. But we must submit patiently to the allotments of life, trusting that a wise Providence will in His good time reunite us in happiness and health. . . .

Your Affectionate Father,
A.S.W.

◆

HORRORS OF THE MUD MARCH

Stafford Court House,
January 24, 1863.

My Dear Daughter,

Here I am at length at another of those old Virginia Court Houses, which means, generally, nothing but an old tumble down courthouse with a few dilapidated dwellings around it. I reached here through much toil and tribulation, Heaven only knows how, through seas and oceans of mud and over multitudes of angry, swollen streams. We left Fairfax Station camp on the 19th, weather cold and road frozen in the roughest state. My division led. I encamped that night about two miles beyond Wolf Run Shoals, at Beacon Race Church, near the camp of our first march this way. The next day (20th) the road was still rough and the weather cold and threatening snow. We started by daylight and reached Dumfries (fourteen miles) before night, encamping on the south side of the Quantico Creek, one brigade on the north side. I took my headquarters at a house on the south side upon an elevation where Stuart had put his battery during his recent raid. In consequence the house had been greatly mauled by our batteries in Dumfries, receiving no less than nine shots, one of which tore down the chimney. The women and children of the house took to the cellar during the cannonading and were, of course, terribly alarmed, especially so when the chimney fell. We found nobody at the house but women and children, one married woman and her sister, who was very pretty. There was but one room which could have a fire. In consequence, we had not much spare room.

A cold northeast rain began before dark with a very tempest of wind. The few tents our men had were soon flattened. All night the cold rain dashed on the windows and the wind howled. In the morning we had a precious sight. The frost had all gone and mud of the stickiest and nastiest kind had taken its place. The rain was still pouring, but we began our march at 7 o'clock, and such a march! On either side of the road was the densest forest of scrub pines, a perfect thicket. There were no side roads, no turning out, no getting into fields, but right on-ward through the saturated clay man and beast were compelled to travel, every wagon deepening the profound depth and every drop of rain soft-ening the lower depth profound. After an infinitude of floundering, my infantry and artillery reached the Chopawamsic Creek early in the afternoon (five miles). We found it not fordable for ammunition wagons, and news was brought from the rear that the Quantico had risen above fording. So here we were between two rising streams, our supply train cut off, rain still falling, and the heavens indicating a con-tinuation beyond a guess of fair weather.

Our only resource was to bridge the Chopawamsic. So at it went a hundred or two of our men, and at it they worked by details all night. In the meantime, I unloaded what wagons had arrived and sent back for the stalled ammunition train and other be-mudded vehicles. The five miles of miry clay back to the Quantico seemed like fifty, but by 9 or 10 o'clock the following morning all my trains except some ammunition wagons were up, and I began to cross the creek over our rough but stout bridge. We were, however, on our last day's rations, and the supply train, which is managed by the corps quartermaster, could not be heard from. At length, however, before the last of my division crossed it was reported as across the Quantico and coming up. So onward we went, full of hopeful appetites, and reached the Aquia Creek soon after 2 o'clock and found it not fordable! Here was another bridge to build, or wait till morning in hopes of sudden subsidence of the waters. Wait was the word, but preparations for bridging were made.

Fortunately, the water fell and early in the morning we were able to ford the artillery. By noon I began my march towards this place, moving forward my infantry (who were without rations) and leaving trains with small guards. I reached here in time to get one day's rations from Sigel's commissary and so was able to feed my men after 24 hours fasting. Horses and mules were worse off. Dozens died on the way, wagons abandoned, ambulances broken down, contents thrown away. But after all, the wonder is that a single wagon or gun was got through, but today I have got up my ammunition train and all other wagons except the broken-down ones and order begins to reign again. I fear, however, the effects on officers and men. For three days there has not been a dry foot nor dry skin nor shelter scarcely at night, and for one day and night the rain was so pelting and heavy that fires could not be built. Such exposure must produce more deaths and disability than two pitched battles.

We are here now in the mud, striving to get food and forage over such roads as I have described from Brooke Station on the railroad, or [Hope's] Landing five miles away on Aquia Creek. How we shall succeed is yet a problem, as, indeed, is the fact whether there is either to be had at either place. Such is campaigning in Virginia in the winter. If a few of our "Onward" people could try the experiment, I think they would vote backward till spring comes. Tonight it looks like more rain. If it comes, the Lord help us, for I don't exactly see how we can help ourselves. The roads will be literally impassable. In truth, they are so now. One can't go a mile without drowning mules in mud-holes. It is solemnly true that we lost mules in the middle of the road, sinking out of sight in the mud holes. A few bubbles of air, a stirring of the watery mud, indicated the last expiring efforts of many a poor long-ears.

I don't know, of course, how the world's surface looked after the flood in Noah's time, but I am certain it could not have appeared more saturated than does the present surface of this God-forsaken portion of the Old Dominion. Our whole line of march, almost without exception, has been through pine barrens with scarcely a house, certainly not one to a mile, and those [there were] of the most forlorn look with starved-looking occupants. It is neither a decent country to fight in or to fight for. I would [not] accept as a gift the whole of Prince William County, and yet this was once a rich part of Virginia, the great tobacco-raising region, and Dumfries, now the most wretched of worn-out places, was once a great mart importing from Europe largely. There are traces now of splendid old estates, with enormous trunks of cherry and pear trees standing amidst the pine forests all along the road. One can hardly fancy, however, that so desert a region could ever have been fertile or populous. This Stafford Court House is a small group of poor houses and one dilapidated thing called a courthouse.

We are now within eight miles of Falmouth in the most direct line, and may be said to have joined Burnside. We belong to Sigel's grand division. His headquarters are here. Where we shall next go, no one knows. I suppose some grand movement is in contemplation. If we find, as I think probable, that the enemy has fallen back from Fredericksburg we shall have a tedious and exposed forward movement with a long line of supply communication, which the whole army could hardly protect. If we attempt this during the wet months it will be a dead, if not disastrous, failure. Indeed, the efforts already made to campaign in the winter have greatly destroyed the spirits of the men. Other causes have combined, but the exposure and hardships of such a camp life has done the most. In consequence, the desertions from Burnside's troops are very large. I arrested some thirty on the march, who were straggling in the wood. In truth, Rene, I fear it is done with the Army of the Potomac for any vigorous operation. I think the commander has very little confidence in himself and the army generally reciprocates the feeling. This is a critique not for the public. . . .

> Love to all,
>
> Your Affectionate Father,
>
> A.S.W.

❖

VIRGINIA MUD AND SOLDIERLY AFFECTION

Stafford Court House, Jan. 27, 1863.

My Dear Daughter: . . . .

I wrote you as we were about to march from Fairfax Station. Our march on the 19th and 20th was tolerably fair; weather cold and roads exceedingly rough, frozen after having been cut up in the deepest mud. On the evening of the 20th a severe northeast cold storm began with wind and rain, prostrating the few tents we had, putting out camp fires, and exposing the whole command to the pitiless peltings. It was a savage night. In the morning everything looked afloat. The rain still fell heavily, the frost was all out of the ground, and the deepest mud was substituted.

We worked all day to get four miles; such floundering in bottomless holes; such whipping and hallooing and boasting and swearing. Many of our wagons stuck fast inextricably and many mules were drowned in the middle of the road, fairly swallowed up in the mud. It was, in places, really difficult to force a horse through the tenacious stuff. The road on both sides was for the most part hemmed in by dense and impassable pine thickets. Of course man and beast were obliged to flounder along the best way possible. Towards night the head of the column reached a stream called Chopawamsic. We had encamped the night before on the Quantico, opposite Dumfries. The rain had so raised the Chopawamsic that it was not fordable. So we sat down before it in the pine barrens, unloaded what wagons had got up, and sent back to relieve others and began building a bridge.

All night we worked at it and until 10 o'clock the next morning, when it was fit to pass. We got over the angry stream pretty well and worked on all day through similar mud and country to Aquia Creek. Here we found another unfordable stream and again encamped. I sent back wagons again and prepared to bridge, but the rain had stopped and the stream was falling, as they do rapidly in this country, so we waited for morning and found that we could ford. From Aquia to this place (five miles) we were nearly all day in getting through the men and a few wagons. It was not till next day that all my wagons got up and some of the supply corps train is, I believe, still behind. I say, 'all my wagons'; I mean all that were not lost in the mud. We had to abandon several wagons and ambulances broken down or from loss of mules. Such a march! such destruction of property, throwing away of loads, dying mules and horses, the old "Cyropedia" wasn't a circumstance! Black Swamp or the old Chicago Road twenty-five years ago was a pleasant race course [compared] to the quagmires of the Old Dominion.[3]

This part of Virginia, through which we marched, used to be its most fertile and populous portion. It was worn out by tobacco raising and fairly abandoned. All along in the midst of the pine barrens are traces of old estates and of splendid mansions; stumps of old cherry and pear trees; outlines of large gardens and ornamental enclosures. But the houses are now very few and very dilapidated, and what few farms there are are very sterile looking and the people apparently very poor. Northern people in several places began settlements some years ago and a few still remain. They say the land can be reclaimed, but the instances we saw would not warrant much outlay. Dumfries, now the most forlorn of all old towns, was once quite a mart for importation as well as exportation, one of the largest in the South, and in Colonial days second to but few in the country. They pretend to show the house where Patrick Henry made his great war speech before the Revolution. The present appearance of the town would chill the eloquence of Demosthenes!

This Stafford Court House, near which we are encamped, is like most of Virginia's "Court Houses," a place of three old homes, a small, dilapidated court house, and a jail about eight feet square. It is surrounded by the same interminable stunted pine and evergreen thickets, though now pretty well thinned out by Sigel's troops, here before us. There is, amongst other evergreens, a most beautiful one called the holly, the same that I saw in Tennessee two years ago. I wish I could send you a live plant.

We are now only eight miles from the main camp opposite Fredericksburg. There was to have been another crossing, but Burnside's army, after floundering two days in the mud, was obliged to return or starve. They could not draw an empty wagon through the roads after a few trains had passed. . . . We are five miles from the Aquia Creek at Hope's Landing. We have all we can do to draw supplies for man and beast. I would I could have some of the winter "Onward" people one day at work on these roads. They would get some faint idea of Virginia winter roads. . . .

Did I tell you of the handsome gift I received from the officers of my 'Old Third Brigade'? Though it had partly leaked out through Rene months ago, I had quite forgotten it and was quite taken aback the evening before we marched by being invited into the office tent by a committee and finding it lit up and decorated with evergreens and full of officers, some sixty. Col. Knipe, now commanding the brigade, received me with a very flattering speech, opened a box, and took out a most magnificent sword and a belt and sash, which he presented on the part of the officers. I was so taken by surprise, so affected by the manner and mode the testimonial was made, so filled with recollections of the past several months that this gallant brigade has been under my command, of the many changes that death has made, that I fairly broke down and for the second time since I have been in the service, tears flowed freely. You can hardly realize how attached I have become to many of these officers who have been with me through so many trials, privations, and dangers. Of course it makes me very happy to know that they love me, as I know they do, sincerely. The sword is the most gorgeous thing I have seen, costing nearly four hundred dollars. Nobody but the officers of my old brigade was permitted to subscribe. The sword has been sent to New York for some inscriptions and will then be sent to Rene for present safekeeping. It is altogether too fine for the field.

Perhaps almost a more touching compliment was started by this. The enlisted men of the brigade, hearing what the officers had done, got together, I am told, and resolved that they would make me a present and I hear they are busy in getting one up. A testimonial of privates is not a usual thing. I have had hundreds of occasions to know that those of my old brigade have great affection for me. I will give you two instances on the recent march. On the first day's march in rain and mud, I stayed behind to see the rearmost brigade start. Afterwards I went forward. On reaching the front, I found the old brigade just halting after a most fatiguing march. I was myself wet and cross as could be, hardly able to speak a kind word. As I rode down the hill where the men were lying, they all sprang up and gave me three cheers. This, from tired men with wet feet and wet skins, was something.

On the last day's march our rations gave out, as the supply trains were stuck in the mud. In riding by a rear regiment with the brigade commissary the men set up a cry of "Crackers, Crackers." The old brigade was just in advance and a halt was sounded soon afterward. As soon as it halted the men went back in crowds to this new regiment and told these cracker fellows if they ever insulted their general again they'd "lick the Devil out of them." The cry was undoubtedly intended for the commissary, but the men of the old brigade saw me only and thought I was being insulted.

I should hardly dare say these things to anyone but you, but I confess and feel that the love of these men, whom I have taken through snow and rain, [who] have marched thousands of miles for the last year and a half under all circumstances that try the temper and disturb the amiability, is worth a great deal. It is my chief support and encouragement amidst the trials and dispiriting circumstances that surround me. Poor fellows! Their ranks are terribly thinned. At Cedar Mountain nearly one-half of this brigade was killed or wounded, every field officer and every adjutant included. In one regiment every company officer was numbered in the casualties. At Antietam they lost every fourth man. Many of the wounded have come back, some quite disabled, but sticking to their ranks. I met one the other day whose left arm was so disabled at Antietam that he could only carry his musket in his right hand. Still he does not ask for a discharge.

I see another list of major generals and my name not included. Amongst them are several who have seen no service, one a captain on duty in my command six months ago. He has seen little or no service. I have been now nearly a year commanding a division, a major general's command, longer than any officer in the service. How long I shall be able to hold out under this oversloughing is very doubtful. Every such promotion over me, as Carl Schurz and the twenty others in the last list, is an insult.[4] Of course it greatly dispirits and discourages me. I am not so annoyed that I am not promoted, as I am that others are promoted over me, especially as the President has months ago announced in general orders, published to the Army, that no promotions to general officers would be made except for services in the field. And yet he promotes over my head men who have not seen a tenth part of the service I have. So much for grumbling! My officers swear worse than I do on this point and I hear are getting up a petition. Love to all. . . .

Your Affectionate Father,
A.S.W.

❖

DECAYING GRANDEUR OF VIRGINIA

Stafford Court House,
February 16, 1863.

My Dear Jule:[5]

Your kind and welcome letter enclosed in Minnie's last deserves a prompt answer. . . . We are still in the mud in this most God forsaken of all holes that human eye ever rested upon since Noah first looked out of the ark. I doubt if his prospect wasn't more inviting. He could have seen more mud, and if my memory serves, he had a hill or two and some rocks, like Ararat, to look upon. We have a broad waste, slightly rolling, once covered with a thicket of stunted pines, which have pretty much disappeared under the joint operations of Sigel's Teutonics and our own corps.

Houses, there are none in sight. What few decayed and dilapidated ones there were, have found their way into the cabins of the men and the bricks and stones have followed the boards. For example, my headquarters are on the site of what was one of Old Virginia's most stately stone mansions. Not one stone is left upon another, save one chimney which we use for an office fireplace and around which an Aroostook company from one of my Maine regiments have built me a very neat and comfortable log office. One tall brick chimney we tumbled down to accommodate the multitudinous little fires of our quarters. Our location is on the summit of quite a high knoll in the center of my fifteen regiments. There are still on its slopes traces of the garden paths and old adornments, solitary-looking fruit trees and other evidences of decayed wealth and grandeur. Gen. Kane, who has kindred hereabouts and who spent some boyish days in these parts, gives us great stories of its ancient wealth and of the pure blood of its former denizens. In my rides about I occasionally meet an old decayed mansion, with bushes and pine thickets growing up where was evidently once splendid parks and fruit yards. Often venerable old fruit trees are standing in the midst of these pine barrens.

Just over the hills east is what is called Stafford Court House. One old tavern, awfully used, one small courthouse, windowless, one smaller jail, a blacksmith shop for mule shoeing, and one tolerably looking house terraced in front, where "Mit Sigel" has his headquarters and around which barbaric Dutch is uttered with most villainous vehemence and gutturalness.

You probably think living in tents in the winter is a killing thing. But it is vastly more pleasant and comfortable than you in a warm house imagine. You are obliged to stoke the little stove pretty briskly, for the moment the fire stops the cold air slips in. It is something like living out of doors with something to keep the wind off. But I prefer the tent to one of these nasty houses, or one that has been occupied by some of our men. Those little creeping things will stick to the tenants in spite of water and soap.

[*The remainder is missing.*]

❖

BAD WEATHER AND CAMP LIFE

Stafford Court House, Feb. 22, 1863.
My Dear Daughter:
It is a most tempestuous day, snow, cold, and a very high wind. I have never seen at the North a more disagreeable day. I find it hard

work to keep my tent comfortable and am kept very diligent at my little sheet-iron stove. The front of the tent, which is tied together by strings, is not easily kept tight in this gale. It is one of those storms when at home one would not willingly go out of doors. Think of my poor 600 men on picket out in front, and the thousands around so poorly sheltered. To add to our troubles, the wood has been so cut away that it is not easy to get a supply for our large camps. We consume fuel at an enormous rate with these large camp fires.

Today is the anniversary of Washington's birthday. We expected to have a grand division parade and review, with salutes. I hear now the big guns going in all directions (12 M.) but I ordered mine to be omitted on account of the weather. . . .

Yesterday I took a long ride to see a road I have 600 men corduroying toward Falmouth, I don't know for what purpose, unless we are about to corduroy up to the Rebel position. I dined with the Baron Von Steinwehr, a general in Sigel's corps, with whom I spent a couple of hours. He is a remarkably intelligent and agreeable person. I have not seen him since we were at Sulphur Springs last summer, where we passed through that terrific artillery fire. . . .

I rode yesterday my "Yorkshire." I have not been on his back for over a month, preferring to ride "Plug Ugly" over these rough and muddy roads. "Yorkshire" never looked so well as now. He has grown large and muscular since we left Detroit. Considering his thin skin and soft hair he stands exposure wonderfully, though Charley is as careful of him as a mother of a baby. The horse is admired by everybody and pronounced by all as the finest animal in the army.

Have I described to you our location? Our headquarters tents are pitched upon the summit of a pretty high knoll where once stood a large stone house, one of the mansions of the old F.F.V.'s. There is not a stone of it left now, save a chimney around which the Aroostook boys from one of my Maine regiments have built me a nice log cabin, which is used as an office. It is roofed with canvas, but is quite comfortable. When we came here the ground was saturated, I think, to the center of the earth, as I have not been able to get my ground floor dry. Yesterday some of the men got me boards enough to cover half my floor. Our tents are pitched in a square and we have some evergreen bushes outside to break the high winds, not very successfully.

I am almost in the center of my three brigades (fifteen regiments) and can overlook nearly every camp. Of course I get the benefit of all the calls and am awakened every morning by the reveilles on drums or trumpets on every side of me. The ground is so broken into short hills that we have no space for drill grounds, even when the mud partially dries up. These short hills, which two months ago were covered by a heavy growth of yellow or pitch pine, are now stripped and naked in all directions, save the log huts and shanties with the shelter tent roofs of the regiments, which are generally placed on the slopes. We have an old log barn for our private horses. All the rest, horses and mules, are obliged to stand out in this terrible snow storm. . . .

Your Affectionate Father,
A.S.W.

◈

MILITARY OPERATIONS AND OPINIONS

Stafford Court House, Mar. 7, 1863.

My Dear Daughter:

I am stopped on my application for leave, as the enclosed paper shows. Whether I shall succeed hereafter is very doubtful, and depends upon the weather, as we shall undoubtedly move as soon as the earth dries up. Spring is so rapidly advancing that this must come soon. Ergo, I think I shall not get leave. Besides, after the mud and exposure of our winter life there is much to do to prepare for a march. Everything gets out of order. Mules and horses are used up, harnesses destroyed, accouterments injured, guns and muskets need repairs. Everything is at sixes and must be looked to. We have a stupid old ass for chief quartermaster of the corps, through whom all these requisitions must pass and who makes no more headway than a man on a treadmill, always fussy and tramping but never getting ahead.

We are having the preparatory reviews. Day before yesterday I reviewed my division and yesterday Gen. Hooker was to be here to review it, but it rained and the affair is postponed. Today it is foggy and showery. Our duties continue arduous. I have 2,000 men on duty daily on pickets, road building, guards, etc., and the mud is so deep yet that we can hardly fix up. For a season I am obliged to cram my whole division into a space about big enough for a regiment, such is the broken nature of the country, full of deep ravines and rolling hills. . . .

Aunt Rene writes that Letty Larned (Mrs. some other name now) reports in Norwich that she saw letters of mine in Detroit in which I represent myself as greatly disgusted with the war and awfully discouraged. She says she saw them at Uncle Lew's. Now as I write to you all a good many things I don't wish to publish, I hope you will all be careful how you show my letters. I sometimes 'bile up' on first impressions, but it won't do to make the 'bilings' public. From what I hear you are all too excited up North and everybody is in an extreme state on one side or the other. I don't remember writing such doleful accounts, though I have felt irritated enough at times to say most anything in confidence. I suspect Mrs. Letty has exaggerated my opinions. I have never felt otherwise than fighting out this war to the bitter end, or at least to the point of teaching Rebels that there is a power of heavy chastisement amongst the loyal people of the country. Just now I feel like letting slip the dogs of war in any way that will most effectually subdue Jeff. and his myrmidons. Goodbye, and God bless you. Love to all.

Your Affectionate Father,
A.S.W.

❖

DETROIT RIOT AND MILITARY INSPECTIONS

Stafford Court House, Mar. 20th, 1863.
My Dear Daughter:

I have not heard from you for an unusual time but I get now and then a Detroit paper, in one of which I see you have had a great riot, which, however, looks to me from this distance to have been a very small one, and very easily stopped if there had been any efficiency and vigor in civil or military authorities. These mobs are generally composed of nine-tenths spectators, whose presence serves to encourage the rioters and to disperse them by their own flight when vigorously attacked. This Detroit riot was about as absurd an affair as I have read of, only equalled by the weakness and want of action on the part of somebody in power. The provost guard rather inflamed than quelled it.[6]

We are still having bad weather; quite a snow storm today. Our best weather so far has been cold, high winds, with gleams of sunshine. Still, we are preparing for good roads and a movement. Reviews and inspections are frequent. Yesterday Gen. Hooker reviewed my division and pronounced it a "splendid division." The regiments certainly never looked better or did better. The day before I was reviewed by Gen. Slocum, and the day before that I reviewed a brigade. Inspections of regiments go on when it don't rain or snow. There are so many things to look after by the way of supplies before taking the field that everybody must be active, each one above inspecting to see that those below are doing their duty. Among the multitudinous officers of a division of fifteen regiments it is not easy to keep all up to their duties. . . .

I suppose we shall move soon, or as soon as the roads are practicable for artillery. It looks very little like it today, as snow is falling heavily. We have symptoms of alarm almost daily now and as my division is on the right of the Grand Army I am expected to look out that we are not surprised and our flank is protected. It takes a large number of men to do picket and fatigue duty, nearly 2,500 men out at all times. The news today looks not as pleasant as I could wish from Yazoo and Vicksburg and Port Hudson. . . .[7]

Love to all,

Your Affectionate Father,
A.S.W.

❖

COMMENDATION AND PROSPECTS
OF PROMOTION

Stafford Court House,
March 31, 1863.

My Dear Daughter: . . .

I wrote you last that Gen. Slocum was away to attend Gen. Sumner's funeral, and that Best was with him as far as Philadelphia, I supposed.[8] Do not believe all you hear about my modesty in applying for leave. I tried all manner of strings, private and official, and should have succeeded but that Gen. Geary got in an application when I was in command of the corps in the first absence of Gen. Slocum. I did not approve of his leave but was obliged to forward his application, hoping, however, it would die in the pigeon holes of the adjutant general's office. Unfortunately, my application unhoused his, and as he was ahead of me in date he succeeded. Before his return the weather began to look favorable and orders were issued for inspections etc. preparatory for a march. I applied privately to Col. Dickinson, adjutant general on Hooker's staff, who offered to help me, but it was decided that we should probably move before I could get back. In such a case, I did not wish to go. I enclose Williams' last letter, by which you'll see they were courteous if not obliging. I am sorry, for no one can tell how I weary to see Minnie. Indeed, it became a thing which made me very unhappy. However, my whole reputation depends upon my being on hand when the army marches. Did I tell you how highly my division was complimented by Gen. Hooker and staff at the recent review? He pronounced it the best he had seen in the army. The other day I called upon Gen. Meade and others six or eight miles away. He also spoke of the high praises we had received, as did other general officers. Gen. Butterfield, chief of staff, was especially flattering. I am glad I was not away. I should have lost some of the fame of a splendid division. Gen. Meade spoke of having passed you with Cousin[?] Brooks, but did not recognize you till he was by. He wonders I am not promoted, and says the fault must be with Gen. Banks. He owes his own, he thinks, to the recommendation (active) of his commanders. I feel, however, that there is something deeper, a want of army prestige and not having been on the Peninsular [Campaign]. The whole thing is so smothered in army influence that not to have its aid is quite death to one's hopes. Every military bureau in Washington is in the hands of army officers and Gen. Halleck thinks nothing else can be valuable.

However, patience and perseverance. I have a letter from Senator Howard who says he shall continue to urge my promotion. I met Parson Hunter at Gen. Meade's. He is chaplain to some regiment.

Capt. Beman has come back to me, so we are nearly all together again. Capt. Wilkins has tendered his resignation, but I doubt if it will be accepted. He acts foolishly just now, on the eve of a movement.

[*The remainder is missing.*]

1. He led the Army of the Potomac to senseless slaughter at Fredericksburg four weeks later.
2. The battle of Fredericksburg, one of the worst Union defeats of the war, occurred on December 13, 1862. About 10,000 Union soldiers and one-half as many Confederates were killed or wounded in the battle
3. The infamous Black Swamp embraced portions of a dozen present-day Ohio counties at the western end of Lake Erie, occupying the drainage basin of the lower Maumee River. Prior to the construction of improved highways it was impassable for wheeled vehicles during a large part of the year, constituting an effective barrier to travel between southeastern Michigan and the settled portions of Ohio. The Chicago Road was the highway which followed the old Sauk Indian trail from Detroit to Chicago. See "The Black Swamp Road," *Burton Historical Collection Leaflet*, I (September 1922), 45–52, and M. M. Quaife, *Chicago Highways Old and New* (Chicago, 1923), Chap. II.
4. Carl Schurz, like General Sigel, was a participant in the German Revolution of 1848. In America he attained outstanding influence as a German-American spokesman and an enthusiastic advocate of Unionism and Emancipation. Without a background of military experience, on April 15, 1862, he was appointed brigadier general and within a few weeks was given command of a division in General Fremont's army. The feeling of such contemporaries as Williams is wholly understandable. It was Schurz' misfortune, perhaps, that his division was driven in panic flight by Stonewall Jackson at Chancellorsville. Controversy with General Howard, his superior officer, developed both here and at Gettysburg, two months later, in which the majority of authorities tend to exculpate Schurz. See *Dict. Am. Biog.*, sketches of Schurz and Howard.
5. Mrs. Lewis Allen, sister-in-law of General Williams.
6. The anti-Negro riot of March 6, 1863 has been characterized by Silas Farmer as "one of the darkest pages in the history of Detroit." It was precipitated by an alleged outrage by a mulatto named Faulkner upon a little girl. Although Faulkner was promptly tried and sentenced to prison for life, a mob which vainly attempted to lynch him vented its wrath upon the Negro residents generally, many of whom were beaten and their dwellings burned, some eighty-five buildings in all being destroyed.
7. The "news" concerned the efforts of General Grant, wholly unsuccessful as yet, to capture Vicksburg.
8. General Sumner, who had commanded the right grand division at the battle of Fredericksburg, December 13, 1862, died on March 21, 1863.

VI

To
Chancellorsville
and Back

TO CHANCELLORSVILLE AND BACK

The distance from Stafford to Chancellorsville is short, hardly a dozen miles as the crow flies. For an earth-bound army the distance was somewhat greater, of course. Like General Burnside, General Hooker, the new commander of the Army of the Potomac, was unequal to the responsibility of so large a command. Yet he proved to be an excellent leader of smaller military units, and not for nothing had he won his nickname of "Fighting Joe." With the renovated Army of the Potomac, 130,000 strong and, as he declared, the finest army on the planet, he set forth on April 27 in quest of Lee and Richmond. His initial maneuvers proved highly successful and May Day 1863 saw the main portion of the army united on the south side of the Rappahannock River. Chancellorsville was a single house whose place in history is due to its position at the crossing of two main highways. General Hooker made it his headquarters, and around it surged the terrific battle of May 1 to 3. With its progress General Hooker's self-confidence fell ever lower and because of this General Lee won his greatest victory, over an army twice the strength of his own. By May 7 General Williams was back at Stafford Court House, whence he had departed less than two weeks before. About the same time, too, General Lee was meditating a second invasion of the North. On June 3, only a month after Chancellorsville, he set his army in motion toward the Shenandoah Valley.

PREPARATIONS FOR A NEW OFFENSIVE

Stafford Court House, April 14, 1863.

My Dear Daughter:

We have had ten days of such continuous reviews that I have hardly written a letter. The President and Mrs. Lincoln and family and a long string of satellites came down and spent a week or more, reviewing the troops. First, all the cavalry that could be spared from duty—over 12,000—were reviewed together, then the artillery, then four corps (probably 60,000) infantry together, and then the other corps separately. Our corps was the last reviewed, as we are on the extreme right. We had difficulty in finding open ground enough in this broken and pine-barren country to get our two divisions into reviewing positions. As it was, we were obliged to mass each regiment by two-company fronts. But we made a very fine show, as the ground, from its undulating surface, gave a conspicuous and picturesque appearance to the masses moving over the crests and down the slopes.

The President and Gen. Hooker were greatly fagged, as they had been almost every day on horseback for hours and had on that day reviewed one corps (11th) before ours. Mrs. Lincoln and other ladies came over (in spite of bad roads) in ambulances. I doubt if any week in the history of our country has ever witnessed such a large display of fine troops. The army never looked better and but for the small regiments in some corps would certainly impress one with its invincibility. If properly handled I feel that it must carry everything before it.

I met a great many old acquaintances at these reviews; Gen. Meade, Col. Stockton, Gen. John C. Robinson, Col. Morrow and his field and staff officers, who are known in Detroit, besides many others.[1] I have been living for months comparatively near all these persons and yet have not met them before. Indeed, the roads have been so bad that it was quite an impossibility to look up your old friends, even when but a short distance off. It is often strange, too, that in the army you may be almost near neighbors to a friend without knowing it. For instance, I met H. G. Lacey, Gen. Witherell's son-in-law, who told me he was on duty as staff officer in the 11th Corps, which adjoins me on the left.

We have had several fine days and the roads were getting in good order for this country, but today it is pouring again and the mud will be back again. We shall move, I think, in a few days, as preparations have been ordered which indicate that we are to march; I have no idea in what direction, nor has any one beyond Gen. Hooker's confidential staff. The cavalry command is now up the Rappahannock and we hear firing in the direction they have moved. It is a mere reconnoissance, I think, to divert the attention of the enemy while we get ready to strike somewhere else. I shall write you as often as I can. Tell Uncle Lew that I shall write him before we march, probably tonight.

[*The remainder is missing.*]

April 16th, '63.

My Dear Daughter:

The jewel in the sword Maj. Sherman thinks is with the engraver in New York. It was replaced and sent to him. By observing you will see that the jewel can be removed with a small portion of the hilt. The sword made slow progress but it is now in your possession and I hope is safe. I sent you yesterday by Maj. Sherman, a box containing some papers which I wish to keep and a valuable military book with autographs of my officers mainly.

I sent you another lot of photographs. Did you get two I sent of Lt. Dutton and Maj. Blake, 5th Connecticut Volunteers, both killed at Cedar Mountain? I have been much occupied for the past ten days with Gen. Jackson commanding one of my brigades, who had his leg broken by his horse falling with and on him. He was going to his quarters from mine about ten o'clock of a very dark night. It is a very lamentable affair, as he is a superior officer and though with me but a few weeks was greatly liked. I send his photograph with others.

◆

THE ARMY COUNTERMARCHES

Stafford Court House, May 7, 1863.

My Dear Daughter:

You will be startled to see that I am back to the old camping ground. But so it is, and sadly so. After ten days of great hardship, exposure, and privations we are back again with a diminished and dispirited army.

We recrossed the Rappahannock yesterday morning, the whole army moving after midnight over two pontoon bridges. My division was the last to escape, except the rear guard.

I have not time to write you at length. I sent you a long pencil scrawl which I fear you will be troubled to read, as it was written after a week of watching and fasting and fighting and under the nose of Rebel pickets.[2] The mail carrier waits, so I must say goodbye. All my staff are well and safe except Wilkins, who, I think, is again in the hands of the Rebels. I have heard nothing as yet from any of our prisoners. I am by no means cheerful, because I think this last [battle] has been the greatest of all bunglings in this war. I despair of ever accomplishing anything so long as generals are made as they have been.

Love to all,

Your Affectionate Father,
A.S.W.

◈

CHANCELLORSVILLE

Stafford, May 18, 1863.

My Dear Daughter:

I have been reading over today the newspaper accounts of our recent operations south of the Rappahannock. Such pure fictions are not to be found even in this fertile age of romancers. Either they have most deliberately lied for hire, or not one of them saw what he describes and gets his story from some interested narrator. We had a reporter near us for a while, on the march; but as soon as we reached the sound of cannon he departed and was seen no more. We heard of him with our train on the north side of the Rappahannock. Yet his letters have been full and rich; the rehash of tales told by some skulking officer.

I promised you a detailed account of our ten days' campaign, and yet after so many days of fatigue and heat I undertake it with dread and fear that I shall make you a dry story. But as I can give you personal experience and the incidents of my own command, it will probably prove more interesting than these newspaper accounts, which really cannot be understood by those on the ground. I have seen in the illustrated news-papers and in the *Herald* diagrams and drawings of furious onslaughts made by troops which never fired a gun. Sickles' corps, which, as it was near me, I can speak of with confidence of being truthful, did less than any of all under fire, except the 11th Corps, I see carries off all the glory (if there was any) of the contests about Chancellorsville. Berry's division of this corps fought well. The rest of it ran from a position which enfiladed my whole line and cost my division hundreds of men, killed and wounded. But I will not anticipate, but take up the narrative of my ten days south of the Rappahannock seriatim.

April 27th: My division struck tents at daylight, carrying on the person of each man and officer eight days' light rations, which means hard bread, coffee, and sugar, which filled not only haversacks but knapsacks. All our trains were left behind with orders to follow, we knew not where, but wherever the chief quartermaster should order. Our ammunition was packed on seventy-odd mules, two boxes on each. I had had them in training for some weeks, but as they were jacks of the smallest pattern I anticipated nothing but a dead loss of mules and ammunition on the first day. The day was pleasant, but the roads, after we left the open country, were terrible, and my pioneer corps was busily at work cutting new roads all through the pines, which cover the whole face of this ragged and broken country. However, we reached Hartwood Church at 3 P.M. (twelve miles) and encamped, each brigade in the woods, on a pretty little rivulet. The 11th Corps, which took another route, reached the same point about the same time and encamped in advance of us, and about dark the 5th Corps (Meade's) came up and encamped on our left. It was rather a "bivouac," though most of our men carried their shelter tents. I had been informed before marching that our destination was Kelly's Ford, but with the exception of Gen. Slocum I think everybody else was ignorant of our destination.

April 28: We marched at sunrise, following closely the 11th Corps toward Kelly's Ford. I had not moved more than two miles before I ran against the rear (artillery and trains) of the 11th Corps (Howard's) and was obliged to halt for an hour and a half, massing my three brigades in some open fields where the 11th had bivouacked. Starting again, I reached about noon a place called Grove Church, from its situation (isolated) in a pretty grove of evergreens and poplars. Here I was crowding Howard's corps again, and massing my men I ordered them to cook dinners and make coffee, giving them an hour to do it.

I had just begun to move out when down the road came Gen. Hooker and a long staff train and the inevitable lancer escort. He didn't stop, but merely saluted me as he passed, wherein I was more lucky than others, for as he passed Geary's 2nd Division, our corps, he gave him a sound scolding for not being closed up, and when he overtook Gen. Slocum in advance he reversed the complaint, and seemed full of dire anger, swearing heavily at somebody or something [on] which he was not very clear headed. His general complaint, however, was that the 12th Corps had not kept its interval closed and that Meade's corps was delayed, when in truth I had crowded the 11th Corps all day, and in a half hour afterward overtook its rear guard and was obliged to halt for over an hour to have it clear the way.

Knowing of the anger of our commanding general, I despatched a note forward to the effect that my advance was greatly delayed by the artillery and trains and rear guard of the 11th Corps and begging that the road might be cleared. It had begun to rain and the roads were exceedingly slippery, but in spite of all delays and hard traveling I had my three brigades encamped in the woods near the ford by 3 o'clock P.M. (fifteen miles) and everything as comfortable as the misty, drizzling, cold rain would permit. We pitched a tent or two for headquarters and had the honor of *finding* two stray reporters of the *Herald* (Carpenter and Buckingham) and one artist of some illustrated paper (Lumley), which said artist, by the way, drew some very pretty sketches of our crossing the Rappahannock and fording the Rapidan, all of which he lost with his portfolio before reaching Chancellorsville.

After encamping, a general order was published which told with grand confidence the line and results of our further march. We were to cross the Rappahannock on pontoons, two corps ([the] 11th and 12th) taking the route to Germanna Ford on the Rapidan, and one (Meade's 5th) the route to Ely's Ford on the same river. Once at Chancellorsville the whole Rebel people were to submit or be at once overthrown, or words to that effect.

Two considerable rivers were to be crossed and several large and ugly streams in face of the enemy, or where it was believed the enemy's face would present itself. It was not a pleasant prospect, but obstacles always grow less as you approach them with confidence and vigor or with a feeling that you must meet and overcome them. We saw the pontoons going down and in the course of two or three hours it was generally known that the bridge was laid without much opposition and that Gen. Howard had passed over one brigade to protect it. Gen. Hooker was not to cross with us. Ergo, Gen. Slocum, as ranking major general, commanded the three corps until they were united at Chancellorsville, and I, for the sixth time, became commander of the 12th Corps. I was notified that my corps was to have the advance on the morrow, and that we must at all hazard pass the Rapidan.

April 29: I slept soundly, but I was up long before daylight and before it was fairly light my 3rd Brigade (Ruger's), which was to be the advance guard, was moving toward the bridge. As we approached the river the sound of cannon and small arms not far to our right up the river became more and more frequent and distinct. We were, however, all across by 6 o'clock and I hurried to see Gen. Howard to learn what was going on and to find guides to show me the road to Germanna Ford. He seemed in profound ignorance but had sent out a cavalry picket. Presently an officer reported that it was a Rebel cavalry attack with a battery of artillery, and that they were retiring.

As my whole corps (I was corps commander for three days) was massed in columns on the low ground bordering the river, around which rose an amphitheater of hills, the picture was indeed exciting. Across the river long lines of infantry were winding down toward the river and on the south side brigades were breaking masses and filing up the hills. Batteries of artillery and heavy columns of cavalry were forming large solid squares, which, seen from the elevations in advance, looked like great black blocks on the green surface, massed by some unseen power.

Something less than 200 cavalry preceded us as an advance guard, and soon began the crack of carbines with the cavalry pickets of the Rebels. I moved with a long line of skirmishers stretching a mile on either side of the road and then two regiments marching in the fields by the head of companies. Other regiments and brigades followed the road, which we found better than on the north side of the Rappahannock. The country, too, was less broken and hilly, but as usual, greatly wooded and not much cultivated, at least poorly cultivated, though with more farms.

A few miles out we had to ford a small stream swollen by yesterday's rain, wetting the feet of the men, but no obstacle to our march. Just beyond this Lt. Col. McVicar, 6th New York Cavalry, our advance, came hurrying back with a report that the enemy's infantry was massing in the woods in our advance. Columns were halted and infantry closed up, but it proved to be a false alarm. No masses of infantry were found, though the skirmishers in advance kept up a brisk popping of small arms. Our section of artillery, which followed the advance regiments, made no reply nor any challenge.

Poor McVicar! He was a bluff, red-haired Scotchman, somewhat excitable and apt to see mountains in mole hills; but the next afternoon he was shot dead while leading his fellows forward beyond Chancellorsville and thus gave the last best proof of his pluckiness and fidelity to his command. We had begun to laugh at him for seeing so many infantry where none were found, but when told of his gallant death our hearts paid homage to the bluff old trooper, if they did not upbraid us for injustice to his character.

About 2 o'clock we began to approach the hills which overlook the course of the Rapidan. The crack of the rifles increased in volume. Ruger was ordered to deploy his two leading regiments to the right and left and move rapidly down to the river bank. This was done with a rush, picking up some thirty prisoners, who had not time to ford. On the opposite bank a hundred or so of bridge builders and armed guards had posted themselves in the trench of a road which runs from the ford almost parallel with the stream up the bank to the plateau above. In this trench they supposed themselves safe and able to pick off our advance, but to their astonishment they found our deployed skirmishers were able to enfilade their hiding place, and that they were anything but safe. A few attempted to escape by running up the road, but our riflemen brought them down every time, and in a few minutes they hung out a white cloth and the whole batch surrendered, though they had a rapid and rocky ford between them and us. We counted 125 prisoners. Most of them were engaged in rebuilding a heavy and high bridge upon stone piers. The old bridge was burned a year or more ago. In the mill nearby we found a large quantity of new tools (English) and a pretty good supply of provisions and forage for a cavalry guard which had been there.

The Rapidan at this point is not very broad, but its banks are high and the ford deep, rocky, and rapid. I dashed in with some of the foremost cavalry to cross and tumbling over a rock came near being submerged in the angry flood. In the meantime the infantry came up and finding the shallowest track went in with a scream and a yell, holding one another's hands and wading to their armpits with cartridge boxes slung on their bayonets. Now and then one would tumble over in the rapid stream, but in all cases their companions fished them out and my division all passed without loss, except some wet ammunition.

The scene was a very spirited one and Lumley made a pretty sketch of it, which unfortunately was lost afterward. A foot bridge was afterward made on the feet of the piers, over which the 2nd Division and 11th Corps passed after dark and across which we backed our ammunition. It was after midnight before all was over and one of our headquarters wagons was found at daylight fast between two rocks in the middle of the river, with the rapid current flowing freely through the box. We got it out, however, without serious loss.

The rain began to fall before night, but as we were all pretty wet and my boots full of water, it mattered little and the men were as cheerful as in gayest sunshine. We had crossed the two rivers and were on equal terms. I posted my division in a strong position through the woods, across the peninsula formed by a sharp bend of the river at this point, but it was long after dark before I could leave my saddle, quite tired enough for a sound sleep on the bare ground with two blankets. We got up a tent, however, and were comparatively comfortable, even in wet feet, wet clothes, wet blankets, and on the wet ground. How much our comforts depend upon surrounding circumstances. I slept soundly till broad daylight, probably never with more real enjoyment of "nature's sweet restorer."

April 30th: "The morning lowered and heavily in clouds brought on the day." It was a dismal, drizzling morning, but at 8 o'clock I was ordered to start the advance toward Chancellorsville and feel carefully the way. Nothing definite had been heard from Meade's corps, which was to cross at Ely's Ford below and coöperate with us. We had heard the evening before of his arrival at the ford. Geary's 2nd Division led, followed by the 1st Division and then by the 11th Corps. We met with no opposition of consequence until near Old Wilderness Church. The road was an old, worn-out plank road, full of holes and gullies and very slippery from the rain, the mud on what planks were left being a foot or so deep. It was a very hard march, as on previous days, but the men bore up splendidly and there was absolutely no straggling.

Near Old Wilderness (which, by the way, is no wilderness but the best-cultivated part of Virginia I have seen outside of the valley), the enemy opened with artillery on our right. As I was in advance, I detached a regiment of infantry, which deployed as skirmishers and got up a very brisk engagement, in which we lost a few men and the Rebels more. A second regiment succeeded in brushing away both skirmishers and artillery and we were not further molested during the day. While this was going on I stopped at what had been a country store near Old Wilderness, on a strong elevation, where I could watch and supervise the skirmish on the right. The people had abandoned their store in some haste, but left little behind except quack medicines. We found, however, some curious letters to soldiers, one of which, from a clerk of Gen. Stuart, I have since seen published in the *Tribune*. The Rebels tried one shell on the house and made a very good shot.

We reached the vicinity of Chancellorsville about 3 o'clock and found that Gen. Meade had also arrived behind the place on the Ely Ford Road. Chancellorsville is (or was) simply a Virginia "ville" of one large brick house on the northwest corner of [two] cross roads, built by one Chancellor. You will see on most of the maps its situation, seven or eight miles west of Fredericksburg and on the plank-road route to Orange Court House and Culpeper. It is in close proximity to two good fords (in dry season; now ten feet deep) over the Rappahannock, the U.S. Ford six miles and Banks' Ford four miles off. They are of no advantage as fords at this season, except the advantage of roads leading to them. I will send you a sketch of the roads and our positions during the operations around this place as soon as it can be copied.

We commenced taking up position as soon as we arrived. Our left was directly in front of the Chancellorsville house in some rifle pits made by the Rebels, running in a circular shape through a belt of woods and crossing a deep ravine near a place called Fairview; ran through the woods beyond and struck the plank road, on which we had been marching, a mile and a half west of Chancellorsville. Geary's division occupied the left and my division the right of this line and the general direction of our front was southeast. Meade's corps was to continue the line eastward and the 11th Corps (Howard's) was to connect with us on the west and continue the line down Hunting River to the [blank in MS.]. Banks' Ford was still in possession of the Rebels, while we held and covered with our line the U.S. Ford. It was intended to cover Banks' Ford, too, and our trains and reserve artillery had been ordered there, but somehow the Rebs. got the start of us and seemed determined to hold possession. So our trains and artillery went to the U.S. Ford.

It was a pleasant, moonlight night. Chancellorsville house became the center of hundreds of officers (generals and staff). It was a gay and cheerful scene. We had successfully accomplished what we all supposed would be the great work of the campaign. Everybody prophesied a great success, an overwhelming victory. Everybody was full of enthusiastic congratulations. Gen. Hooker came over during the evening and issued a flaming order complimenting the splendid operations of the 5th, 11th and 12th corps. We began to think we had done something heroic, we didn't exactly see what, except we had put three of the smallest corps on the flank of the Rebel stronghold. But it was rumored that others were coming to help us, and that others had crossed and driven the enemy from his entrenchments at Fredericksburg. All was *couleur de rose!* How many joyous hearts and bright cheerful faces beat and smiled happily for the last time on that delightful moonlight night at Chancellorsville!

I went back to my division (my corps command was gone on the return of Gen. Hooker), pitched my tent near the old log house on Fairview, and went to sleep to the music of the rifle crack of the pickets and the sound of the axes and falling trees of men at work making barricades in the adjacent woods.

Friday, May 1st: The morning was foggy but soon cleared up before a strong sun. I went early to Chancellorsville house, where the headquarters of the army and several corps commanders were concentrated. Hundreds of horses held by orderlies filled the broad space in front, and the piazza and rooms were filled with general staff officers.

185

Everybody supposed it was the beginning of a day big with the fate of the nation. Meade, Sickles, Couch, Howard, [besides] corps commanders and dozens of division commanders were floating around talking anxiously but still confidently. It was known that Hooker had boastingly declared the night before that "God Almighty could not prevent his destroying the Rebel army." The blasphemy did not please the most irreligious as appropriate to any, and least of all to an, occasion so momentous, but allowance was made for excitement. Still, there was an uneasiness in the best military minds. There was too much boasting and too little planning; swagger without preparation.

At length I was ordered to move my division up toward the Chancellorsville house and to move out on the left-hand side of the main road towards Fredericksburg. I never saw my troops in better condition, never more anxious to meet the enemy. The poor fellows, marching on an average of fifteen miles a day over hard, muddy roads and carrying sixty pounds on their backs for four days, were not only not weary or disheartened, but they seemed panting to meet the Rebels. They had marched without stragglers and they went out to battle without skulkers. Such, I believe, was the condition of almost every corps of the army. Surely we had promise of success.

We marched out some two miles, my division on the left of the road, Geary's on the right. I had two brigades, Knipe's and Ruger's, deployed and Jackson's (Ross commanding) in reserve, moving through the densest kind of pine thickets and underbrush. The Rebels were throwing shells at us and their pickets popping away at our skirmishers, but on we went and finally came to an open field, across which Knipe rushed his brigade and seized a belt of wood beyond. Here the engagement on my right became brisk and I had halted Knipe to connect my line on the left and put the reserve in position. The Rebel earth-works were just ahead, and their forces were being marshalled to resist us. We had lost but few men, for luckily their shell and shot had gone over us, following generally the line of the pike. Ten of my regiments lay close behind the woods and the men were eager and cheerful to joking, when up came an order to countermarch and go back to my original position.

Everybody asked why, and the best accepted reply was that Meade, who had been pounding hard on our left, had driven the enemy from

Banks' Ford and the object of our advance was fully accomplished. Still the men went back disappointed, not without grumbling, and it really required some policy to satisfy them that there was not mismanagement somewhere. Back we went three miles or more to our old camp, and began again to cut logs and construct our barricades, but in trying to replace our picket line to the front, we had some severe conflicts and lost two field officers and several men. And the Rebels had brought up on an elevation to our left and front, which opened on our headquarters plateau, a few pieces of artillery and began shelling my position strongly.

They were soon silenced by my artillery, and my picket line cleared them out in front but not before they had planted several shells through my Fairview log hut and one through one flue of the chimney, the shell dropping down into the fireplace unexploded. As good luck would have it, there was no fire and the next morning the cooks built fires outside. Accidentally one of the staff officers, in a spirit of curiosity, discovered the unexploded shell in the ashes of the fireplace. If the cooks had, as they had done the morning before, used the fireplace for cooking, we should have had an explosoin which would probably have spoiled our breakfast and lessened the number of headquarters cooks materially. Such are the slight accidents that make or mar small as well as great matters.

The night passed as before with an almost constant popping of picket riflemen, but our tents were still up in front of the log cabin. I sat quite late enjoying the brilliant moonlight. A long line of artillery was in battery just in front, on the brow of the hill which overlooked the ravine and the woods beyond, in which lay two of my brigades. The whippoorwills, which are thicker here than katydids up north, were whistling out their "whip-poor-wills" as if there was nothing but peace on earth, and save the occasional crack of the rifle away off on the left there was a solemn stillness which was almost oppressive. Two immense hostile armies, over two hundred thousand armed men, lay within almost the sound of one's voice, and now and then away off in front I could fancy the sound of wheels and the tramp of men. It proved afterward to have been no fancy, for Jackson was then moving his artillery and infantry by a crossroad around our front towards the right and rear of the 11th Corps, which on the following day developed itself in a most disastrous discomfiture of our Dutch friends, "what fight mit Sigel," or did until Gen. Howard was made a major general and sent to teach these fellows how to fight after Sigel quit for want of more men.

Saturday, May 2nd: The morning was of the densest fog. We breakfasted, as on every morning during the operations, before daylight and as a battle seemed inevitable, we ordered our few tents struck and everything packed for a movement to clear the front. By sunrise I was out along my lines. The whole front was covered by a very good breastwork of logs. The map which I shall send you will show its direction. I also rode up the "dirt road" which runs south from a short distance in advance of my line on the plank road. Here I found Birney's division lying along the road with a battery or two of artillery, Birney himself stretched on the grass under an evergreen shade.

All night the noise of the enemy moving along our front was distinctly heard, and it was reported that his columns could be distinctly seen a short distance in advance. The rumor was that at Gen. Hooker's headquarters it was believed the enemy were retreating toward Orange Court House and quite a number of prisoners brought up the road was taken as evidence of the fact of haste and confusion amongst them. I went back to an unfinished church on the plank road, where Knipe had his headquarters, and as no orders came I took a long nap. I found Gen. Slocum there with his staff, and what with his and mine and Knipe's we formed a large group of officers and orderlies, all of us pretty much engaged in sleeping.

I was a disbeliever in the retreat, and finally made Knipe send out two or three well-known scouts of his command. They returned after an hour or so and reported that they had gone beyond the 11th Corps and by climbing into a tall tree had seen the columns of the Rebels passing across the Orange Court House road and massing to the right of the 11th Corps, the front of which, by the way, was nearly due west. I was then entirely satisfied that we were to be attacked from that point, and so reported to Gen. Slocum, who, I believe, reported the facts to Gen. Hooker.

Soon after, I saw Whipple's division moving down to the road on which Birney was found, but I fell asleep again in the shade of the church on a plank which I had given an easy inclination to on a sill of the building. My posture and an unlighted cigar in my mouth at-

OVERLEAF:

General Williams' Map
of the Battle of Chancellorsville

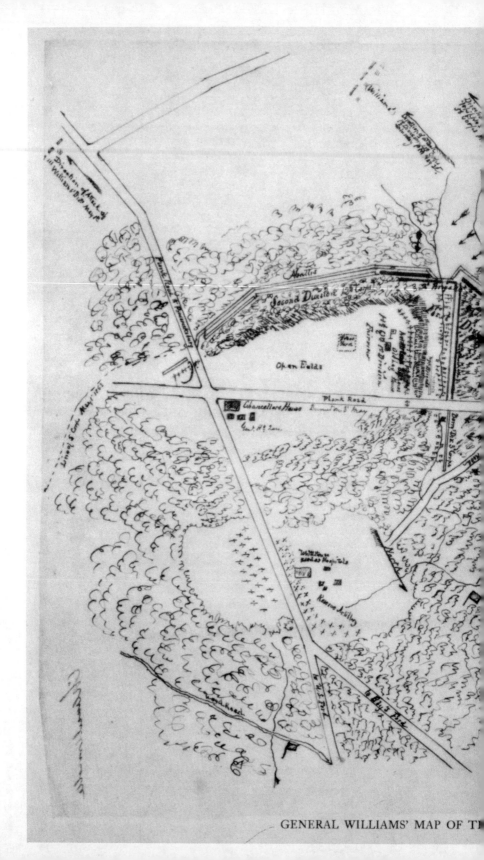

GENERAL WILLIAMS' MAP OF TH

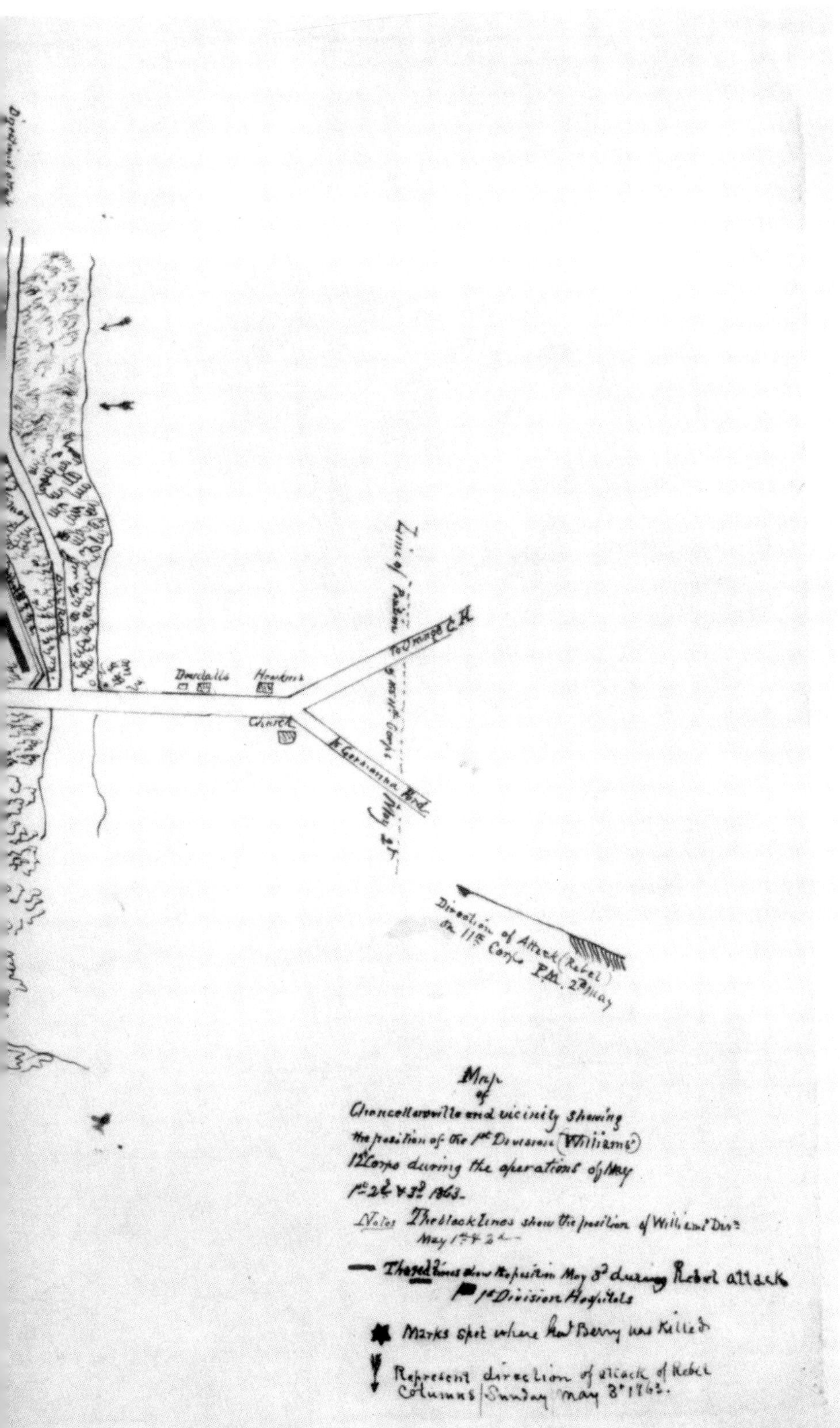

LE OF CHANCELLORSVILLE

PHOTO: JOSEPH KLIMA, JR.

tracted the notice of a passing artist, who took a sketch of me as I slept and presented it to me on waking up. I enclose it that you may see me as reposing on the spot around which twenty-four hours afterwards lay thousands of dead and dying, Federals and Rebels, and as an interesting memento, as well as a striking evidence of how easily and carelessly the heart beats on the very eve of scenes of battle and carnage. Jokes were played; the laugh and the jest were as common as if we had been a party of picnickers instead of armed men awaiting the onslaught of thousands in deadly conflict.

Now and then those not asleep would speculate on the probable movements of the day or guess the cause of the rattling of musketry or the booming of cannon not far off. And so with sleep and talk the day wore through until after 1 o'clock P.M., when I was roused up and told to get my command under arms. I dispatched the orders and went off through the thick underbrush to see that my brigades were ready to move. Presently came another order to move out towards my left and front, go two or three miles down through the woods and strike the Fredericksburg plank road as far as possible from Chancellorsville, and then sweep both sides of the plank road towards the Chancellorsville house.

The intention was to strike the Rebel breastworks and entrenchments on this road in flank and rear and thus place them between two fires as I drove them towards Geary's barricades. The old story of a flying enemy was repeated to me, and I was to help "gobble" the Rebel rout. Geary had been sent out early in the day directly on the road, but he had found a force too large for him and was compelled to get back to his entrenchments. All these things did not prove to me a flying enemy. In moving out to my position in the open field at a point where I designed to enter the thick woods, mostly of stunted pines, I came in contact with Whipple's division.

You will remember Gen. Whipple as Capt. Whipple of the Topographical Engineers at Detroit, living for a while in Mrs. Campau's house on Woodward Avenue.[3] Finding I was to form on his left, he came to arrange with me the order of formation. My brigades were already deployed with two regiments front in line and the rest in reserve for each brigade. Poor Whipple was red with heat and excitement, and I fancied then, and have recalled my fancy often since, that he felt the shadow of the Dark Angel's wing over him. I am by no means superstitious, as you know, but it seemed to me that I could read in his face—misfortune! He was killed, you know, not that day but the next, and I never saw him again. From what I hear, his death was strangely accidental, or, more properly, unaccountable, occurring after the main action was all over and apparently by a stray musket shot.

To return to my attack: The underbrush was densely thick, almost impenetrable to man, and I had the greatest difficulty in finding a place to crowd my horse through. The skirmishers were soon engaged in front, showing that the Rebels were well posted on our movement. We had proceeded forward perhaps two miles from our camp; Knipe's brigade on the right was sharply engaged, and we were driving the enemy before us. I was in the act of getting Jackson's (3rd) brigade (Col. Ross, commanding) into shape, as it had fallen into some confusion, to push to the support of Knipe, when an order was brought me to return at once and reoccupy my old line.

I had for some time heard rapid firing in the direction of the 11th Corps, which in the direction we were attacking was almost directly in my rear, but until this order came it never once occurred to me that any disaster of a serious nature could have taken place. I had left the knapsacks of most of the regiments in our breastworks, as the day was hot and our probable duty severe. My apprehensions were now greatly aroused, though I had no definite information of what had taken place. With the one or two staff officers who had not been sent away on duty I hastened back to see what was occurring.

As I cleared the underbrush where the open space lies in front of Fairview and behind the woods where were my entrenchments, I saw the immense mass of fugitives and heard the yells of the pursuing Rebels. After some difficulty in getting over my own barricade, which lay between that point and the open ground, I rode rapidly to the right near the plank road, where some officers of the general staff had arrested a group of a few hundred men and were trying to get them into order. Lt. Col. Dickinson of Hooker's staff was riding fiercely about, pistol in hand, and occasionally discharging it at some flying Dutchman. Swords were out and flashing in the setting sun. Such a mixture of Dutch and English and oaths! Such a rolling in and out of frightened men (the first really frightened mass of men I ever saw)! Such a swinging of arms on the part of officers, who evidently were quite as much stampeded as the men!

I saw at once that all effort to organize such a body of men was fruitless. They were like a flock of scared sheep driven into a corner; not one thought of defense. In the meantime, the pursuing Rebels were rapidly advancing. The crack of the musket was close at hand. Fortunately my two leading brigades, as soon as they cleared the underbrush, saw the disaster and came down at a double-quick. I rode back to meet them, and leading them by flank along the inner edge of the woods at right angles to the line of the Rebel advance, they faced by the left flank and thus presented the front of a line of battle of two brigades directly towards the Rebels.

Without a halt, and with a cheer that made the woods and the open space ring, the whole line rushed into the woods. The Rebel advance was checked at once and fell back within fifteen minutes, almost without resistance. This is the true story of the first checking of Jackson's pursuit of the 11th Corps. The New York papers are giving immense glory to Sickles for this very act. But he was at least two miles away and did not get back to the vicinity of this affair till some time after dark.

I sent at once by Lt. Pittman to report to Gen. Hooker (Gen. Slocum not being at hand) that my right (north side of the plank road) was uncovered and that I should be flanked and driven out if not supported there at once. It was at this time that Gen. Berry was sent with his division to occupy the woods on the right in prolongation of my line. Gen. Berry was at Gen. Hooker's when Pittman reached there, and it was at least an hour and a half before he got into position on my right, and yet newspaper reports I see have given that division the credit of driving back, first of all, Stonewall Jackson's advance. What I have written to you is capable of proof in any court, except the court of reporters, but history will probably give the absent Sickles and the gallant 3rd Corps whatever of reputation belongs to that body of our troops; [4] and it was the 1st Division, 12th Corps, which stopped an exulting enemy pursuing a disorganized and broken corps and which had reached within half a mile or less of the headquarters of the commander of the army! So much for the truth of contemporaneous history at least!

Thus far all had gone well with my division, but unfortunately an

order was now sent me to push into the woods and reoccupy my log
entrenchments, which you will see by the map ran diagonally to the front
and towards the line of Rebel advance. They were built with reference
to an attack from the direction of Fredericksburg, which direction the
Rebels had not seen fit to follow. I protested against the movement as
useless and very risky. It was now quite dark, especially in the woods,
dense with underbrush. There was quite a slough hole in the center of
the road which would break my line of advance and separate my regiments. The enemy might conceal himself at any point on my right flank
and thus take me in reverse. The order, I understood, was from Gen.
Hooker, and there was no help. It must be tried. So, cautioning Knipe
to push his skirmishers well out, and look to his right flank, he was
ordered to move through the woods.

What I feared happened. No one could tell friend from foe nor see
a hidden enemy a rod away. In consequence, the right regiment (128th
Pennsylvania, Col. Mathews) got fairly enveloped and lost its colonel
and lieutenant colonel (Smith) and nearly 200 men killed, wounded,
and prisoners. The 5th Connecticut lost its colonel—Packer—prisoner,
and a good many men. Maj. Strous commanding the 46th Pennsylvania
(Knipe's old regiment) was mortally wounded. It was a conflict of great
confusion and came near losing me all of Knipe's brigade. We had
already lost Lt. Col. Cook, 28th New York, who was left as a guard
in the barricades with four companies of his regiment. He had arrested
nearly 2,000 fugitives of the 11th Corps and got them behind breastworks, but they fled at the first sight of the Rebels' approach and breaking through Cook's small guard left him to combat as best he could
the exultant enemy.

Cook obstinately held on and lost nearly half his command. All these
misfortunes had lost Knipe every field officer but one of his brigade and
left him but three broken regiments. Of course, we withdrew as best we
could to the north and south line of the woods in front of Fairview,
where we had first entered. The Rebels attempted to follow, but we
punished them severely. Best, whose batteries were on the Fairview
Ridge, opened with his artillery, shelling the woods with appalling vigor,
and our whole infantry line hailed upon them with a simultaneous
storm of bullets. The Rebels fell back, and in fifteen minutes there was
a silence that was almost painful, after the roar of the short combat.

It was in this advance of Knipe to recover our old position that Wilkins was made prisoner. He had gone with me to the right to help stop the fugitive Dutchmen, as I have mentioned, and when I returned to meet my brigades I remember him swinging his sword vigorously, especially at the time the cheer was given when my troops entered the woods. He writes me that I ordered him to follow Knipe's brigade and directed him to look towards his right flank and that he was dodging through the underbrush when he was surrounded by those he supposed were his friends and ordered to dismount. He writes me a piteous story of his forced march from Richmond to the gun boat and says his feet are blistered and his leg rheumatic. He is still, I believe, in Washington on parole and expects to be exchanged within thirty days.

To come back from this digression: Our new line being taken up (as shown by the red line on the map) the men were set to work making log breastworks. We knew there was hard work ahead. Our pack-team of ammunition was sent for and every man fully supplied. I went down to where my line crossed the plank road and had an interview with Gen. Berry, arranging the connection of our two divisions. I met him almost exactly on the spot where he fell the next morning. I had never seen him before, and it was too dark then to see him, but I had another interview with him early the next morning. He was a tall, heavy, coarse-looking man, but I believe a good officer and faithful to his duty. The result of my first interview was that I replaced two of his regiments on the south side of mine by two of mine, taken from my extreme left, where the line connected with Geary's division. He was anxious I should take up my headquarters with him that we might act in concert, and I should probably have done so but for after events which kept me till late in the night busy elsewhere.

Somewhere about 10 o'clock a staff officer came from Sickles' headquarters with information that he had reached the open hill seen to the left and front, about 400 yards across the ravine before Fairview, with Whipple's and Birney's divisions and that he should attack the enemy's right flank during the night with at least one brigade. Gen. Slocum was still absent at general headquarters, but the danger of such an attack, which would bring his troops directly in front of my line of infantry and artillery, was so palpable, and a great mishap and miscarriage so inevitable that I requested this officer to ask that the matter be deferred until the return of Gen. Slocum, who would probably arrange with Gen. Sickles so as to avoid doing injury to ourselves. Luckily, I dispatched messengers to my infantry line that such an attack might take place, and cautioned commanders to withhold their fire.

It was lucky, indeed, for scarcely could the staff officer have got back to his general before the tumult began. There was a faint, misty moon, just enough of its light to make darkness visible. A tremendous roll of infantry fire, mingled with yellings and shoutings almost diabolical and infernal, opened the conflict on the side of Sickles' division. For some time my infantry and artillery kept silent and in the intervals of the musketry I could distinctly hear the oaths and imprecations of the Rebel officers, evidently having hard work to keep their men from stampeding. In the meantime, Sickles' artillery opened, firing over the heads of the infantry, and the din of arms and inhuman yellings and cursings redoubled. All at once Berry's division across the pike on our right opened in heavy volleys and Knipe's next to the pike on the south followed suit. Best began to thunder with his thirty-odd pieces. In front and on the flank shell and shot and bullets were poured into these woods, which were evidently crowded with Rebel masses, preparing for the morning's attack.[5]

It was at this time, as we subsequently learned, that Stonewall Jackson received his mortal wound, and prisoners taken subsequently say that if we had continued the storm of fire a few moments longer the whole of Jackson's corps would have been stampeded. I can conceive of no spectacle more magnificently and indeed awfully grand and sublime than this night attack. Along our front and on Sickles' flank probably 15,000 or more muskets were belching an almost incessant stream of flame, while from the elevations just in the rear of each line, from forty to fifty pieces of artillery kept up an uninterrupted roar, re-echoing from the woods with redoubled echo from the bursting shells, which seemed to fill every part of them with fire and fury. Human language can give no idea of such a scene; such an infernal and yet sublime combination of sound and flame and smoke, and dreadful yells of rage, of pain, of triumph, or of defiance.

Suddenly, almost on the instant, the tumult is hushed; hardly a voice can be heard. One would almost suppose that the combatants were holding their breath to listen for one another's movements. But the contest was not renewed. It was after midnight and the air had become unpleasantly cold. I went back to my log shanty at Fairview. It was full of wounded, and around the fires were fellows boiling coffee in their large camp kettles. One poor fellow was moaning piteously that "he was so cold." His were probably death chills, but I directed some warm stones to be put to his feet. After awhile I got myself warm by an out-door fire, behind the shanty. The night wore away rapidly as I dozed or half slept by this camp fire, roused every now and then by the rattle of picket firing. It had been a strange day of sleep and excitement of the highest character, winding up with a pyrotechnic display which furnished certainly a magnificent finale, and but for

"The shout and groan and saber stroke
And death shot falling thick and fast
Like lightning from the mountain cloud"

it would have been one of immense admiration and beauty.

Sunday, May 3rd: We breakfasted before dawn, as we anticipated at the earliest daylight we should have a very poor chance for meal-taking. We were not disappointed. Our appetites were not bad, considering the time and circumstances, and probably we were not without forebodings that it would be some time before we got the next regular meal.

The Rebels opened with infantry alone, pushing their heavy columns at the same time against my front and upon the two divisions of Sickles in the open fields to my left front (as marked on the map) and against Berry's division in prolongation of my right, across the plank road. I think the heaviest attack was against me, but as I was nearer and could see my own position best, and *hear* there the most, I may be mistaken. At any rate, the fire of musketry was incessant for quite four hours, al-most without cessation or intermission. But in all that time they were never able to reach my front line. Three times they were driven back and their masses (in column) thrown into great confusion, but almost immediately replaced with fresh troops. Our batteries on the ridge a few hundred yards behind my line opened through the entire line of thirty-four pieces, I believe, and for a while Sickles kept up the fire with great animation. Soon, however, his division began to give way and some of his troops came back diagonally through our lines in great confusion. The Rebels captured one or more of his batteries and turned them upon our artillery and infantry at short range, besides bringing up several batteries of their own, which were placed in this commanding position.

It was a great misfortune to us, the loss of that position; as great, I think, as the discomfiture of the 11th Corps. They were able to enfilade our lines and place their infantry masses on our left flank. It was about half-past 2, I think, that they got full possession of this hill. The din of war was never more violent than for the next two hours. My division could do nothing but hold its own, and this it did splendidly. I had withdrawn two regiments from my left between the angle of my breastworks and Geary's division, both to strengthen my right center and because I supposed Sickles' division would hold the hill and hence prevent any infantry attack upon that point. But when they abandoned that position the Rebels followed down over the ravine in heavy masses and pitched in a run upon the line east of the angle. Only two regiments (20th Connecticut and 145th New York) were at hand to resist, but they drove them back in confusion, aided somewhat by a left oblique fire of Ruger's regiments, which held the angle. The strangest part was that the 145th Regiment had attempted to run and had actually marched away from its post without orders. I, fortunately, saw the movement and checked it in time to replace the regiment in its position before injury was done. It fought valiantly afterwards. The same thing happened to a New Jersey regiment, moving back without orders. I halted it and merely said they were disgracing the state of "Jersey blues." The regiment at once marched back and fought nobly.

No man can give any idea of a battle by description nor by painting. If you can stretch your imagination so far as to hear, in fancy, the crashing roll of 30,000 muskets mingled with the thunder of over a hundred pieces of artillery; the sharp bursting of shells and the peculiar whizzing sound of its dismembered pieces, traveling with a shriek in all directions; the crash and thug of round shot through trees and buildings and into the earth or through columns of human bodies; the "phiz" of the Minie ball; the uproar of thousands of human voices in cheers, yells, and imprecations; and see the smoke from all the engines of war's inventions hanging sometimes like a heavy cloud and sometimes falling down like a curtain between the combatants; see the hundreds of wounded limping away or borne to the rear on litters; riderless horses rushing wildly about; now and then the blowing up of a caisson and human frames thrown lifeless into the air; the rush of columns to the front; the scattered fugitives of broken regiments and skulkers making for the rear. If you can hear and see all this in a vivid fancy, you may have some faint idea of a battle in which thousands are fiercely engaged for victory. But you must stand in the midst and feel the elevation which few can fail to feel, even amidst its horrors, before you have the faintest notion of a scene so terrible and yet so grand.

My personal experiences, for which you will probably care more than for generalities were these: As soon as the battle opened I rode to the right to consult with Gen. Berry, for the maintenance of his line was my safety. Poor man! He was probably dead within fifteen minutes after I left him, killed by a rifle ball, and thus it happened that two general officers who had supported me on the right on two successive days were both victims of this battle. Leaving Gen. Berry, I rode down my line, giving such instructions as seemed necessary to my brigades. My line was well sheltered behind logs and a slight depression of the ground behind the woods. This artificial and natural protection saved me hundreds of lives.

I then took position on a knoll which overlooked my whole division from the left of the battery. Of course I remained stationary nowhere, as the changing tide of affairs kept me moving from right to left to see that all was firm and safe. In one of these movements I had a most extraordinary escape. I was passing from the left to the right when I saw one of Berry's regiments giving way, which I was afraid would expose my whole line to a flank movement of the enemy. I was passing through a low, muddy spot, when a shell struck in the mud directly under my horse and exploded, throwing up the mud like a volcano. I felt as if I was lifted ten feet in the air, and supposed, of course, my horse (old Plug Ugly) was clean gone in all his under-works. I dismounted in haste and found he was bleeding pretty freely, but strange to say not seriously wounded, and only in three or four places. It was probably a percussion shell which buried itself below the mud so deep till it reached the hard earth, that the superincumbent pressure gave a low direction to the pieces, and thus saved both horse and myself.

During this terrific contest I saw two or three small regiments coming up behind our batteries and in an exposed position. I rode to them to advise a better shelter, when I encountered two Michigan regiments, the 3rd, Col. Pierce of Grand Rapids, who was wounded by a musket ball as I talked with him, and the 5th, Lt. Col. Sherlock, formerly of the theater proprietorship, who came out from behind his regiment to shake hands with me. He was killed a few moments afterwards by a piece of shell. Indeed, it seemed a wonder that anything could live on that slope and hill-brow in front of Fairview. Shot and shell and musketry swept it from end to end and side to side, and the columns of destructive missiles seemed to increase every moment.

At length, after four hours or so of this incessant strife and turmoil, it was reported to me that every regiment was nearly out of ammunition. I sent a staff officer to Gen. Hooker or to Gen. Slocum, who was at general headquarters, with the report and that I should soon be flanked on both sides unless fresh troops came to my support and to replace my exhausted regiments, half of whom had been without food for nearly twenty-four hours. Hooker replied that I must furnish my own ammunition, which, of course, was not possible through that volcano of flame and roar with a mule pack-train. At length I saw Sickles not far in the rear, and as he had, or ought to have had, two divisions which had been but little engaged, I went to him and was told that he had just sent forward his troops to replace mine.

I hurried to the front to order my regiments to withdraw as soon as other troops came up, but the relieving troops never reached my line. The right (Berry's division) was giving way. The artillery was already nearly gone with empty chests. The Rebels had already occupied the woods far in front of my line on my left flank. There was no time for delay if I would save anything of my command. Oh! but for *one* of the four corps which lay behind me unengaged. But I do not intend to express opinions. I am giving facts. The getting away was worse than the staying. Our line of retreat was over the ravine, up an exposed slope, and then for three-quarters of a mile over an open plain swept by artillery and infantry of the Rebels as they pressed forward. There was no shelter on our side of the Chancellorsville House, and no reinforcements appeared to stay the pursuers. But we had punished them severely and the infantry pursuit was feeble, but the artillery thundered its best—or worst—upon us, and the mud of the slough holes over this plain was thrown up in huge columns on all sides from exploding shells and round shot falling in our midst. Many a poor fellow lost his life or limb in this fearful transit. You remember Lt. Crosby, commanding Best's battery, a young officer of superior merit and fidelity. He was shot dead by a musket ball just as we were leaving the front. In the confusion his body was left on the ground, but has since been recovered.

Reaching Chancellors House, I formed line behind some rifle pits made by the Rebels before we reached C. and facing down the plank road toward Germanna. Here I was ordered by a staff officer of Gen. Hooker to hold this place at all hazards, who to my protestation that I had no ammunition, replied with immense pomposity, "Use the bayonet"! As we were suffering hugely from artillery shells thrown from a half mile to a mile distant, I didn't exactly see how my bayonets were to be effective. No reinforcements or new troops had yet shown themselves.

I knew the 1st, 2nd, 5th and 11th corps were within a mile to three miles of us and yet here my poor devils were ordered to suffer, after a fearful conflict which had in reality kept them under arms all night and in which they had expended eighty rounds of cartridges per man. At length I found Gen. Slocum, and through his protest I was finally ordered to move down the U.S. Ford road and to pass the second line and halt in the woods beyond. The Chancellors House, set on fire by the Rebel shells, was already in flames. Eight or ten women who had been for three days hid in the cellar of the house made their escape, half-starved and half-dead. They were sent over the river and well cared for. The building was full of our wounded, but I believe every one was safely removed. Not so fortunate were the poor fellows lying wounded in the woods, which, taking fire during the battle, burned fiercely in all directions, covering the country for miles with dense smoke and flames.

At the White House, where is marked the reserve artillery, we met the 2nd Corps just moving into position to meet the Rebels. A few rods behind we formed line of battle in a crossroad and my poor fellows disposed themselves for rest, their first chance in twenty-four hours. I caught a stray team of pack mules, deserted by their drivers, and was thus able to replenish, in part, my ammunition. The day was very warm, and what with excitement, dust, and heat my tongue was parched by thirst. I found the hospital of my division and got the most refreshing drink of cinchona and whiskey that was swallowed by mortal throat.

All day we lay in line on our arms. The sound of battle pretty much subsided after we fell back. Now and then a brisk cannonade would open and a fusillade of infantry which, however, was always of short duration, showing that no real engagement was taking place but a mere encounter of opposing skirmishers or patrol parties. Towards evening we could distinctly hear the artillery combat between Sedgwick's corps and the Rebs. toward Fredericksburg, and yet no attack began on our side.

After dark we were ordered to relieve a portion of the 11th Corps on the extreme left of our line, our left directly on the Rappahannock. It was long after dark before we took up our position, but it was a strong one on two high bluffs, forming a kind of natural bastion, separated by deep ravines. We spread our blankets under some evergreens and slept with a soundness which might have been expected after our long fatigue and many nights of broken sleep.

May 4th: Another warm, sunshiny day. The men were put at work strengthening the rifle pits, partly made before, and making traverses for our artillery guns, of which we had sixteen pieces on the two bluffs. We determined to make an impregnable position, as we had one of great natural strength. As the 11th Corps was on our right, we thought it not improbable that the enemy might break through there and turn our right, thus separating us from the U.S. Ford. We made up our minds to hold our post at all hazards to the last. Nothing was seen of the enemy except a few cavalry and infantry pickets, with which ours exchanged occasional shots.

Early in the morning some artillery had opened fire from a high point formed by a short bend of the river a few miles below. We could not imagine at what it was firing. It turned out afterwards that they had the range of our train camp on the other side of the river, and pretty effectually stampeded all our non-combatant staff and made several wounded officers, who could only move on litters the day before, take to their legs with the speed of a scared Indian. It happened that several hundred Secesh prisoners were in the same camp. They set up a loud yell for Jeff Davis and, I fear, laughed somewhat at the general skedaddles on the part of our officers and men. However, it was a pretty sharp specimen of shell practice, and as it found most of them in bed, the notice to quit was to men unused to the sounds rather startling, it must be confessed. Three or four men were killed in the camp.

May 5th: This day passed pretty much as yesterday. It opened pleasantly. No one disturbed our front, but on our right the Dutchmen kept up night and day pretty frequent popping, varied now and then by heavy volleys. It was generally reported that they were firing at imaginary Rebels. It gave us no uneasiness. We constructed evergreen bowers for shelter under the slope of our natural bastions. For food, we broiled pork on the sticks and with hardtack (soldier's hard bread) we made the sweetest meal of the season. About 3 o'clock we had a heavy storm of thunder, lightning, and rain, and it ended off in a regular heavy, cold rainstorm.

Orders had been communicated to me to be ready to recross the river soon after dark, but as ours was the last corps to move, it would probably be 10 or 11 o'clock before we should fall in. The rain poured down heavily. Soon after dark our artillery moved to the rear, so as to clear the bridges early for the infantry. Some of my regiments had been ordered out of the trenches so that the division might be speedily formed. It was darker than Erebus. We gathered around a big camp fire and piled on the wood, but the cold rain poured, and done up in our rubber coats and hats we looked most forlorn and felt quite so. Gen. Slocum had gone about dusk, no one knew where. Finally, tired with waiting I dispatched a staff officer to Gen. Couch to get instructions about withdrawing pickets. He returned with the information that the bridges had been carried away by the flood and that our march was counter-manded! Here was a fix. I ordered my regiments back to the rifle pits and sent for the artillery to return. Back came the messengers after an hour with information that the bridges would be repaired in an hour or so, and that I was to move when Gen. Howard sent me word that his corps had moved.

Wearily wore away the rainy, cold hours. At length, about daylight, came a messenger that Gen. Howard had marched. Silently and sadly we fell in and took the road to U.S. Ford. As I came out on the plateau overlooking the river bottom, a magnificent sight of three or four of our corps moving over the plain presented itself. There were two bridges, made out of four before the freshet. The river looked broad and angry. I was obliged to wait for at least three hours as my division was the last but the rear guard (Meade's corps) to pass the bridges. Time wore heavily and I was terribly anxious, as the guns were booming heavily in the direction of the enemy and our skirmishers were already engaged. Our rear regiment and line of pickets, [which] left a half hour after we marched, at length came up. The bridge was cleared, over went my division, and we took the shortest cut towards Stafford Court House, where we were all encamped by dark the same day. So ended the last day's campaign in Dixie.

I have written you a hurried and yet, as far as I can, a faithful account of this campaign. You will see how poorly it agrees with newspaper stories, which so far as I have seen are mainly fictions. Indeed, most of the pretended writers see nothing. They are safely in the rear. At least it was so with one who pretended to report for the 11th and 12th corps for the New York *Herald*. He went over the river on Friday and never appeared, as far as I could learn, on the south side again.

I have no time to read over what I have written, so you must make the best story you can of it. I have really so much to attend to that I have no thought nor time for outside work. Of thirty-one field officers engaged in these operations, fourteen are numbered with the casualties, nearly one-half. All are absent. All the adjutant generals (including my own) are wounded or missing. Almost all the adjutants of regiments and a great many of the line officers. In consequence, everything is deranged and it requires a great deal of work to get reports and to move things forward smoothly.

My aggregate of casualties in the division is nearly 1,700. I had less than 5,000 in the Sunday battle, consequently I have lost more than one man in three! The absence of many intimate friends and the sad results of our promising campaign have made me almost melancholy. I should like to get away, to restore my spirits, but I cannot just now, as I have but one brigadier left and very few field officers. Knipe [illegible] after the excitement was over and has gone home to Betsy, sick. My division has gone down to a zero of numbers by battle and the discharge of two-years' and nine-months' troops. I have less than half [the number] I had when we first encamped at this place. Heaven knows what are the intended future movements, but it requires no great genius to say that if with all the advantages of position and numbers in the recent operations we made a failure, our chances will not be regarded as promising with diminished numbers and a defensible river to cross. However, I do not propose to criticise the past nor speculate on the future. I have most decided opinions on both, but do not choose now to put them on paper. I enclose you several extracts from newspapers which please file with this letter. I shall need them sometime. Also the map and sketch of the sleeping brigadier! . . .

Your Affectionate Father,
A.S.W.

◈

LAURELS OF GENERAL SICKLES

Stafford Court House, May 23, 1863.
My Dear Daughter:
I will write you in a day or so. I send this note to let you know I am well. I shall come home if I can, but don't forget that I have lost half of my field officers, all my adjutant generals, more than *one-third* of all my command, and hence have unusual duties and difficulties to encounter. . . .

I shall write to Rene to visit Detroit this summer, but I don't know as I shall be able to get away. No one can 'weary for rest' more than I do, and I think I deserve a vacation, but these matters are not settled by merit but by impudence and brass and well paid reporters. A "Sickles" would beat Napoleon in winning glory not earned. He is a hero without an heroic deed! Literally made by scribblers. But justice is sure, if slow, and patience and perseverance will succeed. I think a man as old as Methuselah would on his death bed say he had to regret his short life, that he might see more of human character.

People at home are fancying this war is waged for the Union and for a stable and united government, but it is a mistake. It is carried on exclusively to make heroes of charlatans and braggarts!

Tell Aunt Jule that I lost not a single piece of my artillery, but that the major general whose name fills the New York papers shamefully abandoned his guns in my face and gave up to the Rebels a position which cost my division 500 lives. I'll write more soon.

Your Affectionate Father,
A.S.W.

DESPONDENCY OVER CHANCELLORSVILLE

May 29, 1863.

My Dear Daughter:

I have been hoping for some days to get leave for fifteen days to go to Detroit but am again disappointed. I applied a week ago, on the suggestion of Gen. Slocum, but was met, as before, by an order suspending all leaves except for five days; too short, of course, for me. . . .

I suppose now it is expected that Lee will cross and try his hand on us. At least, I cannot believe that the most extravagant self-conceit nor the wildest lunacy could bring anyone to the belief that with our reduced army we can, with the least prospect of success, cross the Rappahannock just now. We have lost physically and numerically, but still more morally, not by being dispirited, but by a universal want of confidence in the commanding general, growing out of the recent operations. I have not met the first officer who does not feel this, from the highest to the lowest. Of course, with such a feeling offensive operations are out of the question. . . .[6]

I am greatly dispirited and almost disposed to resign. "Whom the gods wish to destroy, they first make mad!" That our government shows symptoms now, as in the past, of being prepared in this way, as the instruments of our natural destruction, seems to me clearly manifested. I could tell you most astounding things, but cannot write them. I will write you again by next mail. Gov. Blair visited me yesterday and I rode all day with him to visit the Michigan regiments. . . .

Your Affectionate Father,
A.S.W.

❖

COMMENDATION OF GENERAL WILLIAMS

Headquarters, 12th Corps,
Army of the Potomac.
June 5th, 1863.

Sir:

Brig. Gen'l. A. S. Williams entered the service at the commencement of the war and has been constantly in the field ever since, and for more than a year past he has been the senior brigadier general in the U.S. volunteer force, has during all this time been performing the duties of a major general, having been in command of this corps at Antietam and for several weeks subsequent to that battle.

Since I was assigned to the command of the corps, Gen. Williams has been in command of the 1st Division. I have found him in camp as well as on the field a most valuable and efficient officer. I cannot speak too highly of his conduct during our late movements under Gen. Hooker. His division marched over sixty miles in three days, and forded the Rapidan during the time. In all our engagements with the enemy, his division did its full duty, as is attested by the loss sustained by it, which exceeded one-third of the number he took into the field. He, as its commander, was constantly at his proper post, both by night as well as day. I know of no officer in the service who has in my estimation so well earned promotion as Gen. Williams.

He has neglected to follow a custom which has become quite general in the army, that of calling the press to his aid, by employing reporters to sound his praise at the close of any engagement, in advance of official information on the subject, but I think in the estimation of every true soldier he will be more honored in the breach than in the observance of such a custom. I most earnestly hope he may be promoted.

I am Sir,
Very Respectfully,
Your Obedient Servant,
H. W. Slocum,
Maj Gen'l Vols. Comd'g

To his Excellency
A. Lincoln,
President of the United States.

◈

PROSPECTS OF PROMOTION

Stafford Court House, June 7, 1863.

My Dear Daughter: . . .

We have been under orders to be ready to move at a moment's notice for several days, but we don't move. Two regiments of my division went to the front yesterday, detached for some secret service. I think we shall have hot work very soon, but in which direction is very uncertain.

We have had the dustiest and warmest of days, so oppressive that it was fatiguing to sit under an awning. Today is cooler and pleasanter. I have kept very shady and to my tent. Indeed, I am almost without assistance. Not more than six or seven field officers out of thirty-three, and all adjutant generals gone. I am the victim of constant annoyance and anxiety, especially as my small division holds the extreme right and pickets a front of over four miles. My letter writing, ergo, is not brisk. Indeed, it is quite as much as I wish to do to look over papers and decide upon them. Knipe is still absent. I have not heard from him. Jackson does not get over his broken leg, and my only brigadier is Gen. Ruger. My command has run down to less than one-half [the number] I arrived at this camp with.

Gen. Slocum has *voluntarily* sent me a splendid letter recommending my promotion. I will send you a copy. It is a very gratifying testimonial from my corps commander.

I have been down to visit Krzyzenowski, commander of a brigade in the 11th Corps, and dined with him and Madame S. He is a Pole but a good officer and speaks English well. . . . I have received a very kind letter from Mr. J. M. Howard, U.S. senator from our state. He wrote to the Secretary of War urging my promotion and sent me a copy of his reply, which was as "wish a washy" as everything which comes from that Department. Just think of the promotion of *Birney* over me for the battle of Chancellorsville!! An officer who has been once tried for misconduct or something else in face of the enemy. I believe he was found not guilty and have no doubt he is patriotic and valiant enough, but he is my junior a year and a half and I have seen more service than he ever can.

All leaves are stopped now. I could go to Washington for five days and get an extension, doubtless, but in the judgment of honest men this practice is regarded as sneaking. I confess I desire still to keep my self-respect. Perhaps something may turn up by which I can get away before summer is over. . . .

Your Affectionate Father,
A.S.W.

1. John Stockton of Mount Clemens, who was appointed colonel of the Eighth Michigan Cavalry Regiment upon its organization October 3, 1862. John C. Robinson of Ann Arbor was appointed colonel of the First Michigan Infantry Regiment on September 1, 1861. He became a brigadier general on April 28, 1862 and a brevet major general on June 27, 1864. Henry A. Morrow of Detroit was appointed colonel of the Twenty-fourth Michigan Infantry upon its organization, August 15, 1862. It was attached to the famous Iron Brigade, in which on the first day of Gettysburg (July 1, 1863) it sustained a loss of 80 per cent of the 500 men engaged. Twenty of its twenty-eight officers were killed or wounded, among the latter being Colonel Morrow, who became a prisoner but was left behind when the Confederate army began its retreat.—O. B. Curtis, *History of the Twenty-fourth Michigan of the Iron Brigade* (Detroit, 1891).

2. The "scrawl," written on May 4, was a 2,400-word description of the campaign and battle to that time. Since its contents are necessarily repeated, in the main, in the more detailed narrative of May 18, it is not included.

3. Amiel W. Whipple, a West Point graduate in the class of 1841. From 1856 to 1861 he was engineer in charge of the ship channel through the St. Clair Flats, and of the channel through Lake George and Neebish Rapids in the Saint Marys River. Mortally wounded at Chancellorsville, he died on May 7, 1863, having been brevetted major general of volunteers the day before.—Cullum, *Register of Officers and Graduates of the U.S. Military Academy.*

4. It has. See sketch of Sickles in *Dict. Am. Biog.,* where we are told that (with the Third Corps) he "attacked the victorious Jackson and after bloody fighting stopped his advance."

5. They were crowded, also, with the Union troops whom Sickles had ordered to make the night attack upon the Confederates and who found themselves under fire from the enemy in front and from their own colleagues in the rear. General Slocum, in reporting the action, expressed the fear that they had suffered heavily from the fire of the latter.—*Official Records,* Series 1, XXV, Part 1, 670; General Williams' report, 679.

6. This analysis of the current situation proved entirely correct save for the forecast concerning General Lee's intentions. Instead of an assault upon the Army of the Potomac he detoured its position, beginning the march which led to Gettysburg.

VII

Gettysburg

GETTYSBURG

Barely a month sufficed to determine the issue of the Gettysburg campaign and the war. In early June General Lee's army set forth from its encampment around Fredericksburg upon its second invasion of the North, hopefully anticipating the capture of Baltimore and Washington and the dictation of a peace on Confederate terms. To checkmate this design General Hooker also moved northward, keeping the Army of the Potomac as a shield between the invader and Washington. Whether he would lead it to another Chancellorsville and the probable loss of the war was the question at issue when on June 27, in response to his own request, he was relieved of his command. Upon General Meade, whom the President appointed to succeed him, now devolved the responsibility of defeating the invading Confederate army. How he did so at Gettysburg in the three-day battle of July 1–3 is known to the world. Less known, however, is the role of General Williams in the campaign, described in part in the letters to his daughters which follow. Once more in temporary command of an army corps, it was his lot to defend the right flank of the Union army, stationed on Culp's Hill. But for his successful performance of this task in a desperate struggle of several hours duration during the forenoon of July 3, there would have been no Pickett's charge and no Union victory. It is our present misfortune that the concluding portion of his narrative describing the battle is missing from his papers.

BACK TO MARYLAND AGAIN

Fairfax Court House, June 16, 1863.
My Dear Daughter:
You will be astonished at my locality, but our changes now are *magical.* Joseph says "presto" and to the charge! I doubt if he is any wiser with the operation than some of our traveling magicians by their legerdemain. I have no time to describe movements, but simply to tell you where I am. We left Stafford Court House Thursday night, (the 11th); marched all night to Dumfries; lay there all next day and left there yesterday morning at daylight; made a march of twenty-five miles with my division in the hottest, dirtiest day I ever saw and reached here last night. I lost a good many men, I fear, by sunstroke. It was a terrible day and my poor fellows suffered greatly.

We have all sorts of rumors and no facts; but I suppose, as the newspapers say, we shall have "stirring times."

Your Affectionate Father,
A.S.W.

❖

RETURNING TO MARYLAND

Leesburg, Va., June 20th [and 23rd], 1863.
My Dear Daughters:
I write to you jointly, as I shall probably have little time to write you separately for some time, at least if the past week is a specimen of what we are to expect. I sent to Rene a short pencil note from Fairfax Court House, but I will begin from our old camp.

Saturday, 13th: We received the evening before orders to take up a new line in rear of the old one, to cover the railroad from Aquia to Fredericksburg. The day was hot and we were busy moving the regiments from sunrise taking up a line from Aquia Creek some four miles long toward Potomac Creek and in establishing in front a long line of pickets. It was a hard job in a country so densely covered by thickets and broken by deepest ravines. I had just got to my new camp about

3 o'clock P.M., very pleasantly located on a grassy knoll near Brooke's Station, and was anticipating a day or so of freedom from dust, under cool shades, when lo! up came an order to put my division in march towards Dumfries without delay.

Here was a pretty duty, after a laborious day! A line of pickets four or five miles long to be taken up; our wagons over a line of encampments covering four miles to be repacked, and all the preparations for a permanent breakup and a rapid night march to be made by a wearied and heated body of men. All the long trains of regimental, brigade, division, and corps wagons, with ten days' supplies, were to be sent ahead. There was hurrying in hot haste and mounted orderlies stirred up a big dust in all directions. It was near sundown before I had massed my whole division around the barren-looking knoll, which had for so long a time been the site of my headquarters. It looked sad and forsaken, for in leaving it in the morning we had stripped everything portable for our new quarters and some of the men had made bonfires of the debris. Here we found the wagon trains blocking the way and it was hours before we could resume our march. And what a dark and dreary night march it was.

Almost the whole way to Dumfries is lined by the densest pine thickets and as the night was cloudy the darkness was as thick as that of a subterranean dungeon. The road in the daytime is at this season quite passable by avoiding the deep gullies of the water courses, but at night it was impossible to choose the side roads. In consequence we had a continuance of upsets in our wagon trains, causing vexatious delays in the marching column in the rear. It was over this route that we made our slow march through the mud last winter, through the worst of obstacles. We made more progress in the night march, but with a condensation of vexatious occurrences. Staff officers were tumbled into deep ravines; wagons went over steep ledges or turned bottom upward in deep gullies and were abandoned. We forded Aquia Creek and Chopawamsic Creek and about daylight, after various calamities and a sleepless night, the head of my column reached the Quantico Creek and pitched our shelter tents on the north side near the antique village of Dumfries.

This place, once so noted in the commerce and politics of Virginia, which boasted in colonial times of its dozens of importing warehouses, which was the theater where Patrick Henry made his great war speech, is nothing now but a straggling and deserted village of a dozen or so tumbling down houses, with not a store or a shop. Even its river, where heavily freighted vessels once unloaded their cargoes, has so filled up that our troops forded at the very landing place of olden times. It was a part of our program to have crossed at Occoquan village, the 3rd Corps passing us here and crossing at Wolf Run Shoals; but after staying all day Sunday (14th) at Dumfries we got orders to march to Fairfax Court House via Wolf Run Shoals over our old route of last winter. . . .

[*A four-page section is missing at this point.*]

June 17: We left Fairfax Court House just as day was breaking, my division leading. Our march was over a new route via Hunter's Mills near Vienna, and striking the turnpike from Alexandria to Leesburg. The morning was pleasant, but by 8 o'clock exceedingly warm again. We halted an hour at Hunter's Mills in a nice shady ravine on Difficult River, to let the men breakfast. The country through which we marched was more fertile and better cultivated and [had] a good many nice farm houses. It was a great contrast to the country from Fairfax to Stafford. We found a few cavalry pickets on the route as far as Hunter's Mills belonging to the 6th Michigan Cavalry. A Captain Weber from Grand Rapids, a very gentlemanly young man, introduced himself during our halt and gave me information as to [our] route.

We intended to pass Dranesville but were met by an order to halt short at a small stream about two miles south of Dranesville and found a good camping ground. We pitched our tents in the pleasant yard of a farmhouse where we found the unusual luxury of sweet butter and fresh milk. Our march was only ten miles and was completed about 11 o'clock A.M. The afternoon was intensely hot, so that we could not be comfortable on the green grass beneath the densest shade. Either by accident or design the dry old grass of the fields and woods got on fire, and filled the air with smoke and additional heat. Altogether it was an afternoon of great discomfort, and I was quite glad that our march was a short one.

June 18: I was ordered at 6 o'clock to move my division towards Leesburg. The early morning was the hottest we had felt. One perspired freely standing still at sunrise. We were ordered to reach Leesburg but as it was understood that we were not to march, there was some delay, and it was past 7 o'clock before we were fairly on the road. We had reached the pike, which was hard enough, but rough with unbroken boulders and very hard on the feet of men and animals accustomed to dirt roads. We passed through Dranesville, a small, insignificant village, and made our first halt at Broad River, over which we found a stout stone bridge. The country along the pike is well cultivated and farmhouses are thick. We had all sorts of rumors of Rebels in front, but none appeared except a few horsemen on our left, which we paid no attention to.

About 1 o'clock a brisk shower relieved our tired and over-heated soldiers and we soon reached Goose Creek, where we found a deep and rocky ford, the bridge having been destroyed long ago. My division forded at once, waist deep, with their usual yells and jokes. The storm of rain, hail, thunder, and lightning had become terrific, but the men felt new life from the cool wetting, and we marched directly on this town, three and a half miles, which my advance reached about 4 P.M. and found no enemy. The 2nd Division (Gen. Geary's) had fallen behind and did not get over the ford until dark, and our trains were unable to pass at all. This place we passed through last December on our march from Harpers Ferry. It is a place of considerable importance in peaceful times, though very old and not at all prosperous in appearance. It lies in a natural bowl or circular valley, around the rim of which the Rebels built last year three or four strong forts. These we have occupied, though they are somewhat dilapidated.

The famous Ball's Bluff is within four miles of this, as is Edwards Ferry, to which you will remember I made my first march in October 1861. The original order of Gen. Stone to Col. Davis, upon which the movement was made, is now in the possession of a landlord of this town, named Williamson. He was at the time adjutant of a Virginia regiment and in the battle, I think. He told me the order was found in the hat of Gen. Baker, who was killed. I have seen the original when we went through last winter and could not but feel that it exonerated Stone from much of the blame put on him. A copy was made at the time, by one of our officers and published. From the accounts of this officer, I think that unfortunate disaster to our troops arose mainly from the neglect or ignorance of green colonels who commanded our regiments and from the rashness of Gen. Baker himself. The government has restored Gen. Stone to duty and I suppose considers him blameless in the matter. It is quite certain from the stories of both sides that we ought not to have suffered the disaster we did and might have occupied Leesburg with ordinary care and sagacity.

As it was raining when we reached town I halted at the head of a street, while my advance passed through, and finally took up my quarters in the house, occupying two large rooms, one for a sleeping room for a dozen or so of us, and one for an office. I slept for the first time for months under a roof, but in my blankets on the floor. The woman of the house is named Grover. No men are seen, but lots of children, white and black. On returning from a ride through the town to see to the position of my troops I found a young lady dressed up very finely in white, with red and blue ribbons. She had come to see the general, and show one Union lady. It was indeed a rarity for a native in this state, where the women are the fiercest of all Secessionists. Her name is Honda, and her family live about a mile from town. As it was raining and very muddy I sent Pittman to escort her home, after doing her up in an India rubber coat, but I fear her Union finery was not a little drabbled in the mud and wet.

June 19th: Today we had the most unpleasant duty of shooting three deserters, about the first capital punishments which have taken place in the army for this offense. Two of them, of the 46th Pennsylvania Volunteers, deserted about two weeks ago when we were under orders to march towards the enemy. They bought citizens' clothes, but were apprehended while trying to get off by Aquia Creek. The other (13th New Jersey Volunteers) deserted a year or more ago and was sent back from home. He neglected to avail himself of the pardon offered by the President in April last. The sentence of court martial was approved by Gen. Hooker just as we were leaving Stafford, and they were ordered to be shot between 12 and 4 o'clock yesterday. Officers of regiments went to ask a commutation, but he would not see them and so the sad business had to go on. The whole corps was paraded in a large field and formed three sides of a square. By Gen. Hooker's orders the execution was under my direction as commander of the division to which the men belonged. The carrying out of details

I put, of course, on my provost marshal. Three graves were dug some two feet apart in a slight depression of the field, and on the gentle swell of the ground the troops were formed so that every man could see the execution. . . . [*The succeeding portion of the journal is missing. It was resumed by General Williams in a letter dated at Leesburg, June 23, whose opening lines are omitted.*]

Saturday [20th] was a calm day. No sound of guns, and I spent most of it in making disposition of my troops and establishing outposts and picket lines.

Sunday, June 21st: Firing began on our left early and seemed about 7 or 8 miles away. Our outer pickets could hear volleys of musketry. The cannonade was kept up all day at intervals, but seemed to recede towards Ashby's Gap, by which token we concluded our cavalry with an infantry support was driving the Rebels. I dined with Gen. Slocum at the hotel in town, kept by an ex-Rebel officer (Williamson). In my rides about town I find many pleasant residences and a great many indignant and explosive Secesh women, but very few men except old ones. The country about is very fertile and beautiful. I came through here for the first time with Alf Coxe in 1850 or '51 after visiting his sister—Mrs. Lewis—in the Shenandoah Valley. A great many years ago when I was a boy (eight or ten years old) an old shoemaker and farmer, with whom I boarded in Madison near the academy, had a son in Leesburg keeping a shoestore. Of course, I heard a great deal of the place and my boyish fancy was quite excited about Leesburg. It was at least forty years ago. Strange are the occurrences of our lives. My earliest ideas of Virginia towns were of a peaceful shoestore and here I am as a belligerent, in manhood, dictating terms of ingress and egress to its people!

Monday, June 22nd: I mounted my horse early in the morning to take a long circuit of the town on the out hills, which rise above the lesser hills near the village and command it. Indeed, all around the town there is an amphitheater of hills like seats which rise as they recede. Towards Edwards Ferry the country is more level, though spurs of mountains run towards the pass in that direction. For perhaps two miles towards Ball's Bluff the country is comparatively level, with immense fields of grass and corn, a very fertile soil and not looking like famine. One corn field we estimated had 400 acres planted. I rode down to the pontoon bridge which has been laid over the Potomac at Edwards Ferry, which is over a quarter of a mile broad. Indeed, in appearance nearly as broad as the river at Detroit.

I went over the scene of the contest which you may remember I described as taking place on Tuesday after the Ball's Bluff fight. From this I visited the scene of the Ball's Bluff disaster, which is some three miles higher up and opposite Harrison's Island. One is filled with astonishment that any man of the least military pretensions should have crossed at such a place and with such means. The island divides the river so that the stream on this side is narrow, but at the landing place the bluff is covered with woods and thickets to the river's edge and is cut deep with water courses, and gullied into deep ravines to the river's edge. It was with difficulty I could get my horse down the narrow footpath, where our troops went up. For three-quarters of a mile back, the woods and underbrush are very thick with small cleared patches, into which, after defeat began, our troops by a monstrous fatality were collected to make slaughter sure and certain from the adjacent woods held by the Rebels. Gen. Baker was killed near the river bank in one of these small clearings. I found a long trench without sign or headboard where our dead were buried. I confess I felt all through the ride over this unfortunate ground that somebody should have been exemplarily punished for permitting the slaughter that occurred there. It is a singular fact that while they were killing and taking prisoners of so many of our men, we had at Edwards Ferry, not over three miles distant and on the flank of the Rebels, a larger force than they brought into the fight. They made no demonstration to relieve our overwhelmed forces. . . .

I finished my day's ride by visiting Fort Johnson, where I have posted two regiments and a battery. It is on a very high hill north of the town. On the south we have Fort Beauregard and on the southeast Fort Evans, but they are miles apart and are nothing but dilapidated earthworks which we are repairing somewhat, though we don't know we shall stay here a day. On the west there is no work. The country slopes away gradually towards the hills and is a good deal exposed. Indeed, our location is by no means a strong one or easy of defense with the force we have. There are too many hills and we have too few men away up in advance of the other corps. But I suppose it is the post of honor, even if we get used up!

I have several times intended to send you an account of my visit to the division hospital after the battle of Chancellorsville, but other things have prevented. All our wounded—700 or 800—were taken back to Aquia Creek and put in large hospital tents on the high hills overlooking the Potomac River. They were made as comfortable as the severely wounded (and none others were kept in hospital) could be. It took me all day to go through and I saw and talked with every man of my division. I need not say that they all seemed pleased to see me, but I had a terrible surfeit of looking at amputated legs and arms, and of all imaginable kinds of severe wounds. It was wonderful how men could survive some of them. Several had been shot through the lungs; one through both eyes and was stone blind; many had had several inches of bone cut out of legs and arms (ex-section) and were doing well. One poor fellow had had his leg amputated by the Rebs. on the field and the flesh had sloughed off, leaving a long bone sticking out, and he was much reduced by secondary hemorrhage; but strange to say, with this one exception, all had healthful, and many cheerful faces, and talked to me cheerfully and happily. One poor fellow had been wounded through the hips, and his feet had lain in the water until they gangrened and more than half the flesh had fallen off, leaving the bones of the feet protruding fleshless, nothing but skeletons of toes and outer bones. I intended to have sent you a full account of these terribly wounded [men] and of the heroic manner they bore up under these distressing injuries, but it is too late now. I was gratified after my visit to get repeated messages from the surgeons from the wounded that my visit had done them so much good and that they had said that the general's medicine was better than the doctor's. It was four or five miles from my camp or I should [have] gone often. . . .

We have no certain information of our future movements. They depend upon the enemy, but I fancy we shall not be here long. When armies approach one another, fighting is sure to follow pretty soon. In this case there is a momentous issue, for if we are badly defeated there is but little hope, I think, of saving Washington. The troops held so sacredly about that "corruption sink" would make a poor show before the victorious Rebels. God save our Republic! For I sometimes think that human heads and arms are working for our destruction. I suppose, however, they are but instruments of divine will, though why He should use those who most blaspheme his authority, it is hard to imagine. I have seen dark times, but none where before I could not see some superior intellect that might probably be brought to our safety.

Your Affectionate Father,

A.S.W.

◆

FOREBODINGS OF DEFEAT

Frederick, Md., June 29, 1863.

My Dear Daughters:

I have a moment in the office of Dr. Steiner of the Sanitary Commission to tell you where I am. We left Leesburg on Friday last, the 26th inst., and marched across the river at Edwards Ferry on pontoons and encamped that night at the mouth of the Monocacy. The next day we marched to within a mile of Knoxville, which Rene will remember is within two miles of the Longbridges on the Baltimore & Ohio Railroad, where we generally took the railroad for Baltimore. The Saturday's march was too tedious and fatiguing for me to go to the Longbridges. Besides, I did not get my brigades in camp until after dark. The whole line of march was crowded by baggage wagons and trains. I expected to march through Sandy Hook towards Williamsport but during the night was ordered to march my division towards Frederick. I reached this [place] yesterday afternoon, when a change of commanders was announced, Meade superceding Hooker.

It was intimated that we should remain at this place a day or so, but at 2.30 this morning I was awakened by a messenger ordering my division to march towards Taneytown at 5 A.M. I was camped in a fine grove and had a great desire for sleep after three days' fatiguing marches, but there is no help under orders. Besides, we are filled with an idea that the Rebels are getting into Pennsylvania, and of course we are bound to go on, cost what of human flesh it may. For myself, I am rejoiced at the change of commanders. I have said very little in my letters, but enough for you to guess that I had no confidence in Hooker after Chancellorsville. I can say now, that if we had had a commander of even ordinary merit at that place the army of Jackson would have been annihilated. I cannot conceive of greater imbecility and weakness than characterized that campaign from the moment Hooker reached Chancellorsville and took command.

I am not much of a military genius, but if I could have commanded the Army of the Potomac at Chancellorsville I would have wagered my life on being in Richmond in ten days! All we are suffering now in shame and mortification and in the great risk of losing the whole fortunes of the war is the legitimate result of the weakness which characterized that campaign. Since then, and as the results of that campaign, our army has been reduced over 50,000 men, two-thirds by expiration of term of service of three-months' and two-years' troops, and yet not one soldier has been added to our forces. All winter, by the natural disintegration of armies, we have been running down at the rate of 20 per cent per annum; add to this 35 to 40,000 men discharged by expiration of service and 25,000 killed and wounded in battle and you have at least 85,000 men in this army less now than last December, and this, too, at the season when active field duties commence. I have in my division less than half the men I had in January last, when I reached Stafford Court House. I think my division is a fair sample of the Army of the Potomac.

You see we have a great task before us to preserve the Republic. It is reported that the Rebels are 110,000 strong in infantry, with 20,000 cavalry. I think the report is greatly exaggerated, but they have been all winter recruiting by conscription, while we have been all winter running down. Still, I don't despair. On the contrary, now with a gentleman and a soldier in command I have renewed confidence that we shall at least do enough to preserve our honor and the safety of the Republic. But we run a fearful risk, because upon this small army everything depends. If we are badly defeated the Capital is gone and all our principal cities and our national honor. That this dilemma could have been suffered by men deputed to care for the safety of the Republic is indeed disheartening. That our northern people could sit down in search of the almighty dollar, when their all is depending upon this conflict, is indeed passing strange. If we fail in this war, be assured there is an end of northern prosperity. The Rebels in Baltimore and Washington will dictate terms and these terms will humiliate and destroy us. I would I had an archangel's voice to appeal to the patriotism (if there be any left) in the North!

I sent you a sort of journal of a few days we were in Leesburg, excepting two or three of the last. Those were devoted to putting the forts in good condition for the Rebels and making several miles of rifle pits and breast works.

Love to all; my column has passed and I must follow. This is a hasty scrawl, but I know with you better than none. Keep writing me. I am full of faith and yet fearfully anxious. There must be a decisive battle, I think, soon, but you will hear of it before this reaches you, probably. Possibly the enemy may withdraw, and I am not without hope that we may strike them on a weak flank exposure.

Whatever may happen, be contented and resigned, and believe it is all for the best. In nations, as in individuals, we must believe there is a "Divinity which shapes our ends, rough hew them as we will."

Your Affectionate Father,
A.S.W.

◈

GETTYSBURG

Halt near Littlestown, Pa.,
July 6, 1863.

My Dear Daughters:

I wrote you a hasty note on the 4th from the battlefield in the rear of Gettysburg and previously a hasty scrawl from Frederick on the march up. I am now at this "halt," moving back over the same road we advanced, for the purpose, I suppose, of hanging on the flank of Lee's army, reported on the retreat. My division lies in the fields hereabouts, and I have borrowed a very poor pen and poorer ink to take advantage of the occasion, for the prospect of quietude is not promising. How long I shall remain at this temporary halt is very uncertain, as we are watching the Rebel movements, so may be off in an hour. There can be little rest until Lee is driven out of Maryland, or we are amongst the armies that were. I wrote you so hastily from Frederick, that I will briefly resume my journal.

Friday, 26th: Left camp at Leesburg and crossed the Potomac on pontoon bridges at Edwards Ferry four miles; marched to mouth of the Monocacy, passing 5th Corps near Edwards Ferry. Day drizzling and disagreeably sultry fifteen miles.

Saturday, 27th: Marched from Monocacy to within a mile or so of Knoxville through byroads which led near Jefferson. Abundance of cherry trees; day cloudy and not oppressive. Marched eighteen miles, the men coming in cheerful. After dark rode to headquarters in Knoxville for consultation on order to advance to Williamsport to burn pontoon bridges. Countermanding order came and we were directed to march for Frederick next morning. Headquarters at Mr. Tighlman Hillyear's—a fussy old fellow of seventy, who was greatly disturbed at the destruction of his rail fences. Got supper at Hillyear's, who has a splendid large brick farmhouse and is an old Secesh.

Sunday, 28th: Marched at 5 A.M. for Frederick, passing through Jefferson. Reached camp near the town. Twelve and a half miles; pitched headquarters tents in a nice grove and anticipated a nice day's rest. Worked all afternoon, after fifteen miles march. In the night got orders to march at daylight towards Taneytown, Md. Received, on arrival, news of the removal of Gen. Hooker and appointment of Gen. Meade to command the army. Very general satisfaction expressed in our division.

Monday, 29th: Marched through Frederick and took the road to Taneytown. March much obstructed by trains of different corps. Day cloudy and occasionally drizzling. Encamped on Little Pine Creek and got our supper at a farmhouse. Wagons behind. March eighteen miles.

Tuesday, 30th: Marched at daylight, my division in advance. Reached vicinity of Littlestown about noon, twelve miles. Found great excitement, growing out of cavalry charge upon our cavalry in the town. Moved through the town, the people turning out en masse with great curiosity and apparent joy that we had come in season to protect them. All along the road since leaving Frederick the people have assembled in country wagons to gratify their curiosity to see the Army of the Potomac. Their comments have been very entertaining. Our cavalry, having chased the Rebels off a few miles, returned, and Gen. Slocum came up and ordered us to encamp, which was done in the fields above the town.

Our whole march from Frederick, as indeed since crossing the Potomac, has been through a very rich and highly cultivated country. Indeed, it was not easy to find a lot upon which we could encamp, so universal were the cultivated fields by the roadside. On our march today we passed the line between Maryland and Pennsylvania. The inhabitants are Dutch descendants and quite Dutch in language. The country is full of Copperheads, more so than the southern part of Maryland, and the people are rich, but ignorant of everybody and [every]thing beyond their small spheres. They have immense barns, looking like great arsenals or public institutions, full of small windows and painted showily. Altogether, they are a people of barns, not brains.

Wednesday, July 1st: Marched at daylight towards Gettysburg, my division leading. Halted at Two Taverns, a small village, where my division massed in the fields. The people all along the road manifested great curiosity to see us and assembled at all road crossings. The country was beautiful and most richly cultivated. The same big barns and hayhouses. After an hour or so halt, got a dispatch that our troops of the 11th and 1st corps were engaged with the Rebels near Gettysburg. My division was at once put in march. Some two miles south of the town we turned off to the right on a narrow, winding path or country road, and after a couple of miles reached a dense wood, behind which was a high, bald hill on which a good position could be had in sight and rear of the town.

I had pressed my men for five or six miles over very muddy and slippery roads in order to reach the hill before the Rebels, who, it was reported to me, were advancing in that direction in heavy column. As I reached the woody screen, officers I sent forward reported that the enemy had possession. I, however, drew up in order of battle and went forward myself to reconnoiter under the cover of the woods. I reached the ravine at the bottom of the hill and from behind a tree (leaving my horse and staff behind) I could see Rebel cavalry on top, but no infantry. There might possibly be a battery there, but I determined at once to take it by assault. Some of my regiments were already at the foot, and the skirmishers were in advance, covered by bushes. I gave the order to advance at double-quick, when I was overtaken by a staff officer of Gen. Slocum's directing me to withdraw, as the Rebels had already driven back our troops in front of Gettysburg and occupied the town, and we were in danger of being cut off from our line towards the main road.

My men were halfway up the hill, but I withdrew them at once and returned to the vicinity of the main road to the town, where we had diverged. Here we passed the night without any information on the condition of the 11th and 1st corps, which we had very indefinitely heard had been repulsed. We had plenty of rumors, and had reliable information of the death of Gen. Reynolds, commander of the 1st Corps. I had been notified that I was in command of the 12th Corps, Gen. Slocum temporarily taking command of the right wing, in place of Reynolds. Gen. Meade had not come up. I was in considerable dilemma, as I could learn nothing of the 2nd (Geary's) Division of our corps.

At length a staff officer came with information that it had been ordered to the vicinity of Gettysburg to support the right of Wadsworth's division, 1st Corps. So I put out strong pickets in all directions, as it was dark and I literally knew nothing of the topography or geography of the country. In my rear was a broad, cultivated country, but all along the front and on both sides of the road I was on was a dense wood, and in front (toward Gettysburg) a considerable stream called Rock Creek; properly named, as it was built up on either bank by high hills of huge boulders; and farther on a high ridge, densely covered, and of irregular form, ran toward Gettysburg on our right.

The country people seemed stupidly ignorant of the Rebel movements, here, as everywhere on our route. They had plenty of stories of huge bodies of cavalry and infantry, from 100,000 to 1,000,000, and thousands of pieces of artillery. These stories, which are repeated and swelled through a long line of timid imaginations, become exceedingly laughable, especially when heard from the chattering lips of the frightened men and women. It is not strange that they are alarmed for their property and themselves. Their peaceful lives in these retired spots have not been calculated to prepare their hearts for "war's stern alarms," and the sound of cannon and the movement of troops on all sides must fearfully disturb their fancies. I pitched my bivouac (for I had neither tents nor blankets) under a big oak near the edge of the woods, and after making arrangements against surprise and "giving audience" to several farmers, rolled myself in an india-rubber poncho and slept most splendidly until daylight.

Thursday, July 2nd: Woke at daylight and soon after began to put my troops in better order than the dark permitted last night. Borrowed a little coffee from an orderly and a piece of hardtack, which made an excellent breakfast. Gen. Slocum came out from the front early with general directions as to the positions the 12th Corps was to take up. As I was placing the 1st Division, the head of the 5th Corps began to arrive and took up a position on our right, all of us facing to the east. I met for an instant on the ground Capt. Chipman, who is on Gen. Sykes staff.[1] We had scarcely got into position before I was ordered to change a couple of miles or so toward the town and form the 1st Division on the right of the 2nd, already in position along the wooded ridge I have before mentioned. I was soon there, following up the pike to within half a mile of Gettysburg and then taking a bridle path which led to about the center of the ridge. Here I found the right of Geary's division and I placed the 1st along the rocky crest, extending south until I struck Rock Creek, and then following it to a rocky knoll near the pike, where it crosses the creek.

This ridge was a wild position, full of great detached masses of rock and huge boulders. I ordered at once a breastwork of logs to be built, having experienced their benefits at Chancellorsville. Looking at the spot, it seemed almost absurd that the enemy could attack there, as the approach was so rough and broken. Besides, the creek, dammed near the pike bridge, became almost the whole length of our front a stream quite unfordable, as far as we had been able to follow it. Still, though ridiculous the work, we were there, and our men had learned to love entrenching with logs. So at it they went and in a couple of hours had covered themselves with a good, substantial breastwork.

Matters went on all day pretty quietly. I had lost a few men in the morning in my skirmishers, sent out to feel the enemy, and on our left towards the front the artillery had been occasionally exchanging shots. Nothing to indicate the intentions of the Rebels had occurred. They

had got the better of us the day before, rather through our own rashness, I think, as it was not intended to have a general engagement until
the several corps could concentrate from the many routes they were
obliged to take. Reynolds, I fancy, precipitated a large action by under-
rating the strength of his opponents. In consequence, both the 1st and
11th corps were badly cut up, and it is reported that a considerable
portion of the latter corps behaved badly, almost as much so as at
Chancellorsville, falling back without firing and thus uncovering the
flanks of that corps, which suffered terribly in killed and wounded.[2]

In consequence the two corps which fought in advance of Gettysburg
were driven nearly through the town, the Rebs. holding the north side
and we the south with our headquarters in the cemetery adjoining the
village. We had the considerable but gently rising ridges on the center
and left of the town; the Rebs. similar ones, with the high hill I spoke
of yesterday, on the right of the town. Wadsworth's division, 1st Corps
and 12th Corps held the wooded and rocky ridge from the town to
Rock Creek. Gen. Meade had concentrated to a narrow circuit all his
troops which had arrived. He held the center or interior lines, and the
enemy were on the outer lines or circumference. The diameter of the
circle was not two miles, I think, while the circumference, in its
irregular shape, was six or seven, or more. The Rebs. were for once at
a disadvantage, as we could reinforce any part of our line rapidly, while
the "Secesh" had a long outer line to march over to bring aid to an
overpowered point.

During the morning, as we were taking up a position, a new brigade
of two pretty large regiments, the 1st Maryland Home Guards and
the 150th New York Volunteers, reported to our corps. They were
under command of Gen. Lockwood, of whom I know as yet very little.
He appears to be a very pleasant gentleman and I believe has had some
command for a long time on the Eastern Shore of Maryland.[3] Another
regiment (1st Maryland Eastern Shore) will join the brigade tomorrow,
quite desirable reinforcements to our weakened corps in matter of
numbers, but I fear not very reliable, as none of them have seen much
active duty.

It was as late as 3 o'clock P.M. when the Rebels began heavily with
artillery at our front and then with infantry on our left, attacking at
first the 3rd Corps. The battle raged fiercely until dark and several

corps or parts were ordered up to reinforce our line; the 5th, part of the 6th, and finally my division of the 12th Corps. I was in command of the corps and could properly have left the division with Gen. Ruger, temporarily commanding, but as I had also the new brigade of Gen. Lockwood, I preferred to accompany the division. We took the route promptly and marched rapidly, following the sound of the battle, for I could find no one on the way to give me intelligence as to the point I was most needed.

On we went, therefore, following up the main line of the returning wounded and the skulkers. We soon came to signs of battle; broken-down fences, trodden fields, broken gun-carriages, scattered arms, knapsacks, blankets, and clothing of all kinds. I reached a considerable elevation upon the center of which heavy woods came down to a point, and in the rear spread out broad both ways. I followed the side where I heard infantry volleys, and as I came near the wooded apex an artillery officer rode rapidly towards me begging for assistance to protect his battery. It proved to be Maj. McGilary of Maine, who once commanded a battery in my division. He was delighted to see me and I heard, with the rapidity that such occasions require, that the infantry supports had just left him and that in the woods in front the Rebels had just captured several pieces of our artillery, or rather dragged them there after capture. I had the new brigade leading and one regiment of it had fallen behind. The 1st Maryland Home Regiment, Col. Maulsby, was ahead and I ordered him to pitch into the woods. So he did, indeed, without waiting to form line of battle, but rushing forward in column. Fortunately, he met little resistance, for the Rebs. ran and left the catpured guns, which were thus recaptured without firing a gun.

Leaving this regiment, I passed to the other side of the wooded triangle where the main road runs and after placing my 1st and 3rd brigades in the woods went forward to learn what was to be done, but it was fast growing dark and the battle was really over. I chanced, however, to meet Gen. Meade and a good many other officers on the field and to learn that we had successfully resisted all the Rebel attacks and had punished them severely. There was a pleasant gathering in an open field, and gratification and gratulation abounded. One must see these events and anxious scenes to realize the joy of a successful ter-

mination, even of a single day's work, no matter how uncertain may
be the morrow.

I returned toward my entrenchments after dark and was met with
the astounding intelligence that they were taken possession of by the
Rebels in my absence! Gen. Geary (whom I left to guard them) had
been ordered out after I left by Gen. Slocum, and though he did not
reach the front, by mistaking his way, he was gone long enough for the
Rebs. to seize upon two-thirds of our line, which we had prepared with
so much care. Fortunately, Gen. Greene was left on this extensive left,
adjoining Gen. Wadsworth, and on the highest part of the ridge at a
point where our line made an abrupt angle, along a pretty high cliff.
The angle of the line came almost to the edge of a low morass, or
swale, leaving but a narrow, rocky pass for the Rebs. to move up
against Greene's position. They tried hard to drive him out, but failed,
though keeping up [the attack] until nearly my return. I had had
experience in trying to retake breastworks after dark, so I ordered all
the brigades to occupy the open field in front of the woods, put out a
strong picket line, and waited daylight for further operations.

In the meantime as temporary commander of the 12th Corps, I was
summoned to a council at Gen. Meade's headquarters. I found present,
Gens. Slocum, Sedgwick, Hancock, Howard, Newton, Sykes and Gibbon. It was to decide upon the next day's policy. I have no right to tell
others' opinions, but mine (the second given) was to remain the following day, hold a defensive attitude, and await events. This was the
decision, as the day showed. It was rather a serious question for one
great reason, if not many others. We had but one single day's rations
for the army. Many corps had not even one. We had outrun our supplies, and as all the railroad lines which came near us were broken,
there were no depots within reach. But it was thought that what with
beef cattle and flour, which possibly could be got together, we could eke
out a few half-fed days.

Few appreciate the difficulties of supplying an army. If you will
calculate that every man eats, or is entitled to eat, nearly two pounds a
day, you can easily estimate what a large army consumes. But besides
what men eat, there are horses and mules for artillery, cavalry, and
transportation in vast numbers, all which must be fed or the army is

dissolved or made inefficient. There is another all-important matter of ammunition, a large supply of which for infantry and artillery must be carried, besides what is carried on the person and in the ammunition chests of guns and caissons. Our men carry forty rounds in boxes, and when approaching a possible engagement take twenty more on the person. Of this latter, from perspiration, rain, and many causes there is great necessary waste. It is an article that cannot be dispensed with, of course, and the supply on the person must be kept up. The guns cannot be kept loaded, therefore the diminution is constant from this necessary waste. My division, at present numbers, will require forty to fifty wagons to carry the extra infantry ammunition. You should see the long train of wagons of the reserve artillery, passing as I write, to feel what an item this single want is.

But to come back to my narrative! After returning from the council I met Gen. Geary and Col. Best and made arrangements for retaking our entrenchments in the morning. The plan was simply to open upon the ridge they occupied with several batteries of artillery at daylight, and after a cannonading of fifteen minutes to attack them from the left (Greene's position) while the 1st Division held a threatening position on the right and felt them cautiously by skirmishers. The cannonading was to be kept up on the right woods so long as it could be done and not interfere with the advance of our troops.

We had high and admirable positions for our artillery, but the defense of the Rebs. on our right (opposite the 1st Division) was quite impregnable for assault. There was, besides our log entrenchments along the crest of the ridge, a strong stone wall parallel to it about one hundred feet on our side, but inside the woods, which was also in possession of the Rebels. They therefore had two lines of strong defenses against a front attack and the flank toward the creek could not be turned, as a morass and impassable stream protected it; and across the creek they had filled the woods with sharp-shooters behind rocks and in a stone house near the bank.

Thus unfavorably stood matters. It was 3.30 o'clock at night before I got through duty and then got a half hour or so of sleep on a flat rock sheltered by an apple tree.

[*The remainder is missing.*⁴]

ONCE MORE ON THE POTOMAC

Pleasant Valley, Md.,
July 16, 1863.

My Dear Daughter:

I reached this place today from Williamsport. I have hurriedly continued my journal from where I left off at the halting place. I have been so long on marches and so much deprived of sleep and rest that I am obliged to send you a stupid account of our share of the great battle.

The newspapers will give you the intelligence that Lee has reached the Virginia shore with most of his army. His invasion has doubtless cost him 40,000 men in killed and wounded and prisoners. I doubt if he ever tries the game of invasion the third time.

I am now encamped within a few rods of my headquarters of last autumn. Rene will remember the rolling hills towards Sandy Hook, near Maryland Heights. I am on these.

I have not yet seen Miss Longbridge nor any of the family, but propose to go over today. I judge from the orders that we shall be here but a day or so and then cross into Virginia again, and so do the campaign over and over. Our troops require rest, shoes, and clothing. They have been some five weeks on the march. None but veteran troops could stand it, especially as we have not had a dry day for nearly three weeks. It is pouring in torrents today, but I think the Army of the Potomac is simmered down to the very sublimation of human strength and endurance. I will bring up my journal to date, if I stay a day or so. . . .

Love to all,

Your Affectionate Father,
A.S.W.

1. Henry L. Chipman of Detroit, who became lieutenant colonel of the Second Michigan Infantry upon its organization in April 1861. He served with distinction throughout the war, being brevetted for gallantry at Chancellorsville and again at Gettysburg. Following the war, he remained in the regular army until his retirement in 1887. In May 1881 he became lieutenant colonel of the Seventh Cavalry, General Custer's old regiment.—*Record of Service of Michigan Volunteers.*
2. In the battle of July 1 the First and Eleventh corps, commanded respec-

tively by General Doubleday and General Howard, were alone opposed to the vastly superior numbers of General Lee. Although they were driven from their positions and compelled to retreat through the town of Gettysburg to the new position selected by General Howard on Cemetery Ridge, the desperate fight they had waged made possible the assembling of the Union army in the favorable position it occupied during the second and third days of the battle. Although Pickett's charge on July 3 still captures the headlines, the fight made by these two corps on July 1 contributed as much as anything to the ultimate Union victory. The reports of Generals Doubleday and Howard concerning the action of July 1 do not support the statements of General Williams, who apparently was still smarting over the rout of Howard's Eleventh Corps at Chancellorsville, two months earlier. The losses sustained by the regiments of Doubleday's First Corps sufficiently attest the desperate nature of the fight they waged. The Twenty-fourth Michigan Regiment of the Iron Brigade, in particular, sustained a battle loss of 80 percent of the number engaged, of which 64 percent— practically two men out of three—were either killed or wounded. At the Gettysburg semi-centennial celebration fifty years later, survivors of the regiment welcomed their ancient foemen of the Twenty-sixth North Carolina Regiment, which had sustained a battle loss of over 800 of its total of 900 men engaged. For the reports of Generals Doubleday and Howard see *Official Records*, Series 1, XXVII, Part 1, 696– 711 and 243–257.

3. General Henry H. Lockwood of Delaware, a West Point graduate in the class of 1836. Following the Florida War of 1836–37 he resigned his army commission and in 1841 became Professor of Mathematics in the U.S. Naval Academy. His service here continued, save for the interruption occasioned by the Civil War, until his retirement in 1876. In August, 1861, he became a brigadier general of volunteers, continuing in the army until August 24, 1865.

4. The remainder of General Williams' letter, describing the action of July 3 in which the Confederates were driven from Culp's Hill after seven hours of continuous fighting, is unfortunately missing. A summary account of the action is included in Williams' report upon the battle, published in *Official Records*, Series 1, XXVII, Part 1, 772–76.

VIII

To the Rappahannock Once More

TO THE RAPPAHANNOCK ONCE MORE

For whatever reason, the will to fight displayed by General Meade prior to the battle of Gettysburg seemed to have vanished following that event. Contrary to President Lincoln's desire, General Lee was permitted to withdraw his army across the Potomac without interference by Meade, who continued to sadden the President by his procrastination throughout the autumn months of 1863. On October 16, Lincoln proposed that if Meade would attack Lee on a field "no more than equal" to the Union army, the honor, if successful, would belong to him, while the blame, if defeated, would be shouldered by Lincoln. Prior to this proposal, however, on September 29 an order was issued which brought General Williams' career with the Army of the Potomac to a sudden end. The Union defeat at Chickamauga (September 19–20) led the government to order the transfer by rail of the entire Eleventh and Twelfth corps (some 16,000 men) from the Army of the Potomac to the western arena, the operation constituting perhaps the largest transfer of troops over so great a distance that had ever been performed. The letters which follow relate General Williams' closing activities with the Army of the Potomac.

IN PURSUIT OF GENERAL LEE

Snickersville, Va., July 21, 1863.

My Dear Daughters:

The change of my whereabouts is almost as magical as the Rawls[?] performances, appearing through the stage floor in one instant and mysteriously disappearing in the scenic clouds above in the next. We literally have no rest now, for our stoppings are so full of duties that we can hardly be said to rest. We remained in Pleasant Valley two days, exclusive of the day of our arrival, one of them very rainy. I sent you my journal up to the 16th. I visited the Longbridges and took tea there. Miss Ella and the old folks were in good health, the former as sweet as ever.

The fields which we left last winter all forlorn and desolate-looking, are now planted all over with corn and grain, but are for the fifth time terribly cut up again, as two or three corps encamped on them and whole acres of wagon trains. I pity the poor people who live where armies encamp. Pleasant Valley has suffered worse than any other spot. This time our visit was especially destructive, as wheat, corn, and potatoes were all standing and as far as the eye could reach were being desolated by horses, herds of cattle, tramping men, and crushing wagon wheels. It is absolutely an impossibility to keep up in the minds of soldiers and employees the least respect for private property. They drive through fields of ripe wheat and over acres of growing corn without one thought of the destruction they are causing.

I sent you from Pleasant Valley a conclusion of our Gettysburg campaign and battle. It was stupidly done, as absolutely I could not get my fatigued mind up to the subject. I forgot also to tell you of a narrow escape I had on the road. I was passing a column of our soldiers and endeavored to take the side of the road, passing along a deep roadside or ditch on a narrow strip between a stone wall on one side and the deep ditch on the other. I finally came to the end of the wall where a rail fence had been partly thrown down. Here I tried to jump my horse over, but in turning him on the narrow ledge he slipped and tumbling down the bank landed flat on his back in the bottom of the ditch. Fortunately, as he slipped I jumped from the saddle and landed safely on the bank. Old

Plug Ugly must have fallen eight or ten feet and as he groaned hugely I supposed he was finished at last, after passing through divers[?] battles and one heavy fall into the pontoon boats. The men got his saddle off while he lay as quiet as a lamb and turning him round, with a big grunt he got to his feet and was led to the upper end of the ditch to terra firma, apparently as sound as ever. My saddle, which I supposed was crushed beyond repair, came out scarcely injured, saved I supposed by the overcoats and blankets strapped before and behind. Altogether, it was a lucky escape for man, beast, and saddle.

Old Plug was somewhat stiff the next day, but I rode him every day. He is a regular old soldier, however, and takes great advantage of my indulgence and his long service and five or six wounds. As we march along he grabs at every knot of grass, corn, shrub, or any vegetable substance that presents itself on his way. No amount of spurring or whipping can break him of this habit of laying in a supply against short rations. He is an odd, lazy old fellow, sometimes pretending to be very scary, especially after every battle, at other times apparently afraid of nothing. For a year and a half we have been daily companions. We get up a great love for even brutes under such circumstances. I should grieve to part with old Plug Ugly, with all his faults.

Sunday, 19th July: We marched from Pleasant Valley at 9 o'clock, the 2nd Division leading. The 2nd and 3rd corps had crossed the day before. We crossed at the same place as last winter, over the pontoon bridge into Harpers Ferry and round the foot of Loudon Heights. The corps trains in advance delayed us so that we halted for the night about eight miles up the valley.

The guerrillas troubled the advance considerably, coming down from the passes in the Blue Ridge. We sent out patrolling parties, and as some firing had been done from houses, we arrested several citizens and copying Lee's example we gathered up all the horses and cattle we could lay hands on. Our first camp was in the vicinity of the pass through "Short Mountains" near Hillsboro. From this point we went last winter through Hillsboro to Leesburg. Our present march will be toward Snickersville.

Monday, July 20th: Marched at 7 o'clock, in the rear as before; road very rocky, muddy, and crooked. Men and teams were obliged to find new paths through fields and woods. In an hour or so, ran against the trains of the 2nd Corps and halted for several hours. Day very hot and sultry.

At 2.30 P.M. marched again. Passed through Woodgrove, a village of half a dozen houses, and struck the Leesburg Pike about four miles from Snickersville. Encamped in the vicinity of Snickersville at 6.30 P.M.

This village is just in the mouth of Snicker's Pass through the Blue Ridge. It is the main route to Winchester from Washington.

You may remember that I marched my division up to the pass on the other side just before the battle of Winchester, and was obliged to go back and go through Jackson up the Shenandoah Valley. Years ago I passed over this same route from Berryville to Washington. It was before the days of pikes in this section. I found the most execrable roads, such as we came over yesterday; roads in which small mountain streams find their courses, making an alternation of rocks and mud as the nature of the soil changes. Roads are never repaired in this state, except the pikes.

It is now 9 o'clock A.M. and we have as yet no order to march today. Our destination was supposed to be near Warrenton. What the grand program is, I cannot say, but if it be another "onward to Richmond" we shall make another failure, simply because our army is still outnumbered by the Rebel army under Lee. He is constantly falling back on reinforcements and his base of supplies. We are moving away from both and daily decreasing in numbers. Besides, as an invading army, we must almost of necessity attack, and the odds are always greatly against the attacking party in two armies like those now opposed. We have, I hear, received some reinforcements, not as many as we lost men at Gettysburg, nor are they the same hardened troops, but rather of that kind which have been enervated by garrison life on the sea-coast. These long and daily marches will break them down in spirits and strength.

I see that our real strength at Gettysburg is greatly exaggerated in the public prints. I have no doubt the public generally think that our army wears longer than a railroad track, with not half the wear and tear! It never takes into account the fact that this army has lost nearly 40,000 men by expiration of term of service within the past two months. That in the same time at least 40,000 have been put "hors de combat" in battle and engagements, and that sickness and intercessions of friends are continually draining our ranks. It is a fact, I know, that at Gettysburg we had less than 60,000 fighting men. The lowest estimation of the enemy's force was 85,000, and from that to 120,000. I think they crossed the Potomac with at least 90,000 men, and they lost in killed and wounded, prisoners and deserters, at least 40,000, an expensive invasion, from which they cannot soon recover. It vexes us here, however, to see the constant disposition of people at home to overstate our numbers.[1] There never was a better army, because from long service and few recruits we are hardened down to the very sublimation of muscle, health, and endurance. The men can march twenty-five to thirty miles a day with sixty pounds—if necessary. They seldom grumble, and come to camp after a hard day's march with jokes and songs. They are absolutely without fear, and if ordered forward as skirmishers against entrenchments they go with cheerfulness and generally cracking jokes. Such an army can only be made by long service and exposure in the field and at a great loss of original numbers.

If recruits had been constantly sent to old regiments they would have [been] assimilated, in a good measure, to these old soldiers, and in a short time caught their spirit and daring. It is wonderful how soon a recruit becomes a good soldier when placed amongst old troops. Our government should never have relaxed for a minute its recruiting. It takes a great effort to keep a large army from decreasing, and it can be kept fully efficient only by constant additions. When regiments fall below a certain number their efficiency is greatly destroyed. The details and daily-duty men oppress the soldier, and their thin ranks discourage and dishearten him. But enough of this!

I hope a new policy is inaugurated of filling up old regiments who have experienced officers with the new drafted men, and that our armies will never again be permitted to lose half their men in the beginning of a campaign, and at a moment when the enemy has just filled his ranks with hordes of conscripts.

Love to all,

Your Affectionate Father,
A.S.W.

❖

STILL FOLLOWING GENERAL LEE

Camp near Warrenton Junction,
July 27, 1863.

My Dear Daughters:

I sent you my journalizings from Snickersville up to the 21st inst., I think. If the mail escaped the guerrillas, who watched our flanks and rear pretty closely, you have received the package before this.

We remained at Snickersville two days, expecting to move every hour and therefore uncomfortably packed up, ready for a start. We were encamped near the mouth of the pass over the Blue Ridge. Some of the officers went up the mountain ridge and found a splendid view of the Shenandoah Valley, embracing Winchester, Martinsburg, Front Royal, Berryville, and other towns of the valley. A sight of the Rebel camps and their moving columns and trains was also had.

On account of the repeated annoyances of the guerrilla bands, firing at our men from houses or their vicinity, we sent out scouting or patrolling parties to sweep in all cattle, horses, and forage that could be found. The country was pretty well cleaned out before, and our gleanings were of a poor character. Lame and worn-out horses, poor cattle, and mixed wheat, corn, and oats. But the gatherings were followed by all sorts of people begging for the return of horses and cattle, as the last left them to carry on their farms. Women (all widows, by their own accounts) were generally successful, as they gave piteous stories of their necessities. The men in some cases were handed over to the provost guard to be carried on a few days. They were generally in concert with these roving guerrilla bands, although they swore to entire ignorance of anything of the kind.

July 23rd: My division marched at 6 o'clock under orders to encamp at Paris, which is in the entrance to Ashby's Gap. These gaps, you know, are low places in the mountain range through which roads have been made. They are generally deep gullies or ravines cut by the passage of small streams or rivers; sometimes simply low depressions in the mountain. They occur in the Blue Ridge Range at pretty regular intervals, commencing within a short distance of Harpers Ferry in the following order, southward: Vestal, Hammond, Gregory's, Snicker's, Ashby's, Manassas, Chester, Thornton's, Swift, etc. If you have Lloyd's official map you can follow our lines of march pretty accurately, though the roads and relative positions of villages are by no means correctly laid down. For general purposes and for names of small places it is the best map you can get.

Our first halt today was near Upperville, a small village on the stone pike which runs through Ashby's Gap to Fairfax Court House and Alexandria. I halted here for several hours to avoid the heat of the day, myself and staff taking a nap under the shady oaks of a Mrs. Fitzhugh's lawn. It was a beautiful broad lawn of a very dilapidated old Virginia residence. Mrs. Fitzhugh was in great distress about the vegetables of her small garden, which I protected by a guard. Several grown daughters took observation of us from a ricketty old stoop of the decayed mansion.

I moved on toward Paris at 3 o'clock, and when about half way to what I supposed would be my night halt, up came an order to countermarch through Upperville to Piedmont, and thence to Markham's Station on Manassas Gap, fifteen miles distant. I had already marched nearly fifteen miles in a very hot day. The order was not a pleasant one, but there was no appeal. I countermarched the whole command, infantry, artillery, ambulances, and ammunition trains, leaving the supply train to follow the 2nd Division, which was going by the way of Paris. We had a pike road all the way to Piedmont, but a terrible one for the men as it was covered all the way with small boulders and sharp stones which cut their feet badly. As the side of the road every few rods was springy and miry, I was obliged to keep the stone pike.

About sundown we reached Piedmont, an abandoned railroad station with two or three ruined buildings. There was nobody about to give us information as to the route beyond, but after some delay one of my staff found the residence of a Mr. Marshall (who said he was a son of the late Chief Justice Marshall) from whom we got information as to the road to Somerset Mills, one of the designated points of my march.[2]

We found this road very bad. At its outset it ran along the bed of a creek, which recent rains had overflowed. It was very rocky and full of deep holes. Dusk had come pretty deep, and the very small crescent of a moon helped us but little. We splashed along this dismal way, winding about in great uncertainty as to whether we were on the road or not, the troops going along the fields as much as practicable. After much labor the head of the column reached Somerset Mills. Regiments straggled in, having lost connection in the woods. It was 10:30 o'clock. There was just moon enough to find a campground. I massed the brigades in the field and having traveled twenty-five miles in the most sultry of temperatures I ordered a bivouac and reveille at 3 o'clock. I put myself on my rubber poncho under a thick sour apple tree with my saddle for a pillow and was asleep in five minutes.

July 24th: Reveille at 2:30 o'clock and marched at about 3:30, as soon as light showed me the road down a deep muddy ravine on toward Markham's. These Virginia roads wind about in all directions; seem to be the chance paths of farms connected by lanes; never repaired; and all the little brooks flow into and along them, cutting out gullies and forming immense mud holes. It is incredible that heavy loaded wagons get over them. The country is not well cultivated, though capable of high cultivation for the most part. The fields now are covered with the largest kind of blackberries, both the vine and the bush kind. We have been surfeited with them. For miles and miles in every day's march since crossing the Potomac the fields on both sides of the road have been, at every halt, covered with men gathering these berries. Before crossing the Potomac, we had feasts of all kinds of cherries. Our orderlies would break off limbs loaded with the most luscious of this fruit, which we ate as we marched along.

We halted at Markham's to issue rations to the troops. The trains which we overtook at Somerset Mills last night had passed on to this point. I found Capts. Whittlesey and Beman (who remain with supply trains) still in bed. They have comparatively easy times in these active campaigns. I went ahead and halted for the troops at a small church in front of Gen. Meade's headquarters. It was full of wounded cavalrymen from a skirmish yesterday. Now and then a gun boomed out of the mountain gap in our front, and it was generally understood that a strong attack was to be made by the 3rd Corps, which our corps was to support. Gens. Meade and Slocum had gone in advance.

I took a long nap and was awakened by a staff officer, with orders to march to White Plains via Rectortown. Took a road to the right, which led below the railroad at Piedmont, to Rectortown. Roads badly blocked by trains of three or four corps, all fighting for the right of way.

THE UNION RETREAT AT BALL'S BLUFF, OCTOBER 21, 1861
Reproduced from a sketch in *The London Illustrated News*, November 23, 1861.

CHARGE OF THE FIFTEENTH MASSACHUSETTS REGIMENT AT BALL'S BLUFF,
OCTOBER 21, 1861
Reproduced from a sketch in *The London Illustrated News*, November 23, 1861. The accompanying article states that most of the officers of the regiment were students of Harvard College, whose conduct was "most praiseworthy."

An "incident" in the life of General Banks' Division in western Maryland. Reproduced from a sketch in Frank Leslie's *The American Soldier in the Civil War*.

MARCHING UNDER DIFFICULTIES

Reproduced from a sketch in *The London Illustrated News*, July 13 1861. The accompanying article describes the tactics of the Secessionists in waylaying Union sentries and officers and mention "our special artist" accompanied the party on the night when the incident illustrated occurred.

"ALL QUIET ALONG THE POTOMAC TONIGHT"

"CONTRABAND OF WAR" IN VIRGINIA

Slaves seeking refuge in the Union Army. Reproduced from a sketch by "our special artist" in *The London Illustrated News*, July 27, 1861.

Got bread and milk at the "house of a widow" in Rectortown. Bad roads to that point; better between Rectortown and White Plains. It was 10:30 o'clock when the head of my column reached the cross-roads from Salem to White Plains, [two and] one-half miles distant from the latter place.[3] The multitudinous mountain streams had all dis appeared, and for hours my men were without water. Found a little stream and good spring at this point and bivouacked for the night, sleeping again under an apple tree, very soundly and very nicely. Marched today twenty miles, making forty-five miles in two hot days for my troops, over all sorts of roads from stony pikes to water courses, and fording lots of small streams.

July 25th: Made a late start, as my staff officer reported that corps headquarters had not arrived at White Plains and I had no orders. Went forward, however, to relieve a brigade of the 6th Corps (Gen. Russell) at the railroad depot. Halted on a broad plain near the village, forming two lines and breaking into column by the right of companies, the usual formation for camping. The men had their shelter tents up at once, supposing we were camped for the day.

Gen. Slocum came up in an hour or so and ordered me to move in my own time through Thoroughfare Gap to Haymarket, enroute for Warrenton Junction! I let the men remain quiet until 1 o'clock; sounded the "generale," a signal to strike tents and prepare for march. It was a sunny, hot day and over acres of ground covered in regular streets by the little white shelter tents you could hardly see a man, but when the drum corps on the right rolled out the "generale" the fields swarmed like a bee-hive with the "blue jackets" in a confused mass of moving humanity.[4] Soon the "assembly" is beaten and that confused and restless mass suddenly forms in regular columns. The acres of white tents have disappeared and motionless columns of men stand in their places. You hear the confused murmur of the roll calls and the responses of the men. Then comes the beat of "to the colors" and those columns wheel into two long lines and the head of it begins to stretch out over the fields towards the route of march, preceded by the colors of the different brigade commanders. In fifteen minutes this city of canvas has disappeared and is moving away as if by a magical power.

So in halting: The order of camp depends upon the space and nature of the ground. Sometimes in masses, sometimes in long lines, sometimes in a front line of battle, with a second line in column. Riding ahead or sending a staff officer, the order of encampment is determined and notice sent to the commanders of brigades. The formation is taken up without delay or confusion, and before you could fancy so many men could be put in position, you will see the little canvas tents formed in regular order and the fires built and suppers cooking. The practice of two years has taught the economy of time and the way to do it.

After leaving White Plains we found a tolerable country road to Thoroughfare Gap, a deep and famous pass through the Bull Run Range. It was through this gap that Lee sent most of his army last summer before the second battle of Bull Run. A stream called Broad Run, has its headwaters north of this gap and tumbles through it in a very tumultuous way. It is a very narrow pass and one cannot help wondering why Ricketts with his division of McDowell's corps did not hold Longstreet in check, when sent there last summer. Had he done so, Jackson's famous corps would have been destroyed. On the east side of the gap, at the base of very steep bluffs, is a considerable group of deserted stone houses and a very large mill, windowless and floorless, several stories high. I believe it was intended for a cotton mill. The road from the gap to Haymarket is a good pike, but the level, fine-looking country is wholly abandoned. We did not see one cultivated farm nor an inhabited dwelling. Even the fences have pretty nearly disappeared.

I encamped near where the village of Haymarket once stood, of which nothing is now left but chimney stacks. The houses were all burned last summer by Sigel's corps in a belief that one of our soldiers had been murdered in the village. On investigation, however, it turned out that the bloody clothes found were those of one of our cavalrymen, mortally wounded in a skirmish, who had been kindly cared for by the people whose houses were burned and who came near being hung by the infuriated soldiers. Such is one of the phases of war. March today, thirteen miles.

Sunday, July 26th: Marched at 6 o'clock via Greenwich, crossing the Warrenton pike two miles below. As we approached Greenwich a church bell rang. It was a sound we had not heard for a long time. The people did not know we were near, and stopped the bell at once. They seemed to fear that we would think it a signal for the Rebels. A very healthy and gentlemanly Englishman has a splendid country place here. As I was halting at one of his tenant houses he came out and invited me to his house, introducing me to his stout and very ladylike wife. On the gate post of his grounds he had a large placard, "This is the property of an Englishman and protected by safeguard," which safeguard he showed me and requested a guard, all which was furnished while my troops were passing. This Englishman was a cotton broker for several large Swiss and French factories, residing in the winter in Savannah and in the summer here. His name is Green. As few of our troops have been this way before, the people were both curious and agitated. I saw a good many female faces peering out of Mr. Green's windows, and Mr. Green was very short of breath when he introduced himself. However, he knew several officers of my acquaintance, had been a good deal in New York and in the North, and was very pleasant, setting out his good things with capital whiskey and ice water! Altogether I was sorry I could not stay longer with Mr. Green.

We reached Catlett's Station on the railroad. Here the whistle of the cars sounded like the tones of civilized life again and we found a newspaper, after a week's fasting. Two miles beyond Catlett's in a large open plain, almost surrounded by woods, we encamped about 4 P.M., from which I am at present writing. It is just south of Cedar Run. Good water is scarce, though we have contrived to find two or three tolerable springs. Two other corps (the 1st and 11th) are at Warrenton Junction, just beyond us. The 6th is at Warrenton. I know nothing of the others. Our march today was fifteen miles. The 2nd Division, which we have not seen since leaving Snickersville, arrived about dark and encamped opposite us.

We are now on our last summer's route of retreat under Pope. The face of the country has much improved in greenness and freshness, as the recent rains and the absence of troops have brought out the grass. Last summer everything was dry and dusty and desolate. There are no inhabitants about here now, but what with green, fresh foliage and herbage and the absence of dead mules and horses and general nastiness, things certainly look better than they did then. The affairs of the country look better, too, I think, though they ought to be much better than they are. But why complain? It is easier to grumble than it is to submit with confidence and good nature. It is hard work, sometimes, to convince oneself that affairs are not most bunglingly conducted, and yet how few of us are on the proper standpoint to judge the best how things can be or ought to be conducted.

I will continue my journal from this point if we stay here, as I hope, a day or so. My men greatly need rest. They have been marched now for nearly six weeks, much exposed, up nights, and always on the march as early as 2:30 or 3 o'clock. It surprises me, often, how they stand it, carrying, as they do, over sixty pounds weight and marching over roads of the roughest and rockiest kind. But they do it, day after day, in the old regiments without a single man falling out. At the end of the two days' march of forty-five miles over the hardest roads, of the old regiments three men was the highest number reported as stragglers, and it is very probable that they were sore-footed or fell asleep on a halt, without waking.

But I must close for the day.

Your Affectionate Father,
A.S.W.

◈

Near Catlett's Station, July 30, 1863.

My Dear Daughter:

We have been here three days but I really have not gathered strength or resolution enough to do much letter writing, and now at 10 o'clock at night comes an order to march at 6 o'clock in the morning. I have just time to acknowledge yours of the 25th and to endorse a check for $100 as a birthday gift. After using what you need you can give the rest to Uncle Lew, as your trustee.

We march to Kelly's Ford, where we crossed in April last, and from there I know not where. My health is perfect, but I am somewhat fagged by six weeks' marching and by sleepless, or nearly sleepless, nights. This sleeping under a "sour apple tree" and being roused at 3 o'clock is not pleasant nor conducive to strong nerves and bright spirits. Love to Rene and all. I'll write you both from Kelly's if I have time.

I suppose some great event is in preparation. I hope it may not prove a repetition of my last summer's campaign on the Rappahannock. I cannot see the policy of our movement just now, but others have a higher standpoint and a broader view, and of course are better judges. We shall see!

Your Affectionate Father,
A.S.W.

◈

BACK AT THE RAPPAHANNOCK

Camp at Kelly's Ford, Va.,
Aug. 6th, 1863.

My dear Daughters:

I wrote you last from Warrenton Junction and enclosed a draft to Minnie for a birthday gift of $100, all of which I hope was duly received.

We left Warrenton Junction Friday, July 31st, marching at 6 o'clock A.M. via Elk River or Elkton and Morrisville to this point, a march of twenty miles on a very hot day. The roads were unusually good for Virginia, but the country poorly cultivated and thinly settled, as it has been since we crossed the Bull Run Mountains. We halted near Elkton for a long rest, and I rode over to a very antique-looking brick house to learn its history. I found it full of Negroes, dozens of which were children of all ages. It was a farm of about 900 acres formerly owned by a Mrs. Blackwell, who, dying a few years since, gave all her Negroes their freedom and the farm for their support. A half dozen or more families live in the family mansion and others are scattered over the estate. The land seems to be good, much of it lying along Elk River, but it is uncultivated except a small patch about the house, in corn, and the premises were sadly dilapidated.

I had a long talk with a very old Negress, who told me all about the family, but could not explain why so many Negroes free could not better cultivate. She insisted they were all fond of work, for their 'Missus' had brought them up to that. A brother of Mrs. Blackwell, a Mr. Fox of Foxville, above this, made the same disposition of his slaves and his estate. He had over 100 Negroes. It would be an interesting subject to look into. I should like to know how these communities of freed Negroes get along, where they have a large property left them. The outside appearances at Mrs. Blackwell's were not very creditable to this colony.

At Morrisville we passed the 2nd Corps. I saw Capt. Smith (formerly of Detroit) of the 7th Michigan Regiment. He is inspector general on the division staff. I have met him several times before. At Snicker's he came up several miles to call upon me. He did not reach the ford here until dark. The moon was just rising and gave light enough to make long shadows of woods and hills, quite a strange look to familiar localities. We encamped here one night last spring on our march to Chancellorsville, and crossed the Rappahannock at the very spot we have laid the present pontoon bridge. It is directly at the mouth of Marsh Run, on all the maps, which at its mouth is nearly as broad and deep as the Rappahannock.

The 2nd Division had the lead today and arrived before us. They were just crossing a regiment in the pontoon boats to cover the laying of the bridge. I was on a slope of ground in the angle between Marsh River and the river. It was reported that only two Rebel pickets had been seen. We supposed all was quiet, and would be, and I was forming my division by the moon-light on the side hill which slopes towards the south bank. All at once quite a volley of musketry belched from the opposite side of the river. The 2nd Division had a regiment in line and they opened in return and for a few minutes we had quite a lively fusillade. The low grounds lay in the shadow of the high hills on the north and east, and though we heard the whiz of the balls, nobody was hurt, nor did my regiments stop their movements into line for bivouac.

In ten minutes the whole hillside was blazing with the countless campfires for cooking coffee. As it was only a Reb. picket of twenty or thirty men, they did not stop to molest us, after one volley. But the cool and unconcerned way in which my troops took the affair, hardly asking what it meant, proves how strangely we get accustomed to all kinds of life of exposure and danger. If such a volley had been fired before our troops had seen the smoke of battle, it would have created an intense excitement, and in the night, as it was, probably great confusion. As it was, not a man moved nor halted to wonder even.

Saturday, August 1st: My division crossed the Rappahannock this morning at daylight, relieving five regiments of the 2nd Division bivouacked close to the stream. I deployed as skirmishers six regiments down and up the river and to the front to clear away the Rebel cavalry which showed itself here and there. We had some skirmish firing but no resistance. The day was intensely hot by 9 o'clock. I was obliged to ride along my whole extended front from the river above the ford, in a circle, to the river below the ford, a distance of several miles. I was ordered to halt my line and hold all this ground by a picket line. I got back to a small shaded hill near the center of my broad circuit well heated and was delighted to find that some of my staff had discovered an ice-house belonging to Mr. Kelly, with real ice in it! Was it not luxurious! Just fancy a day without a breath of breeze and the thermometer about ninety after a long ride, to find yourself most unexpectedly in possession of ice, somewhere where one had not even dreamed of the luxury. I immediately ordered a guard over the ice-house, the contents to be delivered on my order.

Pitched two tents for our headquarters near the small village of Kellysville, which is just above the ford. The Kellys, father and son (seventy and fifty years old) are rank old Rebels and the owners of great acres and vast property hereabouts. At the village is a large brick flouring mill and a woolen factory, both much dilapidated by nonuse for two years. They had over a hundred slaves on the breaking out of the war, most of which they have sent South. One old Negro, whose wife (now dead) was a slave of Kelly's, came in to visit his children, but he found that Kelly had sent them all off last week. The old man's voice was husky as he told me his story. I did not feel very bad that our soldiers had pillaged and destroyed most of Kelly's property and used his hay and grain. The younger Kelly, who looked very seedy and wore a very shocking, bad, white hat, pestered me greatly by his complaints. Today we gathered up all his cattle and horses we could find (some fifty of the former) and sent them to our commissary.

Sunday, August 2nd: Another very hot day. The south side of the Rappahannock here is a triangular shaped plain, a mile or so deep and perhaps three-quarters of a mile broad at its base, enclosed in thick woods. It is perfectly commanded by high hills which come almost to the riverbank on the north side. Our artillery is placed on these hills. Near the river on the south side the land is quite low and in places marshy. The land rises gently as it recedes from the river. Of course the ford and the approaches to it are perfectly commanded from the north side, and to hold it on the south requires a large picket force and an encampment in the hottest and most unhealthy locations. So we have been ordered back to the north bank. I removed the six regiments which have been frying under their little shelter tents to the north side, and after dusk the six regiments on picket quietly withdrew and we all took up a much pleasanter camp ground. The 2nd Division has gone below to Ellis' Ford, and our corps now pickets the river from Wheatley's (a mile and a half above, where we connect with the 1st Corps) to below Ellis' Ford, seven or eight miles. I have all my headquarters tents pitched and my camp bed, a luxury I seldom enjoy nowadays. The river from Wheatley's to the ford here is rocky and rapid, giving an immense water power. There was formerly a canal around the rapids built by the state for slack water navigation, but its locks are all decayed and broken in. Part of the canal is still full of water and used as mill races.

We have been figuring up our month's work to make out the monthly report and find that we have marched, last month, eighteen days; engaged in skirmishing and battles five; in camp, but mostly under arms or packed for march, eight days. Since leaving Stafford Court House on June 13th we have marched over 440 miles, to say nothing of entrenching work, side marches, and small movements. Besides this, we are often up until 11 or 12, and must be around again by 3 o'clock and our men have heavy picket duty which keeps 300 to 400 without sleep after long marches. None but hardened troops could stand this. Their cheerfulness under it is wonderful.

Monday, August 3rd: In withdrawing to this side last night I ordered the provost to bring off the younger Kelly and turn him over to the corps provost guard. He has recently been to Richmond and is a great scamp, I think. My pickets brought over a Negro slave, belonging to a Mr. James ("Jeemes" he pronounced it). His wife is a slave of Kelly's and he had the usual Sunday pass to visit two of his children at Kellysville. His wife and three other children have been sent away by Kelly. The man stays on account of his wife. He was greatly alarmed when first brought to me, for some reason or other, but I was interested in his talk and kept him at it till he told the whole family history of the Kellys and the "Jeemes." Two of his "young masters" had been at home, hid in the woods, all the while we were over the river. He thought they were all very tired of the war. They didn't talk much before the slaves, but he contrived occasionally to overhear what his "Massas" said to other officers. Old Kelly has but one arm. The other was lost by erysipelas caused by a wound on the hand received in giving a slave woman a blow in the mouth!

Righteous retribution!

The old Negro, who was of very pious temperament, kept me entertained by his talk until midnight, every now and then exclaiming, "Why de good Lord, Massa, I'ze had passes to see my chillun every Sunday for years and always back before breakfast, Monday morning. Now I'm here, and de Missus will be mighty anxious." I kept the Negro all night, but let him off in the morning after breakfast, with advice that he leave "Massa Jeemes" at the first chance, but he replied that his wife was the most precious thing to him in this life and he couldn't go without her and the children. When I suggested that his wife might have been sold south by Kelly, he turned away his head, with evident emotion, and after a while replied, "I is feared that, Massa, a long time, but I hope"; and he made some sensible remarks about the uncertainty of his future if he went amongst strangers, and though his "Massa" was only tolerable, he might be worse off elsewhere. There is a wonderful amount of strong sense in many of these uneducated Negroes.

Last evening, indeed all day yesterday, there was a severe cannonading not over five miles away toward Culpeper. It receded at first and then returned until we could hear the screech of the shell and the volleys of musketry. At one time I thought it would reach us and made some preparations for it. It stopped about dark near Brandy Station, five miles away. You will see an account of it in the papers. Deserters and contrabands say that Lee and most of his army is around Culpeper Court House, fourteen miles distant.

What the purpose of our commander is I cannot guess. We keep down the pontoon bridge and have built a rifle pit (very strong) on the opposite bank and have strong ones on this side and guard it vigilantly. We are also replacing the old permanent bridge over Marsh Run by a new one. Matters look like a further advance. If we do, we must attack Lee in his chosen position. Our reinforcements of troops never in action do not yet replace our losses in the recent campaign, and we have as yet no conscripts. People at home would be surprised if they knew how small some of our largest corps have become. Death, wounds, sickness, and discharges are rapidly reducing us to a skeleton army. We must be reinforced or the Army of the Potomac will be of the things that were. If we had 50,000 more men (and there is that number on the Peninsula, at Suffolk, and North Carolina, better here) we could, I think, finish Lee's army and the war within two months. . . .

Tuesday, August 4th: Rode with Gen. Ruger up the river to the right of our line and then to the left, fixing points for strong guards and rifle pits and other earthworks. I don't think I have said much of Gen. Ruger, though he is one of my especial favorites—commander of the 3rd Brigade. He is as modest as a girl but of the most thorough and sterling character. He graduated at the head of his class at West Point, was in the engineers for a while, resigned and went to Wisconsin, and came out lieutenant colonel of the 3rd Wisconsin Regiment. He was promoted last winter at the same time Knipe was. Ruger spends half his time with me.[5]

Did I tell you that Knipe, who has been absent since the Chancellorsville campaign, returned while we were at Warrenton Junction? He has been in command of the militia in Pennsylvania part of the time and tells most amusing stories of the crack New York regiments which were under his command. His health is not good. Gen. Jackson, who commanded the 2nd Brigade, and whose leg was broken before our Chancellorsville campaign, has not yet returned. He has got as far back as Washington. His aide was here and said the general would be up soon.

We have had a furious hot day and my long ride was a fiery one.

Wednesday, 5th: Another hot day, and I spent it under the shade trees in front of my tent. It was barely tolerable in the shade. Paymaster Freeman arrived about noon to pay off part of my division.

Thursday, 6th: National Thanksgiving day, which don't seem to be very generally observed.[6] The regiment directly in my front had some kind of service toward evening. I heard a man holding forth in regular Methodistical roar, and psalm singing and hallooing prayers. There was a considerable confusion of tongues, for the adjoining regiments were singing patriotic songs with uproarious choruses, and the drums of other regiments were beating the adjutant's call for dress parade. The day was very hot again, and I see by the New York papers, which we get now on the second day, that deaths by sunstroke have been large.

I have lost my favorite medical director, Dr. Chapel. He received an order as we were leaving Warrenton Junction to report to Gen. French as medical director of the 3rd Corps. It is a promotion, but the doctor left us with regret and was sorry for what most would have rejoiced at. He has been with us over a year and is, I think, one of the best surgeons and physicians I have ever met and withal a most agreeable and pleasant companion. I feel sad to lose such a staff officer. Dr. Love[?], of the 13th New Jersey Volunteers has been temporarily sent in his place.

I sent sometime ago for Minnie a melanotype group of officers and ladies taken at Stafford Court House and previous to that I sent a similar copy to Rene at Philadelphia. Neither of you have made allusions to them, and I fear they have miscarried. The one sent to Minnie was a laughing scene and we all thought very funny. . . .

Your Affectionate Father,
A.S.W.

◈

FAMILY AND PERSONAL GOSSIP

Kelly's Ford, Va.,
Aug. 31st, 1863.

My Dear Daughter:[7]

I have been rather dilatory in writing and can hardly remember the date of my last letter; but I remember that I was more than two weeks without hearing from you or Rene and that I wrote a short note of complaint. However, I believe your last letter sufficiently explains the delay. It was really too hot for work; but the weather is cooler here now.

I liked the photographs you sent much and it was rather curious that I was just then regretting that I had not asked you to have your photograph taken on your birthday. The full-faced is most liked, though it is not easy to decide. Capt. Pittman has seized upon the full face and several gentlemen have asked for them. Capt. Whittlesey especially wonders you don't send him one. So you'd better do it and send me a half dozen. I don't think your picture shows much change; a little [more] maturity, but I suppose when I get to see you I shall find a tall young lady! [8]

That reminds me that we have very stringent orders about leaves, and must not apply except on a surgeon's certificate of illness, though I judge from the number of general officers absent that the rule is not obeyed strictly. I have been waiting for Gen. Slocum to get off and back before I tried my chance. He has just got twelve days leave and went day before yesterday. I fear it will be too late for me when he gets back. Such has been my luck before. However, I shall try, if we do not get moving orders before.

Our daily routine is so void of interest that I can find hardly enough to make a readable letter. I have one agreeable piece of intelligence. One of my staff has just heard of the birth of a daughter, and he has named it "Minnie Williams Whitney." She is the first daughter of Capt. Whitney, 5th Connecticut Volunteers and provost marshal on my staff. The namesake was born on the 17th of August. You'll have to get up some present for the namesake. I have seen a photograph of the mother, which is beautiful. The father is a most gallant, energetic, and excellent officer, and an especial favorite of mine. So probably your namesake will combine many qualities. I hope she may prove as good a daughter as you have. I, also, have a namesake, for about the same day there was born unto Gen. Knipe a son, which he has named Alpheus Williams Knipe! So you see I have some gift making to do.

Capt. Wilkins has arrived but has sent in his resignation on account of his lameness. I suppose Capt. Pittman will take his place permanently.

Uncle Will Rumsey has a sutlership of one of our regiments. He comes up from Washington once a week or so. He brought up little Will the last time. Henry Colt spent Sunday with me a week ago. He is quartermaster of the 104th New York, in the 1st Corps, about four miles away. I send you photographs of three of my staff. The doctor is the new medical director in place of Dr. Chapel, promoted to a corps. Tell Rene I will write her in a day or so. I shall send the button you want and the Antietam bullets and some papers for safekeeping by Capt. Wilkins.

Your Affectionate Father,
A.S.W.

PROMOTIONS IN THE ARMY

Kelly's Ford, Sept. 4th, 1863.

My Dear Daughter:

I wrote you by Capt. Wilkins and sent a package of papers for safe-keeping. We were all sorry to have the captain leave us. He is exceedingly companionable and very popular as adjutant general with the subordinate officers, with whom he is officially brought much in contact. He has his peculiarities but is an admirable officer in the office, very systematic and thorough. The evening before he left we gave him quite an entertainment, at which the general and field officers "assisted." It was quite the most considerable set-out I have seen in camp. We even had watermelons!

There was a great deal of speech-making, most of which curiously and unexpectedly grew out of my own case on non-promotion. I was rather surprised to find how much feeling there was in my behalf. As a sequel to it all, the officers of the division held a meeting last night and appointed a committee to draw up a memorial to the President to be signed by every officer. I have no idea it will accomplish anything. Such a fellow as Crawford,[9] who skulked at Antietam and knows no more of military than that piebald dog I used to own, will be promoted before I am, simply because he has the impudence and falsehood of the devil, knows well the Secretary of War, is from Pennsylvania, and gives great dinners which he never pays for! He got a small puncture—self-inflicted, I think—(he was an assistant surgeon formerly) at Antietam and he nursed it so vigorously that he stayed away over six months, most of the time in Washington having small puffs prepared for the newspapers. He has recently got assigned to the Pennsylvania reserves and had a big time presenting a sword to Gen. Meade, for his own glorification. These are the fellows that get promotion. . . .

[*The concluding portion is missing.*]

◈

FOREIGN VISITORS AND MILITARY EXECUTIONS

Rapidan River, Raccoon Ford, Va., Sept. 20, 1863.

My Dear Daughter:

I received your letter of 12th inst. (no. 20) on the march to this place. It was indeed a nice long, agreeable letter and very acceptable. I answer it on top of a box, as we are all packed for a moment's move. . . . My command left our camp at Kelly's Ford Wednesday last (16th) and marched to Stevensburg. I pitched my tents in the front yard of a dilapidated F.F.V., who seemed very glad to have me about as a protector. He had a very smart and chatty daughter, to whom some of my staff made themselves very agreeable. I did not make her acquaintance, having absolutely lost all charms for maid or widow.

The cavalry crossed the Rappahannock the day before us and drove the Rebel cavalry beyond Culpeper. From Stevensburg I could see the line of the Orange Railroad down which we retreated from Culpeper last year. The village (a dozen houses or so) is on quite a hill, and the country around is very flat. As we encamped in the afternoon, the 1st Corps was on our right, but nothing on our left. We were the left of the whole army. On Thursday morning (5 o'clock) we marched for this ford. The morning was very foggy, luckily for us, for we struck the Rapidan and marched a mile or so under the Rebel batteries, not 500 yards distant. At length I found out our position from some cavalry and moved my troops into the woods before the enemy found out we were near them.

The whole line of country hereabout is very flat, while the opposite side is a series of high hills rising one above the other from the river bank. It is all fortified and the Rebs. are constantly digging on every hillside and crest. They have all the advantage, especially as a quite high mountain back of them serves as a lookout upon all our positions. Our picket line has been constantly fired upon and is exposed for hundreds of yards this side of the river. It took me all day Thursday, after reaching this, to get my pickets out to relieve the cavalry pickets. Every man who showed his head was sure to be a mark, and in some parts of the line I was obliged to wait until after dark before I could send forward my detail. In the meantime, the heavens opened on us in a terrific storm, which pelted us sadly. I was all day in the saddle and at night pitched my tent in the edge of the woods and by the advantage of some straw for a bed got a good sleep.

Friday (18th) was an equinoctial day, high wind and cold rain, a regular gale, which howled through the woods and poured in torrents. It cleared up about noon, partially, and I had the unpleasant task of calling out my division to shoot a deserter. It began to pour again in equinoctial torrents as my troops were forming, and the gloom of the weather was in concert with the melancholy duty. I have described for you the shooting at Leesburg. It was the same thing over. The poor fellow sat on his coffin and fell back stone dead at the discharge, like one going to sleep. It was his second desertion and the last after our execution at Leesburg and while marching toward Gettysburg. Of course, he had no hope of escape. I have over twenty conscripts who probably will die the same way.

Saturday, 19th: I rode along the whole of our front. The Rapidan is a very narrow stream, but its high banks are all on the side of the enemy. They are as busy as bees throwing up entrenchments and rifle pits. We count sixteen guns in position on my front from Raccoon Ford up to Somerville Ford, two miles or so. The firing has somewhat subsided, as I order my pickets not to reply unless they try to cross. I rode in plain view and at a fair musket-shot, and nobody fired at me, though I could see lots of officers on their works looking to see what was going on. I had with me two mounted officers, Gen. Knipe and Col. Hanley, 2nd Wisconsin, and two mounted orderlies. As I was riding up the river I heard a tremendous firing in our rear, which I supposed was distant artillery near Stevensburg. I hurried home and found an order for the troops to be under arms and the telegraph, which connects with us from headquarters, was working hard to find out the trouble. At length it was ascertained that the cavalry division at Stevensburg was discharging its pieces in volleys.

Sunday, 20th September: This was my birthday, an event which few of you at home remembered, I think. I was obliged to move camp from the wet woods to an open plain farther in the rear, but as I had received a present of a box of sherry I celebrated in the evening with my staff.

An Austrian captain with seven general staff officers called. He was on a mission to see the Army of the Potomac.

Monday, Tuesday, and Wednesday: Three sunshiny but cool days. We have been constantly packed expecting a movement. Night before last we were ordered to put five days' marching rations in knapsacks with three in haversacks. This indicates a long march away from our wagons. Today Sir Henry Holland, physician to Her Majesty, etc., Col. Townsend, and several staff officers, came to see our corps. I was obliged to unpack my only decent coat and do other things to put myself in a presentable look. Sir Henry is an old man. He remained but a short time, but went down to the front to see the Rebel line. . . .

You seem to have a gay time in Detroit. I have not yet learned how the concert went off. . . . Love to all. I have a good many letters to write and while so many things are on my mind I don't make much headway. The news from Rosecrans looks badly. I have feared that he was going too fast for that country. . . .

Your Affectionate Father,
A.S.W.

◈

LAST LETTER FROM THE ARMY OF THE POTOMAC

Raccoon Ford, Sept. 24, 1863.

My Dear Daughters:

We have just received orders to be ready to move on being relieved by the 1st Corps, I suspect to attack the enemy on the flank. The telegraph will tell you of coming events before this reaches you, but I write a word on the head of a box as it is very uncertain when I can write again. Don't be concerned if you don't hear from me. We are supplied with eight days' rations on the person. Love to all.

Your Affectionate Father,
A.S.W.

---

1. General Williams' statements, both here and elsewhere, illustrate a common tendency among soldiers to overestimate the strength of their opponents in relation to their own and the contrary tendency among

civilian and political observers to overestimate the strength of one's own army. At Gettysburg, the two opposing armies were fairly evenly matched, Lee having about 70,000 and Meade about 80,000 men. Of course many factors other than mere numbers operate to determine the outcome of a battle or a campaign.

2. The birthplace and boyhood home of John Marshall was in this vicinity. Descendants and collateral relatives of the chief justice lived in northern Fauquier County in the Civil War period. See W. M. Paxton, *The Marshall Family* (Cincinnati, 1885).

3. Salem and White Plains, both in northern Fauquier County, are now called respectively, Marshall and The Plains.

4. The "general," like many army customs, was probably an inheritance from the British army. Mrs. Lydia Bacon, who in 1812 accompanied her husband on the march of the Fourth U.S. Infantry from Boston to Vincennes and back (via Detroit as prisoners of war) recorded the words which accompany the tune: "Don't you hear your general say, 'Strike your tents and march away.' "—"Mrs. Lydia Bacon's Journal, 1811–1812," *Indian Magazine of History*, XL (December 1944), 374.

5. General Thomas H. Ruger, but thirty years of age at this time, ranked number three in the West Point class of 1854. Number one place was held by G. W. Custis Lee, son of General Robert E. Lee, who resigned his army commission on May 2, 1861 to uphold the fortunes of the Southern Confederacy. From 1856 to 1861 Ruger was engaged in the practice of law at Janesville, Wisconsin. In June 1861 he was appointed lieutenant colonel of the Third Wisconsin Infantry and remained in the army thereafter until his retirement in 1897 with the rank of major general.—*Dict. Am. Biog.*

6. On July 15, 1863 President Lincoln issued a proclamation appointing Thursday August 6, 1863 as a day of national thanksgiving of praise and prayers for the recent victories at Gettysburg and Vicksburg. In Detroit, as in the army, very little attention was paid to it, insofar as an examination of the *Free Press* discloses. Acting Mayor Francis B. Phelps issued a brief statement commending the observance to the local citizenry (dated August 5, but not published until August 6), and a thanksgiving service, to which the public was invited, was held in the Christian Church, corner of Jefferson and Beaubien. Meanwhile the Unitarian Society conducted an all-day excursion to Grosse Ile, featured by picnicking ashore and dancing on the vessel. The *Free Press* contains no further mention of the Thanksgiving service at the church.

7. This letter addressed to Minnie is included in the published collection as offering a sample of the domestic details dwelt upon by General

Williams, which, as far as practicable, have been deleted from most of the other letters.

8. He had not seen his daughter since the breaking-up of his family at Detroit upon entering active service two years earlier.

9. General Samuel W. Crawford of Pennsylvania, who entered the U.S. Army as an assistant surgeon in 1851, serving continuously, chiefly in Texas and the Southwest, until the outbreak of the Civil War. In 1860 he was stationed at Fort Sumter, where he commanded a battery during the bombardment of April 1861 which opened the Civil War. Contrary to General Williams' characterization, his wartime service was conspicuously distinguished. See sketches in Appleton's *Cyclopaedia of American Biography* and in *National Cyclopaedia of American Biography* (New York, 1904), XII, 232.

IX

Guarding
the
Railroad

With the Union army pinned in Chattanooga, besieged by General
Bragg, and in imminent danger of starvation, some effective rescue
measures had to be instituted promptly. The dispatch of 16,000 men
from the Army of the Potomac was one such measure. More important,
perhaps, was the appointment of General Grant, recently conqueror
of Vicksburg, to the command of all military operations in the western
theater of war. He promptly replaced Rosecrans, whose military com-
petence seemed to have vanished, by General Thomas, who grimly
promised that the army would hold Chattanooga until it starved. Yet
starve it must if its line of communication with Nashville and Louisville, whence its supplies were drawn, were to be closed. From Nashville the railroad ran to Bridgeport in northeastern Alabama, distant
fifty-five miles southwest from Chattanooga. From this point supplies had
to be wagoned to Chattanooga over a shockingly villainous highway
which was "strewn with the debris of broken wagons and the carcasses
of thousands of starved mules and horses." October 23 witnessed the
arrival of General Grant, who immediately approved the opening of a
shorter and better route between Bridgeport and Chattanooga. With
the more immediate danger of starvation removed, Grant turned his
attention to raising the siege of the city, and in the actions of November
23–25 (Chattanooga and Missionary Ridge) General Bragg was defeated and driven in retreat, burning his depots and bridges as he
withdrew. Early in March 1864 Grant arrived at Washington to
assume his new position as commander of all the Union armies. The
difficult task of guarding the railroad line from Nashville southward
still remained. To this service General Williams had been assigned upon
his transfer to the western theater. His letters depicting his experiences
and his observations upon the country and its inhabitants comprise the
present section of his correspondence.

REMOVAL TO TENNESSEE

OFFICE OF SUPERINTENDENT

MILITARY RAILROAD

DEPARTMENT OF THE CUMBERLAND

Nashville, Tennessee,
October 5, 1863.

My Dear Daughter:

I am stopped here by a guerrilla raid, which has broken up the track below. My troops are scattered everywhere and our horses and baggage are nowhere that I can hear of. In short, this transportation of large numbers of troops over long lines of different railroads is a tedious and uncertain matter. When my division will get together again in its excellence and unity, such as it was ten days ago on the Rapidan, is more than I can guess.

I wrote you a short note from our camp on the Rapidan on the 24 ult. We had been several days under marching orders and I supposed our destination was against the left flank of the Rebels. Indeed, I had my command under arms before I knew our route lay to the rear. We marched to Brandy Station on the Orange Railroad that afternoon, where we were ordered to turn in all our wagons and public property and prepare to take the railroad cars for Alexandria. Great was the speculation on our destiny and great the bustle and hurry all day Friday. But amidst all I was obliged to shoot a deserter, which [made] the circumstances of our march ten-fold more unpleasant.

Friday night, 25 September, I was ordered to march my command to Bealeton Station north of the Rappahannock. I reached that [place] about daylight and lay there until night waiting [for] cars. I took a train in the night and reached Washington Sunday morning. I was very busy all day, but dined with Maj. Sherman. At night I went as far as the Relay House to superintend my troop trains. I left there Monday morning on the express train, upon which I found Miss Lib Kirby and her cousin Mrs. Pratt, an authoress of some note and wife of an ex-secretary of legation at Paris.[1] Also Gen. Hooker, who took me into his private car and discussed by the hour . . . his military matters. He had been ordered to command the 11th and 12th corps, but Gen. Slocum demurred and sent in his resignation, but the President, I believe, decided to relieve one corps from Hooker's command. I expect that Gen. Slocum talked pretty plain to the President, but of that I can talk to you, not write. At any rate, Gen. Hooker and myself talked on the same subject. I believe you know what I think of Gen. Hooker, a gallant and chivalrous soldier and most agreeable gentleman, but as an army commander his signal failure at Chancellorsville under such advantages as no general officer has a second time will ever prevent any confidence in him as a great commander.

I stopped for the night at Cumberland, a romantic spot where the Alleghanies drop down into the lesser ranges of mountains. A committee called on me proffering a public reception in order to get a speech. I declined peremptorily and they threatened to follow me with a crowd; luckily my troop cars came up, and I escaped.

[*The remainder is missing.*]

❖

GUARDING THE RAILROAD

Decherd, Tenn., Oct. 12, 1863.

My Dear Daughter:

I was very low-spirited after parting from you at Louisville and had a tedious ride to Nashville, which we reached about 7:30 P.M. The country the whole way was without interest or attraction of any kind and seemed poorly cultivated. Perhaps it would have looked better if my feelings had been more joyous. Our reunion was too short for me to get over first impressions. I was really too full to talk; full of joy at seeing you, and full of regret that we were so soon to part, that mixed and conflicting state of the mind that keeps one in constant thought. I was glad, however, to see you for even that short time, after two years' separation.

I found Gen. Slocum and staff at Nashville, but Gen. Knipe and Ruger had gone on. I started to the depot the next morning to take the first train south, but was stopped by news that the Rebel cavalry were south of Murfreesboro and had destroyed a railroad bridge. I remained all day in the depot, but no trains ran and at night I was obliged to go to the hotel again. The next day (Tuesday) I spent the whole day watching the telegraph, receiving all kinds of rumors that the Rebs. were advancing towards Nashville, destroying the railroad as they moved. Toward dusk a train was sent out and we reached Murfreesboro about 10 o'clock without molestation. The town was full, no hotels, no stopping place. Fortunately I took letters from Capt. Irving, formerly of Detroit, to private families and to a quartermaster of the name of Williams, who found us comfortable quarters at the house of a young widow. . . .

I stayed Wednesday and Thursday at Murfreesboro waiting for repairs of the bridge. I was greatly impatient as I was separated from most of my division, which Gen. Butterfield had picked up and was marching up and down in pursuit of Rebel cavalry, which I knew had been chased away beyond Shelbyville by a superior force of our cavalry two or three days before. I left Murfreesboro Friday P.M. about sundown and after a most disagreeable night in a box car, picking up three of my regiments on the way, reached this point the next morning about eight o'clock. I had heard that Rebel cavalry was threatening this place, from which Butterfield had withdrawn all troops, leaving my baggage and Capt. Whittlesey without a guard, or a very small one.

However, I found all safe, except that the mountain tunnel six miles below had been somewhat obstructed by the Rebs. throwing rocks down the shaft. These were soon cleared away. As fortune would have it, a rock had lodged in one of the shafts and when the first train went through with Gen. Butterfield, down it tumbled, without, however, doing damage. Gen. Butterfield imagined the Rebs. were after him and telegraphed a firm order from the first station for watchfulness, etc. I had the whole country around scoured, but found no Rebs., though I am bored to death by incessant stories brought in by citizens that Rebel cavalry is moving to attack such and such points.

This is a monstrous line over which Gen. Rosecrans has to supply his army, over 300 miles of railroad, crossed every few miles by broad streams and valleys and running through and around and across high mountains from this [place] to Chattanooga. The bridge at Bridgeport (where the railroad crosses the Tennessee) has been destroyed and the railroad from that point to near Chattanooga, south of the river, is in Rebel possession. In consequence, all supplies must have land carriage over thirty miles over mountains and on roads of the worst description. This beggars anything we have seen of lines of operations in the Army of the Potomac, and I can't see how the army can be supplied at Chattanooga unless the Rebs. are driven off and the railroad opened in its whole length. Even then, it will be a most insecure line, liable to constant interruptions, and of a length that forbids protection. Even my command is now wholly out of forage and rations, except what I have been able to pick up with four or five wagons. All our transportation was turned in at Bealeton Station and we have received none here, nor do I hear of any.

My horses arrived yesterday. Old Plug Ugly has lost pretty much all his tail. His length is so great that he rubbed at both ends of the car and has bared the bones of his head and his tail, besides having had his neck badly bitten by some indignant horse. He looks worse than after the shell exploded under him at Chancellorsville. He looked at me with most sorrowful eyes on our first meeting. The stallion looks better, though he is badly rubbed on both hips by his two weeks railroad voyage. None of the horses are badly injured, however.

My command extends from Tullahoma south, half way between Cowan and Tantalon, so as to embrace the railroad tunnel which runs through the mountains six miles below this, a distance of twenty-two miles! Of course we can guard only the bridges, tunnels, culverts, water-tanks, etc. Gen. Ruger's brigade is from Tullahoma to Elk River, his headquarters at Tullahoma. Gen. Knipe's brigade extends the rest of the way to Cowan. His headquarters are here. The country about this is not well cultivated and the people who are left look shabby and forlorn. But there is a fine town two or three miles off (Winchester) and the country about it is said to be fertile and well cultivated. It has been pretty well stripped, for Bragg's and Rosecrans' armies have both encamped here. It was near Murfreesboro that the three-days' battle of Stone River or Murfreesboro took place. It was in the same town that Col. Duffield was made a prisoner with most of his regiment.[2] I am anxious to hear of your safe arrival home. Write me all about it and direct at present "Commander 1st Div. 12th A. Corps,

Decherd via Nashville, Tenn." All my staff are well and desire to be remembered. Give my love to all. If things don't move soon I shall apply for leave for twenty days.

Your Affectionate Father,
A.S.W.

◈

Tullahoma, Nov. 11, 1863.

My Dear Daughter:

I wrote Uncle Lew a hasty note yesterday after my return from Bridgeport. . . . I have so many posts now in the ninety miles of railroad I am guarding that my duties are greatly increased at home and away. It is no easy job to travel on this railroad, the way it is managed. The road is in a bad condition and the engines are old and worthless. It is a good day's work to get forty miles. There is a constant struggle to push forward freight cars with supplies for troops in front, but very little judgment is used in putting the road in condition to meet the demands upon it.

I was lucky this time in getting as far as Stevenson (forty-three miles) in one day. I believe I have written you that after leaving Cowan the road begins the ascent of the first Cumberland Range of mountains and passes through the rest of the ridge by a tunnel over half a mile in length. It then descends to the deep valley of Crow Creek, along which, deep down between the high mountain ridges, it follows to Stevenson in the valley or bottom land of the Tennessee River. At this point it unites with the Memphis, Chattanooga and Charleston Railroad and follows the valley of the Tennessee amidst stupendous mountains to Chattanooga.

Gen. Knipe joined our party at Decherd, his headquarters, so we had a quartette of Gen. Slocum, Gen. Knipe, Dr. McNulty, and myself. At Stevenson we found Col. Ross of the 20th Connecticut (whose regiment guards this place) comfortably located in the only decent house there and we were comfortably lodged with him. He had made ready a very stylish bedroom for Mrs. Ross, whom he was anxiously waiting for.

Luckily for us she was denied a pass and we had the benefit of the preparations.

We spent a day at Bridgeport where I have a regiment (123 New York), and where they are re-building a very long railroad bridge over the Tennessee, which was destroyed by the Rebs. in their retreat. The river is very broad here, and is divided into two streams by an island. The bridge makes slow headway as all the lumber is brought from Nashville. I met on my way down several Michigan officers. Amongst others Maj. Wm. Phelps, paymaster, who spoke of seeing you and "Mr. Allen." At Stevenson, Geo. Fellers, who used to keep a grocery store near the oil store, came to see me. He is with the 4th Cavalry, but, with all sutlers, is having a very hard time just now. At Bridgeport the famous Lookout Mountain, now in possession of the Rebs., is in full view, towering high over all the surrounding hills. It must be a grand lookout over the whole country, and I am more than surprised that it should have been given up to the Rebels. It will cost us many lives to regain it.[3] It has already cost some valuable ones to get hold of the valleys at the foot of the mountain.

In my first trip down with my division, when I expected to have been a part of Hooker's advance, I had as companions Capt. Atwell and Lt. Geary of Knapp's Pennsylvania Battery, and I relieved at Anderson a lieutenant colonel of the 111th Pennsylvania Infantry, all of whom were killed in the recent night attack upon Hooker's command. They were attached to the 2nd Division of our corps. It is hard to realize these sudden removals of one's friends, with whom but a few hours before one has talked in health and cheerfulness. But what a long list of them I can recall in this war!

Gen. Greene, whom I think I have spoken of to you, a very warm personal friend, was also badly wounded through the face. He for a while commanded a brigade in my division, and last year was in command of the 2nd Division while we were at Harpers Ferry, and previously at the battle of Antietam. He is a descendant of Gen. Greene of our Revolution. His wound, I hear, is not considered dangerous.[4]

In returning from Bridgeport we were obliged to stop a day at Stevenson where the officers of the 4th Artillery battery gave us an extensive supper. We had oysters and champagne! Just think of that, away down in northern Alabama and over these hard roads! The explanation is, that about fifty purveyors had been ordered away from the front and were all congregated at Stevenson with their unsold goods, and with some they had not been able to get farther toward the main army. It seemed strange, when our soldiers and officers, too, all along the railroad and in front were living on half and one-quarter rations, that oysters and champagne should be abundant at Stevenson. But by bribery and other tricks these sutlers contrive to get transportation often when men are starving for necessary supplies. What an immensity of rascality this war produces or develops!

It makes me sick, sometimes, to hear of the frauds and rascality that are practiced in all departments, often to the suffering and misery of those exposed in the field. These things are found, from the miserable pasted shoes that men pay high prices for to the food they eat. In everything there is proof of contractors' and government agents' fraud and cheating. I think it was Wellington who said that these things could be stopped only by hanging a contractor and inspector every Saturday night! I wish often it could be tried.

I sent you yesterday a few views I found at Stevenson. If I can get more I will send them. I am very comfortably situated now; have a nice cottage for officers and my own private room. The staff are in tents. You will think it strange, but I do not find my large room as comfortable as a tent with a stove. It is more convenient, that is all. . . . How long we shall stay on this railroad no one knows. I rather sigh for the field. I hate this kind of responsible and divided command, and yet those big mountains and rough roads look repulsive. Are we never satisfied?

I shall try to get leave before Christmas, though Gen. Thomas is one of those officers who never leaves himself and thinks nobody should. However, if we set down here for winter, I think I can accomplish it.

Love to all and accept oceans from,

Your Loving Father,
A.S.W.

◈

ROUTINE CARES AND UNFAIRNESS
OF GENERAL MEADE

Tullahoma, Nov. 20, 1863.

My Dear Daughter: . . .

I have nothing of interest to write. One day is like unto another. Only from the multitude of posts I have a greatly increased number of papers to examine and supervise and a great many more matters to think of. The weather has been for the most part mild and Indian summer-like, but from sleeping in a house I have caught a very bad cold, a thing that has never happened to me in the worst weather in a tent! Isn't it strange? Gen. Slocum has moved his headquarters here. Col. Rogers has gone home to get married, it is said; though I think not, for he is on a *real* sick leave and his lady love has been sick unto death's door.

Col. Best spent an hour with me this morning, discoursing about matters and things in general. . . . We are all just now terribly disgusted after reading Meade's report. He not only ignores me as corps commander, but don't even allude to the 1st Division, which lost more men on the morning of July 3rd than the 2nd Division to which he gives the whole credit of the contest on that part of the field. Gen. Slocum, who commanded the right wing, is not named and one brigade of my command is actually given to the 1st Corps! I have read botched reports, but I think Meade's beats all in blunders and partiality. When one reads the conclusion of a loss [of] over 23,000 men, one wonders how it could be from any description of a battle he finds in this report. I am not only disgusted and chagrined, but I am astonished, as I have regarded Meade as one of the most honorable and high-toned men, wholly incapable of unfairness or political bias.

I see, however, that he mentions Carl Schurz for being an hour or so in command of a corps, and Gen. Gibbon and Gen. Birney commanding corps [for] a few hours, but ignores me and my report, too, who commanded a corps the (entire) three days at Gettysburg. To make the matter worse, another Pennsylvanian, Gen. Geary, gets all the credit of the operations on the right during the morning of July 3rd, and myself, who spent a sleepless night in planning the attack, and my old division commanded by Gen. Ruger, which drove the

Rebs. from their double line of entrenchments, are not alluded to. Save me from my friends! I am pretty mad, but I think Gen. Slocum is a mile or so ahead of me in indignation. I do not remember to have passed forty-eight hours in a more vexed and annoyed state.

On the 27th I got back through that Cumberland tunnel, after many delays, and my forty-two miles (up and down eighty-four) seemed to me to have been a voyage equal to the passage to California by the Rocky Mountains. On coming back I changed my headquarters from Decherd to Tullahoma. I have hardly been quiet since I returned, for I am obliged to have a guard at every bridge, culvert, tank, and trestle on the railroad for over ninety miles. So I am kept going up and down to see how they are placed, what defense works, whether patrols are kept up, and generally if the railroad is as well guarded as possible. If important bridges are lost the whole army goes up, as they are just able to live now.

You see the responsibility is immense, without any possible credit. On this long road, bridged over mountain streams and trestled across mountain valleys and ravines for two or three hundred miles, the whole Army of the Cumberland now in and about Chattanooga must get its supplies for man and beast. The country is full of guerrilla parties and the Rebel cavalry are always menacing right and left to pounce in upon a weak point. I got back only yesterday from my last trip of four or five days, going with Gen. Slocum to Bridgeport. At this point the railroad stops by reason of a destroyed bridge where it crosses the Tennessee.

Until within a few days the whole supply of the army at Chattanooga has been carted over the most infamous mountain roads from this point, nearly sixty miles. The recent rains have raised the river so that the boats can now go part way up, to within eight or ten miles of Chattanooga. Gen. Hooker, with the 11th Corps and one division of the 12th Corps, has cleared the intermediate valley. They had quite a smart "skrimage" on the way, a night attack by part of Longstreet's men. Gen. Greene was badly wounded in the face and Capt. Atwell of the Pennsylvania Independent Battery mortally wounded. Lt. Geary, son of Gen. Geary, was shot dead. Both of these officers sat with me during the night I was trying to get over the mountain, as I have mentioned above. Geary's troops were on railroad trains and mine marching. For this reason, and perhaps a little partiality of Gen. Slocum for my division, was the reason mine was sent back to meet, as was supposed, a great cavalry raid. Geary gets the glory, but he suffers, as mine would, in loss of officers. It is singular, but after all and with these hazards, officers complain of being sent to inactive life and *losing* their chances! Strange animal is man!

In going down the other day there were thirty paymasters on the train. Among them, Wm. Phelps of candy store memory, who is now a P.M. I met several Michigan officers, but none from Detroit. At Stevenson on Sunday, Mr. Geo. Fellers, son of the former proprietor of the Exchange, now a sutler, came to see me. On my first trip I should have fasted for forty-eight hours but for a Michigan man who was the telegraph operator. He fed me quite nicely and could not do too much to aid me. Indeed, I find at all points the Michigan officers and men treat me with more than marked kindness and attention.

We have very beautiful moonlights just now and an immensity of whippoorwills, and there are two mocking birds which begin their imitations every night in apple trees close to my tent. They mock everything from a frog to a crow. Some of their notes are beautifully sweet. The boys have tried to capture them but without success so far. . . .

Your Affectionate Father,
A.S.W.

◈

GUERRILLA RAIDS AND POOR WHITES

Tullahoma, Nov. 31st, 1863.[5]

My Dear Daughter:

It is a cold, leaden, cloudy, snow-feeling day. My fingers are so stiff that I can hardly guide a pen; and yet I am away down in the sunny south, close to the Alabama line. Indeed, I have just come from Alabama. I don't see that the skies are more genial or the temperature much milder than in northern Michigan at this season. Indeed, the whole month of October has been mainly rainy and disagreeable, not half as pleasant as those misty, smoky, warm days we generally have up north. . . .

You see I have changed my locality and I must first tell you how. About a week ago I got orders by telegraph to put my division in march for Bridgeport, the place where the Chattanooga Railroad crosses the Tennessee River. They were in motion at daylight in the morning along my whole line. Between Decherd and Tantalon is the first high range of the Cumberland Mountains, and the road over it is nothing but a bed of high rocks and deep mud-holes. The ascent of the mountain begins just beyond Cowan. Having crossed this mountain the road runs down the deep valley of Crow Creek to Stevenson and then turns east toward Chattanooga. The railroad follows pretty much the same line, except that it pierces the mountain crest by a tunnel, three-fourths of a mile long.

I waited for my rearmost brigade to come up and then [went] to the cars, expecting to reach Bridgeport before the advance, but I found that such railroads run in such a way as this one is are not exactly to be relied on. The grades are tremendous, and the locomotives old, worn-out affairs. To this add the fact that no fuel is provided on the road. I started from Decherd in the afternoon and reached Cowan (four miles) without much trouble. But here began the heavy mountain grades and the tug of war. They keep at this point a locomotive called a "pusher" which pushes behind each train. The ascent to the mountain tunnel is about two miles. All night the locomotives tugged and pushed and screeched out signals and blew whistles, but it was "no go." We were obliged to go back to Cowan, where conductors and engineers and firemen all went to sleep. I didn't much blame them, for they had been out several nights without sleep. I rather envied them, as my seat was a board close to a broken window.

The night was very cold and (what is strange with me) I could not sleep. I had received a telegram that Wheeler, Roddey, Lee and other Reb. cavalry commands [6] had crossed the Tennessee to make another raid, and I was ordered to halt my command to meet them. Here I was, unable by rail to reach my command not ten miles ahead of me. I fumed and, I fear, swore, and walked the sidetrack for hours to keep warm and to keep down my indignant spirit. At length day-

**GENERAL BANKS' DIVISION RECROSSING THE POTOMAC AT WILLIAMSPORT
TO ATTACK GENERAL JACKSON, AT THE BEGINNING OF MARCH 1862**
The Forty-sixth Pennsylvania band in the foreground. This was under General Williams' command.
Reproduced from Frank Leslie's *The American Soldier in the Civil War*.

GENERAL BANKS' DIVISION ENTERING FRONT ROYAL, SPRING 1862
The Blue Ridge Mountains and Manassas Gap in the background. Reproduced from a sketch in Frank Leslie's *Illustrated History of the Civil War.*

BATTLE OF CEDAR MOUNTAIN, AUGUST 9, 1862
Reproduced from a sketch by Edwin Forbes in Frank Leslie's *Illustrated History of the Civil War.* General Banks' force, numbering 7,500 men, was defeated by Stonewall Jackson's army of 20,000. Each army lost about 1,400 men. Jackson was so elated by his victory that he declared a day of thanksgiving for the Confederate Army.

light broke on Cowan's Cove (a cove here is a tract of bottom ground in the mountain valleys) and I stirred up engineers, conductors, and stokers with a vengeance and insisted upon another trial. Wood was collected and we started up the grades, luckily made a successful effort, got through the tunnel, and went tumbling fiercely down the slopes into the Crow Creek valleys, where I found three regiments of Knipe's and all of Ruger's brigades. Part of the artillery, after three days' labor, had got over the mountain by the aid of a regiment to each battery. Ten gun-carriage wheels were reported broken and the horses used up.

I was obliged to go on to Anderson to find a telegraph station. Here I began a library of telegrams to Hooker on one side (Stevenson) and Slocum on the other (Wartrace) both sending conflicting orders, Slocum ordering me to move on to Bridgeport, Hooker (through his Chief of Staff, Butterfield) ordering me to relieve certain posts along the railroad. In the meantime, the telegraph wire was so constantly employed by headquarters of the department that it was only now and then I could get in a word. All my baggage, bedding, mess, etc., was left at Cowan. Anderson has a depot building and one or two shanties. Luckily the telegraph operator was from Grand Rapids (a Mr. Atwater) and he saved me from a fast of forty-eight hours, besides exerting himself professionally.

After much tribulation and after collecting my whole division within fourteen miles of Bridgeport, I got an order to retrace my steps, or rather to distribute my division from Bridgeport to Murfreesboro to guard the railroad bridges, tanks, culverts, etc. But the trouble was not over. Butterfield ordered the batteries at Tantalon to be shipped to Bridgeport. So I sent across the horses and put the guns on cars, when I was notified that my guns were not wanted. The messenger, with instructions from Gen. Slocum, was detained by a torpedo-blowing-up of track near the tunnel. I waited another night in the windowless depot, trying to get orders. Near morning a locomotive came along and I hitched on my train of guns and repeated the struggle to get up the grades and through the tunnel to Cowan, which, after many hours, was accomplished; to find, however, at Cowan written orders to leave the batteries at Stevenson and Bridgeport.

These orders could have reached me hours before and saved an immensity of trouble and annoyance if the staff officer of Gen. Slocum had done as he was ordered. My guns were brought on to Decherd and there they stand on the railroad "flats" waiting to be drawn back. My troops were marched back, and now occupy in small posts (just large enough to be gobbled) the railroad from Murfreesboro to Bridgeport, ninety-one miles. I changed my headquarters to this place as being more central, and because the buildings used at Decherd for my offices were occupied in my absence by cavalry officers.

How long this arrangement will last I can't guess. The 2nd Division of our corps has gone to the front and probably crossed the river at Bridgeport with the 11th Corps. They went down by rail, but as I was nearer Bridgeport than they were, with my whole command, I was somewhat annoyed at being countermarched. I went to Wartrace to see Gen. Slocum, and the only satisfaction I got was that he preferred to trust my division with the responsible duty of guarding the long channel of supplies for the whole Army of the Cumberland. Very complimentary, but I dislike this railroad guarding in small posts. The whole country is full of small guerrilla parties who can get to the track and tear it up in spite of anything that infantry can do, over a line ninety miles long. Besides, the posts at important bridges are too small to defend themselves against any serious attack. I prefer the field with my whole division to this kind of duty, and hope I shall get away soon, if I carry nothing but pork and hardtack on my saddle.

This town of Tullahoma, which you have seen in the papers as the headquarters of Bragg and oftimes of Rosecrans, consists of a hundred straggling houses of faded paint and retrograding look. Indeed, it reminds me strongly of some Michigan towns after the speculating fever of 1836 had subsided, a great town-plat with here and there a pretentious frame house of thin boards, half finished and destined to remain so for years. Judge Catron of the Supreme Court has a neat summer cottage in the suburbs, but it is badly soiled by the occupation of soldiers.

All the towns along this railroad excepting Murfreesboro are the veriest pretenses, most of them sounding names and nothing else, and the people—the "poor white trash"—are disgusting: the mere scum of humanity, poor, half starved, ignorant, stupid, and treacherous. The women all "dip" snuff; that is, rub their teeth and gums with a pointed stick dipped in Scotch snuff! If anybody doubts the damning effects of slave labor upon the poor whites, let him come into Kentucky and

Tennessee and see the poorer classes of whites. Of course, there is a rich and educated class, but they are mostly gone and the poor now stand out in bold relief, with not even a bright background. Travel through this country by rail and you will never see this poor class; none but the rich planters and traders. You must stay here and move through the country to see how many there are vastly inferior to the Negro in common sense, shrewdness, and observation, and in the comforts of life. Let us not grieve for the Southern Negro as much as for the poor Southern white man—covered with vermin and rags, and disgusting with the evidences of a cureless "Scotch fiddle," [7] which they dig at continuously. . . .

I must close my long letter as the carrier has just called. I am afraid I can't get leave, as we are expecting to do or suffer great things this fall. If we don't go ahead, and we can't in the present state of supplies, I think Bragg will come ahead on us. It will be an awful country to concentrate troops in, so full of pathless mountains and roadless valleys. How they ever got into Chattanooga is a marvel, and how they will ever get out now the mud roads have begun is a greater wonder. I hope we shan't get out, but things look squally for supplying an army down through this winter. . . .

Your Affectionate Father,
A.S.W.

◈

THANKSGIVING AND REBEL PRISONERS

HEADQUARTERS 1ST DIVISION, 12TH CORPS
ARMY OF THE CUMBERLAND

Tullahoma, December 8, 1863.

My Dear Daughter:

If my memories are correct, I have been very remiss in writing you. I intended to have sent you a letter on Thanksgiving Day, but as the day was very fair I had a crowded levee all the morning of the officers of my division on duty here. First came the general court martial, headed

277

by the venerable-looking Col. Selfridge, and following them the corps
and brigade staff officers and others of the command here. So my day
was used up and I did nothing, except in the quiet of the evening sat
before my fire and thought of absent friends. Of course, the good things
and the good company at Uncle's had a prominent place in my reveries.
Our anticipated feast of good things was delayed and almost lost by the
very mysterious disappearance of our cook. It was nearly 8 P.M., before
we got anything to eat. The cook, making an early beginning of his
Thanksgiving, mistook a Nashville train for his kitchen and went off
in it, not returning for a week nearly. He came back in a very penitential
mood and has been restored to his pots.

Poor Dr. McNulty with a gay cavalcade started for a visit to a very
large cave some seven miles away. The result was that his horse fell
and the doctor was so stunned that he remained insensible for two days
and is still in a very weak and imbecile state, hardly recognizing his
friends. I fear he is done for duty at present. Singular how these things
result. A day or two before, Gen. Slocum's horse fell with him catching
his leg under it and going at a gallop. The general escaped without
serious injury. You have not forgotten my fall with Old Plug into the
Potomac pontoon and more recently his dropping into a deep ditch without injury to me.

We have had for a week past a continuous run of Reb. prisoners, long
lines of railroad trains crammed with them, over 7,000 taken in the
recent operations in front. They are a hard-looking lot of men without
overcoats and very short of dirty blankets, marked generally "U.S.,"
showing that what they have are taken or stolen from us.

But you should see this "chivalry" to appreciate it. A more dirty,
destitute, and diabolical lot of humanities cannot be conceived. We get
in Dickens' novels and in similar works some fanciful sketches of
English poorhouses and poor people, but no imagination can conceive
nor words express the dirty and ragged condition of these prisoners.
Their hands are as black as a Negro's and if their faces are not seen
you would pronounce them Negroes. Such is the pure blood and the
high status of these troops over the destruction of whom by foul Yankees
you see the lamentations of the Southern papers. Their stolid, unex-
pressive, and almost idiotic features are quite in keeping with their dirty
condition. I could not help comparing the neat and orderly appearance

278

of our guards as they stood in the doorways of the boxcars with the stupid foul look of the men they were guarding.

[*The remainder is missing.*]

◈

ERRORS IN REPORT OF THE
BATTLE OF GETTYSBURG

HEADQUARTERS, 1ST DIVISION, 12TH CORPS
ARMY OF THE CUMBERLAND

Tullahoma, Tenn., Dec. —, 1863.
Major General H. W. Slocum,
Comm'd'g 12*th* Army Corps.
General:

In forwarding the report of Brig. Gen. Ruger, Comm'd'g 1*st* Division, 12*th* A.C. at the battle of Gettysburg, (delayed to this late date for reasons stated in the letter accompanying the report) I embrace the occasion to call your attention to certain errors and omissions in Maj. Gen. Meade's official report of that battle, which I think do much injustice to some portions of this corps. These briefly stated are:

1*st*—In crediting Lockwood's brigade to 1*st* Corps.

2*nd*—In omitting all notice of the gallant defense by Greene's brigade of the left flank of our entrenched line on the evening of the 2*nd* July, after the other troops of the corps had marched out to support of the left.

3*rd*—In wholly ignoring the operations of the 1*st* Division.

4*th*—In repudiating most of the material statements of my report as temporary commander of this corps.

1*st As to Lockwood's Brigade.* The following is the notice taken of it in General Meade's Report.

"In the meantime perceiving great exertions on the part of the enemy, the 6*th* Corps (Maj. Gen. Sedgwick) and part of the 1*st* Corps (to the command of which I had assigned Maj. Gen. Newton) particularly *Lockwood's Maryland Brigade,* together with detachments from the 2*nd* Corps were all brought up, &c."

I cannot be mistaken in asserting that Lockwood's brigade was at no time during this battle a part of the 1*st* Corps, or under the command of Gen. Newton. It was a part of the 12*th* Corps, and was brought up under my immediate command, with the 1*st* Division of same corps, to the support of the left.

This brigade (composed then of the 150*th* New York Volunteers and 1*st* Maryland Potomac Home Regiment) coming from Baltimore or its vicinity, reported to me as temporary commander of the corps early on the morning of the 2*nd* of July, while the skirmishers of the 1*st* Division (still on the south side of Rock Creek) were engaged with the enemy. Gen. Lockwood being senior to Gen. Ruger, then comm'd'g 1*st* Division, and a stranger to the division, I directed him to take his orders directly from me as an unassigned brigade, during the pending operations.

When the 1*st* Division and Lockwood's brigade were ordered to support the left on the afternoon of same day, I went in command of the supporting column, leaving [the] 2*nd* Division to cover our entire entrenched line. On reaching the crest of the Cemetery Ridge, Major (now I believe Lieut. Colonel) McGilvery of Maine Artillery, in command of one or more reserve batteries, reported to me that he was threatened by the enemy and was without infantry supports; and that the enemy, but a few moments before, had drawn off into the woods in his front several pieces of our artillery. I ordered Gen. Lockwood to move into the woods indicated, which was promptly done, and our artillery, abandoned by the enemy, was almost immediately recaptured. The 1*st* Division at the same time was ordered into the woods on the left of Lockwood's brigade and both advanced for some distance and until halted pursuant to superior orders, meeting very little resistance at any point from the retiring enemy. Though we passed large masses of our disorganized men, we saw not one line or body of our troops in position. The enemy seemed to have a clear field in that part of our lines and were helping themselves to our artillery until interrupted by the approach of reinforcements from 12*th* Corps and 6*th* Corps, advancing at about the same time. These facts having been fully reported, I am at a loss to comprehend (when all other corps sending supports to the left are especially named) why the 12th Corps should be—not only not named—but deprived of the small credit of "Lockwood's Maryland Brigade," for the benefit of the 1st Corps.

2nd In omitting any mention of the gallant defense made by Gen. Greene's brigade on the left flank of the entrenched line of the 12th Corps on the evening of the 2nd of July.

Gen. Meade's report thus speaks of the manner in which the enemy got possession of our line of breastworks.

"During the heavy assault upon our extreme left, portions of the 12th Corps were sent as reinforcements. During their absence the line of the extreme right was held by a much reduced force, and was taken advantage of by the enemy, who, during the absence of Geary's division of the 12th Corps, advanced and occupied a part of the line."

It was the absence of the whole of the 1st Division and of Lockwood's brigade (supporting the left) and of two brigades of 2nd (Geary's) Division (marching towards Littlestown by mistake) that the enemy took advantage of—not only to occupy our line on the right and center, but also to attack, with great vigor, Greene's brigade of 2nd Division (the only portion of the corps left behind) on the extreme left of our entrenched line. Gen. Meade omits all mention of this gallant contest, which lasted full three hours, and resulted in our retaining this important part of our line of defenses and enabling us to resist for hours, with comparatively little loss, his heavier attacks on the following day and finally to expel him wholly from our line.

Gen. Meade speaks of another attack, in a different part of the field, at about the same hour, as follows;

"On the extreme left, another assault was, however, made about 8 P.M. *on the 11th Corps,* from the left of the town, which was repulsed with the assistance of the troops from the 2nd and 1st corps."

The similarity of time and circumstance leads me to think that there is a mistake in locality of this attack. It is quite certain that Greene was attacked and was reinforced by [the] 1st and 11th corps, about the same hour that the report says the attack on [the] 11th Corps was repulsed by aid of troops from [the] 1st and 2nd corps. Be that as it may; the defense made by Gen. Greene was eminently worthy of notice and commendation.

3rd In wholly ignoring the operations of the 1st Division, 12th Corps.

The active participation by the 12*th* Corps in the battle of Gettysburg was,

1*st* The marching of the 1*st* Division and Lockwood's brigade to the support of the left on Thursday afternoon, the 2*nd* of July.

2*nd* The defense of the left flank of the entrenched line on the evening of the same day, and

3*rd* The long contest on Friday morning (3*rd* July) to recover possession of our line of breastworks. I have spoken of both operations of Thursday. Of those of Friday morning Gen. Meade thus speaks in his report.

"On the morning of the 3*rd* Gen. Geary, having returned during the night, was attacked at early dawn by the enemy, but succeeded in driving him back, and occupying his former position. A spirited contest was maintained all the morning along this part of the line. Gen. Geary, reinforced by *Wheaton's* [a mistake for *Shaler's*] brigade, 6*th* Corps, maintained his position and inflicting very severe losses on the enemy. With this exception the lines remained undisturbed, &c"

This is certainly neither a full nor a fair statement of a conflict which was waged almost without cessation for full seven hours, and in which all the infantry and artillery of the corps were engaged. The idea conveyed by Gen. Meade's Report is a simple defense of one division of the corps. The engagement really began on our side by a heavy cannonading from guns placed in position after midnight. The plan of attack, arranged the night before to dislodge the enemy from our breastworks, was for Geary's division to follow the cessation of the artillery firing by an attack along the entrenchments which he held on our left, while the 1*st* Division was placed in preparation to assault over the marshy grounds on the extreme right, or attack the enemy's flank should he attempt to move beyond the breastworks. The enemy on the other hand had brought up strong reinforcements with the design of carrying the position of our entrenched line, which he had failed to drive Greene from on the previous night, and which would have placed him in the rear of our army and given him possession of our main line of communication, the Baltimore Pike. Both parties started at daylight with plans of attack, each with the expectation of expelling the other.

Not only, as Gen. Meade's report says, did Geary's division (or more correctly the two absent brigades of it) return during the night, but so also did the whole of the 1st Division and Lockwood's brigade, and the whole corps (not Geary's division alone) artillery and infantry "succeeded in driving the enemy back and occupying its former position." It is a noticeable fact, too, that the portion of the corps not mentioned by Gen. Meade lost more in killed and wounded in this contest, from its exposed line of attack, and I think captured more prisoners, than did the division which gets the entire credit in Gen. Meade's report. The commendation given to Geary's division was justly merited, but the same praise might safely have been extended so as to embrace the conduct of the whole corps without doing injustice or giving offense to any portion of it. The entire omission of the 1st Division is so marked, and the report of the contest on Friday morning so meager and so at variance with official statements of the superior officers of the corps, that I am at a loss to conceive from what source Gen. Meade derived his information. Not, I know, from my report as temporary commander of the corps, and not, I think, from yours as commander of the troops of the right wing.

4th The fourth item of omissions stated at the commencement of this communication is sufficiently shown in the comments already made. Gen. Meade either has not seen my report or he has intentionally repudiated all its material statements as to the operations of the 12th Corps at Gettysburg. No commanding general can verify by personal knowledge all the occurrences in his own command in a great battle. But so confident am I of the truth of every material statement of my report in this instance that I could confidently submit its correctness to a decision on proofs, in any respectable court of justice.

There is another omission which in connection with those I have named has a significant bearing. Gen. Meade carefully names all general officers temporarily in command of corps—Maj. Gen. Schurz, in command of 11th Corps for six hours, from 10:30 A.M. of July 1st (when Gen. Howard assumed command of the field) to 4 P.M. same day (when Gen. Howard was relieved by the arrival of Gen. Hancock) is properly reported as such. So are Maj. Gen. Birney, 3rd Corps, and Brig. Gen. Gibbon, 2nd Corps, (Maj. Gen. Hancock, commanding the left center) named as temporarily commanding corps on different days. I was in command of 12th Corps part of July 1st and all of 2nd

283

and 3rd of July, and on the evening of the 2nd (Thursday) attended a council of corps commanders on a summons conveyed to me by a staff officer of Gen. Meade. I may be pardoned, therefore, for expressing some surprise that my name alone of all those who temporarily commanded corps in this great battle is suppressed in Gen. Meade's report. I know Gen. Meade to be a high-toned gentleman and I believe him to be a commander of superior merit and of honest judgment, and I confess to have read that part of his official report relating to the 12th Corps with a mixed feeling of astonishment and regret. I submit these comments to you as the commander of the 12th Corps, not in the expectation that any adequate remedy can now be applied, after the official report of the commanding general has become an historical record, but because I deem a statement of the facts and grievances an act of justice to the corps with which I have been long connected, (and which I commanded on the occasion referred to), and especially to the gallant division which I have had the honor to command for nearly two years.

> I have the honor to be, General,
> Very Respectfully, Your Ob't Servant,
> A. Williams
> Brig. Gen'l of Vols.

◈

HEADQUARTERS, 12TH CORPS
ARMY OF THE CUMBERLAND

> Tullahoma, Tenn., Jan'y 2nd 1864.

My Dear Sir:

I presume you have read Meade's report of the battle of Gettysburg.[8] I can imagine the feeling that its perusal has caused you. I have not met a sensible man who has read it, either a soldier or civilian, who has not felt disappointed on reading it. It purports to be the official history of the most important contest of modern times—a contest in which our troops fought with a valor and determination never before exhibited—and the only evidence in the entire report which tends to prove this heroism is contained in the closing sentence, "Our losses were very severe, amounting to 23,186." Your disappointment must have been greater from the fact that the true history of the operations on the right had already been made known to you by me,[9] and Meade's report is a plain contradiction of almost every statement I have ever made to you. It is in direct conflict with my official report and the reports of all my subordinate commanders. My first impulse on reading his report was to ask for a court of inquiry. I was prompted to this course not so much from personal considerations, as from a desire to have justice done to Gen. Williams and his division.

Although Meade professed the warmest friendship for me, and the utmost confidence in me, not only during the entire battle, but at all times subsequent to it while I remained in his army, yet in his report he utterly ignores me. That he did repose this confidence in me, and that he placed the right wing entirely under my control, I have abundant written evidence now in my possession. In proof of this I enclose a copy of an order sent me during the battle, showing that he had sent part of Sedgwick's corps to me, and that, without visiting me or my portion of the line, he wished me to place it in a central position where he could use it as soon as I could spare it. I also enclose a copy of an order received at 10:20 A.M. on July 2nd directing me to move from the strong position we then held, and the 5th and 12th corps, then under my command, and the 6th, which was hourly expected, to attack the enemy. The latter order was not obeyed because every general officer consulted on the subject deemed it unwise to leave the almost impregnable position we then held. I send you copies of these orders to convince you that although my name is not mentioned in the report, yet I really occupied the position, and had the commands mentioned in my former letters. At no time was I in command of less than two corps, during the entire campaign, and during all the battle the right wing was entrusted entirely to me—a position to which my rank entitled me. Williams commanded the 12th Corps, and was at all times during the battle treated as a corps commander by Meade. He was invited by him to the council with other corps commanders, and yet no mention is made of this fact in the report, nor is Williams' name or that of his division to be found in it.

I finally gave up the idea of asking for a court of inquiry, knowing that the interests of the service could not be promoted by such a course. I wrote a letter to Meade, however, asking him to correct his report, a copy of which I enclose.

There is much secret history connected with the Gettysburg campaign which will some day be made public. The proceedings of a secret council of the corps commanders held the night before the enemy crossed the river was at once divulged, and the remarks of Meade, Warren, and Pleasonton published to the world in full. It was for the interest of Meade that this publication should be made, and there is no doubt that publicity was given to it with his consent, if not through his direct instrumentality. There were other councils, however, the proceedings of which were not made public, and which never will be published with the consent of Gen. Meade. On the evening of July 2nd a council was called, and each corps commander was asked his opinion as to the propriety of falling back towards Washington that night. The majority opposed it, and after the vote was taken Meade declared that "Gettysburg was no place to risk a battle," and there is no doubt that but for the decision of his corps commanders the army on the 3rd of July would have been in full retreat, and the 4th of July, 1863, instead of being a day of rejoicing throughout the North, would have been the darkest day ever known to our country. This piece of history can be verified by the records of that council kept by Butterfield, and cannot have been forgotten by any officer present.

On the 4th of July nearly every corps commander urged an immediate movement, but my corps was kept three days in idleness. In the meantime the enemy had reached Hagerstown, taken up his new line, and had abundant time to fortify. At the council held on the 13th of July by which "Meade was overruled" the following question was proposed to each officer, viz., "Shall we, *without further knowledge of the position of the enemy*, make an attack?"

Previous to putting the question, Meade announced that he could get no knowledge of the position of the enemy. This announcement, together with the peculiar phraseology of the question, indicated the decision which the commanding general anticipated. He offered no remarks until a vote was taken and the question answered in the negative. He then made some general remarks about "the necessity of doing something," which were approved by all. Having "placed himself right on the record," as the politicians would say, he retired. This record he at once used to sustain himself at the expense of his brother officers, although the action of these officers was precisely what he anticipated when he framed the question.

You may think this a hard charge to bring against a soldier, but I believe I am fully justified in it. There are other circumstances which I will make known to you when we meet, which will convince you that I have not done him injustice.

As long as this war continues I shall pursue the course I have thus far followed. I shall ask for no court; enter into no controversy; write no letters. But when the present danger has passed from us, many facts will come to light giving to the public a better knowledge of the real history of this war than can be obtained through the medium of such reports as that written by Gen. Meade.

Very Respectfully,
Your Ob't Servant,
H. W. Slocum

Hon. L. R. Morgan
Syracuse, N.Y.

❖

GETTYSBURG REPORT AND DULLNESS OF RAILROAD DUTIES

Tullahoma, Feb. 25th, 1864.

My Dear Sherman:

I enclose you some correspondence (copies) relating to the battle of Gettysburg and Meade's report. Mr. Thos. M. Cook, formerly of Detroit and more recently of the New York *Herald*, will call upon you for the perusal of them. I have told him he could take notes of all the facts published, but that it won't do to have the letters printed nor extracts from them verbatim.

I do not understand that he wants the facts for the newspaper, but as part of the historical *res gestae* of the battle. At any rate, I do not think I could properly place them in the hands of gentlemen of the press, though I can give him, as I have already, the facts touching Meade's *defective* (unholy) report. Indeed, he was so unjust to me and my command and to Gen. Slocum and his command—so wholly ignored the operations on the right, which he committed to Gen. Slocum and never once took the trouble to look at himself—that I feel a great inclination to open a paper war on him myself. I shall do so if I live through this war. Having let Cook get out the bowels of these papers, will you please forward them to my daughter, Irene Williams, 1605 Filbert St., Philadelphia.

I shall send you tomorrow a copy of a private letter, which you can also show to Cook, and which please also forward afterward to Rene.

Well, I have been home on a thirty-days' leave; expected to have gone on to Philadelphia and Washington, but did not find time. It was the shortest thirty days I ever saw. The winter has been very dull. This railroad guarding is doleful. My command is scattered sixty miles or so, and I have only one small regiment at headquarters. I miss the parades, drills, music, and company of a concentrated division and I weary to get together again. . . .

This town is dolorous; a type of western map cities after the speculations of '36; thin, slabby and shabby houses scattered about, with broken windows and a deserted air. The people are like the houses, poor white trash. The Negro is the only gay dog, keeping up dances every night and having a good time at a cheap rate. . . .

No news not in the papers. Weather has been fine. We shall probably be doing something soon, though a great many of our best troops are out on furlough. All my old regiments re-enlisting. Five are at home; 46th Pennsylvania, 5th Connecticut, 2nd Massachusetts, 27th Indiana, 3rd Maryland.

Goodbye; write us.
Yours truly,
A. S. Williams.

Maj. Sherman.
P.S. Cook is at the *Herald* rooms, Washington.

DEFENSE OF GETTYSBURG REPORT

HEADQUARTERS, 12TH CORPS
ARMY OF THE CUMBERLAND

Tullahoma, Tenn. Mch. 5*th,* 1864.

General A. S. Williams,
Comm'd'g 1*st* Div*n* 12*th* Corps,

The following is a copy of the letter from Gen. Meade, amending his report of the battle of Gettysburg,

Very Respectfully &c
H. W. Slocum
Maj. Gen'l Comm'd'g 12*th* Corps.

❖

HEADQUARTERS
ARMY OF THE POTOMAC

Feb'y 25*th,* 1864.

Maj. Gen'l H. W. Halleck,
Gen'l in Chief,
Washington, D.C.
General:

I transmit herewith the report of Brig. Gen. T. H. Ruger, Commanding 1*st* Division, 12*th* Army Corps, and those of his brigade and regimental commanders, of the operations of his division at the battle of Gettysburg. These reports were only recently received by me, owing to Gen. Ruger's being detached with a large portion of his command not long after the battle; and soon after his return the corps was ordered to Tennessee.

I beg these reports may be placed on file, as part of my official report of that battle. I embrace this opportunity to make certain corrections and alterations in my report, to which my attention has been called by Maj. Gen. Slocum. These alterations are as follows:

I. In relating the occurrences of the 2*nd* of July I state:

"In the meantime perceiving the great exertions on the part of the
enemy, the 6*th* Corps. (Maj. Gen. Sedgwick) and part of the 1*st*
Corps. (to the command of which I had assigned Maj. Gen. Newton),
particularly Lockwood's Maryland brigade, together with detachments
from the 2*nd* Corps, were all brought up, &c"

This should read:

"In the meantime, perceiving the great exertions on the part of the
enemy, the 6*th* Corps (Maj. Gen. Sedgwick) and part of the 1*st* Corps
(to the command of which I had assigned Maj. Gen. Newton), together with detachments from the 2*nd* Corps, were all brought up. Subsequently the 1*st* Division and Lockwood's brigade of the 12*th* Corps,
under the immediate command of Brig. Gen. A. S. Williams, then
temporarily commanding the corps, arrived at the scene of action; the
service of Lockwood's brigade being particularly mentioned."

II. In relating the occurrences of July 3*rd*

"During the heavy assaults upon our extreme left, portions of the
12*th* Corps were sent as reinforcements. During their absence, the
line of the extreme right was held by a much reduced force, and was
taken advantage of by the enemy, who, during the absence of Geary's
division, 12*th* Corps, advanced and occupied part of the line. On the
morning of the 3*rd* Gen. Geary, having returned during the night,
was attacked at early dawn by the enemy, but succeeded in driving him
back, and occupying his former position. A spirited contest was maintained all the morning along this part of the line. Gen. Geary, reinforced by Wheatons' brigade, 6*th* Corps, maintained his position, inflicting severe losses on the enemy."

This should read:

"During the heavy assaults upon our extreme left, the 1*st* Division,
and Lockwood's brigade of the 12*th* Corps, were sent as reinforcements,
as already reported. Two brigades of Geary's division (2*nd* of this
corps) were also detached for the same purpose but did not arrive at the
scene of action, owing to having mistaken the road. The detachment of
so large a portion of the 12*th* Corps, with its temporary commander,
Brig. Gen. A. S. Williams, left the defense of the line previously held
to the remaining brigade of the 2*nd* Division, commanded by Brig. Gen.
Greene, who held the left of the 12*th* Corps, now become the extreme
right of the army. The enemy, perceiving the withdrawal of our troops,

advanced and attacked Gen. Greene with great vigor, who, making a gallant defense, and being soon reinforced by portions of the 1st and 11th corps contiguous to him, succeeded in repulsing all the efforts of the enemy to dislodge him. After night, on the return of the detachments sent to the left, it was found the enemy were occupying portions of the line of breastworks thrown up by the 12th Corps. Brig. Gen. Williams, in command, immediately made arrangements, by the disposition of his artillery, and instructions to both divisions, commanded respectively by Brig. Gens. Geary and Ruger, to attack the enemy at daylight and regain the position formerly occupied by the corps. In the meantime the enemy brought strong reinforcements, and at early daylight a spirited contest commenced which continued till after 10 A.M., the result of which was the repulse of the enemy in all his attempts to advance and his final abandonment of the position he had taken the evening before. During this contest Shaler's brigade, 6th Corps, was sent to reinforce the 12th Corps. With this exception the lines remained undisturbed."

I should be glad, as an act of justice, if this communication could be published.

Respectfully, Your Ob't Servt,

Geo. G. Meade,

Maj. Gen'l Com'd'g

◈

SOCIAL FESTIVITIES AT THE FRONT

Tullahoma, March 26th, 1864.

My Dear Daughter:

Last night as I was reading Kinglake's Crimean War, the cry of fire was raised by the sentinels and looking out of my window I saw our only hotel, a good-sized wooden building, all in flames. It was midnight and raining. As the commissary's store was in the range and the stable of our horses near, I ordered out the provost guard and all was saved except the tavern. While the fire was fiercest, the passenger train from Nashville came in, and when I returned to my quarters I found your letter of the 20th inst., and this was after all the great event of the night! I was delighted with your long letter, especially so, as I have been some days anxious to hear the fate of my letter of the 6th inst. enclosing some photographs and $40 in *greenbacks*. . . .

The photographs were of several general officers of my acquaintance, which I thought good likenesses, but they can be replaced. The cash, in these times, I greatly regret the loss of. However, I will replace it by express in a few days. Somehow or other my salary oozes away very rapidly and I save nothing; what little I get over our expenses is melted on debts and interest money, without greatly reducing my indebtedness. I am pretty economical myself and none of us are very costly, yet it takes money to keep us all. I was unable to get drafts on my last pay, hence I trusted greenbacks to the mail. If I had left out the photographs it would doubtless all have gone safe. I hope it may yet turn up; but I fear not, as complaints are very frequent and safeguards from the army not great.

I wrote you an account of the ball in that letter, I think. I did not go to the first one, as I had no clothes. The last was not very elegant and I think I have greatly lost my taste for the gay world. Several officers' wives were there and some rather dashing ones. One, wife of Lt. Bartlett, 150th New York Regiment, is a daughter of Capt. Andrews on Gen. Morris' staff, a brother of my classmate, W. W. Andrews, a reverend gentleman who visited us once and preached in Dr. Duffield's church. A mild, gentle, classical man, of queer religious opinions, the peculiarity of which I cannot describe, but the main idea of which is, to unite all denominations in the church. He is a sort of bishop of this religious fraternity. Another officer's wife (Lt. Col. Rogers) is fresh from 5th Avenue, New York, a bride. The change must have been marked, but she is sensible and enjoys life as it comes. Aunt Hatty was there but not very well, and Mrs. Capt. Pittman, a little body about as big as a piece of chalk, also a Mrs. Capt. Greene of the 150th New York. The rest were all leather and prunella women who mostly dip snuff and look very thin and gaunt. Music, made up from two bands of the division, was very good.

This is about all I can remember of the ball, excepting that the landlady, a Mrs. Robinson of Kentucky, who entertained me with tales of her high relationship to a great many Kentucky bloods, was immensely chagrined that a private table set apart for herself and guests (myself one) was appropriated by the ignoble vulgar before we could get up the narrow stairway. All the silver and splendor and six bottles of champagne was lost to us and we were obliged to take seats in the very worst spot of the banquetting hall. Poor woman! She seemed greatly distressed, but I contrived to smother my disappointment in a very large quantity of boned turkey and the like. Last night poor Mrs. Robinson suffered a greater chagrin by being burned out, stock and fluke. She was obliged to take shelter in the hospital building. I hope she saved the spoons. Our ball room, not of the most superb dimensions, has gone up and we shall no more transgress in that way during Lent.

That reminds me. We received yesterday preparatory orders for the front. It will be a week or more before we get away, and I think much longer, as we are wanting many things for which we cannot get transportation and we must be relieved by other troops. I look for a long, sorry campaign amongst these barren and denuded mountains below us. As for our horses, I don't see how they can be fed. I wish my Yorkshire was at home, or on Uncle Lew's farm. He never looked so splendid as now, but what will he be beyond the reach of forage.

Mar. 27th: I was stopped here yesterday and could not resume until the mail closed. There is not much new. Capt. Whitney and five lieutenants have returned. Capt. Whitney brought me from Mrs. Whitney a very neat gold locket badge of a Royal Arch Mason. Mrs. Knipe also sent me a very fine military hat, with a gold general officer's hat band. So you see our namesakes' families do not forget me. I think I shall send you the old hat which I have worn so long and which you have so much admired. . . .

I suppose all the ladies will be obliged to decamp soon. I am afraid part of my division will have to remain behind, guarding the blockhouses now being built. Commands are badly mixed in this department. In trying to give places to officers not wanted in the field, a great many useless commands are carried out in the shape of military districts and independent posts. We have in this way a conflict of authority and a want of graduated command which is provoking and alarming, and subversive of good order and organization. I find somebody now and then trying to command some of my regiments on the ground that they fall within their military district. I notice they don't succeed well in this attempt. . . .

I have just got rid of a big job in the way of a personal listing with account of battles, etc., sent to the War Department by order. I have just received a letter from Gen. Greene, who had a talk with Gen. Meade. The latter expressed much regret at the oversight in his report. Said he thought I reported as a division commander and he had not read my report when he made his! I shall send copies of Gen. Slocum's letter to Gen. Meade, as well as mine, for safe keeping, also a copy of my report of services, a volume of some seventy-five pages. . . .

Love to all. I am working up my neglected correspondence to be ready for the front.

Your Affectionate Father,
A.S.W.

◈

ARMY REORGANIZATION AND COMMANDS

Tullahoma, April 15, 1864.

My Dear Daughter:

Yours of the 10th came to hand last night. I have been absent four or five days—two days in Nashville. I went up to see about supplies for my men. It is several months since we have been able to get clothing, for want of railroad transportation. Gen. Knipe went up with me. I saw nothing wonderful in Nashville. It is a very dirty and badly managed place. I met Maj. Fifield of Monroe and saw several Michigan officers. Col. Mizner was down here while I was absent.[10] I think I have writen you since the order consolidating the 11th and 12th corps. As you [may] imagine, we [are] not very amiable over it. Officers and men get much attached to corps names. It is the *espirit de corps* which is a great military power. Besides, we are all very much attached to Gen. Slocum and dislike greatly to lose him. What you say about our new commander may be all true, *though I hope you are all careful about expressing your opinion or judgments on this topic.* It would probably be sent back here by some kind friend, greatly to my injury. The inference would be that if my family said hard things that their opinions were founded upon something I have written or said. So express no opinion about my commanding officers, unless favorable. You

294

will understand, and Uncle Lew, who is very judicious on such subjects, will explain what you may not see clearly. I hear that our new corps commander has not drank for some months, and if he ever was indiscreet that he is now the pattern of temperance.[11]

We have been a week waiting for the new organization. As we have several major generals, it is not at all improbable that I may lose my division. It is said Gen. Butterfield has come back expecting to get one. If so, he will be very apt to choose mine, which is the best in the new corps. Such is the fate of war. It is now over two years since I took command of this division! Would it not be strange if I was sent back to a brigade? [12] . . .

[*The concluding portion is missing.*]

❖

VISIT TO GENERAL HOOKER AND LOOKOUT MOUNTAIN

Tullahoma, April 21, 1864.

My Dear Daughter:

I have been knocking about so much of late that I have not written you, since the breaking up of our old corps. We all feel pretty badly to lose our old name. The badge we shall retain, and Gen. Hooker has applied for the name of 12th Corps instead of 20th.

Gen. Slocum has left us for Vicksburg, taking with him Col. Rogers, Col. [blank] and Maj. Gordon [?] Capts. Mosley and Tracy. The rest of his staff are waiting orders. Col. Best, I fear, will be obliged to go back to a captaincy. We shall miss the general and his staff. Circumstances have thrown our quarters near together for a long time and intimacies and friendships become very strong under such circumstances as we have lived in for eighteen months.

I have been away for most of the past two weeks, first to Nashville for four or five days and last over to Gen. Hooker's headquarters in Lookout Valley this side [of] Chattanooga. I had a very pleasant visit there. The general was quite gracious and insisted upon our stay for a day or so. He went with us to the summit of Lookout Mountain and explained the recent military operations around. I think the prospect from this mountain exceeds in extent and grandeur anything I have ever seen and you know I have seen grand natural scenery. I found Mrs. and Col. Ross of the 20th Connecticut at corps headquarters. They were our companions on the trip to Lookout. I wished often that you were along. I came back yesterday.

In the new organization, I have still my old division (1st) with additions. I exchanged the 20th Connecticut for the 141st New York. I get one entire new brigade.

Gen. Hector Tyndale, an officer you wrote me about after Antietam, where he was wounded, [commands the brigade]. He is a Philadelphian. My division, I think, will number present nearly 9,000 and present and absent probably 14,000. Individually, I cannot complain of the new deal, but somehow I feel heavy hearted and not buoyant. I hope when the weather improves my spirits will amend. . . .

I expect to have a hard summer. The mountainous country in front is so poorly supplied for man or beast and we shall be so far away from supplies that I prepare for a season of deprivation. I really fear more for my horses than myself. We shall probably break up here next week and move to the front. When the fighting campaigning will begin I cannot guess. The season is very backward and grass hardly started, even down in this sunny South; peach trees and apple trees are blossoming. The weather is much like our April in Michigan.

I hear from Best that you are having great concerts. It must be over two weeks since I heard. . . .

[*The remainder is missing.*]

◆

END OF RAILROAD GUARDING

Tullahoma, April 26th, 1864.

My Dear Daughter:

I enclose a sprig of crocus taken from Top Lookout (Mountain), which place I visited lately in company with Gen. Hooker; also, a more acceptable memento of a $20 greenback, picked up in Washington. . . . I wrote you a few days ago. We are certainly off this week. I am glad of it, for I weary to be somewhere, I know not where. I am tired to death of this railroad life, out of spirits, for what I know not. It is a year ago since I started for Chancellorsville, full of hope and confidence. Today I feel sad and blue, though the weather is fine and spring-like. . . .

I have a letter from Mr. Jacob Howard, saying that Meade's supplemental report will be published by Congress. The President promised him that I should have the next promotion. Two have been promoted since. The making of fortunes I do not understand. I could have made one here if I had consented to have sold my self-respect and the good name of my children to the third and fourth generation. While somebody makes $700,000, somebody [else] loses a corresponding sum. The world's cash don't grow as fast as that. We hear of the successful, but of the poor devil who loses his all in the pocket of the other little is said. He returns to shady life. I long more than you can to be gathered with you all in some quiet home, but I don't see clearly how I can get out and not regret it. I want to see the end. . . .

Love to all,

Your Affectionate Father,
A.S.W.

1. Apparently this was Mrs. Sarah Morgan Bryan Pratt, for whose career see *Dict. Am. Biog.*
2. The desperately-fought battle of Murfreesboro, December 31, 1862, to June 2, 1863, is regarded as a Union victory, since General Bragg's Confederate army retired from the field of combat. The capture of Colonel William W. Duffield with a portion of the Ninth Michigan Infantry Regiment at Murfreesboro on July 13, 1862 was another and minor affair.
3. On October 19, General Grant had replaced Rosecrans in command of the army and with the support of reinforcements assumed the offensive against the now discouraged Confederates. Contrary to General Williams' forecast, the recapture of Lookout Mountain on November 24, 1863, in the storied "battle above the clouds" was effected rather easily, marking the initial success of the Union army in the Chattanooga campaign.
4. General George Sears Greene, for whose career see *Dict. Am. Biog.* He attained the age of ninety-eight and in his later years took pride in his distinction as the oldest living graduate of West Point. In 1836

he had resigned from the army to devote himself to an engineering career. In 1894, then ninety-three years old, by special act of Congress he was given the rank of first lieutenant which he had held in 1836, and placed on the retired list—possibly a record of longevity in the American army.

5. Apparently an inadvertent error for November 30.

6. Joseph Wheeler, Phillip D. Roddey, and Stephen D. Lee. For sketches of those notable Confederate cavalry leaders see *Dict. Am. Biog.*

7. More commonly known as the itch, a parasitic infliction common among domestic animals and among certain economic strata of the human race.

8. This report is printed in the *Official Records*, Ser. 1, XXVII, Part 1, 114–19. General Meade's supplementary report, made in response to General Slocum's letter of protest, is in the same volume, pp. 120–21. General Slocum's report upon his role in the battle and campaign is on pp. 758–63. His subsequent letter of protest to Meade (December 30, 1863) and General Meade's reply (dated February 25, 1864) admitting some of the criticisms and rebutting others are on pp. 769–70. General Williams' own report of his operations is on pp. 770–76.

It is interesting to note that both General Slocum and General Williams were concerned over the judgment of future history upon General Meade's misleading report of their roles in the battle. Perhaps it would be a fair statement of that judgment (as of 1959) to say that General Meade, whatever his errors of detail may have been, waged a creditable campaign and battle, on the whole, in marked contrast with the performances of McClellan, Burnside, and Hooker, his predecessors in command of the Army of the Potomac. In particular, all of his forces were thrown into the battle, being moved from point to point as circumstances dictated, instead of permitting a large part of the army to lie idle while the enemy defeated the remainder in detail. Yet Meade was subjected to a storm of contemporary criticism, chiefly inspired by his failure to pursue and destroy Lee's army. One lengthy critique in particular, published in the New York *Times* on March 12, 1864 and signed by "Historicus" (whom Meade identified as General Sickles) stung him into requesting a court of inquiry upon his conduct of the battle. See *Official Records*, XXVII, Part 1, 127–36.

9. From 1858 until he resumed military life as colonel of the Twenty-seventh New York Infantry in May 1861, General Slocum had practiced law in Syracuse. LeRoy Morgan, to whom this letter was addressed, was Slocum's brother-in-law and a fellow-member of the bar of Syracuse, who in 1859 was elected justice of the Supreme Court. See sketch of Slocum in *Dict. Am. Biog.* and sketch of Morgan in D. H. Bunce, *Onondaga's Centennial* (Boston, 1896), I, 349–350.

10. Colonel Henry R. Mizner of Detroit entered the regular service as a cap-

tain in May 1861 and on November 11, 1862, was commissioned colonel of the Fourteenth Michigan Infantry Regiment. He served throughout the war and at its close remained in the regular service until he retired with the rank of colonel in 1891.—*Record of Service of Michigan Volunteers*, Vol. XIV.

11. General Joseph Hooker, who following his resignation of the command of the Army of the Potomac in June 1863 had been given command of the Eleventh and Twelfth corps, was assigned to the Army of the Cumberland, now consolidated as the new Twentieth Corps.

12. His forebodings were unjustified. General Butterfield was given command of the Third Division of the Twentieth Corps, and Williams, although but a brigadier, continued in command of the First Division.

X

To Atlanta
and
Savannah

TO ATLANTA AND SAVANNAH

Three years too late, President Lincoln had at length found a general whom he could trust to wage the war effectively. For himself Grant reserved the direction of the Army of the Potomac, whose repeated efforts since July 1861 to traverse the less than one hundred miles distance between Washington and Richmond had failed utterly. To General Sherman was assigned the task of reducing Atlanta, next to Richmond the most strategic point still held by a Confederate army. The two great invading hosts were to strike in unison, Grant with an army of 120,000 and Sherman with the slightly lesser force of 99,000. The advance from Chattanooga to Atlanta was begun by Sherman on May 6. His progress disputed at every turn by General Joe Johnston's army, 50,000-odd, and subsequently by General Hood, Johnston's successor, almost four months were consumed in the march from Chattanooga to Atlanta. From here, after a considerable delay, Sherman launched his much celebrated and much longer march from Atlanta to the sea (at Savannah) which was reached in time to present the city to President Lincoln as a Christmas gift. This section of General Williams' letters, the longest in the series, is largely devoted to the advance to Atlanta. The six-weeks' march from there to the sea was chiefly a festive military promenade, but since Sherman's army was cut off from all communication with the North no letters could be sent concerning its progress, although a typed copy of the "journal" he kept during the campaign (sent from Savannah to his daughter Minnie) still remains. With the letters written from Savannah in early January 1865, the present section concludes.

FORWARD TO ATLANTA

HEADQUARTERS, 1ST DIVISION, 20 CORPS
ARMY OF THE CUMBERLAND

Tullahoma, April 28, 1864.

My Dear Lew: . . . .

I am off tonight for the front and within the month of May you will hear of stirring events. Almost everything is adverse to us. The face of the country is almost impassably mountainous. I expect to live on hardtack and pork, without tents and roughly as a trapper. But I always feel in the best spirits when so living. So God prosper the right and let it come. . . .

Yours Affectionately,
A. S. Williams.

◈

ROSSVILLE AND CHICKAMAUGA VISITED

3½ miles south of Ringgold, Georgia,
May 6th, 1864.

My Dear Daughter:

I have sat down in the shadow of my tent to tell you of my whereabouts. It is near sunset and at my front canvas door the shadows are most agreeable after a hot day. A hot and busy day! Just in front of me, over the woods beginning to put on a deep green, is seen the almost straight line of Taylor's Ridge, at the foot of which along Middle Chickamauga Creek my brigades are encamped.

I left Tullahoma on Thursday afternoon (28th April) after putting all my troops in motion for the front. I stopped that night at Decherd and took the cars next day for Stevenson, where I passed a night in the "Soldiers' Home." The next morning I went to Bridgeport, opposite which, across the Tennessee, one of my brigades was encamped, the new 3rd Brigade of Gen. Tyndale. I found the general quite ill, troubled with his old wound at Antietam. He has received leave of absence and is now on his way home. His brigade is at present commanded by Col. Robinson of the 82nd Ohio. At Bridgeport I concentrated all my brigades, excepting the 107th New York (left to guard the supply trains which I had sent to Nashville, unfortunately, just before the order of march came) and the 3rd Wisconsin, which had been on duty at Fayetteville and had not come up.

We marched from Bridgeport to Shellmound on Sunday and on Monday to Whiteside. The whole of the route is quite mountainous, though it is spoken of as a valley. I had sent my equipage and staff (excepting Lt. Robinson, A.D.C.) by rail direct to Lookout Valley; my horses [went] with the brigade trains. My destination was quite uncertain and I got them as near corps headquarters as possible. We marched from Whiteside to Chattanooga Valley on Tuesday, passing my headquarters tents on the way, very pleasantly located. I also called at Gen. Hooker's headquarters in Lookout Valley and was very pleasantly received. Our day's march was over the Wauhatchie battle-ground and along the valley in front of Lookout Mountain.

On Wednesday we moved early across Chattanooga Valley to Rossville, crossing the Mission Ridge at that point and then turning south over the Chickamauga battleground to Gordon's Mills, where we encamped. We saw at Rossville the old residence of John Ross, the Cherokee chief.[1] It is, indeed, with its barns and granaries, all that remains of Rossville. On the Chickamauga battleground the torn trees and numerous graves pointed out the scenes of the heaviest fighting. We passed several wagons loaded with disinterred bodies of the victims of the battle. I was surprised to find the battleground so level and almost wholly covered by dense forests. . . . It was a poor spot for a great battle and I am not astonished that the reports show a series of defenses and isolated combats of which the rest of the army seem to have been in ignorance. I think our people must have been forced to accept the battle there, for a far more advantageous spot was near Rossville.

On Thursday (yesterday) we marched from Gordon's Mills to this place, a hot day and a dusty march, miles without water; but the men are in good condition and spirits. On my march I received your letter of 26th April, No. 12; also the *Advertiser* with a long account of the tercentenary. You must have had a rare time for Detroit. I fancy I see little Jule in the mass of young beauties, looking like a cherub, as well as a fairy.[2] So Kitty has gone. You must miss her vastly;

but such is life—meetings, pleasant moments, sorrowful partings! . . .

I send you a flower I picked from near some graves on Chickamauga battleground. We move tomorrow at daylight, I know not in what particular direction, but you will see that we are near where the enemy have held strong positions. Before this reaches you, you will know by telegram if anything has occurred.

God bless you my darling daughter and keep you in health and happiness. Love to all. I write on a box cover and amidst constant interruptions.

Your Affectionate Father,
A.S.W.

❖

CORRESPONDENCE UNDER DIFFICULTIES

Near Snake Creek Gap,
12 m. S.W. of Dalton, Georgia,
May 11th, 1864.

My Dear Daughter:

I write you a line to show you where I am. We are stripped of everything for a vigorous campaign and have few facilities for writing. Besides, we are kept constantly on the *qui vive*, marching nights and always ready to move at a moment's notice. I wrote you from Pleasant Church near Ringgold on the 5th. On the 6th we marched at daylight, crossing Taylor's Ridge on the Nickajack Trace, a rough and dangerous pass over a pretty sharp mountain. We encamped at Trickum Post Office. Gen. Kilpatrick's cavalry accompanied my command. The day was very hot. We were two days at Trickum. The enemy made but little demonstration but appeared strongly entrenched about Buzzard's Roost and toward Dalton, between which and us runs a strong mountain range.

On the night of Monday, the 8th, we marched about 12 o'clock towards this place, marching all night and reaching this at 8 A.M.[3] The whole country is a series of mountain ranges, with intervening valleys densely wooded, a hard country for campaigning. At Trickum

Post Office I received your letter of May 2nd, a most pleasant surprise, and Capt. Pittman received yours also and was greatly pleased with the hits. We have before us a hard campaign, I think, but I am well and can stand anything. I slept last night in the most furious storm of rain, lightning, and wind under a shelter fly. I am very moist this morning and am writing on my knees before a campfire, talking business and supplies while I write.

The enemy are near and we shall have stirring times soon. You will hear it all by telegraph. The postman waits. Love to all.

Your Affectionate Father,
A.S.W.

❖

THE BATTLE OF RESACA

Camp near Cassville, Georgia,
May 20, 1864.

My Dear Daughter:

For the life of me, I cannot recollect whether I have written you since I left Trickum Post Office or not. I scribbled a short pencil note from that place. Since then my mind has been so full of constant duties, responsibilities, and cares, and events have followed in such rapid and varied succession that my recollections are a jumble. Day and night we may be said to be on duty and under anxieties. No one who has not had the experience can fancy how the mind is fatigued and deranged (as well as the body) by these days and nights of constant labor and care.

We left Trickum Post Office on the night of the 9th after much reconnoitering and skirmishing toward Buzzard's Roost and reached the entrance of Snake Creek Gap in the Chattanooga Mountains in the morning. The whole march, as everywhere, [was] through woods, with hardly a clearing. On the 12th, moved the division through the gap about six miles and encamped. On the 13th moved towards Resaca, under arms always from daylight and lying ready for a fight all night. I carry nothing for myself and staff of a dozen but four tent flies and one wall tent for an office. All private baggage is left behind. The wagon with the tent flies is seldom up and consequently we roll ourselves in overcoats and what we can carry on our horses and take shelter under trees every night. The days are hot and the nights quite cold and foggy. Most of us have been without a change of clothing for nearly three weeks.

On the 14th we moved through thickets and underbrush to the rear and in support of Butterfield's division, and in the afternoon received a hurried order to move rapidly farther to the left to support Stanley's division of the 4th Corps. I reached the ground just in time to deploy one (3rd) brigade and to repulse the Rebels handsomely. They had broken one brigade of Stanley's division and were pressing it with yells and were already near one battery (5th Indiana, Capt. Simonson, Lt. Morrison commanding) when I astonished the exultant rascals by pushing a brigade from the woods directly across the battery, which was in a small "open" in a small valley. They "skedaddled" as fast as they had advanced, hardly exchanging a half-dozen volleys. They were so surprised that they fired wildly and didn't wound a dozen men. I was much complimented for the affair and Gen. Howard, commander of the 4th Corps, came and thanked me.

On the 15th we had a more serious engagement. Butterfield's division attacked their entrenched positions on the hills, short steep hills with narrow ravines. I was supporting. While his attack was in progress, information was brought to me that the Rebels were moving towards our left in force. I changed front and in luck had plenty of time to form my line and place my batteries in position before they attacked. They came on in masses and evidently without expectation of what was before them. All at once, when within fair range, my front line and the batteries (one of which I had with much work got on the ridge of a high hill) opened upon them with a tremendous volley. The rascals were evidently astounded, and they were tremendously punished. They kept up the attack, however, for an hour or so, bringing up fresh troops, but finally gave way in a hurry.

We captured one battle flag and the colonel of the 38th Alabama, several other officers, and several hundred prisoners. The flag was a gaudy one and covered with the names of battles in which the regiment had been engaged. It was the only flag taken during the day. But that I was not advised of any supports on the left, I could have charged them

with great success. As it was, I did a good thing, and the division behaved splendidly. Not a man left the ranks unless wounded. In the
language of a private of the 27th Indiana (one of my old regiments)
we had a "splendid fight," and he added, " 'Old pap' (that is I) was
right amongst us."

The fight ended about dusk and in the morning there was no enemy
in front. I went out over the field in our front, not out of curiosity but
to see what was in advance. There were scores of dead Rebels lying in
the woods all along our front, and I confess a feeling of pity as I saw
them. One old grey-headed man proved to be a chaplain of the Rebel
regiment, and it is rather a singular coincidence that one of our own
chaplains (3rd Wisconsin) was seriously wounded directly in front of
where he was found dead. Early in the war I had a curiosity to ride
over a battlefield. Now I feel nothing but sorrow and compassion, and
it is with reluctance that I go over these sad fields. Especially so, when I
see a "blue jacket" lying stretched in the attitude that nobody can mistake
who has seen the dead on a battlefield. These "boys" have been so
long with me that I feel as if a friend had fallen, though I recognize no
face that I can recollect to have seen before. But I think of some sorrowful heart at home and oh, Minnie, how sadly my heart sinks with
the thought.

I put parties to bury the dead Rebels but was ordered away before
half were collected over the mile and a half in our front. I fear many
were left unburied, though I left detachments to gather up all they
could find. As I marched away, I was obliged to go along the line
where my own dead were being collected by their comrades and interred
in graves carefully marked with name, rank, and company. It is interesting to see how tenderly and solemnly they gather together their
dead comrades in some chosen spot, and with what sorrowful countenances they lay them in their last resting place. There is much that is
beautiful as well as sad in these bloody events. I lost in this battle between four and five hundred killed and wounded.

[*The remainder is missing.*]

◈

THE PILLAGE OF CASSVILLE

Cassville, Georgia,
May 22, 1864.

My Dear Daughter:

I wrote you on the 19th [17th?] from camp this side of Adairsville.[4] We moved from that camp at 12 M., hurried up to support Butterfield's division four miles in front. [We] found his skirmishers engaged and a good deal of artillery firing, so after I had formed [a] line of battle I was ordered to move to the front till I met the enemy. We drove his skirmishers before us over hills and down valleys, across creeks and marshes until after dusk when I halted and bivouacked, sleeping myself under a very dense thicket.

During the night I found we were within a few hundred yards of this place, which lies deeply embowered between two ranges of hills. On the hill beyond the town the Rebs. had constructed strong entrenchments and kept popping away until near midnight. They had all decamped before morning, though Johnston had most of his army here the day before and published an order that he should fight and retreat no farther. He had found his "last ditch."

During the night two regiments of another division were sent in to occupy the town. In the morning I was ordered to send in a strong guard and clear away the stragglers. The people had abandoned their houses leaving suppers on the tables. The Rebels fired from the close hill upon our troops in the town and what with vacant houses and irritation every house was dolefully pillaged. Hardly a thing was left not destroyed or carried away. The picture is painful enough. Just as I reached town some rascal had set fire to one of the principal buildings, which bid fair to finish the whole place as it was difficult to find water. I had a lot of New York firemen who wet sheets, etc. and tore down buildings and saved the place. A few women have come back to mourn over the desolation of their houses and the destruction of their household gods.

This was formerly Cass County and Cassville [was] named after Gen. Cass, but the legislature of Georgia in its Confederate wrath changed the county name to Bartow and the town to Manassas! It is still generally known as Cassville.

Gen. Sherman spent an hour or more with me yesterday. He was very frank, pleasant, and communicative, more so than any commanding general I have ever met. Gens. Hooker, Butterfield, and Geary also came to see me, and scores of colonels. It was our first day of real rest for nearly a month.

Tomorrow we are off again with preparations for a twenty days' march. The long line of fortifications (six to seven miles) running N.E. and S.W. beyond this town would seem to indicate that Gen. Johnston did intend to make a stand here. They ran the line straight through a handsome cemetery, cutting up graves and overturning tombstones. The few people who remain are very angry.

I have been very busy and am still preparing supplies of ammunition, forage, and rations for the twenty days, sending back sick, and am hourly interrupted. If my dates are not correct as to my writing before, it is because my head is too full of the thousand and one questions from staff officers, commanding officers, and the like. Captain Whittlesey is now by my side full of wants and queries. He has read your letter and is tickled.

> Love to all,
>
> Your Affectionate Father.

❖

BATTLE OF NEW HOPE CHURCH

> Camp near Rafer's Creek,
> 4 miles north of Dallas, Georgia,
> May 31, 1864.

My Dear Daughter:

I wrote you last from Cassville. We left that [place] at daylight on the 23rd, marching a circuitous route to avoid the other corps. We crossed the Et-o-wah (accent on first syllable) on a pontoon bridge just south of the mouth of Euharlee Creek, and the whole corps encamped along that stream. The next day, the 24th, we moved forward to Burnt Hickory or Huntsville and encamped just in advance of it. Owing to delays and having troops and trains in advance, I did not get into camp until dark. We had a tremendous storm of thunder, lightning, and rain soon after, which lasted well into the night. Neither my wagon nor ambulance could get up. Luckily for me, Gen. Knipe had his with his command and I took shelter in his tent. My staff passed the night on a rather musty pile of straw, enveloped in their rubbers. Some of them got very wet, but all seemed pretty jolly in the morning.

The next morning (25th) my orders were to move in advance of Dallas and encamp to the right. I took a road leading south of the direct road; had rebuilt a bridge over Pumpkin Vine Creek, destroyed by the Rebels, and was within a mile of Dallas when an order came to me to countermarch and move back across the creek to the direct road to support Geary's division. He had met the enemy in force, and apprehended trouble. It was about 2 P.M., the day very hot, and my men much fatigued. Back I turned, and after a march of six miles or more came up with Butterfield and Geary's divisions occupying both sides of the direct route from Burnt Hickory to Dallas, four miles or more south of Pumpkin Vine Creek.

They were in dense woods with considerable underbrush and the ground full of small ravines enclosed in gently swelling hills, which evidently grew higher in front and [on which] was the entrenched line of the enemy. We could see but a few rods in front, but the constant rattle of the skirmish line showed that we had a stout enemy before us. I was ordered to the front with my division and told that I was to push forward and drive the enemy until I found out his force or chased him away from our front. I formed in three lines of brigade front, the 3rd, Robinson's brigade, leading, next Ruger's, and last Knipe's. Two regiments were thrown forward as skirmishers. The bugles sounded the "forward" and on went the three lines in beautiful order, though the ground was broken, bushy, and covered with small stones.

I followed just behind the leading line. We met the heavy supports of the Rebels in a few moments and the volleys of infantry firing became intense. Our lines never halted. As the opposition became intensified, I sounded the "double-quick" and all three lines pounded forward on the trot and the Rebels traveled back quite as quick. Soon we got within range of the enemy's artillery and they poured into us canister and shrapnel from all directions except the rear. My front line, after advancing a mile and a half or more, brought up against the enemy's entrenched line. They had expended pretty much all their ammunition, sixty rounds per man. I sent forward the second line to relieve it, and they expended their ammunition, and Knipe's line was sent to replace it, and thus under continuous shot and shell we held the line close up to the enemy's entrenchments until my whole division had nearly expended its ammunition.

After dark we were relieved by troops of Geary's and Butterfield's divisions and I withdrew my division some three or four hundred yards to the rear. Rain began falling. I found the campfire of Gen. Newton, where I met many general officers, among them Gen. Kimball, who was with us up the Shennandoah and whom I have not met since. Everybody congratulated me on the splendid manner my division made the advance. Gen. Hooker said to me, "It was the most magnificent sight of the war"; that in all his experience he has never seen anything so splendid. He has induced Dory Davis, the artist of *Harper's*, to make a sketch of it. If Dory is not too lazy he will do it,[5] though it will probably be some weeks before it will appear.

I lost about 800 men killed and wounded. Col. McDougall of the 123 New York lost his leg above the knee. I went to see him in the hospital. He seemed cheerful and I hope will recover. He has been a long time with me and I shall miss his pleasant face.[6] Several younger officers were killed, and a good many wounded. None of my staff were hurt. My horse got a ball in his hind leg. I was talking with Gen. Knipe at the moment, just behind the front, when I heard the "sug" and the horse made a tremendous leap. He was hit in the fleshy part of the leg.

We have been here now five days and have not advanced an inch beyond the point my division reached. On some points the troops sent to relieve us did not hold, and some of our dead lie there unburied. There is a constant rattle and has been all these five days on the skirmish line, and now and then tremendous volleys are poured in from one side or the other. Several batteries have been placed in the front in as favorable points as the woods and ground will admit. They occasionally join in the tumult of sounds.

On the 26th we opened with all our guns in position for three hours. I think Gen. Sherman intended to charge their lines. He probably came to the conclusion that the whole Rebel force, with strong reinforcements, were in front strongly posted and entrenched. Two nights ago they came out in some force to attack our position, not more than four hundred yards in front of where my division lies. There was a tremendous hubbub stirred up of infantry and artillery all along our front, extending for miles both ways. I had several men wounded by glancing balls. We have these affairs almost every night and there is not a minute of the twenty-four hours that popping is not going on. We are so near that it seems in our very camp. I have been along the skirmish line several times. Little can be seen through the dense forest. On the extreme right of our corps, from a hill I can see a long line of entrenched hills. The Rebs. have evidently a strong place and I suppose have collected all their forces in the South to give us a final meeting.

I thought I had got quite a hit the other day, but it turned out to be nothing. On the day after the fight I had fallen asleep in front of a tree with all my staff and Gens. Knipe and Ruger with me. A good many "Minnies" had passed over us with their peculiar buzz, cutting the leaves high up in the trees. All at once I was made wide awake by a sharp sting on my elbow joint; I thought somebody had hit me with a stick. Knipe was coolly looking around for the ball, which he soon found. It had struck a tree and spent itself so nearly that it only made a lump on the elbow, without breaking the skin. I had it well rubbed with spirits and have not suffered the least inconvenience. It hit so near the "funny bone" that it quite paralyzed my fore-arm for a while.

I suppose we shall move somewhere soon. It is a very tedious and worrying life as we are situated, for we are kept constantly on the *qui vive* ready for battle. Our rest, you can well fancy, is not of the most refreshing kind. We have had no mails since leaving Rossville.

Love to all,

Your Affectionate Father,
A.S.W.

◈

ADVANCE TO LOST MOUNTAIN

Jackson's House Near Lost Mountain, Georgia,
June 10th, 1864.

My Dear Daughter:

While we are waiting orders to march I pull over my wallet and find two photographs which I enclose. Also a flower plucked in the woods on my line for your herbarium collection.

I wrote you yesterday; nothing new. We are under orders to march towards Marietta. Goodbye, and love to all.

Your Affectionate Father,

A.S.W.

✿

June 10th, 1864.

My Dear Daughter:

I wrote you last on the 27th or 31st ult. in the woods after our engagement of May 25th. We lay in those woods from May 25th to June 1st. The days were exceedingly warm and the air filled with the noisome odors of the dead, man and beast. The tread of so many thousand men had destroyed all traces of vegetable life on the ground. The small stones so thickly strewn over the surface seemed to have been partly converted into powder, which every shuffling mule stirred up in our faces. All the days and nights the same incessant rattle of musketry [continued], so close to us that it seemed in our very camp. About midnight both parties would open in volleys, which in the reverberation through the woods would be redoubled in volume and sounded like a tropical thunder storm twenty times increased in noise.

Of course this was a great interruption to sleep, as when the great din of small arms and artillery began everybody stood to arms, not knowing whether the attack was real or feigned. I think I slept better than anyone. Nothing disturbed me, unless there was an unusual hubbub and artillery joined in the fray. It is wonderful how soon we get accustomed to such confusion and sleep straight through noises that otherwise would drive away our senses.

On the 1st of June I moved about four miles northeast and took position with my left on a considerable hill, which we called "Brownlow Hill" after the Parson's son, who commands a cavalry regiment.[7] From this hill we had a very extensive prospect, but not an inviting one. It was woods and mountain ranges as far as the eye could reach in the direction we wished to travel. To the east, the Kenesaw Hills near Marietta; at the southeast, the solitary Lost Mountain; north, the high Allatoona Range; and between all, nothing but woods, woods, woods!

We remained in this position until the morning of the 5th inst. Three days of it were very rainy and our gravelly soil, we found, had a very large portion of bad clay mixed with it. Brownlow's Hill was quite the resort of general officers. I have seen there, at one time, Gens. Sherman,

Thomas, Hooker, Schofield, Howard, Palmer, corps commanders, besides dozens of division and brigade commanders. A good many old acquaintances came to see me. Among them Gen. John King of the Brady family,[8] who told me to remember him to Aunt Jule; Col. Henry Mizner, who had just reached the army with his regiment; Col. Lum of the 10th Michigan Regiment, and scores of others who had known me at the camp of instruction. These almost always ask after my *little* daughter, whom they saw at the camp.

On the 5th inst. I moved about four miles and took position at the junction of the Marietta and Big Shanty Road fronting southeast. We passed one quiet night, without picket firing or midnight alarms. On the 6th my division took the advance down the Marietta Road two miles and then south two miles to this point. We met and drove in the Rebel skirmishers before reaching this [place] and followed them until I found a ridge running west to Allatoona Creek, where I took post and in half an hour my fellows, as usual, had made a mile or so of very formidable-looking breastworks. It is wonderful how rapidly they will entrench themselves after a halt.

In our front was a group of log houses and barns, from which the enemy's sharpshooters annoyed us much. I spent an hour or so on our line looking at them and being a target for their practice, keeping myself, however, pretty well under cover. After a while I got up a piece of rifled artillery and skedaddled the rascals by throwing a few shells amongst them. For the last few days our pickets have completely fraternized. They have been exchanging papers, coffee, tobacco, and the like. Yesterday morning I found them actually sitting together on the banks of a small stream, a branch of the Allatoona Creek. I was obliged to stop the fraternal intercourse. Isn't it strange that men in mortal strife one hour are on affectionate terms the next! and apparently fast friends. Strange are the commingled events and incidents of war!

I write this early in the morning. We are under orders to march at 9 o'clock. Did I tell you how near Pittman came to getting a bad hit? He had just risen from his blankets under the tent fly, while we were at Brownlow's Hill, when a bullet came through the fly and struck just where his head had been and expended itself on a stone inside, falling on Lt. Robinson, A.D.C., who pocketed the trophy. . . .

I have seen very few reports of our operations. Those I have seen disgust me with their lies. I see a Cincinnati paper gives Hovey's division the credit for what my division did, and yet it is a fact that this division could not get up until we had repulsed the Rebels. I went to Gen. Hovey myself to get him to support my left flank, and he confessed that his troops were new and could not be got through the line of artillery fire. Yet this Cincinnati *Commercial* gives a glowing description of a most gallant charge in which Hovey drove the Rebels like sheep. A pure lie! I see also that they are all careful to speak of a portion of Hooker's corps saving Simonson's battery, when every one of them knows it was my division which came to its rescue at the double-quick, arriving just in time to beat back the yelling and exultant Rebels, who were driving Stanley's division like a frightened mob. However, I have got used to these outrageous reports. They are got up by special scribblers, who are kept in many commands. I don't know but one reporter by sight, and he looks like a jailbird. I wish the whole crew were driven out.

I send you a flower plucked in the woods on my present position. I face south. Lost Mountain is just in front of me, a solitary knob covered densely with trees. The Rebs. have been cutting and digging on its sides for the past three days. My tents are by the side of a house of Mr. Harris Jackson, an old fellow with his third wife and his fourteenth child. He has lost two sons and has two [more who are] prisoners in our hands somewhere. He lives, as all do in this region, in a double log house with an open hall or passage between the two parts. He is a nabob and has two carriages, but lives filthily and ignorantly. . . . Love to all and kisses expressly to little Jule.

Your Affectionate Father,
A.S.W.

◈

DELINQUENCIES OF REPORTERS

In the field, 8 miles from
Marietta, Georgia,
June 12, 1864.

My Dear Daughter:

Yours of the 27th ult. reached me last night. I wrote you and Larned day before yesterday a joint letter. We were under orders to move, but did not until yesterday afternoon and then only a mile or two amid the rain, which pours in real tropical storms day after day with intervals of sunshine. Today it looks like a settled steady rain after pouring all night. The ground is saturated from surface to center and the roads, of course, "awful." It is so cold that I have on my winter coat. Of course, changing camp under such circumstances is no joke for man or beast. All of us have to take to the deeply saturated ground and as our bedding consists of blankets with now and then a buffalo robe you can fancy we sleep rather moist. If we don't all come out "rheumaticy" it will be indeed strange. You speak of not seeing any mention of my division. We don't see many papers out here, but the New York *Herald* of the 25th ulto. had a long and very complimentary notice of the division, and the New York *Post* of about that date another. I don't know by sight but one correspondent. He belongs to a Cincinnati paper. I have seen him once, inquiring about our movements. I never intended to say that I should employ or encourage reporters, but that I should see that the official reports did no injustice. I am not indifferent to the ephemeral praise of reporters, but I cannot sell my self-respect to obtain it. The only other New York report I have seen is the New York *Tribune*. I don't know who writes for that paper but he hardly tells a truth and a great many lies. He gives to Hovey's division, 23rd Corps, the credit of defending our left flank and capturing the gaudy flag of the 38th Alabama, when it is known all through the army that Hovey did not get into the fight and that my division captured the flag and the colonel and many officers of that regiment.[9]

Indeed, Gen. Schofield, who commands that corps, told me yesterday that Hovey did not lose in killed and wounded a dozen men on the day of that fight. Such is the reliability of the correspondent of that pious and patriotic paper, the New York *Tribune!* I see he wholly ignores my division and always speaks of it as "a portion of Hooker's corps," but is careful to name Geary's and Butterfield's divisions. Probably the fellow, whoever he may be, fancies I have neglected him sometime. I have no recollection of ever having seen him and don't know his name. But don't let us fret ourselves over this, Rene. Be assured that my division stands as high as any with those who know and that the truth will appear in the end.

I have lost over 1,200 men killed and wounded since leaving Chattanooga, and on the 14th of May, I believe, as do many others outside my division, that my opportune arrival and the gallant conduct of my troops saved our army from a great disaster. Gen. Howard, commander of the 4th Corps, thanked me in person for the services I had rendered his corps. It was one of his divisions that was being repulsed, leaving a battery in the Rebels' grasp. . . .

I send you the *Herald*'s letter, enclosed—the account of Knipe's charge is a good deal exaggerated. He was only slightly wounded and his nephew mortally.[10] The colors of the 38th Alabama were taken by Ruger's brigade. The account of the 14th is correct and mainly that of the 15th. I have seen no account of our battle of May 25th. Hooker says I made the most splendid charge he has seen in this war.[11]

I send you a photograph of Gen. Slocum which he sent me from Vicksburg, his new post. He writes that he is greatly amazed by speculators and sharps who do not hesitate to sell arms and ammunition to Rebels to obtain cotton. They will find Slocum a hard nut to corrupt.

Tell Larned I will write him a separate letter soon but as a general thing I shall be obliged to write you jointly. We are kept all the while packed and booted and spurred for a conflict. The enemy are doubtless very strong. The petty and miserable failures along our coast enable them now to withdraw everything to help Johnston's army. If these expeditions had started now, they could have drawn away from our front tens of thousands of men.

But I will neither speculate nor criticize, but hope for the best and that a speedy end may come to the rebellion and the war. . . .

Your Affectionate Father,
A.S.W.

◈

PINE MOUNTAIN AND GENERAL HOOKER

HEADQUARTERS 1ST DIVISION, 20TH CORPS
DEPARTMENT OF THE CUMBERLAND

Near Kolb's House 3 miles west of Marietta, Georgia,
June 24, 1864.

My Dear Daughter:

I wrote you last from the house of J. Jackson on the 10th inst. The weather has been so rainy since and our occupations so incessant that I have found no chance to write.

We left our quarters at Jackson's on the 11th and moved a mile and a half to the east, establishing a new line. The weather which had been for some days of alternating heavy showers and sunshine became a heavy northeast storm and lasted without intermission for two or three days, so cold that with big camp fires and overcoats one was hardly comfortable. The earth became saturated like a soaked sponge and the mud was intolerable. Our batteries were established on a ridge 800 yards or so from a prominent knoll called Pine Hill. It was on this hill that Bishop or Maj. Gen. Polk was killed by our shell.[12]

On the night of the 14th the enemy evacuated their line of entrenchments and the hill. We moved southeast and in a few miles came up with another line of the enemy's works. Geary's division was leading. I was obliged to put Knipe's brigade on his right and the other two on his left. We had quite a combat but my loss was not large. Geary lost a staff officer, Capt. Veale, I fear mortally wounded.[13] I was quite near him when he was shot, the ball passing into his right breast. I had gone to the left to look out a position for my command. Soon after, I returned towards the center where my troops were lying and was talking with Gen. Hooker when an enormous explosion burst out directly in front of us, within a few feet. We had heard no ball whiz, nor report of artillery. It was like lightning from a clear sky. It turned out that we were close to a Rebel battery which was concealed by the woods, and the shell bursting and the report of the cannon was probably simultaneous. The Rebs. kept the place all around very hot with musketry and artillery. We lost quite a number of men, as it was impossible to find a place of shelter for troops in reserve even.

320

All day, the 16th, we kept up an artillery duel, and the din of small arms went on as has been the custom for weeks past. In the night the Rebs. evacuated and early in the morning we marched over their works, which we found heavily constructed with flanking works and embrasures for artillery. We followed through the woods, my division being on the left, with orders to connect with the 4th Corps. I had a hard task through the underbrush, up hill and down vale. I finally found Gen. Hazen commanding the right brigade. Returning towards the center to find Gen. Hooker, I saw him ascending an open hill in front and followed with Gen. Knipe. Hooker had his escort deployed as skirmishers and was vigorously at work at the Rebel cavalry down in the valley in front. The Rebs. had a battery on a small hill to our right and front and were firing it over our hill pretty energetically. We at length got up a rifled battery and some infantry and were making pretty rapid work with what was in our front.

Suddenly we saw, half a mile or more on our right, a great cloud of Rebel cavalry flying in disorder to the rear. There must have been a brigade of them and every man was kicking and spurring for dear life. Many horses were riderless. We opened on them with artillery, which greatly increased the disorder. It was laughable to see Hooker's excitement. "Williams," he would cry out, "see them run. They are thicker than flies in a Mexican ranch." "See them go," and we all shouted, to the astonishment of our troops who had not got up. In truth our line of skirmishers that morning had one major general, two brigadier generals, and about fifteen poorly armed cavalry! We found the Rebel works a short distance in advance and took up a new line. The rain came down in torrents all the afternoon and night and the mud seemed too deep to ever dry up.

On the 18th, still in the mud. Our pickets, especially on the right of the 4th Corps, kept up a great noise.

19th. The enemy having withdrawn, we moved early to the southeast, crossing Mud Creek. Just after we had got over on a temporary [bridge] the torrents of rain began again, and our small creek swelled up in an hour to a respectable sized river. I moved my division and got possession of a high ridge.[14]

◈

OCCUPATION OF MARIETTA

[July 7(?), 1864]

[*The first four pages are missing.*[15]]

Entrenchments—the third very heavily and strongly constructed. In the march of three or four miles I struck a byroad which led to the Marietta and Powder Springs Road, not more than half a mile from Marietta. Here I put the division in mass and as the corps was waiting orders I rode into the town. The buildings and grounds in the suburbs looked very invitingly cool and shady though for the most part deserted. It was, indeed, pleasant to see signs of cultivated homes after my exile of two months in camps and woods. The town was almost wholly deserted, not more than seventy-five families remaining out of a population of several thousand, not an article of any kind left in the stores, nor the smallest piece of furniture in the abandoned dwellings. Every street is deeply shaded with pride of China and other large leafed trees. Cavalry horses were grazing in the public square, and altogether this once beautiful place wore an air of complete desolation. Our troops were marching through one end, but stragglers were not permitted.

Aunt Rene had written me that the children of an intimate friend of my youth (Miss Julie Denison, afterwards Mrs. Burr of Richmond) had been living in Marietta, but I found on inquiry that they had moved farther south some months ago.

Returning to my command, we continued our march south three or four miles until we were again brought to a stand before formidable looking works along a high ridge in our front. The Rebel cavalry opened upon us furiously but did very little damage. It was nearly dark before I got my division in camp in the woods.

July 4th I did a day of heavy riding. First over to Gen. Palmer's corps (14th) to see if I could connect lines with him. Then I rode with Gen. Hooker over hill and dale and across ditches and through thickets passing the barricades of pickets (23 corps) looking in all directions until we reached Ruff's and Daniel's mills on the Nickajack Creek. It was an intensely hot day and Gen. Hooker is a furious rider. As soon as I got back, I was obliged to put my division in motion to take a new position two or three miles west. It was nearly sundown before I got into camp, but I had the satisfaction of seeing a brigade of "blue jackets" occupy some heights away off on my right front and on the flank of the enemy's position of defense.

Early on the morning of the 5th we found the Rebels had again vacated their strong line of entrenchments. I followed across the valley and creek in my front and across their strongly constructed works until I struck a north and south road, which I followed for several miles, halting now and then to look after crossroads leading farther east. I met Capt. Poe on my rides, looking sound and cheerful. I did a great deal of riding in a very hot sun. Towards 5 o'clock by crossing over creeks on slight cowpaths we reached the crest of a densely wooded hill from which, over a new line of Rebel breastworks, we could see the tall spires and many of the buildings of the city of Atlanta, twelve to fifteen miles away, looking like a city set upon a hill, for it seems a good deal higher than our high position. Nearer, not over three-quarters of a mile away, heavy columns of "grey backs" with wagons and artillery were marching with a hurried pace towards the river and along their lines of defenses. They were, however, taking up a new position of defense, and between them and us lay a deep ravine and a miry creek. We could only reach them with artillery, and this was not effectively used.

We encamped on the high ridge until the afternoon of the 6th, when we moved towards the railroad in an easterly direction and took position on the right of the 14th Corps. Here the left of my division adjoined two Michigan regiments, the 14th Michigan, Col. H. R. Mizner, and the 10th, Col. Lum. Both of these officers and several others from Michigan have been to see me. Indeed, for the four days I have been encamped here in the woods I have had quite a levee of acquaintances and strangers. The weather has been intensely hot in spite of bowers and shades. The firing between our lines and the Rebs. has not been very active. Indeed, the pickets of my division and the Rebs. formed a truce to cease firing, but yesterday afternoon the 14th Corps opened with a battery of artillery and the rattle of the pickets began again soon afterwards. During the night the battle kept up, and in the stillness of camp seemed to be within a stone's throw of my headquarters.

At daylight this morning the general officer of the day reported that the enemy had evacuated again. I ordered forward the picket line, which reached the Chattahoochee River a mile and a half away without opposition. A good many Rebel stragglers and deserters have been taken on each abandonment of Rebel camps. On some days we have taken some hundreds. They give abundant proof that the Rebel ranks contain thousands who would gladly desert. They are carefully watched and it is a great risk to attempt to escape. These deserters have no especial love for us, but are tired of war, discouraged, and after years of absence anxious to see [their] home, which is generally within our lines. Still, the Rebel army has made a very clean retreat. They leave little behind. Even the inhabitants follow with their slaves, cattle, and furniture. I think we should have punished their army vastly more than we have. From my standpoint occasions have presented themselves during these tedious two months in which large portions of the Rebel army could have been destroyed and the whole virtually broken up. But after all, their losses must have been severe in desertions and killed and wounded. Their falling back has enabled them to recuperate by collecting reserves and guards, while our lengthened line has greatly weakened our numbers.

We have reached a point now where comes the "tug of war"—a broad river to be crossed—strongly fortified at all points, and an advance towards the objective point which has taxed the defensive purposes of the enemy for a year or more. I am not so confident as some, as our real base of supply is far away and the line we depend upon a very long and uncertain one, subject to accidents and to destruction by the feeblest party. And yet with the fair chances of war on our side, I think we will get Atlanta. There is much work and I can't help sometimes envying those who are peacefully sitting under their own vines and fig trees and have none of the heavy cares and anxieties that confront us. . . .

Love to all. I never was so impatient to hear from you and have never been so long without letters.

Your Affectionate Father.

◈

FROM KOLB'S FARM TO THE CHATTAHOOCHEE

On the Chattahoochee River
Near railroad from Marietta to Atlanta,
July 10, 1864.

My Dear Children:

You all complain that I do not write you, and yet if you have received my letters (and a reference to dates will inform you) by measuring the *quantity* you will see I have written more to you than all your combined letters would amount to. I have no easy chair in a nice room with pleasant surroundings to repair to while I write, but with all the cares and responsibilities of my place I am obliged to sit on the ground in the woods, generally amidst the rattle of small arms, the booming of cannon, the braying of mules, the rattle of wagons, and the universal din of large armies. If we halt for a few days it is always in readiness to move at a moment's notice; always in expectation that every mounted orderly bears the order to forward. Sleeping on the ground after a whole day in the saddle, roused up half a dozen times a night, up before daylight to be ready to march at daybreak; all these and a thousand matters, that you cannot imagine, nor have I room to repeat, don't prepare either the mind or body for letter writing, even to those we best love and oftenest think of. Yet if my letters to you all have come to hand you will find I have written a good many very sorry looking pages. . . .

Now for my movements since writing any of you. I wrote last to Minnie on the 24th ult. and to Larned or Rene, I cannot recall which, on the 27th or 28th, ult. My division was then lying on Kolb's farm in the same position in which it was attacked on the 22nd of June, and of which I gave you an account. We remained in the same position until the morning of July 3rd. The corps on our right and left made several efforts to do something, but without much effect, save the loss of men. On June 27th the 4th and 14th corps made a combined attack, but without success and with much loss, especially in officers. Brig. Gen. Harker was killed.[16] I see the papers report his name as Maj. Gen. Hooker.

Our corps was not engaged. We were held in reserve for a *coup de grace* in case the Rebel lines had been carried. But in truth they were very strongly built, with strong abatis and chevaux-de-frise. My division lost a good many men on the picket line, as their shelters were exposed in the open and they could scarcely move without exposure to sharpshooters. We had on one day a grand effort to drive them out of their works with artillery. There was a grand expenditure of ammunition, an immense noise, and great deal of smoke, without results.

On the morning of [July] 3rd we found that the Rebels had left. I immediately advanced my picket line and followed with the division over very rough country, full of thickets and deep ravines. We crossed three lines of theirs which the enemy kept disputing. They held a spur somewhat higher. I arranged a small column of attack and having got a battery in position I pounded the top of the spur and immediately charged it with not over fifty men and took it in ten minutes with a loss of only three men. I captured one young fellow who told me the hill was held by a regiment of Confederate Regulars, belonging to Gen. Cleburne's division. I have taken a good many prisoners from Gen. Stevenson's division. Uncle Lew will recollect him, Carter L. Stevenson, of the 5th Infantry.[17] He married a Miss Griswold of Detroit. The Rebs. tried hard to retake the hill, but did not succeed.

On the 20th I was relieved by Wood's division, 4th Corps and marched down across a broad valley to a wooded plateau beyond, then west along this to a larger plantation, where the elevated plateau drops down to the margin of Closed[?] Creek. We found Rebel pickets at a cluster of Negro houses, but they decamped in haste. We came up with a division (Hascall's) of the 23rd Corps, which lay considerably behind us. As our march was in some way to relieve this corps of a body of Rebs. disputing their crossing, we came to a halt for the night in another pouring rain.

There was no stately mansion on this plantation. A few decrepit Negroes were about, who told us that the master lived in Marietta and had carried off about sixty sound Negroes. The overseer, when here, lives in a very poor log house. There were crops of oats, wheat, and corn, all of which became the coveted food for our animals. All the crops very thin and poor. Wheat about ripe, corn half grown in length of stalk, oats in the milk. You can compare this with your crops.

On June 21st, we remained in camp at Atkinson's farm. It was the first day for weeks that it did not rain. We were expecting to move at any moment. I moved forward two regiments about a mile and took possession of a high ridge with a good deal of open country in front and the two twin mountains of Kenesaw clearly defined about six miles north. The enemy have batteries on the summit of both knobs and keep up a pretty brisk cannonading. McPherson's command (Department of Mississippi) is around its base.

June 22nd: Early in the morning I moved up my whole division and occupied in force the ridge taken yesterday and one in echelon to it, farther in advance, which is partly covered by woods in front. Two brigades, Knipe's and Ruger's, were put on the advance ridge and Robinson's brigade on the rear ridge. Robinson and Knipe and two regiments of Ruger had an open country in front, varying from 500 to 1,500 yards wide. I had previously occupied the Marietta and Powder Springs road several hundred yards on my right. There was savage skirmishing all day, especially on my left where the Rebs. held some log houses and had built rail covers all along the front of the woods.

Every time I attempted to advance my line the enemy would get a flank fire from my left. Geary's division was considerably behind mine and on my left a thousand yards or more. I could see his line of skirmishers, but they could not, or would not, advance so as to cover my left or connect with my advancing line. The enemy gave signs of being in great force in the woods in front. Gen. Hooker was impatient for an advance. I was opposed, until my flanks right and left were protected. I had put a battery of rifled guns on the rear hill and a battery of twelve lb. Napoleons on the advanced hill. Luckily, the rifled guns practiced on all the points in front and got superb range in trying to drive out the heavy skirmish reserves.

About 3 P.M. I rode over to the Marietta road to see Gen. Hooker at Kolb's house. He had just got information that the enemy was massing to attack us. The story was that the whole Rebel army had concentrated. No time was to be lost in getting into position and entrenching. I rode rapidly back along my brigades and in ten minutes my whole command was deployed in a single line and everybody piling up logs and rails for breastworks. Ruger and Knipe formed a continuous line of battle, as I have before mentioned, with open country before most of the line. Robinson was on a parallel ridge a few hundred yards in

327

the rear, his right resting opposite Knipe's left, which fell back around the termination of his ridge towards Robinson. Just in front of Knipe's left was a dense patch of woods with heavy underbrush which I had ordered cut down.

We had just fairly begun to pile rails when the heavy skirmish line of the enemy poured out of the woods all along the open and advanced at a run. Three columns, massed, followed close and deployed in three and four lines. Our artillery opened upon them a most destructive fire. The infantry columns opposite Knipe and Ruger's left moved forward, but as they reached the brow of a ravine which ran parallel to our front, the whole line opened a withering volley. Some Rebs. went back, some scrambled down into the deep ravine, but none ever passed beyond it. One heavy column got hold of the woods in front of Knipe's left, and upon it I turned twelve pieces of artillery, sweeping it with canister and case shot until the devils found sufficient employment in covering themselves behind trees and logs.

Farther toward our left a huge mass of Rebels moved out to attack Robinson's brigade, but three rounds from the rifled guns set the whole mass flying in the greatest disorder. They never reached the fire of our infantry. The attack was kept up from 4 P.M. until near dark. The numbers were formidable, but the attack was indeed feeble. The Rebs. had been badly shaken by our artillery fire before they left the woods. All the prisoners say this. Indeed, after the first half-hour the men considered the whole affair great sport. They would call out to the Rebels who had taken shelter in the woods and in the deep ravines in our front, "Come up here, Johnny Reb. Here is a weak place!" "Come up and take this battery; we are Hooker's paper collar boys." "We've only got two rounds of ammunition, come and take us." "What do you think of Joe Hooker's Iron Clads?" and the like.

The fellows down in the shelters, I regret to say, generally answered with some very profane language and with firing of their guns. In the morning, however, over sixty of them lay dead there. Judging from those they left behind, and from the fact their wagons were all night carrying off dead and wounded beyond the ravines, with our consent, the Rebs. must have lost over a thousand men in this attack. My loss in killed and wounded was not far from 120, many of them, slightly. I was in a single line of battle without reserves, and had little or no breastworks. They had four lines of attack and a division in reserve in the woods. I captured one battle flag and could have taken a thousand prisoners, but that I dared not break my single line to advance, especially as I had been officially informed that the enemy was in great force in my immediate front. I took prisoners from Stevenson's, Stuart's and Cleburne's divisions. I lost but one field officer, a Maj. Becket of the 61st Ohio, killed. Several other officers were wounded, but none of the staff. Capt. Pittman had quite an independent fight of his own on the right, in moving up the skirmish line to occupy the Marietta Road. He accomplished the affair with great success.

Altogether, I have never had an engagement in which success was won so completely and with so little sacrifice of life. Considering the number of the enemy sent against my single division, the result is indeed most wonderful and gratifying. Dory Davis (T.R.) has been here making a sketch of the ground for *Harper's;* but he says that *Harper's* don't put in half he sends and those are bunglingly and incorrectly copied. He sketches beautifully and the pictures he has sent give a most correct idea of the field of fight, so far as landscape is concerned. We are now lying in the woods and have possession of the ground the enemy charged over. They have strong works not a mile in our front and our pickets keep up the usual popping of small arms. . . .

And now I'll close. The day is hugely hot, and as I write I circulate around a big oak to get the shadiest spot. Just think of two months of the campaigning we have had with the two weeks of deluging rain. Since the 1st of this month my division has been every night in line of battle and under fire. There has not been a night or day that Rebel musketry could not have reached my headquarters and hardly a day that the projectiles of their artillery and infantry have not made solemn music over my head. Love to all. . . .

Your Affectionate Father,
A.S.W.

◈

FRATERNIZATION AND LIES OF REPORTERS

Near the Chattahoochee, Georgia,
July 15th, 1864.

My Dear Daughters: . . .

Nothing particular has occurred since I last wrote you. I spent one afternoon, the day after I wrote you, along the river with the picket line. The Johnnies were pretty thick on the opposite side, a few hundred yards away, and kept us dodging behind our log defenses so briskly that our sight-seeing was by no means agreeable. One fellow, especially, was an excellent shot and would graze the top of our log defenses at almost every pop. We were quite safe, as we could drop at the smoke of his gun and hear the whiz of the bullet before it reached us. Since that, our "boys" have got up an armistice and they bathe on the opposite banks of the river and meet on a neutral log in the center of the stream and joke one another like old friends, making trades in tobacco, coffee, and the like, and exchanging newspapers. It is a curious fact that while the pickets on both sides of my front are popping away at one another, those of my division have not fired a shot for several days, but are on the most quiet and joking terms with the opposite Johnnies. I had a man mortally wounded yesterday in the picket reserve, which is kept quite in the rear. The fact was reported to the Rebel pickets, with a threat of retaliation. The Rebs. in front opened a volley of hard words on their reserve, which fired the shot, and an explanation was sent down that it was a mistake. The sharpshooter mistook the reserve for one of the 14th Corps, which keeps up its firing. I am always glad when picket-firing stops. It has no effect upon the results of war and is a miserable and useless kind of murder. Pickets are mainly intended to give notice of an advance or movement of the enemy. This constant popping obviates or destroys this valuable purpose. . . .

I have never seen more lying by the letter-writing fraternity than in this campaign. We have no correspondent in this corps, but we have had one division commander who, I judge, has kept a corner in the notes of every correspondent in the army, besides keeping his staff busy at the same work. He claims pretty much everything. I see the New York *Times* gives him the credit of my attack at Dallas. He was hardly near enough to hear my guns. He is not the only instance of lying humbugs in this army who contrive to keep their names connected with battles which they were not near.[18] It sickens one to see what efforts are made by officers high in rank to steal undeserved honors, and how much thirst for false fame preponderates over real love of country and an honorable ardor to serve the great cause, irrespective of personal reward.

Have you seen T. R. Davis' sketches in *Harper's?* He has drawn several of my division; one, the attack in the woods at Dallas, has been published. The other is the Rebel attack on my division on June 22nd near Kolb's farm. I see by the papers that everybody is claiming part of this defense; Geary and Butterfield's divisions and the twenty-third Corps. The truth is, that there was not a musket fired on the Rebels in this attack except by my division, and all the claim for artillery services from other commands is all bosh. My own artillery and infantry did the whole thing, for I stood on the slender rail piles in the front rank and saw all, directing even the fire of my artillery. But enough of complaint! I have been made exceedingly mad, I confess, to read the meanness which would rob another division of its well-earned reputation, to bolster up some ambitious fool to a major generalship. These stories in the press originate in the envy and jealousy of commanders, and I know them.

Gen. Butterfield, commanding the 3rd Division of our corps, has gone home. He says [he is] sick, but I think he was disgusted and tired. Brig. Gen. Ward of Kentucky commands the division. Butterfield was a much more honorable officer than Geary, but he "hankered" after newspaper fame, and was uneasy that as a major general he had a subordinate command to others he ranked. In many respects he is an excellent officer, but cannot stand the hard service of such a campaign as this. Indeed, few can. Many of our general officers are going home and more intend to go, but hope to hold out until we reach Atlanta.

Gen. Hovey, the officer whom the newspapers gave the credit of my defense near Resaca, resigned soon after that affair and started for Washington. I have it from a prominent staff officer of Gen. Sherman's that his only reason was that the President had promised to promote him, and had not, and he would not stand it any further. This he did in face of the enemy and within sound of his guns. I see he has been made a *brevet major general!* The same gazette announces the dishonorable dismissal of a captain for resigning in the face of the enemy, for reasons not satisfactory. Hovey is my junior by two years at least.[19] He resigns in face of the enemy and is promoted; I stay and am never thought of at the War Department.

I write all this for your private eye. I don't wish my grievances made public, but I have made up my mind to quit when I can do so honorably, when the present active campaign is over. The whole system of promotion is by the practice of a low grovelling lick-spittle subserving and pandering to the press, who can lie you into the favor and notice of the war authorities. I might stay a long life in hard service, as I have done for over three years, and I never could seek the polluted steps to preferment and should never reach it.

Theo R. Davis, the artist for *Harper's,* spends most of his time with us now. He sits sketching now, just before me, sketching "Vining Station" and the Chattahoochee River. A smooth-faced, handsome-looking youngster, full of good humor and wit. His sketches are beautiful, much better than copies seen in *Harper's,* and he does them with the rapidity of a ready writer. His mother is traveling in Europe. He reads me long passages from very long, well-written letters, descriptive of men and things. He is an only son, and she a widow.

I have written Minnie several times that Capt. Beman has been detached and is in charge of some commissary depot. I have not heard from him for several months. Capt. Whittlesey is here, as fat and jolly looking as ever, but rather grouchy at times on account of the trouble of large trains. I am going over to tea with him. He lives as only quartermasters can, very luxuriously, for the woods. Has *spring chickens* and soft bread and pies and *butter* (a thing I have not had for two months) and all other luxuries. Living behind us with large trains, they contrive to carry anything, while we eat hardtack and hog meat salted. . . .

Your Affectionate Father,
A.S.W.

◆

KOLB'S FARM AND AGGRESSIVENESS OF HOOKER

Near the Chattahoochee, Georgia,
July 17th, 1864.
My dear Lew:

We cross the river this afternoon, so I employ a few moments to tell you of my whereabouts, as you have not Minnie's letters now to inform you. I hope you opened my last to her as it would give you information of my movements up to the 25th ulto. or thereabouts including a "right smart" fight my division had on June 22, in which I licked Carter L. Stevenson's division and other Rebel troops right soundly.[20] Do you remember C. L. Stevenson of the old 5th Infantry, who married a Miss Griswold of Detroit? He is the man. His division is a part of Hood's corps. I had moved my division to a line of small hills in an "open" where Master Hood thought he had caught me, and he moved his whole corps straight on my front. But I had my twelve pieces of artillery admirably posted and my whole line was deployed before he could get out of the woods. I had no defenses save a few rails thrown down in a hurry, but before they could get within reach of my infantry their columns were awfully ploughed through and through and thrown into great confusion. Then his advanced lines became commingled and badly confused when they reached a point where one brigade could reach them. It opened a volley of two thousand muskets! The devils, what was left of them, took refuge in a deep ravine, into which I plunged shot and shell for an hour from a whole battery. Another huge column (covering ten acres, I should think) further to our left was broken up and thrown into a rolling mass by my artillery alone and finally fled like scared sheep back to the woods. The fight was kept up by fresh troops for nearly four hours. The Atlanta papers acknowledge a loss of three brigade commanders and 1,200 men. Another paper says one brigade lost over 700 men out of 900! I have no doubt their loss was over 2,000! *Mine was only 120!* That is what I call a glorious success. So few men lost and the enemy so badly punished. I could have taken a thousand or two of prisoners, but as I was deployed in a single line without supports and without connection on my left, and as I had been advised by Gen. Hooker that two corps were on my front, I dared not venture from my strong position to pursue their broken columns. Prisoners say that they thought to catch me before I could get into position.

We have had a hard and wearisome campaign. For more than a month we have been day and night literally under fire, and day and night the din of war has ceaselessly gone on. From our crossing the Etowah, the Rebs. have entrenched themselves every five miles. Driven from one line, they would fall back to another and each one seemed stronger than the last. If you could see the obstructions they place in front of their strong lines of dirt and log breast works you would wonder that any attempt should be made to carry them. The country is all woods, deep ravines, muddy creeks, and steep hills, the most defensible positions by nature I have ever seen, and they most skillfully bring art to aid nature. Rods and rods of abatis, trees, and bushes cut down and intertwined in front, and chevaux-de-frise of strong pointed stakes, fastened firmly in the ground in the midst of the abatis, making a network through which a man could hardly crawl in an hour. Just imagine a line of armed men making their way through and thousands of rifles firing upon it!

Our corps has had the fighting share. It seems to me we are always in advance. In truth, the impetuous Joseph, surnamed Hooker, hates to be behind—is restless, prompt, sometimes impatient, and always "Fighting Joe." He is not so reckless of his men as the world thinks but is exceedingly reckless of his own safety. You will always find him in the front. He sometimes drags us division commanders a little farther on to the advance picket or beyond than we would think it judicious to go. On one occasion, Hooker, Knipe, and myself encountered the Rebel line of skirmishers. Hooker deployed his fifteen or twenty mounted orderlies with carbines and actually drove a strong line of mounted infantry and we held a hill, notwithstanding the Rebs. opened a battery upon it!—until I could get up a battery and a regiment or two of infantry. Just as we had accomplished this, a whole brigade of Rebel cavalry came pouring from the woods on our right in the greatest confusion and disorder, every man spurring over the soft ground as if for dear life. We helped the confusion by pouring into their flanks salvos of case shot from our battery. Hooker was as tickled and excited as a boy and fairly shouted with delight. He is indeed a strange man, but the men like him as he is always seen when a fight is on. When we came from the Potomac, the troops here called us the "paper collar troops."

Now they call us the "iron clads," and I have requests from dozens of regiments and some brigade commanders asking transfers to our corps. I think none stands higher than Joe Hooker's corps.

I want to write you about the probabilities of this campaign, but I have a call and must mount horse. We are a long way from our base and if any loafer or body of Rebs. happens to burn an important bridge, we are in a bad way. We can thrash Johnston at all times if we can keep up supplies. The recent fuss in Maryland which gave "conniptions" to all Pennsylvania and the whole country makes one sick. A thousand old maids with broomsticks ought to have driven the enemy over the Potomac. It seems, however, that all the forces we have there are divided up into squads and put in charge of a lot of fussy and incapable major generals, decayed and fossil remains of political appointments. Love to all. I'll write you again when I have time.

Yours Affectionately,
A.S.W.

◈

INVESTMENT OF ATLANTA

Near Atlanta, Georgia,
July 26, 1864.

My Dear Lew: . . .

We are now *near* Atlanta, but there is a big gulf or gulfs I fear between us. Unless we can starve the Rebs. we have hard work ahead. I had a severe fight on the 20th, was attacked in the woods and lost nearly 700 men and six good officers, killed and wounded.[21] I have recently written to you but such are the occupations of my head and heart that I really cannot remember whether it was since the 20th or not. We have little rest, as my division lies near the Reb. entrenchments and the din of arms is kept up night and day. A battery of twenty pieces is posted near my headquarters and is booming away night and day into Atlanta. Every report cutting the air along a ravine in front of my entrenchments reverberates and gives out a volume of sound like the falling down of many houses. In the night it is particularly noisy and rest-breaking. In return, the Rebs. throw round shot and shell on all sides of my tents. Yesterday they spoiled one of my water buckets. I lost one of my aides (Capt. Newcomb) killed and one (Capt. Bennett) badly wounded in the head on the 20th. My veteran division has been sadly cut up, so that I am reduced in numbers to a brigade. We have had so wearisome and long continued a campaign that I sigh for rest. My health has been perfect until within a day or so. I begin to feel debilitated and broken down and am taking quinine to build. Shall be all right I hope in a day or so.

     Love to all,

                               Yours Affectionately,
                                    A.S.W.

◈

                               Outside Atlanta,
                           August 11th, 1864.

My Dear Daughter:

     I have been unusually occupied for some days and have neglected to write you. . . . I have been in command of the corps since the 27th, which coming suddenly has put upon me a great deal of new duty, especially in our close proximity to the Rebel lines. I am obliged to be on the front line almost every day and it is an all day and laborious job. We are constantly moving up some part of the line, which for this corps extends over three miles along the northwesterly side of Atlanta. We are now face to face with the outer Rebel works, and one has to be very cautious of sharpshooters and very steady nerved to get into and out of our line of works through the picket bullets and the tornado of artillery missiles.

     There is scarcely a cessation night or day, and as some very large guns are in position very near my headquarters on both sides, I have a constant irritation of the tympanum kept up through the twenty-four hours, to say nothing of that irritation in the shape of Rebel shells which are at times whizzing and exploding on all sides. I have twice been fairly shelled out, the rascals throwing projectiles of fifty and sixty pounds weight directly amongst my tents and wagons. It is strange how few, comparatively, are injured by these heavy guns. Now and then a shell explodes inopportunely and a few men are injured. The stray bullets and the sharpshooters do more damage. Still, I don't think one will ever get so used to the shrill and sometimes roaring sound of shot and shell as to enjoy it as a serenade. It is decidedly disagreeable, and the different varieties and calibers give every possible variation of unearthly noises.

The Northern papers speak of the country between the Chattahoochee and Atlanta as level and open. It is, on the contrary, full of deep ravines and steep, wooded hills, and directly around the town the elevations command each other. Tangled bushes and underbrush fill the gullies and obstruct the hillsides. In going to the front I am obliged to leave my horse in a deep ravine as near to the picket line as it is safe and then ramble through the tangled undergrowth over muddy rivulet banks and up steep hillsides under the hottest sun's rays, with occasional pouring showers, and in this way trace out the next best line for our advanced works.

It has been a most fatiguing business, but we have now reached hills on my front which stand face to face (but a few yards distant) with the more elaborate entrenchments of the Rebels. I am now principally occupied in straightening my line and seizing upon favorable advanced points held by the Rebel outposts. Almost every day we stir them up and drive back their pickets. A day or so ago I captured 138 in one haul by the picket line of one brigade. We have thus far always succeeded in dislodging them from their small entrenched picket posts and their stronger reserves. But they show no signs of yielding the town, though it must be a very uncomfortable place, as every day we treat the occupants or the vacant edifices to a thousand or so of shell and shot, and now we have several guns of very large caliber in position, within close range.

Last night they opened for the first time and made the woods and ravines howl with the heaviest reverberations. We had got used to ten pounders and twenty pounders but these eight and ten inch fellows throwing elongated shells of sixty-odd pounds are a new element in the general thunder. The Rebs. have thrown into my camp several weighing over forty pounds, and of all varieties of French and English invention; some of about the shape of a large iron pot, though much more solid. They come with a noise of most portentous and ferocious import, and I notice that Christian and Sanitary agents and all non-combatants make rapid tracks towards the rear at the first sound thereof. . . .

Gen. Hooker left us on the 28th, much to the regret of the whole division. He asked to be relieved because Gen. Howard, his junior and often his subordinate in command, was placed over his head in command of the Army of the Tennessee, in place of Gen. McPherson, who was killed on the 22nd inst. He thought it was intended as an indignity. Gen. Hooker has certainly been a superior corps commander. He is full of energy, always courteous and pleasant, and has a great faculty of winning the confidence and regard of all ranks. It was a blue day when he left us so suddenly, after the many days of hard service we had been together.

I was placed temporarily in command [of the corps] until an assignment is made by the President. We hear now that Gen. Slocum has been ordered here. I hope it may be so, for my rank precludes a chance for myself, even if I desired it, which I really do not. I am satisfied with my old division and I have long given up all hope of promotion from the present powers. When officers can quit the army in the face of an enemy and get promotions in Washington, those who stay may well despair! . . .

I have seen several newspaper notices of my division in western papers and one in the *Herald*, but not the *Times* article. You had better keep it. I will send you some others. The division deserved all that was said of it, and more, for it saved one of the other divisions from a great repulse and flight. But it has deserved as much on five or six occasions during this campaign, for which others got the credit. All at once it seems to be discovered that it is a great fighting division. It has been so at Cedar Mountain, Antietam, Gettysburg, and dozens of other places, always fighting without skulkers and always repulsing or driving the enemy. I think it the best division in the army! A good portion of it has been under my command for more than two and a half years. If I had, as others have, paid puffers, it would have had a name of marvel and its commander would probably have been promoted! Did you see

THE BATTLE OF CHANCELLORSVILLE

Reproduced from a sketch by A. R. Waud in *Harper's Weekly*, May 23, 1863. The sketch shows General Couch's corps forming a line of battle to cover the panic flight of General Howard's Twelfth Corps on May 2, 1863.

VIEW OF DUMFRIES, VIRGINIA

Reproduced from a sketch by A. R. Waud in *Harper's Weekly*, August 29, 1863. The town was occupied alternately by Union and Confederate armies. "It has been the scene of many a savage skirmish," wrote artist Waud.

GENERAL HOOKER'S ESCORT CHARGING CONFEDERATES AT THE BATTLE OF DALLAS, MAY 25, 1864

Reproduced from a sketch by Theodore R. Davis in *Harper's Weekly*, July 2, 1864.

my likeness in the last *Harper's?* (dated the 13th). Capt. Pittman thinks your comments on it will be entertaining. I recognize nothing but my mustaches! I suppose Dory Davis sent it to *Harper's,* but I have no knowledge about it. . . . I send you some little trifles for your scrap book. No. 1, sample of maps sent to division commanders to indicate routes on march; No. 2, a note from Gen. O. O. Howard, written at Gettysburg and carried in my pocket until today. No. 3, sketch of position of my division (in red pencil) 21st and 22nd June. On last day was attacked by Rebels; see letter account. No. 4, sketch of my position of the 2nd Division taken a few hours before the attack at Peach Tree Creek, July 20th, '64. It was drawn to enable me to find the road through the division after I had crossed the creek. My division moved up the road towards what is marked "open fields" and was lying both sides of the road close to the house indicated in N.E. corner in the woods. My advance engaged with Rebel pickets, when the furious onslaught was made. I send you also a map of the vicinity of Atlanta, on which I have indicated as nearly as practicable the position of our corps relating to the town. *We stretch out over three miles.* These are not very valuable additions to your collection; but I have no doubt will greatly interest you, trifles though they be.

I am now at corps headquarters and have with me of my old staff only Capt. Pittman and Lt. Robinson. All the rest of the mess are new. We have three or four messes here and live more expensively than at the division. Indeed, one can hardly avoid living expensively in the humblest way, for we depend upon caterers and sutlers who bring everything from Nashville at enormous prices. I have seen green corn but once; new potatoes once; no butter for weeks. The country is stripped about this. We get what we call desecrated [dessicated] potatoes now and then, canned milk and fruits at outrageous prices. But all the fruits of the season as well as vegetables are not seen. I hear peaches and watermelons are plenty below this. I weary to get there. The postman waits and I must close. . . .

Your Affectionate father,
A.S.W.

◈

OCCUPATION OF ATLANTA

In Atlanta, Sept. 3rd, 1864.

My Dear Daughters:

I have dated my letters so long from *Near* Atlanta that it is quite a change to write *"In* Atlanta." Most of our corps came in yesterday evening, the Rebels having evacuated the night previous. We remained in our old camp and works in front of Atlanta until the night of the 25th, when the 20th and the 4th corps on our right were withdrawn to cover important operations of the army. Our corps moved to three crossings of the Chattahoochee; Pace's and Furness' ferries and the railroad crossings. We did not march, except to move out of the trenches, until the 4th Corps had withdrawn across our front and taken a new position. It was after 2 o'clock at night before we got away. The Rebs. never fired a shot at us and we quietly took up our new positions on the south side of the Chattahoochee. We entrenched ourselves strongly and awaited the progress of events by the rest of the army, which moved southward to strike the Macon Railroad. We heard little from it, but every day we made reconnoissances in force toward Atlanta, getting up to our old line, where the enemy appeared in force.

On the night of the 1st inst. I was awakened from a dream of heavy thunder in which the earth seemed to tremble. Heavy reports of what I thought artillery firing followed in rapid succession, and for two hours or more the roll of artillery firing seemed to increase, while a red glare lit up the skies in the direction of Atlanta, with fitful shooting up through the clouds that hung over the town. After listening and wondering for an hour or more I concluded that Sherman had driven the enemy near the southeast part of the city and had attacked or was being attacked.

I was strengthened in this belief as toward morning the firing was renewed with more regularity. I inclined at first to the opinion that the reports were explosions, but I had heard distant firing so resembling this, and the line of sound seemed to recede, so my judgment settled down on artillery. We know now it was the explosion of powder shot and shell from eighty-two carloads of Rebel ordnance stores, and the burning of a large car factory. At daylight we started out reconnoitering parties and about noon our advance had entered and occupied the town. I brought up two brigades of my division, reaching this [place] after dark. We entered the town with bands playing. The people say that the Rebel army has gone toward Macon, avoiding the position of Sherman. A good many people are still in town, but my duties on the lines which the Rebs. built to protect the town have not yet given me much chance to see this town of greater distances than the original city of Washington. It appears to be scattered over leagues, having a thickly-built business center.

Many [residents] are said to be sincerely Union. As I was marching at the head of my column last night through the dark streets, made intensely so by the heavy shade-trees, I heard a window shoved up and a female voice cry out, "Welcome!" I cried back, "Thank you, and the more so as it is a rare sound down here." It did, indeed, seem strange, that voice of welcome where we have met little but battle and carnage, coming so suddenly from the impenetrable darkness. For more than a month we have lain face to face with the heavy works thrown around this city, and day after day have I peered over our trenches to catch some new idea of the position of affairs. Three high, broad parapets seemed to bid defiance, and my curiosity was generally met with sharp efforts to plug my head. Week after week their heavy guns and ours have kept up a roaring, during which we have thrown thousands of projectiles from the twenty-pounder Parrott to the sixty-odd-weight ball into this city.

It seemed, therefore, very strange to march unopposed, as I did last night, through these same hostile works, and especially right alongside of one of those frowning fortresses that lay in my original front and which had killed or maimed hundreds of men of my division. I rode along full of queer sensations and exciting emotions. It was too dark to see much, but there was the principal battlement which had caused so much trouble and injury and not a sound came from it. I could hardly realize that its strong and defiant voice had really been silenced.

I forgot to mention, in its place, that Gen. Slocum joined us just after we withdrew to the Chattahoochee. He brought with him his three aides, Maj. Guindon and Capts. Moseley and Tracy. I was glad to turn over to him my command and go back to my division. The general seemed to fear that I would be greatly disappointed in not getting command of the corps.

On arriving here last night I took quarters at a very imposing-looking house, as seen by the dim candle light. A very large room with a broad bed and white counterpane promised a splendid rest, after a fatiguing day. It was the first time in four months I had slept in a house. You will laugh when I tell you that I found the air oppressive and could not sleep. To add to the troubles, the bugs (bedbugs I suppose) worked on me from head to foot. I have never, during the campaign, sleeping under trees, on the ground, or in straw, suffered anything like it from the numberless variety of wood-ticks, jiggers, and other festering biters that fill every atom of the dirt of this section. The consequence was, of course, a very disturbed night and the getting up at daylight with a resolution to have my tent pitched and go back to the luxury of my cot and blankets.

I took a long ride at sunrise along my lines and came back in an hour or so to my breakfast, with a hearty appetite. This afternoon we have a huge storm of thunder, lightning, and rain, with a cold wind. I doubt if we have had as hot weather down here as you have had. Our nights are always cool. There has been but one or two that I have not slept under a blanket. The days are hot, very, outside the shade.

Capt. Pittman has sent in his resignation, which will doubtless be accepted. He will go home soon I suppose. [Illegible] left us day before yesterday for home, after three years' service with us. It made me homesick to say good-bye. He has been a very faithful and useful man. When Capt. Pittman goes, all my Detroit associations will be broken up. I shall have no one about me from home. These matters affect me very unpleasantly. But three years have taught me sad lessons of sudden and painful partings and of friendships swept away by hundreds in an hour of bloody battle. I don't know that the heart grows callous, but it learns to bear the heaviest blows with but a passing pang.

What a retrospect! What a mass of mixed recollections is embraced within the compass of three years! How merriment and agony and death; pomp and parade; the battle struggle; the excitement of the charge and rush; the despondency and sinking sensation of retreat; the proud feeling of success; the oppressive and disheartening thought of failure; the dead and dying friends; some with cheerfulness, crying you a "Farewell" as they are borne away; some—so many indeed—with the glassy eye and speechless tongue! How all these recollections and a

thousand others fill the mind in an hour of meditation such as I have
had tonight, looking out of my window into the dark night and for-
getting the present and living alone in a retrospect of the now almost
three years of my active war life! Who can tell, but he who has passed
through such a weird life of excitement and joys and sorrows?

Sunday morning, 4th September: I got so far last night. Fearing I
was getting rather too sentimental for a soldier, I stopped. Now the mail
messenger says the bag goes in a minute. We hear the Rebs. have
burned the Bridgeport bridge. If so, it is a very bad thing for us, and
this letter may not reach you for weeks, if at all. Love to all.

Your Affectionate Father,
A.S.W.

❖

Atlanta, Georgia, Sept 21st, 1864.
My Dear Daughters:

Pittman left us day before yesterday [22] and I celebrated my fifty-
fourth birthday by a review of my division. I don't think I should have
called them out for that purpose, but Gen. Slocum's order did the thing,
unconsciously. We had tried it the 18th in a big rain and so on the 20th
the Heavens let up, though very cloudy, long enough to let us through.
After the review the troops marched by the headquarters of Gen. Sherman and Gen. Thomas. Sherman came out in his careless manner,
standing in the middle of the street and emphatically declaring that
such soldiers could never be beaten. He is indeed a queer one. A genius
indeed!

I feel pretty blue today. These changes of one's old comrades are not
pleasant. Besides, we are having the meanest kind of rainy weather. I
believe I shall never feel in good spirits while in the service, except on
active duty. I think I shall journalize for a while, so adieu for today.
The review was a good one and the division appeared well. I was surprised to see how neatly the fellows had got themselves up.

September 24th: Rain every day at intervals, pouring down. I was
out almost every day, in spite of the rain.

343

25th: Geary's 2nd Division was reviewed and made a good show. From the high works of the Rebs. behind his review ground I could see our old line from which for weeks I had watched this same Rebel works. It looks less formidable inside, than out, but along the whole line is a very strong line of obstacles; sometimes three or four lines of abatis and chevaux-de-frise. It seems fortunate that we did not attempt a direct attack.

26th: The 3rd Division was reviewed and did not appear as well as the other divisions of the corps. It is of more recent organization and its principal officers are away. A colonel was in command of the division and seemed a little at loss. My old inspector (Lt. Col. Buckingham) was in command of a brigade. I forgot to say that Gen. Knipe left us on the 22nd, having been detailed as chief of cavalry of the Army of the Tennessee. I am grieved to part with him, after three years' service together.

October 1st: More rain; more cloudy, dull weather.

October 3rd: Rumors of trouble on the railroad. Have reports for several days that enemy was moving towards our communications. The 4th and part of the 14th corps moved toward the Chattahoochee. Railroad cut somewhere. All mail and papers stopped a day or so ago. Trouble ahead, unless we catch the rascals. Met Gen. Sherman today in front of corps headquarters. He was evidently uneasy. A day or so before I had been to his headquarters to call upon Mrs. Rousseau and daughter and two other ladies. Sherman was in a distressed state that ladies should intrude upon his precincts without permission. I have been riding all round the Reb. works twice in the past few days, no easy job, as it must be over ten miles. Took a look at several points where I had been to establish [entrenchments].

October 4th: Great moving of troops yesterday and today toward the Chattahoochee. This morning Gen. Sherman followed with all the corps but ours, and a few thousand convalescents, wagon guards, and the like. Day cloudy.

October 5th: Cloudy and more rain in the afternoon. Was obliged to ride half around the outer works to make new dispositions of my command, and to look out the many small camps and squads left by other corps.

October 6th: Raining all day. Out again on horseback. I have half

344

the circle of the town to picket. The number of small squads left behind is very annoying.

October 7th: Clear and cool; first signs of frost and first real fires of the season. We had one early morning fire in September. More long rides; horses on half forage. Lt. Harbaugh came to see me.

October 8th: Clear and cool; no doubt that Hood has badly cut the railroad; have been days now without letters or papers. Two orderlies sent to the Peach Tree Creek were gobbled (Snow and Ransom), both mounted. Sent out a party and found that they had been taken prisoners by about twenty-five cavalry.

October 9th: Weather keeps cool, but pleasantly so. The rascally signal fellows sent in a story that Richmond was captured. Whereat there was great rejoicing and hurrahing all over the camps. A band came to serenade me, late in the evening. I didn't believe the story and didn't get up to rejoice. I have serenades now almost every night, as the moon is shining finely.

October 10th: The Richmond news is pretty much blown up by a report from Gen. Sherman. The Pennsylvania and Ohio regiments vote today for their state tickets. I stayed an hour or so at one of the polls. The vote seemed to be pretty much all Union. I think this army will vote strongly for Lincoln. I think full four-fifths, not counting the Missouri and Kentucky regiments. Something may work a change or the vote may be lost by Hood's impediments. Sent out a long train today for forage.

October 14th: We have actually got a mail. It was carted around the railroad break. Got letters from Rene, Minnie, Larned, Capt. Pittman, and others. Latest date from Detroit Oct. 1st, Pittman's letters. You will all be anxious to hear from me. I am anxious to hear from the railroad for I think Hood is on an audacious raid and will do great harm. No mails have gone forward north since Oct. 1st. I am told. It seems queer to be cut off from all news and all letters so long. It is like being at sea. No enemy has appeared near the town and we are all greatly mystified. I see Jeff Davis prognosticates a Moscow defeat for our army. I think he will find things different, even if we have to retreat!

Saturday October 15th: The Department photographer came and took a picture group of myself and staff, with headquarters for a background. After several trials made necessary by someone's moving his head at each trial, we finally succeeded in getting a picture pronounced satisfactory, though Capt. Whitney's face is badly blurred from movement. Col. Boughton had himself and all his officers (twenty-two) taken in one picture. In the afternoon went to see Col. Ketcham, 150th New York, off, going home to attend to his election to Congress. Found Lt. Duffield at the cars going home, mustered out. Went back to headquarters and made up two packages of pictures and a short letter with $200 Pittman's checks for my daughter. Reports from the rear bad. Hood seems to be getting hold of the railroad where he pleases.

Sunday October 16th: In all the forenoon, lots of officers called. In the afternoon called on Dr. Batewell, at 14th Corps Hospital and on Col. Inness, 1st Michigan Engineers. Evening at home. Col. Robinson, 3rd Brigade, in command of three brigades from different divisions and two batteries artillery left with over 600 wagons for foraging. Rather a lonely day. Telegraph from rear shows that Hood is still at work on railroad. Track all up from Resaca to Dalton. Day fine.

Monday October 17th: No further news this morning. Our suspense is great, and our condition by no means pleasant. We are pretty hopeful that Sherman will give Hood a big coup, but it is not pleasant in our isolated condition to reflect that if he fails, or Hood out-maneuvers him, we are badly isolated. The morning is very pleasant. Artist shows first impression of our staff group. Capt. Whittlesey could not be present, which I greatly regret. All the rest are in and good, save Whitney's. I close here as one of my clerks can send it outside mail. I saw Capt. Poe this P.M. Wrote to Rene yesterday.

◈

REASONS FOR THE RE-ELECTION OF LINCOLN

Atlanta, Georgia, Oct. 18th, 1864.

My Dear Daughter:

I sent you a special letter, though as things look just now it may be a long time getting to you. It was good and affectionate of you to remember my birthday. I forgot yours only for the day. Then I have a great deal more to think of than you, and expecially at that time while in command of the corps. . . .

Give my love to Syl. and tell her that I have hunted all along Marietta Street for that female who cried, "Welcome!" But the night we came in was so dark that I have never been able to locate the spot of female patriotic welcome. Most of the houses in the vicinity are small and of humble pretensions. Gen. Sherman's order was made necessary from the fact the people could not stay here and subsist. The moment we took the city all supplies from the country stopped. North of this there are no people left but the very poorest, and the country is literally stripped. South of this in Rebel hands. It became a matter of necessity and mercy, therefore, to send them away, north or south as they choose, where they could be fed.

You seem to be in doubt on political matters. I am no politician, nor have I been for some years. Fortunately, too, I have been for years at a distance from the political contests which excite the passions and prejudices of men and so dethrone their reason. I think I am, and have been, in just the position to make a dispassionate judgment between the contending parties. McClellan is patriotic enough, but the great weight of talent and energy and shrewdness of the party which is going to control him (especially in the western states) belongs to men who hold that one state can not coerce another or that the de facto government has no rightful power to compel a state to remain in the Union.

These kind of politicians control the Democratic party in a majority of the western states and they really controlled the Chicago convention. They did not dare present one of their own men, for it would have so shocked the masses that their game would have been up. They, therefore, yielded the man, but took the platform. They got in the clause for an immediate armistice, well knowing that an armistice or truce, unless sought for by the Rebels, is nothing more nor less than absolute submission to the Rebel government. They know that Rebels in arms must be so subdued by arms as to be driven to ask terms themselves; that no rebellion was ever put down by gentle means, after severe ones had been tried; and that especially in this rebellion the Confederate government and its President and Congress has repeatedly and officially declared that they will accept no terms short of absolute independence.

Now I think that to abandon the war now, to submit after all that has been done and suffered, would be disgraceful to us of the North, who now live, and would entail dishonor and disaster upon our posterity for many generations. We cannot stop now and concede all we have been fighting for without bringing upon our heads the contempt of foreign governments and of the Rebel government itself. Personally, I should certainly wish to find a home where the finger of scorn could not be pointed at me.

Now from what I have written you will understand that I do not favor the McClellan-Pendleton ticket. I have no particularly strong personal reasons for loving the existing Administration, nor do I, in everything, admire its policy or measures. Still its great aim, in the emergency which absolves small things, is right. It goes for fighting this rebellion until the Rebels cry, "Enough!" Therefore, without making pretensions to any very large amount of Roman virtue, which prefers country to self and forgets personal grievances in the thought of the general good, I do not hesitate to say that if I was at home I should vote for "A Linkum" and his party. So much for politics. I catch up these themes as I read over your letters. . . .

I have missed Capt. Pittman greatly. He was always near me and more a confidential officer and friend than any of the others. I sometimes get so *lonely* when surrounded by thousands that I feel sorry I did not resign and go home also. But for a great desire to see this war through, I should have done so long ago, and don't know but I shall do so now. I feel at times as if my duty to the government demands it, as well as my own self-respect. You will not appreciate the feeling, because you can never know all that I know of the facts of my case. It has become in my mind a question, often mooted, whether the discouragement and depression the government has put upon me is not unfitting me for that zealous and ambitious discharge of duty which is properly due from every man holding the responsible position I do. So you see I either feel, or am trying to argue myself into the belief, that on every account, public as well as personal, I ought to quit the service. Some fine morning you may see me at the front door a *citizen!* . . .

People at home can't see why a man's pride and spirit is wounded and diminished. Let them work and toil long months under every exposure, doing, in the written judgment of their superiors, their full duty in all respects, and then let them see dozens of sneaks and drivellers put over their heads. Ah, Minnie, in civil life honest labor and faithful services unrewarded or unacknowledged chill the heart and depress even the efforts of the benevolent Christian spirit, but there is something, especially in military life, where the gradations of command are violated and the shirking junior is foisted over the heads of long-serving and faithful officers, that falls with especial weight upon one's pride and self-respect. It can't be denied nor concealed, and he who does not feel it is not fit to hold a commission! . . .

Oct. 20th: No mails go out today. Several guns heard this morning toward the river. About 200 Reb. cavalry appeared on the track. Yesterday a train of cars was burned at Vining's Station, just beyond the river. Things begin to look rather mixed for us down here. However, we keep in good spirits and hope for better news. If this gets through you will know that matters are improving. Again love to Rene and family.

Your Affectionate Father.

The ring enclosed was made by Capt. Whittlesey's blacksmith out of the brass plunger of a percussion shell, thrown into my camp by Rebs. in Atlanta.

◆

GENERAL HOOKER'S OPINION OF SHERMAN

Cincinnati,
October 31, 1864.

Brig. Gen. Williams,
Dear General:

I have just received yours of the 23d and have only time to reply that [I] am rejoiced to learn that my letter was in every way satisfactory to you. It is not in [my] power to do as much for you as I would like to, or as much as it is my duty to do. If you were here, I could make application for you to be assigned to the command of the district of [?] Michigan, but until you are, it will do no good, as you know. It might not if you were here, but whether so or not it would afford me happiness to have an opportunity to press it. I leave for Detroit tomorrow and wish that you could be with me.

I am a good deal amused as well as annoyed at Sherman's cunning. He is a fool or a knave. I think the latter, and I know that he is crazy. The superior administrative ability of Howard required him to discover. He knows better or ought to, and it is only made use of as a cloak to cover his d——d rascally treatment of me. This matter is not over. It will have a long tail to it. The indignation of the Army of the Potomac at the treatment I received from Sherman was deep and violent. Sherman's conduct is fully understood by all and his motive of action. The truth was he was afraid of me.

Excuse my writing so much of myself.

His excuse in his report for ordering the assault of the Kenesaw is rich—that the enemy might know we could do it. He ought to have known this from their experience with him in his first attack at Vicksburg, also at Missionary Ridge, in all of which he was whipped out of his boots. But damn him, let him go at present.

Adieu, Your Friend and Servant [?],
Joseph Hooker.

◈

EVACUATION OF ATLANTA

Journal, 1864:

November 5th: A beautiful day again. Sent box and letters home with pictures and a remittance in 7 2/00 and $250 to Lew Allen, and to Larned a check for $100 by Maj. Stone, paymaster. About 12 M. got an order to move the division on the McDonough Road about three miles out and encamp. Marched at 3 o'clock and encamped with trains and all before sundown. The order was unexpected and the hurry of packing up was great. I passed the night in a log-hut, occupying the *top* of a bed in a room full of men, women, and children.

November 6th: Was awakened at daylight by the firing on picket line and the beating of reveille along the whole line. The attack was on the 3rd Division just to the right of me. Our pickets ran in without much resistance, losing one man killed and one mortally wounded. The ground was at once recovered and the firing soon stopped. The morning was very cool and soon clouded over with high, disagreeable November winds, not very much like the pictures of the sunny South. It was not easy to keep comfortable around the largest campfires. At 12:30 M. received an order to move back into town and occupy our old camps. Moved at once. I went back to my old quarters. Sharp rain in the afternoon and pretty much all night. No news, but all manner of rumors about the future.

November 7th: Cloudy again and rainy at intervals. Temperature mild. Gen. N. J. Jackson, who is here awaiting orders, called.[23] Gen. Ruger left with the probability of commanding a division of the 23rd Corps. This leaves me without a general officer. All my brigades are commanded by colonels.

November 8th: Election day. Went with Capt. Whittlesey to the polls of the 1st Michigan Engineers and Mechanics and deposited my vote, the first time within four years or more, I think. I voted for Lincoln electors. After voting, went with Col. Robinson, 3rd Brigade to several Ohio and Pennsylvania regiments. Everything going on quietly and orderly.

Reports that the last train runs north to-morrow morning. We are then to be cut loose and find a new base of supplies. Doubtful if some weeks don't elapse before we hear the election news. The weather is quite mild, but showery, and the prospect of bad roads is not amusing. The roses have pretty much disappeared from our yard; now and then one blooms forth. I enclose one, very fragrant, which was solitary and quite alone.

There is a great scramble at the depot to get away. Thousands of Negroes are striving to get transportation. We sent away a family of blacks which came in about forty miles soon after we got here. Part of them have been with us. There are two women and one boy that I should like to get to Detroit. They are the best and steadiest Negroes I have ever seen. One of the women washed and sewed for our mess and cooked part of the time. She cooks, sews, and washes splendidly, and withal is a steady home body and a most excellent character. She calls herself "Pibby," not *Phoeby*. If anybody wants a superb house-servant let them get her or her sister also with her. I gave them a letter of commendation to Lew Forsyth at Louisville.

These may be my last notes for sometime. I will write as soon as possible. And so, Goodbye!

[A.S.W.]

BATTLE OF GETTYSBURG AGAIN

Tullahoma, Tenn., Dec. 30, 1864.

Major General George G. Meade
Commanding Army of the Potomac
General:

I enclose herewith the report of General T. H. Ruger of operations of the 1st Division, 12th Corps, at the battle of Gettysburg, together with the reports of his brigade and regimental commanders. General Ruger, with a large portion of this division, was ordered to New York City soon after the battle, and immediately after his return from New York the corps was ordered to this department. The reports of General Williams and myself were delayed with the hope of recovering General Ruger's report in time to forward it with them. I deeply regret the necessity which compelled me to send my report and that of General Williams unaccompanied by any report of the operations of the 1st Division. For although an account of the operations of this division was given in the report of General Williams, who commanded the corps during the battle, I think the absence of Ruger's report may account for some of the errors contained in your report as to the operations of the 12th Corps.

I enclose a letter from General Williams calling my attention to these errors, to which I respectfully invite your attention, and if anything can be done at this late day to correct these errors I trust you will do it. Your report is the official history of that important battle, and to this report reference will always be made by our government, our people, and the historian, as the most reliable and accurate account of the services performed by each corps, division, and brigade of your army.

If you have inadvertently given to one division the credit of having performed some meritorious service which was in reality performed by another division, you do an injustice to brave men and defraud them of well earned laurels. It is an injustice which even time cannot correct. That errors of this nature exist in your official report is an indisputable fact. You give great credit to Lockwood's brigade for services on the evening of July 2nd, but state that this brigade was a portion of the 1st Corps, while it never at any time belonged to that corps, but was a portion of the 12th Corps, and was accompanied in its operations on the evening of July 2nd by General Williams in person. A portion of this brigade (150th New York Volunteers) is still in General Williams' division.

I copy the following statement from your report: "During the heavy assault on our left, portions of the 12th Corps were sent as reinforcements. During their absence, the line on the extreme right was held by a very much reduced force. This was taken advantage of by the enemy, who, during the absence of General Geary's division of the 12th Corps, advanced and occupied part of the line. On the morning of the 3rd, General Geary's division having returned during the night was attacked at early dawn by the enemy and succeeded in driving him back, and re-occupying his former position. A spirited contest was maintained all the morning along this part of the line. General Geary, reinforced by Wheaton's brigade of the 6th Corps, maintained his position and inflicted severe losses on the enemy."

From this statement it would appear that Geary's division marched to the support of your left—that Williams' division did not—that his (Williams') division, or a portion of it were guarding the entrenchments when the enemy gained possession—that General Geary returned and with his division drove the enemy back—that the engagement on the following morning was fought by Geary's division, assisted by Wheaton's brigade. This I know is the inference drawn from your history of these operations by every person unacquainted with the truth.

Yet the facts in the case are very nearly the reverse of the above in every particular, and directly in contradiction to the facts as set forth in the report of General Geary, as well as that of General Williams. Geary's division did not march even in the direction of your left. Two of his brigades under his immediate command left the entrenchments under orders to move to the support of your left, but through some unfortunate mistake he took the road leading to Two Taverns. Williams's entire division did move to the support of your left, and it was one of his brigades (Lockwood's) under his immediate command, which you commend, but very singularly credit to the 1st Corps.

Greene's brigade of the 2nd Division remained in the entrenchments, and the failure of the enemy to gain entire possession of our works was due entirely to the skill of General Greene and the heroic valor of his troops. His brigade suffered severely but maintained its position and held the enemy in check until the return of Williams' division. The "spirited contest maintained by General Geary reinforced by Wheaton's brigade" was a contest for regaining the portion of our entrenchments held by the enemy, and was conducted under the immediate command of General Williams, and was participated in by the entire 12th Corps, reinforced not by Wheaton's, but by Shaler's brigade.

Although the command of the 12th Corps was given temporarily to General Williams by your order, and although you directed him to meet at the council of other corps commanders, you fail to mention his name in your entire report, and in no place allude to his having any such command, or to the fact that more than one corps was at any time placed under my command, although at no time after you assumed command of the army until the close of this battle was I in command of less than two corps, and I have now in my possession your written orders dated July 2nd, directing me to assume command of the 6th Corps, and with that corps, and the two then under my command (the 5th and 12th) to move forward and at once attack the enemy. I allude to this fact for the purpose of refreshing your memory on a subject which you had apparently entirely forgotten when you penned your report, for you have not failed to notice the fact of General Schurz and others having held, even for a few hours, command of above that previously held by them.

I sincerely trust that you will endeavor to correct as far as possible the errors above mentioned, and that the correction may be recorded at the War Department.

I am General,
Very Respectfully Your Obedient Servant,
H. W. Slocum
Major General Vols. Commanding

◆

ARRIVAL AT SAVANNAH

Savannah, Georgia, Jan. 6th, 1865

My Dear Daughters:

I don't know when I shall be able to send you my promised description of our "promenade militaire" through Georgia. It seems as though I had not a moment to myself. What with visitors, business, reports, reviews, and what not, I have not a moment from getting up to going to bed.

We have been having a series of reviews by corps, all done in the broad streets of Savannah. My corps (or the 20th, more properly) was the last reviewed and all the world and his family came to see it. They call us the "paper collar and white glove fellows" and of course said we would beat them in show. And we did! Hundreds of officers have told me it was the finest and most splendid review they ever saw. Gen. Sherman confesses it was the best of all. The other corps commanders acknowledged the same. My old division (the 1st) was especially elegant. We have three or four of the best bands in the army, and we managed to have it all tell. I was quite a lion! Think of it—a lion! I—a lion!

We are without mails and almost without food for man or beast. This will sound strange to you, knowing that we have had communication with tidewater for nearly a month, but so it is. Few supplies have reached us. The country has none, and we are almost starving our animals on rice straw. And yet we are within three or four days' sail of New York.

While we were on the march through Georgia, supplying ourselves from day to day and not knowing whether tomorrow would furnish the supplies, the men used to say, "We can live on beef twenty days" (and we had plenty of it) "but when we get to the coast won't we find plenty. Lots of ships full of stores waiting for us." And yet, we have been poorer fed here than I have ever had my men during the war. I really begin to fear that we shall suffer for food with a dozen good ports close by us. I know that my artillery horses and wagon mules are already reduced to a dying state! I have in the corps 7,000 of them to starve and they can't be replaced here.

Tell Aunt Jule that I hear in this place of two daughters of Mrs. Clitz, wives of Secesh officers (Sallie Clitz one) [24] and a daughter of

John Kinzie of Chicago a *ditto wife*.[25] I have not been to see either, because I hear they are rabid "southrons." Old army officers talk of them.

I have just finished my official report and am having it copied. To-morrow I will begin a series of letters to you about our march. I hear Gen. Butterfield is coming back. If so he will rank me and command the corps. I shall ask to be relieved and probably shall get leave to come north. I have been strongly recommended by Gen. Sherman for pro-motion, but shall not accept brevets junior to the hundred who have recently been promoted. The mail leaves tonight and I write this merely to let you know I still live. Love to all.

Your Affectionate Father,
A.S.W.

◈

DEATH OF A SOLDIER

Savannah, Georgia Jan. 15th, 1865.

My Dear Minnie:

My dear daughter, your pious and hopeful spirit, as it breathes through your letters, gives me new strength for the labors and dangers which are before me. I shed tears sometimes when I read them, but I always feel refreshed and have a renewed vigor when I reflect what pure souls are praying for my safety. I ought, indeed, to be grateful that I have been so miraculously kept from harm. I have seen so many struck down by my side, so many who have fallen, as it seemed, in the very tracks I had left, that it seems like a miracle that I have always escaped.

The case of young Ahrett of my staff, a boy of twenty years, im-pressed me greatly. I had been over the same ground carelessly, trying to see the Rebel works and not imagining any particular danger. He goes out a few hours afterwards and in the same spot is struck dead by a ball through his heart and is brought back to my quarters a corpse. Accus-tomed as I have been for three years to like scenes, I know of no similar event as the death of this brave and beautiful boy, which has so long and so deeply impressed me. Dozens of times each day on the march he brought me messages, always with a cheerful face and a happy air, and always ready for any duty. It was not easy to believe that the boy with the curly hair and the smiling face could be so early a victim of war.

But goodbye. Love to all.

Your Affectionate Father,

A.S.W.

1. John Ross, notable chief of the Cherokees, had a white father and a mother who was three-fourths white. From early manhood he chiefly devoted his life to the public service of his tribe, of which he was principal chief from 1828 until its removal to Indian Territory in 1839. Thereafter, until his death in 1866 he served as chief of the united Cherokee nation. See F. W. Hodge, *Handbook of American Indians North of Mexico*, and Bella Armstrong, *History of Hamilton County and Chattanooga, Tennessee* (2 vols., Chattanooga, 1931), I, Chap. 5. The latter contains a picture of Ross's house at Rossville.

2. The celebration was in honor of the three-hundredth anniversary of the birth of William Shakespeare. The Detroit *Advertiser and Tribune*, issue of April 23, 1864 contains a nine and one-half column report of the elaborate day-long proceedings. Five addresses by eminent Detroit citizens were delivered, along with a musical concert and tableaus which the reporter characterized as "the finest exhibition ever gotten up in Detroit."

3. Here, as occasionally elsewhere, General Williams' chronology is inaccurate. Monday fell on May 9, 1864, instead of May 8. The succeeding letter (of May 20) correctly indicates that the march was made on Monday May 9.

4. This letter is missing from the collection. Presumably it described the desperate battle of Resaca, May 14–15, 1864, which is briefly described in his letter of May 20, 1864. His official report of the battle is in the *Official Records*, Series 1, XXXVIII, Part 2, 27–29.

5. Theodore Russell Davis, illustrator and artist-correspondent for *Harper's Weekly* during the war and afterwards for many years. See The New York Historical Society, *Dictionary of Artists in America, 1564–1860* (New Haven, 1957). The illustration showing the advance by General Williams' division was published in *Harper's*, July 2, 1864, p. 928.

6. Colonel Archibald L. McDougall died of his wounds in the officers' hospital at Chattanooga on June 23, 1864.

7. Colonel James P. Brownlow, commander of the First Tennessee Cavalry Regiment. His father was "Parson" William G. Brownlow of Knoxville, notable upholder of the Union cause, and subsequently Governor of Tennessee and U.S. Senator from that state.—*Dict. of Am. Biog.*

8. General John Haskell King of Detroit, whose son, Charles Brady King, developed the first automobile ever seen on the streets of Detroit (in 1896). In a letter of February 9, 1944 to Mrs. Elleine Stones, chief of the Burton Historical Collection, Detroit Public Library, Mr. King states that his father in boyhood lived for some years in the General Hugh Brady house on Jefferson Avenue at Hastings, where subsequently the former Detroit Museum of Art was built, and that this association with General Brady inspired him to adopt a military career. General King's wife was Matilda Davenport, member of an old-time Detroit family.—Data compiled from the Charles Brady King material in the Burton Historical Collection.

9. This was the battle of Resaca, May 14–15, 1864. General Ruger's official report of the action states that the flag, commander, and some thirty prisoners of the Thirty-eighth Alabama Regiment were captured by the Twenty-seventh Indiana Regiment of his command. Ruger's brigade formed a part of General Williams' First Division, Twentieth Corps. General Hovey, without mentioning the capture of the flag, affirms that his division fought brilliantly, rolling the Rebel force back "like smoke before the wind." Compare *Official Records*, Series 1, XXXVIII, Part 2, 29, 59, and 541. Obviously General Williams' statements and those of General Hovey are squarely contradictory.

10. The nephew, Lieutenant John H. Knipe, was a member of General Knipe's staff. The latter reported that his dying words were: "I have endeavored to do my duty. If you were satisfied with my conduct, I am ready and willing to die."—*Official Records, Series* 1, XXXVIII, Part 2, 44.

11. Described by General Williams in his official report in *Official Records*, Series 1, XXXVIII, Part 2, 29–30.

12. Leonidas Polk of North Carolina, a West Point graduate in the class of 1827, was "converted" through the influence of the chaplain, during his final year as a cadet. Following graduation he resigned his commission to devote himself to a religious career, in which he achieved marked distinction. A friend of Jefferson Davis and an ardent supporter of the Southern Confederacy, he resumed military life in 1861 with the rank of major general. Until his death in 1864 he was active in the western theater of warfare. On June 14 at Pine Mountain a Federal artilleryman fired a shell at a group of Confederates, and Polk, Episcopal bishop and Confederate lieutenant general, was slain. See *Dict. Am. Biog.*; report of General Geary in *Official Records*, Series 1, XXXVIII, Part 2, 127; Wm. H. Polk, *Polk Family and Kinsmen* (Louisville, 1912), pp. 181–83.

13. Although shot through the lungs, Captain Veale survived his injury.—*Official Records*, Series 1, XXXVIII, Part 2, 129 and 147.

14. The remainder of the letter is missing. Presumably it described Williams'

triumphant repulse on June 22 of the Confederate attack at Kolb's farm, which is also described, later, in his letter of July 10.

15. On June 27 at Kenesaw Mountain General Sherman made an all-out assault upon the Confederate entrenchments, only to be bloodily repulsed with a loss of 3,000 men. Resorting again to flanking movements, he compelled Johnston to abandon Kenesaw Mountain and Marietta in the night of July 2. The first four-page section of General Williams' present letter is missing. The remaining portion takes up the story as he entered Marrietta on July 3, 1864.

16. The battle of Kenesaw Mountain. General Charles J. Harker, a graduate of West Point in the class of 1858, colonel of the Sixty-fifth Ohio Regiment, November 11, 1861 and brigadier general of volunteers September 20, 1863. On May 14, 1864, he received a wound from a shell in the battle of Resaca. He was shot from his horse, mortally wounded, in the battle of Kenesaw Mountain on June 27, while leading his brigade and within fifteen paces of the Confederate entrenchments.—Cullum, *Biographical Register of Officers and Graduates of the U.S. Military Academy*, Vol. II; *Official Records*, Series 1, XXXVIII, Part 1, 369 and 888.

17. Carter L. Stevenson of Virginia was a West Point graduate in the class of 1838. From 1841 to 1844 and from 1847 to 1848 he was stationed at Detroit. Upon the opening of the Civil War he supported the Confederacy, attaining the rank of major general and of corps commander in the defense of Atlanta in 1864.

18. Apparently the officer alluded to was General Geary, commander of the Second Division, Twentieth Army Corps. His thirty-five-page report of the operations of his division during the Atlanta campaign contrasts markedly both in length and in tenor with General Williams' similar ten-page report. His one-page account of his role in the battle of Kolb's farm affirms that his artillery completely enfiladed the ranks of Hood's assaulting force, and "literally" swept them down by his "fearful" cannonade; yet Williams characterizes such claims as "all bosh." For the reports of Williams and Geary see *Official Records*, Series 1, XXXVIII, Part 2, 26–36 and 112–47.

19. Alvin P. Hovey, brevetted major general of volunteers, July 4, 1864. General Williams' official report of the battle of Resaca, May 14–15, 1864 is in the *Official Records*, Series 1, XXXVIII, Part 2, 27–29, General Hovey's report of the battle is in the same volume, pp. 541–42. Williams was made a brigadier general on May 17, 1861; Hovey, on April 28, 1862.

20. For the battle of Kolb's farm see the letter of July 10. For General Williams' official report of the battle see *Official Records*, Series 1, XXXVIII, Part 2, 31–32.

21. The battle of Peach Tree Creek, July 20, 1864. For General Williams'

official report of the battle see *Official Records*, Series 1, XXXVIII, Part 2, 33–34.

22. He had resigned his commission and left for Detroit. The official record shows that he was mustered out of the service on September 7, 1864. On March 13, 1865 he was awarded a brevet of major in the U.S. volunteers, and on the same day a second brevet of colonel. He had enlisted with the rank of first lieutenant in the First Michigan Infantry upon the reorganization of the regiment in September 1861. He served as aide to General Williams until May 1863, when he was promoted captain and assistant adjutant general U.S. volunteers. He died at Detroit, March 30, 1922 at the age of ninety-one. Much of his energy during his final decade of life was devoted to procuring the erection of the equestrian statue of General Williams on Belle Isle, whose unveiling he witnessed in October 1921. At his death the flag on the City Hall was displayed at half-staff, reputedly for the first time in honor of a civilian. Perhaps his foremost distinction in life was accidental. It was he who obtained the famous lost order of General Lee, outlining his plans for the invasion of the North in 1862, which, carried to General McClellan, led to the battle of Antietam.

23. Nathaniel J. Jackson, commissioned colonel of Fifth Maine Infantry, September 3, 1861; brigadier general of volunteers, September 24, 1862; mustered out of service, August 24, 1865; died, April 21, 1892.

24. The Clitz family story is a Detroit saga. John Clitz entered the army as an ensign from New York in 1814 and a year later was transferred to the Second U.S. Infantry, attaining the rank of captain, December 31, 1829. For many years prior to his death in November 1836, he commanded Fort Mackinac, then a place of much importance in the Great Lakes area. Following his death his widow removed to Detroit where she conducted a boarding house, which remained the family home for many years. From it came John M. B. Clitz who attained the rank of rear admiral in the U.S. Navy, and Henry H. B. Clitz, member of the West Point class of 1845, who attained the rank of brigadier general in the Civil War. In line with army tradition, Mary Clitz married Capt. Henry C. Pratt of the regular army. Hattie married Lieutenant Henry B. Sears, a West Point graduate in the class of 1846; Sally married Richard H. Anderson of Georgia who graduated from West Point in 1842 and during the Civil War became a lieutenant general in the Confederate Army; and Frances married another West Point graduate, Gustavus A. DeRussey, who became a brigadier general in the Civil War. The mother of this brood (several not mentioned here) lived to the age of ninety-one. Misfortune clouded the closing careers of two of her sons. General Henry H. B. Clitz disappeared from his Detroit home in October 1888 and supposedly committed suicide by drowning at Niagara Falls.

Admiral John M. B. Clitz late in life became hopelessly insane, and was committed to an institution in Washington.

25. John Kinzie, of early Detroit and Chicago background, popularly accorded the title "Father" of Chicago, had a son, John Harris Kinzie, who, following a varied career from infancy (1803) onward, settled permanently at Chicago in 1833, where he remained for a generation a well-known citizen. He married Juliette Magill of Connecticut, author of the much-celebrated narrative of frontier life, *Wan Bun the "Early Day" of the Northwest*. Their daughter, Eleanor, born at Chicago in 1835, who married William W. Gordon of Savannah, is the "ditto wife" of General Williams' letter. The lot of these Northern-bred women, now allied with the Confederacy, in opposition to their brothers and other relatives who were fighting in the Union armies, affords one of the poignant illustrations of the consequences of the Civil War.

XI

Through
the Carolinas
to Washington

THROUGH THE CAROLINAS TO WASHINGTON

In mid-January 1865, while Lee at Petersburg continued to baffle General Grant, Sherman set out from Savannah northward to rejoin his chief. Rain and Rebels conspired to make the march through the Carolinas a nightmare for the Union army. Despite both forces, however, the army moved northward as relentlessly as a glacier in its descent to the lowlands. Columbia occupied and burned, Charleston and Wilmington effectively separated from their interior bases of support, Raleigh, another state capital, taken—these were but landmarks high-lighting the success of the campaign. Meanwhile Richmond fell and Appomattox followed. With the surrender of Lee's army, the doom of the Confederacy was patent to all observers. The surrender of Johnston to Sherman followed in due course and for all practical purposes the war was over. It only remained for Sherman to continue the march to Washington, there to share in the pageant of the Grand Reunion. Upon its conclusion, with the heartfelt farewells of his official staff and the warm commendations of his superiors, weary warrior Williams sheathed his sword. Ended at last were his four years of service in the field with but a single leave of absence. Ended, too, were his letters home, written often times amid scenes of carnage such as only America's bloodiest war could produce. Hidden from the world for almost a century, they comprise a revealing picture of that war and an enduring monument to the memory of the man—soldier, patriot, and gentleman—who recorded it.

FLOODTIME ON THE SAVANNAH

Headquarters, Twentieth Corps,
Savannah, Georgia, Jan. 23rd, 1865.

My Dear Minnie:

Your journal letter to January 1st. was received last Wednesday, the 13th inst., while I was under orders to move and all packed up to go into South Carolina. . . . I sent you a long journal of our campaign down to the entrance here, but I fear you will find it dull. As I think it over, I am conscious that I left out the most interesting parts of such a march, especially for home reading. I am afraid it is too much for my own memoranda. I send you by this mail my official report, with maps of our daily camps, embracing each division of the corps. This is sent for safe keeping. It is of no consequence to you, except perhaps the statistical parts showing how much we punished Georgia. You must remember that this is only what one corps of four did, and all the estimations are understated.

Now I will give you a brief account of my three days' experience in South Carolina. For two weeks or more one of my divisions (Ward's) has been encamped on the opposite side of the river, beyond the rice plantations, some six miles inland. On Wednesday last Ward was ordered to move up to Hardeeville on the Charleston and Savannah Railroad and the 1st Division (Jackson's) to cross and take Ward's position; both to move forward the next day and take position from Hardeeville and Purrysburg on the Savannah River. Pontoon bridges had been laid from the upper part of the city to Hutchinson Island and from this across two other channels to the mainland, or rather the rice field, in South Carolina. Hutchinson Island and the intermediate one beyond are old, abandoned rice plantations and are kept from overflow solely by the dikes or banks of the old fields. The north bank of the river for three to four miles inland is equally low as the island and are the rice plantations of the Langdon Cheves, Huger, and other rich and old Carolina families. The only way we could make roads was to corduroy the dikes, which are barely broad enough for a single wagon.

Two of my divisions had been for weeks at work at this corduroy and had probably laid seven miles of it across the island and the low ground on the Carolina shore to the causeway road from [illegible]

Ferry to Charleston. The weather had been excellent and the road was pronounced all right. So on Wednesday, the 18th, Jackson's division crossed successfully. On the 19th the 15th Corps, or rather two divisions, were to follow, and I put my headquarters team in their train and started across in advance, expecting to encamp some ten or twelve miles inland. The river for days had been very high and well up to the tops of the banks or rice-field dikes, and the weather was threatening. Before we reached the woods on the Carolina shore, which skirts the broad belt of rice fields, it began to rain heavily. We hurried on, thinking to find a safe shelter for the night in the Cheves mansion, four miles ahead.

Alack for expectations! We found the Cheves house a heap, a mass, of smouldering ruins, hissing and laughing at our dilemma as the heavy rain poured on the mass of burning timbers. We were without blankets or overcoats except rubbers, and our only shelter was a Negro hut or shanty which had been occupied in turn by Reb. and Fed. soldiers, and would have been a very foul pigsty.

There was no alternative; outdoors in the cold rain and mud, or indoors in dirt and, possibly, vermin. We chose the latter; set the orderlies at work cleaning as far as practicable; built up a big fire in each of the three small compartments, and despatched the orderlies back for blankets and food. There were at least twenty of us, not counting servants or escort, and twice that number of horses, man and beast without food and most of them without shelter. About 10 o'clock of a very dark night the orderlies returned with some blankets, but no food. My pack of white blankets, carelessly enveloped in a rubber, had been dropped in the mud and badly besmeared, and the rain had pretty thoroughly saturated them. As the general, I was honored with the only bunk, and rolling myself in my only blanket and sheltering myself as well as possible by the rubber from the rain dripping through a bad roof, I went supperless and dinnerless to bunk!

I thought myself pretty fortunate, compared with the troops, the mules, and the mule drivers, who were stuck in the mud on the dikes of the rice plantation, and there were at least five miles of these unfortunate ones, not one of which could move forward over these greasy roads until the leading team was out of the way. You can get a pretty good idea of what these rice swamps are by imagining the Grand Marais in

Hamtramck [1] or the marshes in Ecorse spread out from three to four miles in width, and then ditched and diked by the fat, black unguinous soil. The river here, however, at high tides rises almost to the top of the dike and quite above the surface of the marshes or fields. Standing or lying on these narrow, slippery, and treacherous dikes were hundreds of wagons, including my headquarter's wagons, and thousands of men, who could not get past the vehicles or were left to help them out. A few broken-down wagons had greatly helped to obstruct the march, until the rain and darkness stopped all progress.

I slept soundly, waking up, however, now and then to hear the rain beating heavily on the shanty and drizzle in big streams down the timber near my head. It was one of those dismal nights that surroundings make more dismal, but I slept soundly in spite of weather and the occasional wakings to think of the poor devils on the muddy dikes. I mounted early without breakfast or face washing, for I had neither soap, towels, nor hardtack. Sending part of the staff forward towards Hardeeville, I turned my horse's head, with a dozen others, towards Savannah, to learn the prospects of my train. I felt an inward satisfaction that all the trains of two divisions were on what I supposed [to be] terra firma and that, excepting my own headquarters and Gen. Jackson's headquarters wagons, all the stalled trains belonged to other corps. So as I sploshed down the Union Causeway Road to the point where our dike road intersected it, I was thinking of the best method of getting up a cup of coffee when I should reach the wagons; and I thought, too, of the comfortable and delicious breakfast that was probably coming off at Aunt Jule's about that hour. I had been twenty-four hours without food, and my fancy was pretty active, to say nothing of my appetite.

Presently we began to find our farm path which led through the woods, the great, moss-bearing live oaks covered with water, and as we went forward it grew deeper and deeper and spread out wider and wider. Our wonder and concern grew fast, for, supposing that some one had cut the dike or destroyed a sluice, I saw that at least some days would pass before our road would be passable. But on we went, splosh, splosh, splosh, following one another to avoid the treacherous mudholes. In spite of all our caution, however, many a horse went down, pitching his rider to his middle in mud and water. After a couple of miles or so of this mysterious and perplexing aquatic equestrianism we came out upon the open rice field.

Just fancy our consternation when we saw before us, as far as the eye could reach, an almost uninterrupted sea of water. Nothing of land, but here and there the projecting points of the dikes, looking as one can fancy the backs of sea monsters may have looked in the great deluge. Away off, three miles distant, we could indistinctly see the white covers of our wagons, and in the background the upper portions of the tall storehouses of Savannah, like the great houses of sea-girt Venice over the Laguna. It was a rich spectacle, especially as the rain was still pouring, and more especially as from the broad canal, the bank of which we had reached, was pouring over its whole length a volume of water which was rapidly making its way to our road in the rear and making problematical whether our retreat was not doubtful.

Ahead no part of the long road we had passed over yesterday was visible above water. We drew up on the only semi-solid piece of ground we could find and after some consultation decided to try [to make] our way through to the pontoon bridges. We could see the corduroy sticks bobbing and floating ahead, but we were pushed to desperation by our empty stomachs, our wet feet, and the bad chance behind us. So we formed a *queue* again, and in single file tried to find the road over this waste of water. It was a bad beginning, for several orderlies' horses and one or two officers' went down into deep holes and riders were left floundering in the water before we had gone a hundred yards.

So I gave up the attempt, and ordered all to turn back. In turning round to get back, my horse, a tough, Canadian-looking racker, slid into a hole so low that the water ran into my boots. I sat quite still, and with wonderful sagacity the animal felt forward and sideways with his forefeet and finding a firm spot he planted it and making a spring we landed on the upper crest again, unharmed, but with my boots full of water.

A further consultation was had, and two or three staff officers determined to try again, taking the opposite side of the canal, which was crossed by a bridge. We watched them from our eyrie for a long distance, saw rider and horse repeatedly floundering in the water, and we shouted with great laughter, notwithstanding our real apprehensions and the very dolorous prospect of our next meal. I decided for the rest that we should turn back and overhaul some wagons I had seen stalled on the road toward Semmes [?] Ferry. There might be food for man and beast in them; besides I had made a water mark and saw that the flood was rapidly increasing. So back we turned into the woods and without serious mishaps reached beyond the sea, at a point where the Cheves family have built up a large village of Negro quarters for the slaves of their rice plantations. There were fifteen to twenty Negroes left and "the smoke that so gracefully curled" above these very dismal-looking pens reminded me that my feet were very wet and cold. So I dismounted, entered, unseated an "old Aunty," had a big fire stirred up, and entered into a long talk with a bright-looking Negress who had lost a right arm in a rice mill. A very smart old Negro soon joined in the conversation and about a dozen young ones snuggled close up to their colored people, gaping in wonder at a live Yankee general.

These people told me that we were witnessing the beginning of the annual freshet of the Savannah, larger this year than usual, but that ordinarily all the rice plantations were overflowed, and that in a day or so, probably, the high cause-way road from Semmes [?] towards Charleston would be submerged, and that last year they had lost over four hundred sheep by the freshet. On the whole, we were satisfied that we were just beginning to feel the rise of waters and that we should lose no time in getting our wagons on terra firma.

But how? As usual with these people, they talked a great deal of family matters; told me a history of matters about old Mr. Langdon Cheves, so long a member of Congress from South Carolina, and about Mr. Charles Cheves, who died before the war, and young Mr. Langdon Cheves, who was killed on Morris Island by a ball "that cut him right in two"; about the two widows and Mr. Langdon Cheves' daughters, who had not been on the plantation for years; about the extent of the rice plantation—over 3,000 acres; the ordinary annual amount of rice crop, over 90,000 bushels; or "ninety million thousand," as the woman said; of the hard life of incessant labor a rice-planter's slave lives; of the great amount of sickness amongst slaves, of which I expressed a doubt, but which she confirmed by opening a large cupboard or room and displaying an array of quinine bottles which she said they had to take in great doses. They told me that over 200 able-bodied slaves were worked on this plantation, and that most had been sent above Abbeville; that men and women labored alike in the field; that their only food since the war was rice, which they threshed and pounded clean themselves; that the Rebel troops had taken all their corn and drove away all the cattle from the place.

THE CAPTURE OF LOST MOUNTAIN BY GENERAL HOOKER, JUNE 14-16, 1864
Reproduced from a sketch by C. E. F. Hillen in Frank Leslie's *The American Soldier in the Civil War*.

THE MARCH TO THE SEA BEGINS
Sherman's Fourteenth and Twentieth corps moving out of Atlanta, November 15, 1864. Reproduced from a sketch by Theodore R. Davis in *Harper's Weekly*, January 7, 1865.

THE MARCH TO THE SEA ENDS

General Sherman's army entering Savannah "at sunrise," December 21, 1864. Reproduced from a sketch by Theodore R. Davis in *Harper's Weekly*, January 14, 1865.

I kept them talking for an hour while I dried my feet. At last I said to the old man, "Have you heard that they are going to put your people into the Rebel army?" He had heard of it, but he added, "Massa, they can't make us fight de Yankees, I habe heard de colored folks talk of it. They knowd all about it; dey'll turn the guns on the Rebs." "Then," I said, "you prefer the Yankees?" "Ah, Massa," and he said it with his hands raised and an expression of earnest feeling and a pious soul, "Efery night when me and my woman say our prayers we say the biggest part for de Yankees"!

I have no doubt there are hundreds of thousands of honest old pious Negroes all over the South who are nightly putting up the same heart yearnings and petitions for our success. I have been astonished to find how widespread amongst field hands, as well as house servants, the idea is that the Yankees are coming to set the captive free, and how long this feeling has existed. The Millerites [2] never looked with more faith for that certain and final ascension day than have these Negroes, especially the old ones, for their certain deliverance from bondage.

After my Negro confab we mounted, and learning on the causeway road that a portion of the 1st Division train was stuck in the mud toward Semmes [?] Ferry, where it had gone after subsistence stores, I turned my horse's head that way. I found a portion of the 5th Connecticut Regiment and some stalled wagons, with pork and hardtack. Perhaps I have eaten more sumptuous meals, but none with a heartier relish than that slice, or those slices, of pork, which I toasted myself on the point of a stick to a beautiful brown color, and then laid across a section of hard bread, as both plate and condiment, or vegetable accompaniment. Around a campfire, myself, [my] adjutant general, and two aides toasted and toasted, until I think we had made up, in quantity at least, for the previous long fasting. A tin cup of strong coffee finished the perfection of breakfast. I felt compassion for poor Billy, who wandered about near me cropping the leaves from a few stunted bushes and nibbling away at some rice straw in the road, as the best substitute that could be got up for his meal after nearly thirty-six hours of faithful unfed services.

I found some forty-odd wagons stalled, and the roads so bad that six mules could not draw through an empty wagon. Indeed, the mules themselves were nearly drowned in mud. It was now 2 o'clock, and we had fifteen miles to ride to the camp of the nearest division with unfed horses, over the heaviest road, and in regular pour-down rain, which, after a brief respite had begun again with renewed force. But on we went. Billy began to look upon spur and whip with indifference. Now and then, as some one tried to pass him, his pride would come up and he tried his best rack. The road was flat and marshy almost all the way, save now and then a sandy ridge upon which the Rebs. some time ago, probably about the [time of the] Port Royal capture, had constructed extensive field works.

Before reaching the point in the road where the Hardeeville road turns sharp to the left from the Grahamville Road, I met Gen. Smith of the 3rd Division, 15th Corps, going back to look after one brigade and a part of his train which had passed the night on the dikes. He was surprised to hear of the extent of the deluge, and expressed an opinion that he was in a bad fix, but he started to reach Savannah. I find since I got here that he has not reached it. What has become of him no one here knows.

I reached General Ward's headquarters at Hardeeville about dusk, found a good supper waiting, spread my blankets on the floor of a shell of a house, and I don't think I rolled over until daylight. My horses got a good feed. The venerable Yorkshire, who is generally carefully attended to, looked supreme disgust, as he was obliged to stand in the rain all night unblanketed, and for thirty-six hours un-fed. Major, the chestnut horse I have generally rode since last spring, as tough as a knot, looked quite resigned. The worthy and war-worn old Plug Ugly, I believe I have told you before, gave out last summer beyond even strength to be led, and was ignominiously sold for $50. I would cheerfully pay more for his bullet-bored skin, if I had it at home. I hear that he died soon after I disposed of him.

On the next morning (Saturday the 21st) I rode over to Purrysburg on the Savannah River; still raining and water all around. I found the two divisions (Geary's is still here) encamped wherever they could find some solid ground, and often obliged to move camp. In the river the "double ender" man of war *Pontiac*, Capt. Luce, was at anchor. I went aboard. He kindly gave me a boat and in it I descended the most unpicturesque Savannah in a dense fog and rain to this city, reaching this about 4 o'clock P.M. I was rejoiced to learn that my wagons had got safely out of the mud back to the city, and that my provost marshal,

Maj. Parks, whom I had sent across the river from Semmes [?] Ferry had them in charge. The staff officers who left me to try the submerged rice fields got safely through, after many mishaps and plunges. My supply wagons were still embargoed on the causeway and the [illegible] Whittlesey was transporting forage to the mules in boats! I took quarters in the comfortable apartments of the medical director of the corps, Dr. Goodman, and today have reestablished my own mess, only for a day or so until I can collect my scattered trains and troops. I shall probably go back to Purrysburg and Hardeeville on Wednesday, and if weather permits we shall soon advance again. I fear, however, we have a terrible job before us.

[*The remainder is missing.*]

❖

PUNISHMENT OF SOUTH CAROLINA

Fayetteville, North Carolina, Mar. 12, 1865.
My Dear Daughter:

After long and weary marches we entered this town yesterday. A gunboat came up this morning by which I am enabled to send you a line in pencil. As soon as we get our "base," or if we linger here long enough, I will copy my journal to this point.

Our campaign has been more arduous, weather worse, and roads infamously worse than on the Georgia campaign. We have had but little fighting, however, so far, the enemy always easily driven away from the strongest positions. He has evidently been confounded by the audacity of our movements. We swept through South Carolina, the fountain-head of rebellion, in a broad, semi-circular belt, sixty miles wide, the arch of which was the capital of the state, Columbia. Our people, impressed with the idea that every South Carolinian was an arrant Rebel, spared nothing but the old men, women, and children. All materials, all vacant houses, factories, cotton-gins and presses, everything that makes the wealth of a people, everything edible and wearable, was swept away. The soldiers quietly took the matter into their own hands. Orders to respect houses and private property not necessary for [the] subsistence

373

of the army were not greatly heeded. Indeed, not heeded at all. Our "bummers," the dare-devils and reckless of the army, put the flames to everything and we marched with thousands of columns of smoke marking the line of each corps. The sights at times, as seen from elevated ground, were often terribly sublime and grand; often intensely painful from the distressed and frightened condition of the old men and women and children left behind.

We saw no young men, save the deformed, the sick or wounded, and deserters (pretty numerous). Everybody else had been forced into the service, even to decrepit old men of sixty and upwards, lots of whom came to us to be paroled or to be sent home. Boys deserted to us, not over thirteen years old. The "Confederacy" has literally gathered its infancy and aged, [its] first and second childhood. If it fails now, all material for reinforcing its armies is gone, unless, indeed, they can make fighting men out of the Negroes.

Our line of march has been across the largest rivers, the broadest swamps, and the muddiest creeks of the state. I think I am within bounds in saying that this corps has corduroyed over a hundred miles of road. For the last fifty miles we have traveled over a shell of quicksand which would not bear up a horse, and through which a wagon would cut to the box. The country was much poorer than I expected to find. Even respectable houses are very rare, and superior ones rarer. The soil, never very fertile, is worn out. The people left at home, mainly sickly-looking and grossly ignorant. How even the politicians of South Carolina can boast a superiority over our hardy and industrious Northern people is more than I can imagine. Everything in that state presents evidence of decay and retrogradation. There is nothing new, nothing that looks flourishing, and the people look like "fossil remains."

So far into North Carolina the country, if possible, is worse and the people worser! This town, you know, is at the navigable headwaters of the Cape Fear River, and is second only to Wilmington in population. One of the largest U.S. Arsenals is here, which the Rebs. have used as their largest. Only one U.S. Arsenal stolen by Rebeldom now remains to them, that at Augusta. Our march in the rear of Charleston made necessary the evacuation of the first fort upon which the Rebels fired, and Wilmington and all their seaports follow as we interpose between them and their interior communications. How much more effectual this has proved than all the costly attempts to take these places from the sea front!

I suppose we shall move on tomorrow or next day. Gen. Sherman announces that we have new duties before us. I have no doubt that his great objective point is Richmond, but we shall probably halt this side to replenish and refit our army on the Charleston and Savannah Railroad. I received a letter from Rene of January 24th and Minnie's journal to January 17th. This is the last I have had from home. It was a pleasant surprise, brought to us from a rear corps.

I will write you again if I have time. We are sixty miles from Goldsboro and shall probably halt there for some days, if we get it, as I doubt not. Love to uncles and aunts and cousins, and believe me as ever,

Your Affectionate Father,
A.S.W.

P.S. My health has been and is excellent. No exposure seems to affect me.

◈

A TATTERDEMALION ARMY

Two miles north of Goldsboro,
North Carolina, March 27th, 1865.

My Dear Daughters:

Today brought us our first mail for sixty-five days; three from Minnie—regular journal series to February 17th, three from Larned, but *not one* from Rene! What is the matter with my eldest daughter? With the exception of one letter received on our march, I have not a line from her since the date of November 17th. I have written her several individual letters and she has a joint interest in all I send to "My daughters." Reflect, how much my mind is constantly engrossed with the care of nearly 20,000 men. No sooner do I reach camp after a most arduous campaign than my labors begin in making preparation for the next. No one who has not experienced it can comprehend the anxiety and watchfulness that this creates. Everything from wagon grease to the armament of artillery has to be attended to. With all the agents and assistance I have, I am still responsible that it is all done and done right. It must all be supervised. If it fails, or is neglected, I am the responsible man. In consequence, my mind is never at rest. My anxieties never cease. I dream of the work at night and I ponder and inquire and sometimes fret all day. I doubt if these stops to rest are not more harassing to me than the actual campaign.

You can see, therefore, that it costs me something to stop my cares and present responsibilities to write you long letters. I often think they must be very incoherent, as I catch myself, even while writing, thinking of something or other that ought to be at once attended to. Besides, I am every moment interrupted by all manner of applications, petitions, references, papers for approval, accounts to be examined and certified, and the thousand and one matters which the head of a large force must always supervise and decide. You must appreciate my letters, therefore, rather by the difficult circumstances under which they are written than by their intrinsic merits. I prove my love and constant remembrance somewhat, at least, in this way.

I wrote you a brief note telling you of my safe arrival here on the 23rd. Since then we have been daily changing camp and taking up positions of all the corps and making preparations to get supplies up from below, all of which we greatly need. We have had but little clothing since we left Atlanta, nearly six months ago. We started from Savannah with twelve days' rations of coffee, sugar, and hard bread (no meat) and were out sixty-seven days before reaching this base. All that we have had to support us, besides this, has been taken from the country. Our clothing is worn and torn. Many men are shoeless, and few have a decent pair of breeches. Every man's face is as black as a Negro's with the smoke of the pitch-pine fires. A more begrimed and war-worn looking army I fancy was never seen.

I doubt if your worthy "Pop" would have made a very presentable appearance in a drawing room. His pants, which were originally of light-colored corduroys, had assumed a very dirty and burnt-black color. The coat, torn in numerous places and badly patched, would have been an excellent "habit" in the *Beggar's Opera*. The vest had lost all but two buttons, and the shirt of brown woolen had undergone a three weeks' wear and tear. The hat, which was new in Savannah, having braved forty severe rain storms, had lopped down all round and the

376

yellow cord turned to a dingy yellow gray. His beard, of a three-months' growth, never once in that time reflected from a looking glass, really seemed frightfully grizzly as first seen from a farmhouse mirror.

Altogether, it would have been gratifying if I could have sent you a true photograph of him and a panorama of the troops as they marched through town on the morning of our arrival, with the long train of pack mules, darkies, mounted bummers, and the thousand laughable and grotesque collections of a large army after a two-months' march. It was amusing to see the gaping wonderment of not only the few citizens, but of the 23rd Corps and other strange troops in the town. We were hardly conscious ourselves, I think, of the strangeness and war-worn appearance of our columns.

You can fancy something of the pleasure we felt at reaching a point where we could hear from home again, and yet, with what mingled feelings of apprehension, hope, and suspense. What calamities might not have happened to our friends at home during our two-months' wanderings. How we longed and watched for the first mail. How we pored over the few stray papers we could find, and when the mail came—tons of it—how impatiently we watched for the opening of each package, fretting at the seeming delay of the corps postmaster. How we grumbled that the mail was so old, a month and over! How eagerly letters are clutched at and torn open; read in silence, or rather skimmed over at first, to see if any sad event has occurred. And then follows the slow and careful reading, the exclamations that John Jones has married Fanny Smith. Tom Snooks has been brevetted for staying at home valorously. Peter Spike has resigned. Somebody has another heir or heiress; and alas! now and then the silent going aside with sad face tells of mournful and heavy tidings, such as unfit the heart for the general merriment and take away all the anticipated joy of getting, as it were, after toilsome marches, *near home!* Who can describe these scenes and these heart beatings? Not I.

But I shall send you my journal in a few days, if I can find time to transcribe it. In the meantime, I can only say that the fatigue and labor of the last campaign has far exceeded that of Georgia. The officers, especially, were well worn, though, like the men, looking tough and hearty. We were glad to get to a point where we could replenish and refresh our strength. Judging from Minnie's letter, you have had a gay winter, so in contrast to my life in the pine barrens and swamps that the description almost strikes one harshly. Still, yours is the season for rational amusements and I only ask that it be used and not abused. But are you not all, up North, running mad with a sort of ephemeral prosperity? Is everybody rich? We in the army feel poor, for as everything advances our salaries proportionally decrease. Our pay now, measured by prices, is not half [what] it was in the beginning of the war; our labors and exposures never half as great. It is a year now that I am absolutely without rest. How I weary for it; for absolute retiring in some most secluded spot where for months I should not see an army wagon nor hear the bray of a donkey nor feel that mental anxiety which sits perpetually upon me now. I might consent to go out to those fine operas, or musicales, or plays, but the parties and balls—no, I think I have had my day of these. . . .

I fear that my journal must have been sorry stuff to the reading club. I can't recall anything of it, except that I transcribed from brief notes in great hurry and under constant interruptions. Uncle Lew must be the judge as to reading these things, for you daughters are too partial and do not always see the fitness of Pop's productions as a more disinterested and cool eye would. The "curious letter" which you forwarded was from a colored servant girl, a most excellent cook, washer, and sewer. Indeed, the best colored servant girl I ever saw, pious, steady, industrious, and wonderfully intelligent. She came to my headquarters with her sister Ann and two brothers-in-law, and a nephew the day after we entered Atlanta, having walked thirty-odd miles with what worldly goods they could carry to get away from slavery. We took this girl as cook and the boy nephew as a servant. I tried to induce "Phibby," as she calls herself, to go to Detroit with the Michigan Engineers, but she has a husband, slave to an officer before Richmond, and a son eight to ten years of age, who was carried away into the interior of Georgia. She could not make up her mind to go so far away from them and lived in hopes to get them with her before we left Atlanta. At length the order came to evacuate the place, and with it her struggles of heart as to which way to go. I advised her to try to get North; got her a pass to Nashville for herself and sister and nephew; gave her Uncle Lew's address, and told her to write me if she got into any trouble. The boy nephew decided to go with us, but the attack of Wheeler's cavalry a few days after so disturbed his nerves that he gave up the idea. The brothers-in-law are still with the command and are excellent servants. I wish she and her sister could get to Detroit. The whole family is the best collection of Negroes I ever met, but "Phibby" is the leading spirit of them all. I see she calls me "Pap"; a term she got from the soldiers and no doubt thinks it both a respectful and affectionate expression of her gratitude and love. Her name is Phoebe Simms. "Old Tom" she speaks of is my Negro servant, whom everybody in this army knows for his grotesque costume, his cheerfulness, and his active and intelligent spirit. He is a great favorite, a decided character. If anybody in Detroit wants a steady faithful and most superior servant, let them get Phoebe from Nashville. When she wrote she was in a hospital, I judge, with somebody whose address was "Lock Box No. 75.". . .

I see by the papers that Gen. Willcox's brevet is dated August 1st, six months, nearly, before mine! The same paper has an abstract of the court of inquiry which censured him, I know not how justly or unjustly, but I can't help feeling that he had no claim for promotion over me and that the people at home and our delegation in Congress have done me great injustice and personal dishonor. But that my brevet is necessary to retain rank in my own corps, I would send it back. It is in other respects perfectly valueless. It gives the bauble of vanity to wear two stars! . . .

Love to all.

Your Affectionate Father,
A.S.W.

◆

DEMOTED ONCE MORE

Near Goldsboro, Apl. 5th, 1865.

My Dear Daughter:

I was right glad to get your two letters yesterday, one of March 7th and the other March 24th. I began to think you had cut me dead, but you see how irregular our mails are with a straight and quick communication with New York. . . . I have lost the corps again and go back to my old division tomorrow. You know I have been commanding the corps during the two last campaigns by *seniority*, Gen. Slocum being the regular corps commander assigned by the President. We have had a new organization, making the 14th and 20th corps into a new department, the Army of Georgia, of which Gen. Slocum was given the command. This made vacant the command of the 20th Corps and as we have a great many full major generals it of course threw me. It is one of the curses that I have to bear for not getting my proper rank years ago, but I shall go back to my division without grumbling. I was gratified yesterday, when the three brigade commanders called on me formally and announced that they spoke the wishes of every officer and man in the division that I would resume command.

Maj. Gen. Mower has command of the corps. He is a very pleasant, gentlemanly man of the old army and has been with Sherman during all his Mississippi campaigns. This is about the fortieth time that I have been foisted up by seniority to be let down by rank! But no matter. Sherman told my brigadiers yesterday that I should have a corps. I prefer my own division to any corps except the 20th. . . .

This morning (6th April) we got the news of the evacuation of Richmond. The regiments are cheering all around me. I do not feel so much rejoiced. I think if Lee had held on a little longer it would be better for us, as we should have made a junction with Grant. Now the whole Rebel army I fear, will get between us. I could have come home after being relieved, but it would have left me out in the cold and Sherman would have been angry. Besides, there was such a pressure from the old division for me to come back that I could not resist. At one time I made up my mind to go for thirty days. I have just finished my official report—will send a copy in a day or so. I am so busy and occupied that I really have found no time to copy my journal and now I have to do a great deal with the division in getting ready for a new move.

Your Affectionate Father.

◈

NEWS OF LEE'S SURRENDER

Raleigh, North Carolina, Apl. 15th, 1865.

My Dear Daughters:

I had so much to attend to, to meet our sudden march from Goldsboro, that I did not get the maps of my reports ready to send. . . . The news of the capture of Richmond and the retreat of Lee made it important that we should hurry towards Johnston, who lay in the vicinity of Smithfield on the Neuse, twenty-six miles from Goldsboro. Our corps left Goldsboro on the morning of the 10th inst., my division leading. We passed through the town and recrossed Little River, passed over the same road we went in on, as far as Beaver Creek, then north on Smithfield Road. We crossed the Moccasin Creek, after much opposition by Rebel cavalry. Indeed, we skirmished all day, but drove the enemy rapidly. At the Moccasin, which is a broad swamp with two deep streams, we were obliged to travel the men to their arm-pits to get possession of the bridges which had been thrown into the creek. Loss, two killed and three wounded. I got into a very hot place on one of the bridges, looking after the skirmish line. The day was drizzling and most disagreeable. Marched sixteen miles.

On the 11th we marched to Smithfield without much opposition. Found the large covered bridge over the Neuse on fire and was obliged to lay the pontoons. The country between Goldsboro and Smithfield is much better than any we have seen in North Carolina, better soil and better cultivation. The houses are of better character and the people at home generally profess to be Union and rejoice at the probable end of the war.

On the 12th we crossed the Neuse early. I had the rear, and before I got over heard of the surrender of Lee's army from a dispatch to Gen. Sherman. I have never seen Sherman so elated. He called out to me from a bevy of mules and as soon as I could reach him through the kicking animals he grabbed my hand and almost shook my arm off, exclaiming, "Isn't it glorious? Johnston must come down now or break up!" I confess that I felt and expressed a pretty large sized "Laus Deo" at the prospect of an early end of this great Rebellion and a return to my family. Our long and tedious marches, for now nearly a year, with but little cessation, has quite filled me with a yearning for quietude and repose.

We marched this day on the left road to Raleigh, twice crossing Swift Creek. It was a sultry, showery day and I don't know when I have seen the men so fagged and disposed to straggle. For old marchers of thousands of miles, it seemed singular. I think our new corps commander was a little too impetuous in his mode of marching. We encamped about sixteen miles from Smithfield. Road was heavy. Smithfield is a dilapidated old village.

On the 13th we moved at daylight, my division in advance. We hoped to reach Raleigh early, but we ran against the 14th Corps and had to flounder about on crossroads and byroads. We reached the southwest side of town about 12 M. Miles away we had heard that the enemy was gone and Kilpatrick in possession. We passed through some fine country today, our march over sixteen miles. We encamped near the Insane Asylum. While waiting orders Gen. Mower and myself visited the inmates. Dr. Fisher, the superintendent, was greatly distressed at the presence of our troops, but as we saw a strong line of Rebel works running directly through the asylum grounds we concluded he had other motives. Our men gathered pretty close about the building and were greatly entertained by the Union speeches and songs of several of the inmates. We saw a good many strange cases inside, several of whom made quite eloquent talks of the old flag. Indeed, the prevailing sentiment of these insane seemed to be for the old Union.

After the troops were encamped I rode into town with Gen. Mower. We found a large, straggling, well-embowered village, with a respectable State House in the center and a good many pleasant residences about, but no signs of commerce or manufacturing. I could not but feel that the place had got all its wealth and growth, whatever it may be, from the public pap.

The 14th we remained in camp, doing up what we could for a continued march, which it was intimated would be for a month, probably.

15th: This morning we were under orders to move at 6 A.M., marching in review order through town and then on a southwesterly road to—no one knew where, but it rained in torrents all night and poured this morning, and the march was countermanded after we had broken camp and got wet. So we pitched tents again and just now I heard a mail would be sent out this P.M.

Johnston and his whole army left this the day before we arrived, it is reported, for Hillsboro in expectation of meeting at least a part of Lee's army. No one seems to know or tell what his ultimate intention is. I doubt if he knew himself. He heard of the disaster to Lee the day he left but did not credit the extent of it, I think. He can hardly hope to make much headway against all of us, though I think he can, if he wishes, get away into Georgia. It would only prolong the war for a few months and bring great distress on the people of the South. . . .

I don't know and can't tell you where we are to go next. The telegram will let you know before this reaches you. The camps are full of rumors, but I credit nothing not official. Love to all.

Your Affectionate Father,

A.S.W.

❖

MURDER OF PRESIDENT LINCOLN

Raleigh, N.C. Apl. 21st, 1865.

My Dear Daughter: . . .

From a communication with Gen. Sherman yesterday I am satisfied that he has made such a negotiation with the military authorities as will surrender all the Rebel armies to the Rio Grande, if the powers at Washington approve the terms. You will probably have heard all about it before this reaches you. The terms, . . . which we doubt our government [will approve], relate to the state governments assuming power again and taking the oath to our government. Gen. Sherman don't seem to have doubts, as he has published an order that he expects to lead us to our homes again in a short time. The murder of Lincoln, tidings of which without particulars reached us a day or so ago, is likely, I fear, to complicate matters. The tidings were received here with a most solemn and sorrowful feeling on the part of officers and men, I fear not unmixed with bitterness that prompted deep revenge. The details have not yet come to hand. Should they implicate any of the Rebel authorities and this war goes on, woe to the people of the South! The reported assassination at Mr. Seward's would seem to indicate a most nefarious and wide-spread plot. It is to be hoped it will not so turn out. The news of the President's death came directly upon the news of Lee's surrender. I have never seen so many joyful countenances so soon turned to sadness. We have been expecting to march from day to day, waiting the result of negotiations going on between Sherman and Davis. Now we shall remain, at least until the terms are sent back from Washington.

383

We are fixing up camps which are a mile or two southwest of Raleigh. We shall probably march to Washington or Frederick, if the answer is favorable. . . .

Your Affectionate Father,
A.S.W.

◈

CONQUEST OF THE CAROLINAS

Raleigh, North Carolina, April 21, 1865.

My Dear Pitt:[3]

I intended to have written you from Goldsboro, but our stay there was comparatively short, and I had but just gotten through the reports of campaigns when we were ordered to march. I was greatly interested in your letter and for the element of it which you seemed to doubt would interest me—the talk about yourself and your prospects. . . . I think you did well to go to Chicago. Detroit is too old-fogy for an active youth, and it has nearly got its maturity, I fear.

We are likely to have peace soon now, I think, and with it will come the revulsions that always follow the expansions of war. So look out for a year or so, and be contented with direct profits on not very risky engagements.

Sherman told me yesterday that he expected to lead us homeward soon via Washington and Frederick in several columns. But it depends upon the approval at Washington of the terms of settlement that Sherman, Johnston, and Breckenridge have been fixing up for several days a few miles out of town. The only point of probable difficulty to an agreement is that the state authorities shall resume their powers on taking an oath of allegiance, or something to that effect. Nothing is said about Jeff Davis or his government. All troops and munitions of war to the Rio Grande are to be surrendered. But for the unfortunate and damnable murder of Lincoln (of which we have not yet the particulars) I think, and Sherman thinks, the whole subject would be peacefully settled, so far as the military authorities are concerned, within twenty days. Of course, there will be the great swell of the storm for years to come.[4]

I know not how often I have regretted you left us, but it is probably all for the best. It certainly looked so then. Our march through Georgia was altogether pleasant, a "big hunt," as a Wisconsin Indian recruit called it—A "promenade militaire," as a Frenchman would have named it. We swept up all forage, hams, turkeys, ducks, chickens, sheep—everything edible, and burned all the cotton and cotton gins and presses within a belt of from sixty to seventy miles wide. We had beautiful weather and but few days of very hard roads. Supplies were abundant, and we sat down before Savannah with at least one-fourth of the supplies we left Atlanta with. We had no fighting (except around Savannah) beyond some cavalry skirmishes.

At Savannah we lost a hundred men or so, killed and wounded. Col. Ketcham was among the wounded, was brevetted, and has since resigned.[5] Lt. Ahrett, assistant to Asmussen, was killed.[6] In Savannah we had quarters in town at Mr. Cuyler's house, railroad president, etc. and brother-in-law of Sproat Sibley.[7] The town was charming and the weather superb. Good wine of very old vintage abundant, and altogether it was a delightful winter residence. We had the grandest reviews, and by common consent the 20th Corps waxed them all. But, strange to say, we got no supplies of clothing, and on January 17th we crossed the river into the rice swamps of Georgia without stockings for the men and with but few shoes. The campaign of the Carolinas was a decided contrast to the Georgia march. It was all mud, swamps, treacherous quicksand and quagmires—cursed cold, rainy weather, hard work, much swearing, great wear and tear, short commons for days, and altogether a most irksome and laborious campaign. We wound up with two very considerable fights. That near Averysboro, N.C. on 16th March was wholly by our corps and the cavalry.[8] We drove them from two lines of works, captured three guns, and smashed them up sadly before the 14th Corps came up. It came off in the swampiest of country. The Rebs. got off in the night, leaving ambulances, caissons, and wagons sticking in the road toward Smithfield. That on 19th March was begun by the 14th Corps or rather two divisions, each corps having one division guarding trains eight or ten miles away. One division of the 14th got badly punished before we got up and was driven in some confusion. The Rebs. then undertook to carry a new line I established, in the angle of which I left a marshy interval commanded at canister distance by twelve pieces of artillery. They threw a mass into this interval and at the same time attacked in front. They were terribly punished, but tried it five times before nightfall and each time were repulsed in thirty minutes or less. They left lots of dead officers and men, especially when the canister swept them on the left front. It was a worse affair for them than Kolb's Farm, and somewhat reminded me of it. We sent during the night for the other divisions, and the 15th and 17th corps were moved toward their left on the following day. If they had stayed one day longer Johnston's army would have been finished then and there, but they put out in the night. Johnston's force, composed of the debris of Hood, Hardee's, and all the other armies outside Lee, was estimated by prisoners from 30 to 40 thousand. Our two corps, when attacked, had not together 10,000 present. I took nearly 400 prisoners on the 16th, and buried over 300. Lost, killed and wounded, 438. I lost about 250 on the 19th, but no officers of note killed.[9]

I can give you but a faint idea of the devilish nature of the country through which we passed. The streams (across all in the state our course ran) were generally in six to ten channels with the worst entangled swamps between, often three miles wide. Behind these the Rebs. would entrench, and it took a good deal of skirmishing in water waist-deep to get them out. We lost a good many men in these affairs. It rained twenty-one days during the campaign. The roads, mostly sandy loam with a quicksand substructure, would become so saturated that there was no bottom. Corduroy would sink, again and again. But we became expert road-makers, first piling on all the fence rails and then cutting the young pines of which there was an abundance everywhere. For days we corduroyed every mile, and moved the trains from eight to ten miles! Right glad were we after the fight of the 19th to get the order to make for what we knew was our base and resting place, Goldsboro. We reached there on the 24th of March and remained in camp until the 10th of April, seventeen days. We were joined by, or rather found there, the 23rd and 10th corps, Gen. Schofield, Terry of Fort Fisher memory commanding the 10th Corps. He has the only Negro troops (one division) in the command. We had but little rest at Goldsboro, but we got supplies of clothing for the first time since leaving Atlanta. We left Goldsboro on the 10th and reached this [place] on the 12th. Had much skirmishing at the swamps but no severe fighting.

Johnston evacuated this place two days before we got up. On the march we heard of the surrender of Lee's army. There was great hurrahing through the lines. It began to look like the beginning of the end. The day after our arrival Johnston began negotiations with Sherman. The result has gone to Washington. I send you by this mail a map showing the route of our march until we reached North Carolina.

Such in brief is our campaign history. It has been interesting, though often laborious. We have had a chance not often found of seeing the interior of Rebeldom. South Carolina will not soon forget us. A blackened swath seventy miles wide marks the path over which we traveled right through her center and sweeping in the march her capital and her chief commercial city.[10] The first gun on Sumter was well avenged. The state generally is miserably decayed and worn out. Its houses are comfortless and shabby, and the people at home rusty, ignorant, and forlorn. I think the tornado of war may do them good in the end. . . .[11]

Yours faithfully and sincerely,
A.S.W.

◈

END OF THE REBELLION

Raleigh, Apl. 29th, 1865

My Dear Daughters:

Johnston has surrendered his whole army east of the Chattahoochee River. We are back again from our march, and tomorrow we march toward Richmond and Alexandria. I expect to reach Alexandria by June 1st. Write me often via Washington, D.C. If I have a chance I will write you on the way. . . . The main body of Johnston's army is at or near Hillsboro and Greensboro. The newspapers will give you the terms of surrender before this reaches you. We move at daylight tomorrow morning. I expect to be at home by the middle of June. Love to all.

Your Affectionate Father.

◈

EN ROUTE TO WASHINGTON

Near Richmond, May 10th, 1865.

My Dear Daughters:

We arrived within eight miles of Richmond night before last, having marched about 170 miles in nine days. Yesterday we moved camp to this point about five miles south of Richmond. We had very pleasant weather but some hot days. We shall leave tomorrow morning for Alexandria and shall be from eight to ten days on the route. What will be our fate by then, we are not advised. Probably mustered out. . . .

I was visited by one of my classmates yesterday, who had been here nine days waiting to see me, Mr. Jansen Hasbrouck of Rondout, New York. We had not seen one another for thirty years. I did not recognize him at first. We spent most of the day together in Richmond. I am going in again this morning. The mail goes soon, so with love to all, I am as ever,

Your Affectionate Father.

❖

DRAWBACKS OF GRAND REVIEW

Near Alexandria, Va.,
May 21st, 1865.

My Dear Daughters:

We reached our camp some miles behind Alexandria night before last. . . . It was a great temptation that Capt. Poe made you to come here; but it wouldn't pay. Washington is overcrowded and has been for days. Alexandria is nowhere. In camp, as we are now situated, women could not live. I shall be so occupied during the reviews and a few days after that I could hardly see you. Besides, it is nothing but a march through Washington, and [the] tramp of masses, all looking alike, for hours and hours, till everybody will be tired to death of seeing soldiers. So far as show is concerned the review of a brigade or division would be far more agreeable. I say this to console you. You'd be bored to death, as we shall all be tired to death, with this grand show. I do not like the arrangement. One army (2 corps) only should have been reviewed in one day. As it is, I think our corps will pass the reviewing stand about midnight. One hundred thousand men cannot pass a given point in a short time.

I wish I had an available house near here. It is rumored that we are to change camps and to remain some weeks. If so, I may be tempted to get a short leave and bring you both to Washington or Georgetown *malgré* the paucity of pecuniary resources. We will see. As yet all is uncertainty. I have not been to Washington and have seen no superior officers since we arrived, except Gen. Meade, who seemed to know nothing of future policy. He inquired after Rene, and spoke feelingly of the death of his son.

After the review we shall probably know what is coming. As I am a poor figurer I fancy I shall retire to private life early. . . .

Love to all,

Your Affectionate Father.

◈

THE GRAND REVIEW

Near Bladensburg, Md.,
May 29th, 1865.

My Dear Daughters:

Since the "great review" I have been pretty much "horse de scramble" as Gen. McNeil used to interpret the used-up state. I got something into my stomach that has greatly distressed me ever since. Yesterday I was able for the first time to ride into town, with much pain, however, as every step of the horse was a pang. Today I am much better, and have been engaged on my report from Goldsboro to this place. Added to the discomforts of a sore stomach, the most dismal northeast rain storm has blowed and flowed for nearly three days.

I was in Washington a few hours during the review of the Army of the Potomac and saw lots of Detroiters. Amongst others I paid my respects to Mrs. Chandler. I did not see Chandler, as he was out.[12] I wanted to have a little talk with him. His intimate friends (Geo. Jerome amongst others) declare most positively that he has never opposed, but has repeatedly recommended, my promotion. I only know he has never written me a favorable line. The Detroiters and, indeed, hundreds of Michiganders received me with great cordiality. Everybody tells me that I am a greatly abused man. I shall begin to think, myself, that I am a *martyr!* However, it is gratifying to receive these evidences of appreciation, or of flattery. It seems to me I never met so many acquaintances. It took me an hour or more to get from Willard's to the National. . . .

The review of Sherman's Army was a great success. People doubtless thought us a military mob, but I believe it is generally conceded that we were in marching and military appearance at least equal to the Potomacs. I received whole armfuls of bouquets. Indeed, I could not carry them all. Some had names attached and some were sent out and delivered in the name of persons I had never heard of. One had Mrs. Gen. Willcox's name and was presented by a staff officer of the general. It was a very delicate compliment. I have not yet seen her to make my thanks, but shall do so as soon as I can get down town. He commands a district hereabouts. Several of the bouquets came from wives of my old officers. If you want to see the most flattering account of our display, you must read the New York *Herald*'s correspondent of Friday, I think. He says the "Red Star" division took the palm. Others (many) have said the same thing.

[*The remainder is missing.*]

◈

FRIENDSHIP OF SUPERIOR OFFICERS

Near Washington, June 5th, 1865.

My Dear Daughters:

As I have not heard from you for a week or more, I suppose you think I am on my way home, but I can't get away until the mustering out is completed and my remaining regiments are transferred. Nobody seems to know what will be done with us then. Gen. Slocum is an apathetic man in such matters, especially, and our corps commander is both modest and indifferent.

Gen. Geo. H. Thomas, our old commander of the Army of the Cumberland, is here. He sent for me on Saturday night and after telling me that after the campaign of Atlanta he had made a stronger recommendation of me for a full major general than he ever made before, asked me if I would like a command of troops embracing one of the Southern states. I said, "Yes!" He said that he should do all he could to get me such a position under him; that he had watched carefully my command while with him and was eminently satisfied with me; that he intended at Atlanta to ask to have me made a major general for the purpose of securing my command of the 20th Corps, which he thought was due me. He did not doubt that Gen. Sherman had acted for what he supposed was the best interests of the service, etc., etc.

Now to appreciate all this, you must know Gen. Thomas. He has all the gravity and solemnity (and I may add sincerity) of a Washington. Never pays a compliment unless he means it. An officer of great purity and most devoted to his duties, so much so that for four years he has never left the field and never seen his family, until he went back to Nashville just before the battles with Hood. I confess that I was overwhelmed with his good opinion, and could only express my thanks in some confusion. I knew that he had strongly recommended me at Atlanta and had often been told by his staff officers that he often spoke of my command of the corps in high terms, an unusual thing to be heard by his staff, as he talks but little and seldom with his staff generally. As Gen. Thomas is here to see the President on special summons, it is not improbable I may get the detail to report to Gen. Thomas.

I went to see Gen. Sherman to say good-by. He was very cordial and repeated several times, "Williams, if there is anything I can do for you, call upon me freely." It was too late then to ask his influence, and it is doubtful now if it would aid me with Stanton. Gen. Slocum promised to do it for me, but I fancy has said nothing. He is not marked for personal exertions of that kind. I have done nothing for myself because I don't know where to begin. It is dangerous to go high without the aid of those below.

Our corps will be entirely broken up this week, I think, and I shall soon know my fate. If I go west I shall soon see you. If not, I shall send for you when I get fixed. . . . Love to all. Keep writing until you hear that I am coming.

Your Affectionate Father.

391

FAREWELL OF STAFF MEMBERS

Headquarters 1st Div. 20th A.C.
Near Washington, D.C.
June 7, 1865.

Major General A. S. Williams
Commanding 1st Division 20th A.C.
General:

The members of your staff wish to present you before separating a slight testimonial of their esteem and affection. They, therefore, beg your acceptance of the accompanying album.

The marked impartiality, justice, and kindness with which our individual and collective claims and interests have been received and acknowledged, have animated us with feelings higher than regard for our commanding general.

The division is soon to be dissolved, but the officers of the 1st Division staff will ever remember with feelings of pleasure, gratitude, and veneration, one from whom they have always received the kindest personal consideration, and in whom they have had the fullest confidence as an able and energetic commander, and for whom they individually entertain the warmest feelings of affectionate regard.

May the remainder of your days be happy and their close glorious.

[*Letter signed by*]

James Francis, Major 2 Mass. Infantry
H. Z. Gill, Surg. U.S. Vols. Bevt. Lt. Col.
E. K. Buttrick, Capt. and Asst. Adjt. General
E. A. Wickes, Capt. and A.C.M.
S. V. R. Cruger, Capt. 150th N.Y. Vols. and A.A.D.C.
A. Y. Gavitt, Capt. 5th Conn. V.V. and Chief Pioneer
George Robinson, 1st Lieutenant, 23 [?] Aide-de-Camp
A. T. Mason, Capt. 123 N.Y. Vols. and A.A.D.C.
Wm. J. Augustine, Capt. 29 Pa. Vols. and Ord. Officer
C. M. Burke, Asst. Surgeon 46 Rt. P.V. Medical Inspector
H. A. Gildersleeve, Major 140 N.Y.V. and Pro. Mar.
Eugene Weigel, Capt. 82d, Ills. Vols, and A.A.D.C.

◈

COMMENDATION FROM GENERAL SHERMAN

Lancaster, Ohio,
August 5, 1865

General E.O.C. Ord.
Comnd Dept. Ohio
Detroit
Dear General:

If you can favor General A. S. Williams in any way, I wish you would do so. He is an honest, true, and brave soldier and gentleman. One who never faltered or hesitated in our long and perilous campaign. He deserves any favor that can be bestowed.

Your friend,
W. T. Sherman
Maj. Genl.

1. The Grand Marais, or Great Marsh of early Detroit adjoined the opening of the Detroit River and the lower tip of Lake St. Clair. The "Hamtramck" of General Williams' letter was Hamtramck Township, from which the subsequent city of Hamtramck acquired its name.
2. The allusion is to the followers of James Miller, founder of the Adventist religious sect, who aroused widespread excitement by his predictions of the second coming of Christ, first in 1843 and subsequently on October 22, 1844.
3. Apparently the original manuscript of this letter belonged to Samuel E. Pittman. The present copy is from a typed copy of the letter on the letterhead of the Detroit Steel Products Company, with which Mr. Pittman was connected in his later years.
4. The terms agreed upon with General Johnston contemplated the surrender of all the remaining Confederate armies "from the Potomac to the Rio Grande" and the continuation in authority of the existing state governments. Although Sherman had thus assumed a political role, promptly repudiated by the Washington Administration, the nation would have been spared untold discord and misery if his program for reconstruction could have been accepted. For a revealing study of General Sherman's attitude toward the South throughout the war see E. Merton Coulter, "Sherman and the South," in *The Georgia Historical Quarterly*, XV (March, 1931), 28–45.
5. Colonel John H. Ketchum of the 150th New York Regiment, wounded near Savannah, December 20, 1864. He was promoted a brigadier

general on April 1, 1865. Heitman, *Historical Register* . . . *of the U.S. Army*, gives the date of his resignation as December 2, 1865.

6. For the death of Lieutenant Ahrett see *ante*, letter of January 15, 1865.
7. Ebenezer Sproat Sibley was the eldest son of Solomon and Sarah Sproat Sibley, founders of the well-known Detroit Sibley family. A younger brother of Ebenezer was Henry H. Sibley, notable early-day citizen of Minnesota. Ebenezer graduated at the head of the West Point class of 1827 and until 1864 devoted his career to the U.S. Army. In May 1831, he married Harriet Hunt, daughter of Judge Hunt of Washington. From 1838 to 1840 and from 1842 to 1844 he was stationed at Savannah, where, presumably, the family connection alluded to by General Williams was established.
8. The battle of Taylor's Hole Creek, or Averysboro. General Sherman's account of the affair is in *Official Record*, Series 1, XLVII, Part 2, 871. Contrary to his (and General Williams') statements, Confederate General Hardee on March 17 issued an order congratulating his soldiers upon their signal victory over vastly superior numbers, inflicting a loss of 3,300 men upon the enemy, at a cost of "less than 500 men" to themselves. Such are some of the oddities of warfare. For Hardee's order, see *Official Records*, Series 1, XLVII, Part 2, 1411.
9. This was the battle of Bentonville, in which General Johnston attacked the left wing of Sherman's army in a vain endeavor to stay its further northward march. Johnston's loss in the battle numbered "at least" 2,600 men. Some further fighting took place on March 20–21 by which time ample support had arrived to reinforce the Union left wing and Johnston withdrew his army.
10. That is, Raleigh and Charleston.
11. The remainder of the letter is devoted to personal news and gossip.
12. Zachariah Chandler, U.S. Senator from Michigan.

index

Fremont, Gen. John C., 75, 88, 89, 96, 99, 150
French, Gen., 253
Front Royal, Va., 77, 78, 97, 138, 240; letter from, 98
Furness' Ferry, Ga., 340

Geary, Gen. John W., 154, 155, 170, 215, 311, 372; at Chancellorsville, 180-93 *passim*; at Gettysburg, 226, 229, 230, 271, 273, 281-83, 290, 291, 353, 354; troops reviewed, 344
Geary, Lieut., son of Gen. Geary, 269, 272
Georgia: march through, 355, 385; army of, 380
Georgetown, 389
Germanna Ford, Va., 180, 181, 199
Gettysburg: battle of, 222-30, 236, 238-39; errors in report on battle of, 279-91, 352-54; region, described, 224; comment on, 238
Gibbon, Gen., 229, 271
Goldsboro, Ga., 375, 380, 381; letter from, 375, 379
Goodman, Dr., 373
Goodwin, [Gen.], 100
Goose Creek, Va., 25, 152, 215
Gordon, Col., 82
Gordon, Gen., 101, 126, 154
Gordon [?], Maj., 295
Gordon's Mills, 305
Gordonsville, Va., 72
Gorman, Gen., 64
Grand review, the, 388, 389
Grant, Gen. U. S., 380
Green, English cotton broker, 245
Greene, Mrs. Capt., 292
Greene, Gen., 99, 129, 269, 272; at Gettysburg, 229, 230, 281, 282, 290, 291, 354
Greensboro, N.C., 387
Greenwich, Va., 244
Gregory's Gap, Va., 240
Griswold, Miss (Mrs. C. L. Stevenson), 326, 333
Grosvenor, Col., 28
Grove Church, Va., 179

Guidon, Maj., 341
Guns and rifles: Belgian rifle, 28, 54; lack of guns, 28; Parrott, 55, 58, 88, 138, 341; Napoleon, 129; Dahlgren, 138

Hagerstown, Md., 121, 286
Halleck, Gen. Henry W., 106, 170
Hamilton, Gen. Charles S., 20, 28, 62, 63-64
Hammond Gap, Va., 240
Hammond, Mr., 139
Hancock, Gen. W. S., 229, 283
Hancock, Md., 54, 55, 61, 83, 150; letter from, 52, 53, 59
Hanley, Col., 257
Harbaugh, Lieut., 345
Hardeeville, S.C., 366, 368
Harker, Gen. Charles J., 325
Harpers Ferry, W. Va., 32, 131, 150, 152, 215, 237; letter from, 134
Harrisonburg, Va., 89; letter from, 71; advance to, 71f
Harrison's Island, Va., 218
Hartwood Church, Va., 179
Hasbrouck, Jansen, 388
Hascall's division, 23rd Corps, 326
Hatch, Gen., 82, 87
Haymarket, Va., 243, 244
Hazen, Gen., 321
Herndon, Dr., 105
Hill, A. P., 150
Hillsboro, N.C., 387
Hillsboro, Va., 237
Hillyear, Tighlman, 223
Holland, Sir Henry, 258
Honda, a Union lady in Secessionist country, 216
Hood, Gen. John B., 333, 345, 346, 386
Hooker, Gen. Joseph, 167, 176, 216, 220, 223, 264-65, 272, 275, 295, 311, 316, 322, 338; at 2nd Bull Run, 108; at Antietam, 121, 123, 125, 127, 134; praises Williams, 136, 169, 170, 313; at Chancellorsville, 180, 181, 185, 191, 192, 198, 199, 205; Williams' opinion of, 221, 334-35;

DESIGNED BY S. R. TENENBAUM

SET IN CASLON OLD FACE, BOLD, AND ANTIQUE TYPE FACES

PRINTED ON WARREN'S OLDE STYLE ANTIQUE WOVE PAPER

BOUND IN COLUMBIA BAYSIDE LINEN

MANUFACTURED IN THE UNITED STATES OF AMERICA